THE BURNING OF THE VALLEYS

dedicated to
James M. Prideaux
an inspiring teacher of history

Lawrence Park Collegiate Institute
Toronto

THE BURNING
OF THE VALLEYS

DARING RAIDS FROM CANADA AGAINST THE
NEW YORK FRONTIER IN THE FALL OF 1780

GAVIN K. WATT, BASc

with research assistance by
James F. Morrison

Dundurn Press
Toronto

Editor: Mary Beacock Fryer
Designer: Sebastian Vasile
Printer: Best Book Manufacturers

Canadian Cataloguing in Publication Data

Watt, Gavin K.
   The burning of the valleys: daring raids from Canada against the New York
   frontier in the fall of 1780

Includes bibliographical references and index.
ISBN 1-55002-271-7

1. New York (State) – History – Revolution, 1775-1783.   2. United Empire loyalists.   3. Indians of North America – Wars – 1763-1814.*   4. Iroquois Indians – Wars.   5. Canada – History – 1775-1783.   I. Title.

E236. W37 1997   973.3'36   C96-932420-0

2   3   4   5   BJ   09   08   07   06   05

The publisher wishes to acknowledge the generous assistance of the **Canada Council**, the **Book Publishing Industry Development Program** of the **Department of Canadian Heritage**, and the **Ontario Arts Council**.

Care has been taken to trace the ownership of copyright material used in this book. The author and the publisher welcome any information enabling them to rectify any references or credit in subsequent editions.

Dundurn Press	Gazelle Book Services Limited	Dundurn Press
8 Market Street, Suite 200	White Cross Mills	2250 Military Road
Toronto, Ontario, Canada	Hightown, Lancaster, England	Tonawanda NY
M5E 1M6	LA1 4X5	U.S.A. 14150

TABLE OF CONTENTS

List of Maps

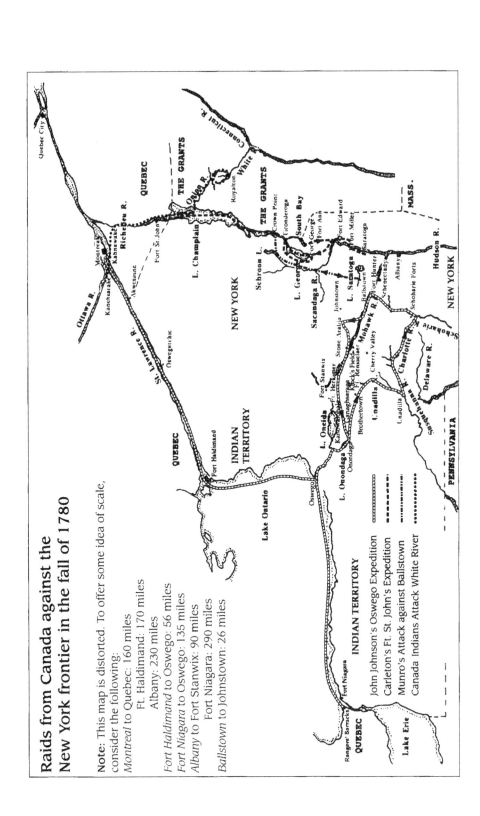

Raids from Canada against the
New York frontier in the fall of 1780

Note: This map is distorted. To offer some idea of scale, consider the following:

Montreal to Quebec: 160 miles

    Ft. Haldimand: 170 miles

    Albany: 230 miles

Fort Haldimand to Oswego: 56 miles

Fort Niagara to Oswego: 135 miles

Albany to Fort Stanwix: 90 miles

    Fort Niagara: 290 miles

Ballstown to Johnstown: 26 miles

John Johnson's Oswego Expedition

Carleton's Ft. St. John's Expedition

Munro's Attack against Ballstown

Canada Indians Attack White River

Preface

To my knowledge, a detailed account combining the four raids from Canada against the New York frontier in October 1780 has never been published. Nor have I discovered an account of any of the raids which covers both sides of the contest in relatively equal depth. This book examines each separate raid as it was developed by the British Command in Canada and from the viewpoint of the men who conducted the campaign. As well, it examines the attempts by the New York State Governor, his military department and the inhabitants of the frontiers to react to each of the expeditions. Of interest to the genealogist, lists of prisoners taken by both sides are included in appendices, as are the names of men recruited by the loyalist regiments during the campaign.

The text has a Canadian perspective which is obvious in the use of certain descriptive terms.

For example, those persons who rebelled against the established government and sought independence for America are called "rebels," just as they were known at the time. I have shunned the term "patriot" as one could justly ask, "who was patriotic?" — those who remained loyal to the government, or those who rebelled?

Those who favoured the government are called "loyalists," and sometimes, to give a contemporary pejorative flavour, "Tories."

I have avoided using the adjective "American" to describe persons or organizations. The rebellion was a civil war of Americans against Americans, not just rebels against the armed forces of their British government. At the time, the word was indiscriminately applied to both rebels and loyalists. For example, Simcoe's famous Queen's Rangers were "raised to the British Army's American Establishment" and distinguished as the "1st Americans."

I have not employed the lurid rhetoric often used to describe either the raiders or defenders — except in contemporary quotations. Where deserved, full credit is given to commanders, soldiers and civilians, irrespective of their politics. Where each side failed or faltered, and where each enjoyed success, is noted equally.

Regarding the native allies of both the Crown and Congress, there are no simplistic judgements made about the morality of their conduct. This was their civil war as much as it was the Americans'.

They fought in their traditional manner for their own political and societal goals using conventions of war developed over centuries of contact with white societies.

The depth of detail in this book owes a very great deal to the research of James F. Morrison of Gloversville, New York. Jim is a life-long student of the Revolutionary War, in particular, the conflict as it unfolded in northern New York State. His intense interest in these affairs was prompted by his ancestry — Lieutenant/Adjutant Lawrence Schoolcraft, 15th Albany, who was in the Lower Fort in Schoharie during Johnson's raid of 1780; Serjeant Jost Mattice, 15th Albany; Lawrance Wrinkle, 4th Tryon, who was killed at Oriskany, 1777 and Rudolph & John Youcker, 2nd Tryon.

Jim's studies are prodigious and his willingness to share his findings is legendary. As I stumbled over contradictory evidence and uncovered an endless stream of questions, I would write a letter to Jim and a staggering flow of paper would be the reply. Jim's method of responding to questions matches the deviltry in his personality — his twinkling eyes and sly smiles. Not for him the simple approach of addressing question #1 and providing answer #1 — instead a horde of photocopied references arrived in my postbox, and then the fun began. I pored over each reference, trying to match what I found against the questions I asked and *always* there were kernels of information, often a whole new line of development was uncovered. Everytime I laid a chapter aside in the belief that every single "fact" had been wrung out, along came another mailing from Gloversville with new revelations. It is only fair to point out — and if I didn't, Jim would — the research is Jim's, but the interpretations are mine.

It may help the reader to know that Morrison and I have been adversaries in the "living" history of the Revolution since 1976, when the recreated Royal Yorkers made their first visit to Johnson Hall at Johnstown in the Mohawk Valley. Jim was "skulking about" in the ranks of the 3rd Tryon County Militia and I "strode" the grounds of Sir John's family home as a Serjeant of the Colonel's Company. Since that time, we have grown in history together and exchanged as many contradictory views as we have hard facts. To use the derogatory term of the Revolutionary War period — twenty years after our first meeting, Jim "styles himself" as the colonel of his battalion, while I "serve" as the colonel of mine.

Jim enjoys the company of other history fanatics in the Mohawk region. Rick Sherman of Schoharie and John Osinski of Middleburgh, who march as officers of the 15th Albany County militia, have cast nasty glances in my direction for many a year. This book began its life as a series of articles in "The Burning Issues", the newsletter of the Burning of the Valleys Military Association. Editor John was in search of some inflammatory material (pun intended) and requested that I write a "Tory" perspective regarding the 1780 raids for the 215th anniversary. My series of articles appeared through 1995 and into 1996. Those rebels, Colonel Rick and Lieutenant John, were very encouraging in bringing this work to fruition.

A source of rich material came from André Fortin of Montreal who wrote to me asking for research assistance for his master's thesis in History. The focus of his dissertation is the Revolutionary War prison camp which was on the island in the St. Lawrence River off Coteau-du-Lac, Quebec. I provided André with material on the garrison there and opinions on his questions and André sent me the two books which had prompted his study — Steele's account of the Indian raid against Royalton and Hollister's memoirs of his capture at Ballstown. André proved the old adage, "one good turn deserves another."

David Putnam, a sergeant in the recreated Royal Yorkers, produced a detailed study of Johnson's 1780 raid. He was motivated by our upcoming anniversary event as his Royal Yorker ancestors, Ephron Putnam of Duncan's Company and Francis Putnam of the Grenadiers, had served during the expedition. From Dave's study, I received some key information and inspiration.

By chance I had a telephone call from Todd Braisted, an officer of the Brigade of the American Revolution and the "Tory" New Jersey Volunteers. He is widely known for his landmark research on loyalist units. Todd had just completed some transcripts of lists of prisoners taken on Johnson's expedition which are in the appendices to my text.

Another piece of good fortune occurred when I received a copy of the incredible Butler's Rangers manuscript collection of LtCol. William Smy. Several of Bill's wonderful finds have been incorporated into my book.

Another friend, Alan Fitzpatrick, whose ancestor Patrick Fitzpatrick marched in the Royal Yorkers, introduced me to a mystery regarding Captain Peter Drummond of McAlpin's Corps. As a prisoner, Drummond was on parole in Schenectady in 1780 and involved in spying. Discovering he was suspected by the rebel commissioners, Drummond broke his parole to "come off" with an unspecified party of loyalists. Who were these men? The question remains unanswered.

My daughter Nancy shares as deep an interest in the history of the Revolutionary War as I. Added to her pertinent historical comments was her exceptional ability to spell correctly (albeit as a Canadian) and her understanding of the esoteric vagaries of grammar and punctuation. And, of course, my wife Gill enjoyed correcting us both. The book was considerably improved by the attention of these two critics.

The series of articles for "The Burning Issues" was entitled "With Consummate Daring." Nancy suggested that a far more appropriate title would be "The Burning of the Valleys." I asked Rick Sherman, as the President of the Burning of the Valleys Military Association, if he thought the society would approve of such a title and he gave me his enthusiastic blessing.

Extremely important advice was received from my friend and editor, Mary Beacock Fryer who is a very successful and prolific writer of Canadian military and social history. Mary's expertise in all aspects of the American rebellion made her critique of the text and notes particularly valuable.

An "Old" business friend, Paul Wallis, was instrumental in rescuing the manucript of the book from electronic obscurity when it was discovered that my software package was too ancient to transfer to the publisher — imagine, all of six years old! Paul's computer skills and his willingness to help on several occasions where all other measures had failed were deeply appreciated.

In addition to those mentioned above, I would like to thank the following people for their assistance. As artists and photographers:
Norman J. Agnew, Brunswick Light Infantry, Stouffville, Ont
Allan Fitzpatrick, 3rd Tryon County Militia, Benwood, WVA
George R.P. Howse, King's Royal Yorkers, Toronto, Ont
Peter W. Johnson, King's Royal Yorkers, Scarborough, Ont
Janice Lang, King's Royal Yorkers, Carleton Place, Ont
Scott Paterson, Butler's Rangers, Port Lambton, Ont
Gavin Alexander Watt, King's Royal Yorkers, Toronto, Ont

In the search for likenesses of key personalities and other illustrations:
Mary Allodi, Royal Ontario Museum, Toronto, Ont
David Anderson, Bethune-Thompson House, Williamstown, Ont
Horst Dresler, King's Rangers, Bedford, Que
Christopher D. Fox, Curator, Fort Ticonderoga Museum
Noel Levee, Congress's Own, First Canadian Regiment, Johnstown, NY
Peter Schaapok, Continental Dragoons, Petersburg, NY
Philip D. Weaver, 2nd NY Continental Line, Highland, NY
Chris Zoetewey, King's Royal Yorkers and Parks Canada, Fort George
The staff of Johnson Hall State Historic Site, Johnstown, NY

Gavin K. Watt,
Museum of Applied Military History,
King City, 1996

Chronology of Some Primary Events of the American Revolution and Key Occurrences Relating to the New York Frontier & Canada

June 1774 to October 1780
(events in bold type occurred in the north)

1774

Jun 22   **Quebec Act passed. Borders of province expanded to Mississippi & Ohio Rivers in the west & Indian Territory in the south. American colonies are outraged.**

1775

Apr 19   Armed conflict begins at Lexington & Concord, MA.

May 10   **Rebels under Ethan Allen & Benedict Arnold capture Fort Ticonderoga, NY.**

May 30   **Col Guy Johnson, LtCol Daniel Claus, Maj John Butler, Joseph Brant etc. leave their homes in the Mohawk Valley.**

Aug 28   **Allan Maclean arrives in Montreal with the nucleus of the Royal Highland Emigrants.**

Sep 4   **Rebels invade Quebec Province; lay siege to Fort St. John's.**

Sep 25   **Indians capture Ethan Allen during unsuccessful attack on Montreal.**

Oct 5   **Rebel victory – Fort Chambly surrenders.**

Nov 3   **Rebel victory – Fort St. John's capitulates.**

Nov 7   Guy Johnson, Daniel Claus & Joseph Brant sail for England.

Nov 13   Sorel, Montreal & Trois Rivières surrender to the rebels.

Nov 15   Rebel army of Benedict Arnold displays outside walls of Quebec City.

Nov 17   John Butler arrives at Fort Niagara to manage Six Nations Indian Department.

Dec 9   Combined rebel armies of Montgomery & Arnold lay siege to Quebec City.

Dec 31   Crown victory – rebel attack on Quebec fails; 1200 men, Regulars, sailors, Canadiens/Canadians & Royal Highland Emigrants save the province.

1776

May 6   Winter-long siege of Quebec City ends; British supplies and reinforcements arrive; Governor Carleton's army pursues rebels.

May 16   Crown victory – rebels defeated at The Cedars by Indians, Regulars & Canadiens.

May 20   Sir John Johnson flees Mohawk Valley with 200 men.

Jun 7   Sir John's men arrive at Akwesasne on the St. Lawrence.

Jun 8   Crown victory – Battle of Trois Rivières.

Jun 18   British reoccupy Montreal; Sir John's force arrives hours later.

Jun 19   Carleton gives Sir John Johnson Beating Order to raise Royal Yorkers.

Aug 27   British invade Long Island, New York.

Aug 30   Last rebel troops driven from Quebec Province.

Sep 16   Crown victory – Battle of Harlem Heights.

Oct 11   Crown victory – Battle of Valcour Island, rebel fleet defeated at Lake Champlain.

Oct 28   Crown victory – Battle of White Plains; British capture New York City.

Nov 4   Jessup brothers, Justus Sherwood and party join Carleton at Crown Point.

Nov   Carleton's army withdraws to Canadian winter quarters.

Dec 26   Rebel victory – defeat of German brigade at Trenton, NJ.

1777

Jan 3	Rebel victory – Princeton, NJ.
Mar	Eben Jessup & John Peters receive orders to raise New York Provincial battalions.
May	Joseph Brant raises his Volunteers at Oquaga, Indian Territory.
Jul 5	Crown victory – Fall of Fort Ticonderoga.
Jul 6	Crown victory – Battle of Hubbardton, NY (now VT).
Jul 30	Daniel McAlpin joins Burgoyne; raises the American Volunteers.
Aug 3	Iroquois Confederacy council at Three Rivers, NY decides to support the British. Most Oneida & Tuscarora opt out. Old Smoke & Cornplanter are chosen joint warchiefs.
Aug 5	St. Leger's force arrives at Fort Stanwix, New York.
Aug 6	Crown victory – Battle of Oriskany, "bloodiest battle of the Revolution." Rebel militia column defeated by Six Nations, Royal Yorkers & Indian Department rangers.
Aug 8	Loyal Indians destroy Oneida village of Oriska.
Aug 9-13	Loyalist "uprising" in the Schoharie Valley led by John McDonell & Adam Crysler.
Aug 15	Francis Van Pfister and his Loyal Volunteers join Burgoyne's army.
Aug 16	Rebel victory – Battle of Bennington, NY.
Aug 22	St. Leger's expedition retreats in disorder from Fort Stanwix.
Sep 11	Crown victory – Battle of Brandywine, PA.
Sep 16	John Butler receives orders to raise Butler's Rangers.
Sep 19	Crown victory – Battle of Freeman's Farm, NY.
Sep 21	Crown victory – Battle of Paoli, NJ
Sep 26	Crown victory – army under Sir William Howe, C-in-C, occupies Philadelphia, PA.
Oct 4	Crown victory – Battle of Germantown, NJ.
Oct 6	Crown victory – Capture of Forts Montgomery & Clinton, Hudson Highlands, NY.
Oct 7	Rebel victory – Battle of Bemis Heights, NY.
Oct 14	Rebel victory – Burgoyne's army of almost 8,000 surrenders to the rebels.

1778

Feb 6   France declares war against Britain; Treaty of Commerce & Alliance signed with United States.

May 30   **Brant's Volunteers & Butler's Rangers destroy Cobuskill, NY.**

Jun 11   **Continental Congress approves a punitive expedition against Indian Territory.**

Jun 19   British withdraw from Philadelphia, PA.

Jun 26   **Governor Frederick Haldimand arrives at Quebec City to take command; Governor Guy Carleton departs.**

Jun 28   Crown victory – Battle of Monmouth, NJ.

Jul 1   **Crown victory – Butler's Rangers & Six Nations invade Wyoming Valley, NY.**

Aug   Crown victory – defence of Rhode Island from rebel & French attacks.

Aug   **Butler's Rangers & Indians devastate German Flats, NY.**

Aug   **Rebel forces destroy the Indian settlements of Oquaga and Unadilla, Indian Territory.**

Sep 7   French capture Dominica in the West Indies.

Oct   **Major Christopher Carleton leads British, Loyalist and Indian raid against Otter Creek, NY.**

Nov 11   **Six Nations and Butler's Rangers attack Cherry Valley, NY.**

Dec 13   British capture Martinique in the West Indies.

Dec 29   British capture Savannah, GA.

1779

winter   **Six Nations and allied Indians scour the frontiers**

Mar 6   **Command of punitive expedition against Indian Territory given to Gen John Sullivan**

Apr 6   **General James Clinton given command of punitive expedition's northern wing.**

Apr 21   **Col Goose Van Schaick destroys the Onondaga villages.**

May 23   **Capt Robert Leake ordered to raise a company from the remnants of the Loyal Volunteers to operate with Sir John's Royal Yorkers.**

Jun 16   Spain declares war on Britain.

Jul   British raid Connecticut ports.

Jul 15   Rebel victory – capture British post at Stony Point, NY.

Jul 20-22 Brant destroys Minisink, NY; defeats pursuit by militia.

Aug   James Rogers arrives in Quebec with the nucleus of the 2Bn, King's Rangers.

Aug 11   Colonel Brodhead, commanding south-west wing of punitive expedition, leaves Fort Pitt, PA to attack the Alleghany Seneca, Mingo, Delaware and Shawnee villages.

Aug 13   Sullivan's army destroys the Senecas' Chemung settlement.

Aug 22   After destroying several Indian towns, Clinton joins Sullivan at Tioga in Indian Territory.

Aug 29   Rebel victory – Battle of Newtown, Indian Territory. Sullivan & Clinton defeat Six Nations & Butler's Rangers.

Sep   Rebels and Spanish defeat British at Baton Rouge in Spanish Louisiana.

Sep 11   Sir John Johnson's expedition for relief of Six Nations leaves Montreal.

Sep 15   Having destroyed the Seneca Genesee settlements, Sullivan's army reaches its western limit; begins return march through Cayuga country.

Sep 30   Having destroyed the Cayuga villages, Sullivan returns to Tioga; reports to Congress that 40 villages had been razed and 160,000 bushels of corn destroyed.

Oct 15   Sir John arrives at Oswego; recognizes his force is too late to assist Indians and aborts the mission.

Dec   The Netherlands ignores treaty obligations with Britain; aids rebels.

1780

Jan-Jun   Six Nations & allied parties range across the frontiers of New York, Pennsylvania, Virginia and New Jersey.

Apr   Negotiations commence with the Republic of Vermont regarding a return to allegiance to Britain.

May 12   British capture Charleston, SC.

May 22   Sir John Johnson's expedition to Johnstown recruits 120 men and destroys parts of the lower Mohawk Valley.

May 29   Crown victory – Battle of Waxhaws, SC.

Jul 19   Crown victory – Defence of the Blockhouse at Bergen Wood, Bulls Ferry, NJ.

Jul 21   Sir John receives approval to raise the 2nd Battalion, KRR NY.

Aug 3   Brant destroys Canajoharie district.

Aug 9   Brant & Seth's Henry attack Vroomansland, Schoharie Valley.

Aug 16   Crown victory – Battle of Camden, SC.

Aug 18   Crown victory – Battle at Fishing Creek, SC.

Sep 26   Crown victory – Battle of Charlotte, NC.

Oct 10   Major Carleton captures Fort Ann and destroys settlements of Kingsbury, Queensbury, Fort Edward and Fort Miller, NY.

Oct 11   Crown victory – Battle of Bloody Pond; capitulation of Fort George.

Oct 12   Munro's force burns Ballstown and captures Col James Gordon.

Oct 16-17 Houghton's Canada Indians attack Tunbridge, Royalton and Randolph, NY.

Oct 17   Sir John Johnson's expedition lays waste to the Schoharie Valley.

Oct 18   Sir John Johnson's expedition destroys the lower Mohawk Valley.

Oct 19   Crown victory – Battles of Stone Arabia & Klock's Field.

Oct 20   Governor George Clinton takes command of the pursuit of Johnson.

Oct 25   Johnson captures Capt Vrooman's detachment from Fort Stanwix.

Oct 26   Sir John Johnson's expedition arrives back at Oswego.

Oct 28   Capt Justus Sherwood lands in Vermont to conduct face to face discussions with General Ethan Allen.

Comparative Chronology of the October 1780 Raids

DATE	CARLETON	MUNRO	HOUGHTON	JOHNSON
SEPT. 20				SIR JOHN ARRIVES AT OSWEGO
22				EXPECTED DATE OF DEPARTURE FROM OSWEGO.
27	ASSEMBLE AT ST. JOHNS.	ASSEMBLE AT ST. JOHNS.	ASSEMBLE AT ST. JOHNS.	
28	SAIL TO ÎLE-AUX-NOIX.	WITH CARLETON.		
29	AT ÎLE-LA-MOTTE.	WITH CARLETON.		BUTLER ARRIVES AT OSWEGO.
OCT 1				BRANT, REGULARS ARRIVE AT OSWEGO.
2	AT VALCOUR ISLAND.	WITH CARLETON. JOINED BY RANGERS & MOHAWKS.		DEPART FROM OSWEGO.
3	AT SPLIT ROCK BAY. JOINED BY CANADA INDIANS	WITH CARLETON. DISPATCH SCOUTS FROM LIGONIER BAY.		
4/5	AT RIVIÈRE BOU-QUET.	WITH CARLETON.		
6	TO BULLWAGGA BAY.	LEAVE BOATS AT BULLWAGGA BAY, MAKE SHORT MARCH, CACHE PROVISIONS.		AT LAKE ONONDA-GA. SCHELL SENT ON COMMAND. LEAKE FALLS ILL.
7	TO TICONDEROGA.			
8	AT BOTTOM OF SOUTH BAY.			AT OLD ONEIDA CASTLE.
9	SECURE RETURN ROUTE. CAMP AT PARKS FARM.	THREE MEN LEFT BEHIND.		AN ONEIDA DESERTS W/COHORN SHELL.
10	CAPTURE FORT ANN.			
10/11	BURN HUDSON VALLEY SETTLE-MENTS.			
11	BATTLE AT BLOODY POND. CAPTURE FORT GEORGE.	AT SACANDAGA RIVER.		MALCOM LEARNS OF EXPEDITION.
12	DEPART FORT GEORGE.	MARCH TO BALL-STOWN.		PRISONERS BROUGHT IN.
12/13		ATTACK BALLSTOWN.	ON ONION RIVER.	

DATE	CARLETON	MUNRO	HOUGHTON	JOHNSON
OCT 13		WITHDRAWS TO NORTH OF SACANDAGA RIVER. MILITIA PURSUE AND ABANDON ATTEMPT.		NEAR UNADILLA. CAYUGA PARTY LEAVES COLUMN.
14		RELEASES 4 CAPTIVES	TAKE NEWBURY MEN PRISONER.	
15	AT TICONDEROGA.		ENCAMP AT TUNBRIDGE.	SUPPLY OF BEEF ARRIVES.
16	AT CROWN POINT.		ATTACK ROYALTON. MILITIA PURSUE.	AT KENNANAGARA CREEK.
16/17			MILITIA ATTACK INEFFECTIVE.	
17			CAMP AT DOG RIVER.	ATTACK SCHOHARIE. VAN RENSSELAER AT SCHENECTADY.
18	CANADA INDIANS DEPART.			DESTROY LOWER MOHAWK VALLEY.
19			AT LAKE CHAMPLAIN.	BATTLE AT & DESTRUCTION OF STONE ARABIA. BATTLE OF KLOCK'S FIELD.
20			AT ÎLE-AUX-NOIX.	MCDONELL ATTACKS MILITIA. CLINTON AT FT. HERKIMER.
21			AT FORT ST. JOHNS	CLINTON TAKES COMMAND. VROOMAN'S PARTY CAPTURED AT GANAGHSARAGA.
24	MUNRO REJOINS AT BULLWAGGA BAY.	ARRIVES AT BULLWAGGA BAY		
25	DEPART FOR CANADA. ORDERED TO REMAIN ON THE LAKES. TRIAL OF SCHELL, VAN DUSEN & MCMULLEN.	WITH CARLETON.		EMBARK AT LAKE ONONDAGA.
26	SCHELL & MCMULLEN EXECUTED.			ARRIVE OSWEGO, SAIL TO CARLETON ISLAND.
29	TO THREE MILE POINT.	WITH CARLETON.		
30	TO MT. INDEPENDENCE, INTO SOUTH BAY.	LANGAN/MOHAWKS AT MILL BAY. RECALLED BY CARLETON.		JOHNSON ARRIVES AT MONTREAL. DAME ARRIVES OSWEGO.
31	DEMONSTRATE NEAR MOUNT INDEPENDENCE. REBELS AT THE NARROWS.	WITH CARLETON.		
NOV. 1-12	REMAIN ON LAKE CHAMPLAIN TO THREATEN REBELS.	WITH CARLETON.		GRAY ARRIVES AT MONTREAL.
14	AT ÎLE-AUX-NOIX, AT FORT ST. JOHNS.	WITH CARLETON.		

General Introduction

(Persons, places and organizations which appear in
this General Introduction are highlighted in italics)

KEY PERSONALITIES

**Lord George Germain, Secretary of State for the American
Colonies 1775-1782**

Many of the most demanding duties of managing the war against the
American States fell to the reserved and lonely Germain. He was
responsible for "the issuing of timely orders, to the Treasury,
Admiralty, Ordnance and Commander-in-Chief of the Army, so that
every necessary preparation was made, and no delay or mismanagement happened when the services took place."

From his earlier life as Lord Sackville, Germain carried the baggage of his supposed mismanagement of the British army contingent
which had served under Prince Ferdinand of Brunswick at Minden,
Westphalia in 1759. Surrounded by many powerful enemies including
King George II, he was unable to entirely restore his reputation. By
virtue of his many talents, he overcame his detractors to emerge in the
significant role of Secretary of State for the American Colonies in Lord
North's Tory administration which held power in the British Parliament
through the years of the war until 1782. While Germain has no direct
role in this book, he is constantly mentioned as the recipient of
Governor Halidmand's reports.

See: **Piers Mackesy, The War for America 1775-1783.**

★★★

**George Washington, Commander-in-Chief of the Continental
Army**

Very little need be said of George Washington, the first President of
the United States. He is almost as well known to Canadians as he is
to Americans. Washington was a man of exceptional ability, energy
and sensitivity. These qualities are attested to by his record of service,
both during the Revolution (rebellion) and as first President of the

United States, and continue to shine through his surviving writings. His great perseverance and astute management in the face of tremendous odds frequently saved the rebellion from disaster both from the actions taken by his British enemy and the inattentions of the Continental and States' Congresses. See Chapter 6 of this book for Washington's views on the army.

See: Washington Irving, **The Life of George Washington** (4 vols, New York & Chicago: Hooper, Clarke & Company, 1855); Richard M. Ketchum, **The Winter Soldiers** (Garden City, NY: Doubleday & Company, Inc., 1973)

★★★

Sir Guy Carleton (Lord Dorchester), Governor of Quebec

Carleton served two terms as the Governor of *Quebec Province*. His first tenure began in 1766 and ended in his resignation in 1777. He left for Britain in 1778 and was replaced by *Frederick Haldimand*. Carleton's second term began in 1786 and ended in 1796. Many decisions that were made by Carleton during his first period of governorship impinge on this book. Of particular note, he was a prime mover in the passage of the Quebec Act of 1774 which greatly expanded the borders of that province (See map) and guaranteed many rights to the Canadien populace. The provisions of the act were viewed with great suspicion by many of the other American colonies which had fought for so hard and so long to reduce the threat of Quebec. These suspicions were well founded as Carleton, and the British government, saw in the expansion of Quebec's borders a method of protecting the Indian nations by blocking the north-western expansion of the American colonies. Whether the *Western Indian nations,* whose settlements and hunting grounds fell within the borders of the expanded province, viewed this increase in Quebec's influence as entirely positive has not been discovered; however, those nations had been "French" in the past and perhaps assumed that little had changed.

The Governor also favoured the enshrining of many rights and privileges for the Canadien population for which he had developed great sympathy and affection. The provisions of the *1774 Act* define the character of Canada even to this day. The guarantees of language, French civil law and other features of the Act are primary sources of political wrangling and anguish in the late 20th century.

See: A.G. Bradley, **Lord Dorchester,** The Makers of Canada (Toronto: Morang & Co., Limited, 1911); The Historical Section of the General Staff, **A History of the Organization, Development and Services of the Military and Naval Forces of Canada**

From the Peace of Paris in 1763 to the Present Time (Ottawa: Government of Canada) Vol.II, The War of the American Revolution, The Province of Quebec under the Administration of Governor Sir Guy Carleton, 1775-1778. Hereafter cited as "General Staff."

★★★

Sir Frederick Haldimand, Governor of Quebec

The duties of the Quebec Governor included both civil and military responsibilities. Frederick Haldimand served as the commander-in-chief of the Northern (or Canadian) Department during the years 1778-84. He was a Swiss-German who had served with distinction as a battalion commander of the 60th "Royal American" Regiment of Foot during the Seven Years' War and the Pontiac Uprising. Haldimand was appointed as military governor of Trois Rivières, Quebec and thereafter as the military governor of West Florida. He was an austere and meticulous personality, who husbanded the meagre resources of the Canadian Department with great skill. Not one to bend rules, Haldimand had no patience with sharp or "clever" practices and many of his subordinates earned his displeasure.

The Governor's firm hand and direct experience of warfare in America created the strategy behind the 1780 expeditions against the New York frontiers.

One of the greatest legacies of Frederick Haldimand's life are the volumes of the correspondence and reports which he accumulated during his service in America. These documents, now available on microfilm, are a tremendous resource for researchers studying 18th Century North America.

See: Jean N. McIlwraith, **Sir Frederick Haldimand,** The Makers of Canada (Toronto: Morang & Co., Limited, 1911); General Staff, **op.cit.,** Vol.III, The War of the American Revolution, The Province of Quebec under the Administration of Governor Frederic Haldimand, 1778-1784.

★★★

Brigadier General George Clinton, Governor of New York State 1777-1794 & 1800-1804

A veteran soldier of the Seven Years War, George Clinton was appointed as a militia brigadier to command the defences of the Hudson Highlands in 1776. While under his command, Forts Montgomery and Clinton were lost to a powerful British & German attack in 1777. That same year, he was appointed a brigadier in the Continental Army and again given responsibility for the defence of the critical Hudson River. George's older brother, Continental Brigadier James Clinton, commanded a wing of the *Sullivan-Clinton Expedition* against the *Iroquois Confederacy* in 1779.

George Clinton was an attorney and an active politician, and after two years in the State and Continental Congresses, he was elected as New York's first state governor in 1777. Thus, he fulfilled two key roles — one civil, the other military. A most capable and energetic leader, he held the confidence both of the people and *General Washington*. George Clinton served as governor of New York State for seven terms and was vice president of the United States from 1805 to 1812. In 1780, his full title was, "his Excellency George Clinton, Governor of the State of New York, General & Commander in Chief of All the Militia & Admiral of the Navy of the same."

When New York's frontiers were threatened in October 1780, George Clinton took to the field and assumed command of the latter stages of the pursuit of Sir John Johnson's army, but he was unsuccessful in bringing that most active Tory partizan and his men to ground.

See: **The Public Papers of George Clinton, First Governor of New York** (6 vols, Albany: The State of New York, 1902)

★★★

General John Sullivan of New Hampshire

John Sullivan, the attorney, veteran Colonial soldier and militiaman, was appointed by New Hampshire as brigadier general at the outset of the rebellion. Sullivan was also an active politician and was elected to the first two Continental Congresses. He served with merit in the Canadian campaign, and in defence of New Jersey and Rhode Island. By 1779, he had established an excellent military record.

Sullivan's destructive expedition against the Indian country was planned by *General Washington* and approved by Congress in February 1779. General Horatio Gates, who had accepted the surrender of Burgoyne's army in 1777, was first offered the command, but declined due to age and health. The aggressive Sullivan readily accepted the task and began preparations. By July 1st, Washington had grown impatient with Sullivan's delays and, in mid-August, the C-in-C wrote a scathing report to Congress regarding Sullivan's sluggishness. Nonetheless, Sullivan retained the command and mounted his expedition later that month, achieving the destruction of the majority of the *Six Nations and allied* settlements.

He retired from the army in 1780 with his health in ruins, but retained his seat in Congress. He was elected governor of New Hampshire in 1786.

See: Louise Welles Murray, ed., **Notes from Craft Collection in Tioga Point Museum on the Sullivan Expedition of 1779 and the Centennial Celebration of 1879 including Order Book of General Sullivan never before published** (Athens, PA: Tioga Point Museum, 1929) reissued 1975; **The Sullivan-Clinton Campaign in 1779, Chronology and Selected Documents** (Albany: The University of the State of New York, 1929)

★★★

Brigadier General Robert Van Rensselaer

Robert Van Rensselaer of Claverack, NY, was promoted from commander of the 8th Albany Regiment on March 20, 1780 to command a second brigade of the *County's militia* (see, Armies, U.S.) This new formation incorporated the remnants of Nicholas Herkimer's Tryon County Brigade which had been grievously depleted in the ambush at Oriskany on Aug. 6th, 1777.

Unfortunately, very little detail of Robert's earlier and later services to the State of New York has been found. The Van Rensselaers were a very large, influential family; they had been part of the early Dutch settlement of New York. They owned one of the more famous land patents near Albany known as Rensselaerwyck and were Patroons under the old Dutch law, a very similar position to that held by the Seigneurs in the Quebec land tenure system. The extended family contributed six field officers to New York's Continental and militia forces during the rebellion.

After Sir John Johnson's October 1780 expedition, negative reaction in the *Mohawk Valley* to Robert Van Rensselaer's leadership of the pursuing forces led to a Court of Inquiry the following year in which the Brigadier was acquitted of any wrong-doing. The testimony recorded in the Court was an important source of material for this book.

See: Franklin B. Hough, **The Northern Invasion of October 1780, A Series of Papers Relating to the Expeditions from Canada under Sir John Johnson and Others against the Frontiers of New York ...** (New York: 1866); J.A. Roberts, **New York in the Revolution as Colony and State** (Albany: 1897). Reprinted by Kinship, Rhinebeck, NY, 1993

★★★

The Seneca, Old Smoke (Sayenqueraghta), War Chief of the Six Nations Confederacy

At the outset of the rebellion, the septuagenarian Old Smoke was the most distinguished warrior of the *Six Nations*. Of great courage on the battlefield, he had an equal reputation for his intellect. He was acknowledged to be an eloquent orator amongst a race of people who were particularly noted for this gift. This great man stood in excess of six feet and exhibited a most commanding presence.

In the early stages of the rebellion, Old Smoke was against *the Confederacy* entering the war as allies of the British. While he recognized the many ancient treaties that bound the Six Nations to the British Crown, he saw the conflict as an internal affair which the Indians would be better to avoid.

John Butler was significant in influencing Old Smoke and encouraging him to "take up the hatchet with the King to punish the errant Americans." When the Confederacy held a momentous council at Three Rivers (the confluence of the Oswego, Oneida and Seneca Rivers) in early August, 1777, the Confederacy accepted the British war belt. By ancient tradition, the Seneca nation held the two hereditary war-chieftainships of the Confederacy, a dual leadership which planned and executed all of the League's military operations.

Old Smoke was appointed as the Confederacy's war chief representing the Turtle Clan. Within days, he and his co-chief, *Cornplanter,* assisted by *Sir John Johnson,* John Butler and *Joseph Brant,* planned and executed the sanguinary ambush of the Tryon County Militia at Oriskany. Old Smoke was at Wyoming where he, Cornplanter and John Butler conducted a very successful series of actions. He was active at Cherry Valley in 1778, against *Sullivan* in 1779, at Canajoharie in 1780 and then with Sir John's October expedition in the *Schoharie-Mohawk Valleys.*

Old Smoke did not always enjoy a warm, working relationship with Brant, whom he saw in the early days as an upstart Mohawk with great pretensions, but little experience. Brant held the role of secretary to Guy Johnson, had received a white education, spoke and wrote English quite well, had been a recognized favourite of Sir William and was a close friend of Daniel Claus (see *Brit. Six Nations* and *Quebec Indian Depts.)* In short, he was in the white orbit and these factors likely gave him a measure of self-assured arrogance, which was quite naturally unacceptable to the Iroquois hierarchy. As the war continued and Brant continuously proved his worth and energy as a native warrior, the older man grew to accept Joseph as a capable partner.

In 1782 with the war drawing to a close, Old Smoke remained very active and with the other Confederacy chiefs was particularly worried that the British would fail to settle an honourable peace for the Indians. In these thoughts, the chiefs were entirely justified, for when the peace treaty was signed the war-exhausted British had virtually abandoned their native allies. While the British claimed that the *Indian Territory* which had been guaranteed to the Indians in 1768 remained theirs to hold, they offered no concrete assistance in the maintenance of it.

By 1789, the Indians had settled their own treaties with the Americans and much of their lands and freedoms had been surrendered under the constant pressure of western expansionism. Old Smoke, who had lived through such momentous times, died before these noxious treaties were accepted.

See: Barbara Graymont, **The Iroquois in the American Revolution** (Syracuse: Syracuse University Press, 1972); Paul L. Stevens, **A King's Colonel at Niagara 1774-1776** ... (Youngstown, NY: Old Fort Niagara Association, Inc., 1987)

★★★

The Seneca, Cornplanter (Gayentwahga), War Chief of the Six Nations Confederacy

In 1777, at the Three Rivers, NY, council, the half-blood, Cornplanter (Captain Abeel), representing the Wolf Clan, was appointed to act as a traditional, joint war chief of the *Confederacy* with *Old Smoke*. Like Old Smoke, Cornplanter was strongly opposed to going to war in the early stages of the rebellion. Both men clung to a treaty of neutrality which the *Six Nations* had accepted with the Americans, but like the older man, Cornplanter was swayed by the persuasion of *John Butler* and many other pro-British activists who emphasized the Confederacy's ancient treaties of alliance with the Crown and the attendant substantial benefits.

Sources disagree as to the date of his birth. Some suggest he was only 25 when appointed as the Confederacy's joint war chief. This is most unlikely for a man selected for such a critical role. Another source reports that he was born in 1732 at Conewaugus Castle on the Genesee River and that he had distinguished himself in fighting against the British in the French & Indian War. If so, he may also have been active with those Seneca who rose against the British in the Pontiac Uprising, perhaps participating with his nephew Blacksnake in the action at Bloody Hole on the Niagara portage road in 1764. However, such an early birthdate would make him 104 at the time of his death. Whenever he was actually born, one can be sure that he was a recognized warrior/leader to be chosen as a joint war chief of the Confederacy.

Once committed, he was as energetic, cunning and sagacious as was expected by his supporters. He was active across upstate New York throughout the rebellion, participating in major actions at Oriskany, Wyoming, Cherry Valley, Fort Freeland, Newtown, Canajoharie and the Schoharie/Mohawk expedition.

During the large raid of August, 1780 against the Canajoharie area, Cornplanter's white father, John Abeel (O'Bail) was taken prisoner and his house destroyed. Abeel had been a trader amongst the Seneca before retiring near the Mohawk River. Some of the older men amongst the Seneca recognized him and informed Cornplanter of the error. The son was most apologetic and offered to take him to his white home where he could be cared for, or if he preferred, he would be released to return to his white folk. Abeel requested the second option and Cornplanter sent a number of warriors with him to safeguard his return. Many other prisoners were also released as a compliment to Cornplanter.

While Cornplanter and *Joseph Brant* enjoyed a close working relationship during the rebellion, the adjustment period after the peace brought them into serious political conflict. The old rivalries for primary leadership of the Confederacy which had always existed between the Elder Brothers (see *Six Nations),* the Mohawks and the Senecas, was personified between these two vigorous men. These disagreements were never entirely resolved. Cornplanter, who had become the chief spokesman for the Seneca nation, moved his home to a farm in the Alleghany Valley, where he died on February 18, 1836.

See: Sources cited for Old Smoke.

★★★

Sir John Johnson, 2nd Baronet of New York — LtCol. Commanding, the King's Royal Regiment of New York

Sir William's (see *Six Nations Indian Dept)* son John, born a bastard to Johnson's first love, the Palatine German woman Catherine (Catty) Weisenberg, followed in the footsteps of the father. After Catherine's death, Sir William married a young Mohawk, Mary (Molly) Brant, and young John was brought up amongst Mohawk step brothers and schooled in Indian affairs and frontier military arts from his first awareness. His stepmother's brother, *Joseph Brant,* was a great favourite of Sir William's and John developed a close relationship with the talented Mohawk which later led to a most effective military alliance.

For his only white son and heir, Sir William wanted a degree of finish and connection within society which he knew himself to lack. Consequently, John was educated in Philadelphia and travelled widely in Britain where he was thrust amongst the nobility and the gentry. The family had always been concerned about the status of John's birth which might preclude his inheritance of the baronetcy, so there was great relief when John was knighted by the King, as part of his father's reward for the Lake George victory over the French in 1755.

Like his father, Sir John had his passions — in his case, blood horses, competitive sport, fine music, impetuous romance, and the prestige of being the brigadier general of the Tryon County Militia — but, above all, his love for his *Mohawk Valley* home where he could enjoy everything he could wish for. The father, not approving of his son's first choice of a mate — ironically, an attractive Palatine German girl from the Valley — insisted upon a marriage of "quality." This led Sir John to New York City where he courted and won Mary (Polly) Watts, a daughter of John Watts, a Scots immigrant prominent in government and society. Sir John was brought up an accomplished, polished individual; but, by comparison to his sire, a man seemingly lacking the fire and drive of the self-made father.

John made clear his intention not to enter the Indian service, although he held their love and regard having been amongst them from his birth and having led them as an *Indian Department* captain in the Pontiac war. He chose to avoid the constant demands of attending to their needs and wants. Sir John also declined a career in the *Regular Army* when *Frederick Haldimand,* the officer commanding a battalion of the Royal American Regiment, offered him the opportunity to purchase a commission. When Sir William died, the position of superintendent transferred to Sir John's brother-in-law and cousin, Guy Johnson.

While he had purposely chosen the life of a gentleman of leisure, Sir John held firm beliefs and principles. His devotion to the King, who had so favoured his father and himself, and to the established system of government in America, ensured a collision course with those who led the rebellion. Once forced from his home at Johnson Hall and committed to an active military role, he became a zealous partizan and tireless worker for the King and the type of country in which he believed. This book will reveal much of the style and quality of his leadership.

Upon arrival in Canada, Sir John was given a Beating Order (see *Armies, Brit.)* by Governor Carleton to raise a two-battalion *Provincial regiment* to be known as the King's Royal Regiment of New York (KRR NY/Royal Yorkers.) His 1st Battalion saw heavy action during the St. Leger expedition and hard service in the May and October expeditions of 1780. Johnson completed his first battalion in 1780 and received immediate authorization to proceed with his second. The 2nd Battalion went on campaign in the Mohawk Valley in 1781; rebuilt the post at Oswego in 1782; its Light Company served under Brant's command in the last raid into the Valley that same year and the next year the battalion rebuilt Fort Frontenac, the old French post at Cataraqui. The first was disbanded in December 1783 and the second in June 1784.

In 1782, Sir John succeeded his cousin, Guy Johnson, as Superintendent & Inspector General of Indian Affairs. Guy had fallen out of favour with Governor Haldimand. On no occasion after 1775 did Guy Johnson join his charges on campaign against the rebels and it is remarkable that he had been able to maintain their regard and good will. Under a changed definition of duties, the *Canada Indians* were included as charges under John Johnson's management. The Baronet continued in this role until his death in 1830.

Later in 1782, Sir John was promoted to a Provincial brigadier general (see *Armies, Brit.*) in recognition of his military services. Then, in 1784, he was named as Superintendent General of Refugee Loyalists and in this role he managed the settlement in Canada (see *Settlement Townships)* of the families of the disbanded troops and the Six Nations allies who chose to exit New York State.

In 1790, Sir John was recommended by Lord Dorchester *(Guy Carleton)* as lieutenant governor of the newly-created province of Upper Canada (see *Quebec/Canada);* however, the home government chose to favour John Graves Simcoe, the former commanding officer of the Queen's Rangers, 1st Americans. As one of Simcoe's first acts on his arrival, the Lieutenant Governor changed the names of a number of Loyalist communities. Butlersbury became Newark and New Johnstown became Cornwall. To satisfy an eccentricity of LtGov. Simcoe, the New York origins of these settlements were lost to posterity.

Devastated by the government's decision not to appoint him, Sir John joined his wife in England where he spent a number of lonely and disgruntled years. He did not enjoy English society, being a thorough American, and he returned to Lower Canada where he resumed his duties as Indian superintendent. He was also a representative of the Provincial Legislative Council and maintained a life-long involvement in the Masonic Order, serving as Provincial Grand Master. Sir John also continued his military career, acting as brigadier general of Quebec Militia during the War of 1812.

Tragedy continued in the Baronet's life as the death of so many of his children preceded his own. His first son, William Johnson, a major of the 24th Light Dragoons and later a lieutenant colonel of the 28th of Foot and finally, the British army's inspecting field officer in Lower Canada, died in 1812. His second son, John, who had been born while Polly Johnson was being held by the rebels after his flight over the Adirondacks to Canada, never recovered from the ordeal and died in 1778. The next son Warren, a major of the 4th of Foot in Jamaica, died at sea in 1801. His second daughter Catherine died an infant in Montreal in 1778. The next son, Christopher, born in 1783 lived less than three months. Sir John's seventh son, James, a captain of the 28th Foot, was killed at the siege of Badajos, Spain in 1812. His third daughter, Catherine Maria, was widowed in the seventh year of her marriage when her husband, a major, was killed at Salamanca, Spain in 1812, only three months after the loss of James. His eighth son, Robert, a captain in the army, was drowned crossing the St. Lawrence River four days before James' death. While the loss of infants was a part of 18th century life, the deaths of so many mature members in the family must have been a very bitter experience for Sir John and Lady Johnson.

When he died on January 4, 1830 at 88, Johnson, who prior to the rebellion had been considered the second richest man in America, was a relatively poor man due to estate losses and family expenses. Sir John had become estranged from his profligate wife, who had never been reconciled to her exile from New York. She preferred the high life in Britain to the provincial life of Montreal, where she could enjoy a more fashionable society reminiscent of her younger life in New York City.

The Baronet died leaving many friends amongst the old soldiers of the Royal Yorkers, the Quebec Militia, the Masonic Order and, most poignant, the native community — the very people that he had wanted to avoid in his younger days. His funeral was the largest that had ever been seen in Montreal, a thriving commercial city. Over 300 *Canada Indians,* male and female, from *Kahnawake, Kanehsatake & Akwasasne* were in attendance. An old Kahnawake chief gave an eulogy expressing his satisfaction that so many brothers and sisters —

> ... so very unanimously and willingly came forward on the present occasion to testify their very great respect for the character of so great a father to the red children as "He Who Made the Roof to Tremble" had been to them ...

Troops from the garrison of British Regulars fired the three traditional volleys to mark Sir John's passing and a fifteen gun salute crashed from the artillery batteries on Île Ste-Hélène. Thus passed the "scourge of the Mohawk Valley", a man who probably loved that land as much as, if not more than, any other who had been born there.

See: Ernest Cruikshank & Gavin K. Watt, **The King's Royal Regiment of New York** (Toronto: Gavin K. Watt, 1984) text first published, Ontario Historical Society, 1931; Earle Thomas, **Sir John Johnson, Loyalist Baronet** (Toronto & Reading: Dundurn Press, 1986)

★★★

Lieutenant Colonel John Butler, Commanding Officer of Butler's Rangers and Deputy Superintendent of the Six Nations Indian Department

Based at Fort Niagara from 1775 to 1784, Butler was primarily instrumental in maintaining the majority of the *Six Nations Confederacy* as British Allies in the early war. Butler had taken post at Niagara at the specific request of Governor *Guy Carleton* when Superintendent Guy Johnson (see *John Johnson)* removed to Britain in the midst of the American attack on *Quebec Province.*

Carleton never forgot the devotion to duty exhibited by Butler, but he had unwittingly made Butler an enemy in the person of Daniel Claus. Butler had risen from a humble interpreter to the most important figure in the *Six Nations Department* at the same time as Claus lost his position as deputy superintendent in Quebec (see *Quebec Indian Dept.)* Claus recognized that he could not hope to wreak his vengeance on Governor Carleton, but, as a convenient surrogate, he sniped very effectively at John Butler throughout the war. While Guy and John Johnson worked closely with Butler on many occasions, it is difficult to believe that Claus' acid was not without its effects.

John Butler was born in New London, Connecticut, in 1725 of an Irish-born father who had come to America as a subaltern in the army. John was educated in Connecticut before his family moved to the *Mohawk Valley* where his father had obtained a substantial land grant. John and his brother Walter served under Sir William Johnson in 1755 at Lake George. Walter lost his life in action and John was noted as performing signal service. In 1758, John was with Abercrombie at the disastrous battle at Ticonderoga and later the same year with Bradstreet in the successful attack on Fort Frontenac. He accompanied Sir William as second-in-command of the Indians in the triumphant seige of Fort Niagara in 1759. The next year he was again 2-I-C of the Indians during the French capitulation at Montreal. Butler acquitted himself extremely well and in the years following the conquest of Canada, he served Sir William as his chief interpreter, being a naturally gifted linguist who had mastered several Iroquoian dialects.

In late 1777, John Butler raised his famous corps of Rangers and by the war's end his regiment had grown to 10 companies of about 50 men each. Serving in small and large detachments and ranging far, wide and deep into enemy territory, Butler's Rangers were unquestionably the single most effective unit in the *Canadian Department.*

Butler's most famous military victory occurred in the 1778 expedition against the Wyoming settlements (modern Wilkes-Barre, PA), where his Rangers and Seneca allies won decisive victories over *Continental* and *militia forces* (see *Armies, U.S.)* After a particularly rigorous and unsuccessful campaign against the *Sullivan-Clinton Expedition* in 1779, Butler's health was in decline. His last active field operation was to command his regiment on the October 1780 raid led by Sir John Johnson. As he did not figure prominently in any of the reports of the raid, one suspects that he was under debilitating physical stress throughout.

Butler's career was marred by tragedy. Like so many loyalists, he sacrificed for his principles a very substantial estate when he left the Mohawk Valley with Guy Johnson in 1775. Of course, this was never recovered. His oldest son Walter, who became the senior captain in the Rangers, was killed on campaign in the Mohawk region in 1781.

With the encouragement of Niagara's commandant, a group of discharged men of Butler's Rangers founded a farming community on the Canadian side of the Niagara River in 1778 as a support for the needs of the garrison of Fort Niagara. Consequently, Butler's Rangers hold the distinction of founding the first anglophone settlement in Ontario. After the war, when a large body of the disbanded Rangers settled nearby with their families, the community became known as Butlersbury. It is now Niagara-on-the-Lake.

John Butler died in 1796 at age 71. He had been the Niagara region's most prominent citizen, acting as a district court judge and colonel of the Nassau (Lincoln) County Militia while continuing in his demanding role of deputy superintendent of Indians.

See: Ernest Cruikshank, **The Story of Butler's Rangers and the Settlement of Niagara** (Welland: Lundy's Lane Historical Society, 1893) reprinted 1975; Paul L. Stevens, **A King's Colonel at Niagara 1774-1776** ... (Youngstown, NY: Old Fort Niagara Association, Inc., 1987)

★★★

LtCol. James Gordon, 12th Albany County Militia Regiment

Born in 1739 in Ulster, Gordon emigrated to America at 19 in the midst of the Seven Years War. His first employment was as a sutler to Robert Roger's corps of Rangers. After the war, Gordon entered the Indian trade and, following a short visit to Ireland, he returned to America in 1774 with his mother, a spinster sister, his brother-in-law, George Scott and his family. All of them settled at Ballstown. In 1775, Gordon married Mary Ball, a daughter of the settlement's founder.

Gordon became a prominent and successful citizen, owning a large farm and mill. He was an inveterate supporter of the rebellion and served as lieutenant colonel of the 12th Albany militia regiment (see *Armies, U.S.)* for the Half Moon & Ballstown district. Gordon was a member of the Ballstown *Committee of Safety* for 1777&78 and sat in the New York State Assembly from 1777-81. He quickly, and deservedly, earned the strong enmity of the area's loyalists.

Gordon was a primary target of Munro's raid on Ballstown. He was captured and taken to Canada where he was held prisoner. He escaped in 1782, travelling overland through Maine (then part of Massachusetts) and arrived in Boston just as hostilities ended.

In 1786, Albany County created a third militia brigade and James Gordon was appointed its brigadier. He continued his interest in politics and was returned to the State Assembly from 1784-86. Gordon represented the State of New York in the Congress from 1791-94 and was elected a state senator in 1798, serving in that capacity until 1804. He died at Ballstown in 1810, aged 71.

See: "The Reminiscences of James Gordon", Josephine Mayer, **New York History, Vol.XVII, No.3 (July 1936)**

★★★

The Mohawk, Joseph Brant (Thayendanegea), a War Chief of the Canajoharie Castle and a Captain of the Six Nations Indian Department

As a boy, Joseph, the brother of Sir William Johnson's Mohawk wife, Mary (Molly) Brant, began his tutelage in the *British Six Nations Indian Department*. Lovingly cared for and nurtured by Sir William, the youth received an excellent education and an exposure to the conduct of Indian Affairs which prepared him for his own greatness. He attained warrior status in action at Lake George in 1755 and was active thereafter against the French as well as during the Pontiac war of 1763.

Joseph was particularly close to Daniel Claus (see *Six Nations and Quebec Indian Departments)*, Sir William's son-in-law, who lived with Joseph's family when he first came to stay in the Valley. Together they translated the Anglican Book of Common Prayer into the Mohawk language. When Guy Johnson assumed the mantle of superintendent, Joseph was his secretary, in which position he held considerable power and influence.

Brant left the *Mohawk Valley* in 1775 and travelled with Guy to Montreal. He participated in the successful defence of that town in late October and then sailed to England to present to the King and government the many grievances of his people. He was extremely well received. His experiences in Britain cemented his adherence to the "ancient alliances" between the Six Nations and the Crown.

Upon his return to America, he set out across rebel country for *Indian Territory* and on arrival immediately raised the King's Standard. Many of his clansmen flocked to join him as did a large number of white loyalists who chose to serve under this forceful man of action. In 1777, Brant, and his unit known as Brant's Volunteers, distinguished themselves in the ambush at Oriskany and, through his indefatigable energy and acumen, his star continued to rise. Prior to the October raid of 1780, Brant had been promoted to a captain of the Indian Department and he led his Volunteers with great success at Stone Arabia. By the war's end, Brant had so grown in stature within the Confederacy that he was recognized as a senior leader. He led a large number of families of mixed Six Nations and allied peoples to settle along the Grand River in Ontario, where their descendants continue to this day.

Brant's last years were embroiled in bitter disputes with his own people, representatives of other native nations, the Indian Department, Lieutenant Governor Simcoe and the governments in Canada and Britain. His dream of a great Indian Confederacy of the Six and Western Nations built on the Iroquois model had slipped away. Joseph Brant died in self-imposed exile at Burlington Bay, Upper Canada in 1807 at age 64.

See: William Leete Stone, **Life of Joseph Brant-Thayendanegea: including the Border War of the American Revolution and Sketches of the Indian Campaigns of Generals Harmar, St. Clair, and Wayne** ... (2 vols, New-York: Alexander V. Blake, 1838) republished Scholarly Press, St. Clair Shores, MI, 1970; Isabel Thompson Kelsay, **Joseph Brant 1743-1807, Man of Two Worlds** (Syracuse: Syracuse University Press, 1984); Graymont, **op.cit.**

★★★

Captain John Munro, 1st Bn, King's Royal Regiment of New York (KRR NY)
Munro was a Scottish-born, veteran serjeant of the 48th Regiment who had served in America during the Seven Years' War. He remained in America and received land grants from New York province in the *New Hampshire Grants* and along White Creek in Albany County. He took residence in Albany and married Mary Brouwer, a lady of Huguenot descent. In addition to amassing considerable wealth, Munro was appointed a Magistrate to defend New York's interests in the fractious Grants district. The fearless, energetic Munro became an anathema to Ethan Allen's Green Mountain Boys.

In the early stages of the rebellion, Munro was extremely helpful to LCol Allan Maclean and was appointed captain-lieutenant of the Royal Highland Emigrants. He was incarcerated for his recruiting activities and only able to escape in 1777. On meeting Sir John

Johnson at Ticonderoga, he accepted an appointment as a captain in the 1st Battalion KRR NY. In 1780, the 52-year old Munro led the raid against Ballstown and, in 1781, he was the commandant of the post at Coteau-du-lac, Que., after the apprehended mutiny there. Both of these events are found in this book. His eldest son, Hugh, served as an ensign in his father's company in 1782 and was promoted to lieutenant in October 1783. Three younger sons, Cornelius, Henry and John Jr. served as Volunteers under their father.

John Munro has been vilified in American historical accounts for the "brutal" order which he gave to his men regarding the treatment of prisoners. He is frequently referred to as a major in American accounts; however, this must refer to his pre-rebellion rank in the militia, as captain was his highest rank in the *British and Provincial armies.*

Munro had established a partnership in an ironworks in Montreal during the war. After the peace, he became a prominent landowner and businessman and a greatly respected politician in Upper Canada. At various times, he was a sheriff, a magistrate, a member of the Land Board, a postmaster and a Judge of the Court of Common Pleas. He served on two government commissions. Munro died at Long Sault, Ont, in 1800 at the age of 72.

★★★

Lieutenant John Enys, 29th Regiment of Foot

Enys was a Cornishman educated at Eton. At 19, as an ensign of the 29th Regiment (see *Armies, Brit.),* he participated in the Battle of Valcour Island in 1776. Promoted to lieutenant, he served under Major Christopher Carleton during operations on Lake Champlain in 1778 and 1780. His detailed account of the actions against Forts Ann and George was an invaluable resource for this book. His journal of his two tours of service in North America is an outstanding document of history. The descriptions of the old St. Lawrence River are remarkably detailed. He was a great sightseer, particularly enjoying waterfalls. John was also an ardent fly fisherman and astonished settlers with his large catches of salmon.

He made his career in the 29th, being promoted to major in 1794. His battalion was assigned to garrisoning the isle of Jersey in 1795, returning to England the next year where it defended the south coast. Enys was promoted to lieutenant colonel that year. In 1798, the regiment was dispatched to Ireland where it assisted in the defeat of Irish rebels and a French army which had been sent to support the rebellion. After a very full, and quite unusual career in the same regiment, he resigned from the army in 1800 at 42 and died in 1818.

See: Bibliography.

GEOGRAPHY

Canada and Quebec Province

During the time period of this book, Quebec Province and Canada were synonymous terms and used interchangeably. People of French and British extraction who lived in Quebec Province were known as Canadiens or Canadians, respectively. When old Quebec Province was divided into two new provinces in 1791, the settled parts of Quebec in the Laurentian region became Lower Canada and the areas in the west, newly settled by the loyalists, became Upper Canada. A similar division occurred on the Atlantic coast where old Nova Scotia was subdivided and New Brunswick, which had been predominantly settled by loyalists from the lower states, was born.

Later, the Province of Canada was formed by melding together Lower and Upper Canada, but keeping those two divisions as administrative regions which were known as Canada East and Canada West. When the Confederation of British North America was approved in 1867, the Provinces of Nova Scotia, New Brunswick and, soon after, Prince Edward Island, joined with the Province of Canada to form the new country which

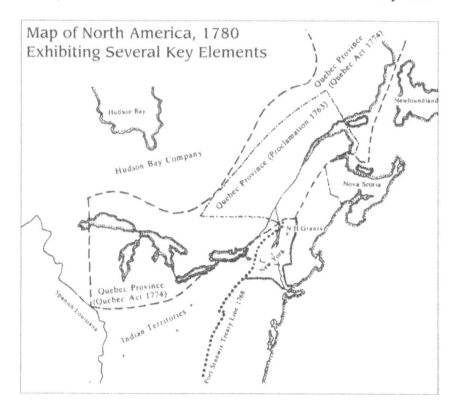

Map of North America, 1780
Exhibiting Several Key Elements

was called the Dominion of Canada. The Province of Canada was once again divided into two distinct provinces, Quebec and Ontario.

See: **The Canadian Encyclopedia** (Edmonton: Hurtig Publishers, 1988)

★★★

The Indian Territories
In 1768, a major treaty was finally confirmed at Fort Stanwix (modern Rome, NY) by Sir William Johnson. On behalf of the British government, Johnson negotiated the geographical limits of colonial expansion. The *Six Nations Confederacy* held a central role in this council acting as the primary speakers on behalf of the Indians present. This position was their historical right as they had developed hegemony over all other native peoples in the north; although their ceding of lands lived in by the Cherokees and Shawnees would prove problematical in the years ahead.

The outcome of this council was the definition of the boundary that was subsequently known as the Fort Stanwix Treaty Line, which divided the areas for colonial settlement from the zone that was reserved for the native nations. This treaty line ran from *Quebec Province* (see map) in the north to the Floridas in the south and effectively prevented the westward expansion of New York, Pennsylvania, Maryland, Virginia, the Carolinas and Georgia. Needless to say, the Provincial governments of those colonies were dissatisfied with this arrangement and did little to prevent new settlements in the Indian territories. Many bloody conflicts occurred as a result. The western boundary of the Indian Territories was the bed of the Mississippi River and marked Spanish Louisiana which stretched from the Gulf of Mexico to modern Michigan.

It will be apparent that after the ratification of the Fort Stanwix Treaty, all of the traditional lands of the Mohawk nation lay within the boundaries of New York Province with only small reserves being set aside for their living space at Fort Hunter, Canajoharie and Schoharie. In order to escape white encroachment, many Mohawks had already moved to the lower Unadilla River area. The river bed formed a natural boundary of the new Treaty Line with New York Province. The Mohawks had bargained away the hunting and "ownership" rights of their lands, and in some case the land of their dependencies, in the faith that the *British Six Nations Indian Department* would favour them with other privileges.

When the rebellion broke out in the Valley, the Mohawks who had remained there found themselves surrounded by hostile elements and unable to hold possession of even the little bit that had been left to them by treaty.

Once the peace treaty was ratified, the Indian nations were theoretically left with their territories intact; however, immediate expansion of white settlements and the resultant serious political pressure from the various American governments quickly forced major concessions. For the Mohawks, nothing was left of their old lands and the majority of them moved north to tracts granted by the British in western *Quebec Province* (see *Settlement Townships.)*

★★★

Indian Castles, Towns, Villages and Settlements

The term "castle" was used constantly throughout the time period to denote major native settlements, particularly amongst the *Six Nations.* A definition of the differences between a "castle" and a town has not been located; however, the term "castle" likely referred to a settlement with a central focus based on traditional longhouses and palisades, although outlying houses and barns similar to white dwellings may have been part of the overall community. It also seems that the term "castle" referred to communities of considerable age in comparison to villages or towns which were more recent in their founding.

★★★

The Mohawk and Schoharie Valleys and the Mohawk Region

The course of the Mohawk River runs from its rising near Fort Stanwix in middle, upstate New York to its confluence with the Hudson River near Albany. The river is bordered on both banks by high hills which form the Mohawk Valley. Not far west of Schenectady, the Schoharie River, or Kill, runs into the Mohawk River. As the Kill flows from south to north, the upper Schoharie Valley is in the south. There were three forts in the Schoharie; the Upper Fort is the furthest south and the Lower Fort the furthest north.

The use of the term, "Mohawk Region" is meant to include all of the lands at one time dominated by the Mohawk nation. Geographically, the Mohawk Valley represents the core of the region. Roughly, the extent of their hunting grounds ran north to *Quebec Province,* east to the Hudson River and the western shores of Lakes George and Champlain, then south into the Schoharie Valley with the Catskill Mountains bordering the eastern margin. The southern boundary was the east branch of the Delaware River and the Pennsylvania border. This accounting of the region in no way suggests that Mohawk influence stopped at those borders. Being a prominent and active member of the *Six Nations Confederacy,* their hegemony reached far beyond this region.

★★★

The New Hampshire Grants ("The Grants") and The Republic of Vermont

The State of Vermont began in a bitter controversy between the provinces of New York and New Hampshire. Both claimed the right to grant title to land in the region and settlers who accepted a grant from one authority invariably ran foul of the other. In 1764, this conflict was adjudicated in Britain in favour of New York. Conditions were set regarding the land grants issued by New Hampshire and many folk were unwilling or unable to comply with them.

Spurred on by men such as Seth Warner, Remember Baker and the Allen brothers, Ethan and Ira, this confusion led to open revolt and a great number of the dissatisfied holders of New Hampshire-issued grants organized themselves into an illegal, paramilitary body known as the Green Mountain Boys. These men hounded all who held New York-issued grants and the Yorker government officials who attempted to apply the law. Acting as vigilantes, they conducted night raids on Yorker homes, destroying property and physically abusing the owners.

When the rebellion began, it was Ethan Allen and his "Boys" who struck the first major blow for the rebels in the north by seizing the legendary fortress of Ticonderoga in a surprise attack on the tiny garrison of British Regulars who were unaware that open conflict had begun. Seth Warner was chosen to take command of an "additional" *Continental regiment* (see *Armies, U.S.*) composed of Grants' men and this unit was prominent in the invasion of Quebec in 1775.

During the Burgoyne campaign of 1777, men from The Grants were active in militia companies raised in the area, as was Warner's Continental unit. But, the rabid politicos in the Grants had set upon a new venture, and even before Burgoyne set out from Quebec, they had proclaimed the New Hampshire Grants as the Republic of Vermont. Under the threat of Burgoyne's invasion, differences were thrown aside and rebels of all stripes pulled together to defeat the Crown's army.

After the surrender of Burgoyne, the Vermonters increased the pressure on the Continental Congress to receive statehood for their republic, but the thorny issues of New York's rights prevented an easy solution and, in the midst of the crises of war, the Congress declined the request. More of the Vermont story is told in this book. Statehood was granted in 1791.

See: Mary Beacock Fryer, **Buckskin Pimpernel, the Exploits of Justus Sherwood, Loyalist Spy** (Toronto & Charlottetown: Dundurn Press, 1981); Henry W. Du Puy, **Ethan Allen and the Green-Mountain Heroes of '76** (Buffalo: Phinney & Co., 1853)

★★★

Settlement Townships in western Quebec (now Ontario)

After the peace, it became apparent to *Governor Haldimand* that the provisions for the loyalists which had been agreed to in the treaty were not going to be honoured by the United States. He recognized that the majority of these refugees had no interest in migrating to Britain. They were Americans and required an American solution.

Haldimand set about examining options for settlement in Quebec and sent a number of trained loyalist officers to survey potential sites for new townships. The loyalist leadership had made it plain to the Governor that they did not wish to live under the French systems of land tenure and civil law which the Quebec Act had guaranteed to Canadiens (see *Canada & Quebec Province.*) Consequently, the new townships were located in western Quebec where there were no previous settlements.

Eight new townships were surveyed along the north shore of the St. Lawrence River west of the Ottawa River. This grouping became known as the Royal Townships. A second set of five were laid out on the north shore of Lake Ontario between, and including, Fort Frontenac (modern Kingston) and Quintes Isle. These became known as the Cataraqui Townships. North of CT#4&5 was the large tract reserved for the Fort Hunter Mohawks.

Throughout the endnotes and appendices of this book, these townships are abbreviated as RT and CT followed by a number which defines their exact location. For example, CT#3 is Cataraqui Township No.3 which later became known as Fredericksburgh. It was the primary settlement area for the 2nd Battalion, King's Royal Regiment of New York and the 2nd Battalion, King's Rangers.

Similarly, there were townships laid out at Niagara and opposite Fort Detroit which were settled by Butler's Rangers, Brant's Volunteers and other loyalists. Between these two surveys lies the Grand River along which the Canajoharie Mohawks and other Six Nations and allied Indians settled under Joseph Brant.

See: Cruikshank & Watt, KRR NY, **op.cit.,** pp.160&161; Brig.-General E.A. Cruikshank, tr.&ed., **The Settlement of the United Empire Loyalists on the Upper St. Lawrence and Bay of Quinte in 1784** (Toronto: The Ontario Historical Society, 1934)

ORGANIZATIONS

The Six Nations (Iroquois Confederacy or League of the Iroquois)
The League of the Iroquois began in the late 14th or early 15th century as a federation of five Iroquoian-speaking nations: the Mohawks, Oneidas, Onondagas, Cayugas and Senecas. The Oneidas & Cayugas were known as the Younger Brothers and the other three as the Elder — the two Younger nations sat on one side of the Grand Council Fire and

the Elder Mohawks & Senecas on the other, with the Elder Onondaga seated between as the balance. Their collective society was matriarchal in nature with the women having an equal say in all realms of politics. Their society was based on a clan system and the clan matrons were responsible for the choice of replacements for vacant council positions, occasioned by debilitating sickness or death, from amongst their wise and experienced clan men.

The valley of the Mohawk River and the territory to its north and south was the country of the Mohawks, the guardians of its Eastern Door. It is likely that they could field no more than 175 warriors when the conflict flared into open rebellion, as this once powerful nation had been so depleted by its contact with the diseases of white society and migration to Canada. Below and west of where the Mohawk River rises were the lands of the Oneidas. This nation was the second most populous amongst the Iroquois at the time of the revolution and may have fielded some 300 hatchets. Amongst them settled the Tuscarora who had been driven from their Carolina homeland in the early 18th Century by white expansion. They contributed some 225 men to the Confederacy. Beyond that nation and lying at the centre of the Confederacy, were the homelands of the Onondagas who could field between 200 – 225 men. Their main settlement, Onondaga Castle, constituted the political centre of the Confederacy where the Grand Council Fire was maintained. At the northern edge of the Onondaga country on the south shore of Lake Ontario sat the ruins of the forts at Oswego. The Cayuga nation lay to the west of the Onondaga Castle; this nation was still strong in numbers at the time of this story and close to 250 men were available for war. And lastly, guarding the Western Door, were the Seneca, mightiest of the five original tribes. Their villages spread to Lake Erie's southern shore and deep into the Ohio country. Fort Niagara was situated in the Seneca country by agreement with that nation. They were broadly divided into two groupings, the Lower or Alleghany Seneca, and the Upper or Genesee Seneca. This Elder Brother was the most populous of the five original nations with perhaps 650 – 700 men and, being quite far from white influences, clung most fiercely to the traditional Iroquoian ways. An independent breakaway group, known as the Mingos, were primarily Seneca in origin and lived in the Alleghany region. While not part of the Confederacy, they could be relied upon in time of need and could bring some 200 men to the field.

The original five nations were not at peace with one another until the formation of the League, or Confederacy. Thereafter, very little armed conflict existed between the members. This remarkable grouping of nations produced what many view as the strongest alliance of indigenous American peoples, even greater than the Lakota grouping led by the Sioux in the northwest that was so prominent in the later 1800's. Springing from this political strength, the Five Nations came to dominate all the other native peoples about them, whether Iroquoian or Algonkian. Often, in Roman fashion, those nations that they conquered were so reduced as to be eliminated, the remnants absorbed fully into the culture of the Confederacy and individuals became valued members of their adopted nations. Those who successfully resisted total destruction became dependencies, or vassals; however, by no means always craven or abject. Thus, the mighty Ottawa, likewise the Sacs and Foxes, the Shawnee — and many, many southern and western tribes as far to the west as the Dakota nations and in the east to Nova Scotia and New England and to the south below Virginia, were under the influence of the Five Nations. These nations were ceremonially referred to as Nephews.

The arrival of the whites disrupted this alliance. The Dutch at first warred with the League, in particular the Mohawks, eventually to find more value and certainly less agony in trade. It was the French who chose to ally themselves with native enemies of the Confederacy and earned their deepest enmity. As the English replaced the Dutch, they readily filled the role of traders and willingly provided the goods and services needed to maintain a changing life amongst the Confederacy's peoples.

Essentially an agrarian society, the Six Nations had come to dominate the central fur trade, not by trapping and curing peltry, but by war. While women, children and the aged tended the fields, the warriors extended the dominance of the Confederacy. On the attainment of economic power through the control of the middle-ground of the trade, they bartered with the whites for tools, arms and cloth and became dependent upon this exchange for their lifestyle. Their culture grew to be interwoven with this trade and, although quite clairvoyant regarding the dangers represented by white expansion onto their traditional grounds, they also recognized the value of this dependency and conducted their affairs with forbearance. The movement of furs developed to such a volume along the river and portage route from Oswego to Albany that by the time of the rebellion, the New York provincial capital had become a serious rival to Montreal as the centre of that commerce.

Of equal significance, the activities of the Christian church reached out to alter their culture. By the turn of the century, the Church of England had made great inroads into Mohawk society and most of that nation which remained in New York province were converted to a devoted practice of Anglicanism. In 1712, Queen Anne made a present of an engraved silver Communion set, which to this day retains immense importance amongst the two communities in Canada which were founded after the rebellion by New York Mohawk refugees.

Accompanying the establishment of New England Protestant settlements to the south of the Mohawk River was the spread of this form of Christianity. As the Johnson family espoused Anglicanism, the Protestant clergy considered that the best location for missions amongst the Six Nations was in the western reaches of the Confederacy, far away from direct Johnson interference. Their first efforts were amongst the Seneca. That nation, due to the proximity of the tireless French Jesuits at Fort Niagara, had already been exposed to Roman Catholicism without success. When the Protestants found the Seneca resistant to conversion, they moved their missions to the Oneida and Tuscarora settlements. With those peoples, they achieved lasting success. This accomplishment was to have great consequence during the rebellion when the Oneida and Tuscorara split from the Confederacy and took side with the rebels.

The government of the Confederacy and its infrastructure was unique in its time. A surface examination suggests a democracy; however, the core of its representation was based upon heredity, often denoted as "kinship." Each nation had a number of civil chiefs, or Sachems, representing the Clans within the tribe; these sat in the Confederacy's central council at Onondaga. At the League's formation, the number of Sachems had been set for each nation, probably based on population and geography. For example, the Mohawks had nine, the Onondagas fourteen and the Senecas eight. Should a civil chief die or be killed, his replacement was chosen from within the tribe by his clan mothers, or matrons, who would choose from amongst their relatives. In consequence, many gifted and astute men were passed over in favour of tradition and heredity. This problem was met with an all too familiar solution. The war chiefs who were chosen for their skill, bravery and deeds upon the battlefield used the force of their personalities and reputations to frequently outweigh the rule of the Sachems. In many cases they became the de facto leaders of the Confederacy.

One other factor is cited as being a flaw in the Six Nations' government, that being the influence of "locality." Similar to the provinces of Canada or the states of the American Union, it was possible for a nation or a grouping of nations to entirely sway the decision making process on the basis of their particular views or needs. For example, it was possible for the war chiefs of the Seneca to foist decisions favouring their position upon the council while the contrary belief was held by a majority of the Confederacy's Sachems and the Matrons, who were either not sufficiently skillful or, at that moment, influential enough to gain the point.

Many of the Iroquois came under the influence of French missionaries and left Iroquoia to build new satellite communities on the edges of *Quebec Province* (see *Canada Indians.*)

When the Tuscarora moved north to Iroquois at the invitation of the League they became the sixth nation of the Confederacy with modified voting rights under the wing of the Oneidas. As the old regime of France drew to a painful, but brilliant end, the Six Nations played a major role, in concert with their European- and American-born British allies, in drawing the curtain closed.

In the 18th Century, the population of the League had reduced alarmingly. The Confederacy's leadership knew that they must offset these losses if they were to protect their hegemony in the north. Their southern and south-west boundary, where white encroachment was extreme, was particularly vulnerable. Many Indian nations had fallen afoul of this expansionism and suffered severely. The League offered a refuge for these people and settled groups of refugees along its southern borders and within the core of the Confederacy as well. These affiliated peoples were given important places at the Grand Council fire, but never a vote. They clearly benefited from their adoption, as did the League from the increase in numbers. Elements of many Algonkian nations such as the Nanticokes, Mahicans, Conoys, Squakies (Foxes) and Shawnees were along the branches of the Susquehanna with some Squakies amongst the Alleghany and Genesee castles of the Senecas. Together, these disparate groups added some 150 men to the strength. The Susquehanna region was Delaware and Munsee territory, closely related Algonkian nations that were strongly under the League's influence. These two closely related peoples added some 150 warriors. Two branches of the Siouian or Lakota linguistic group found their way into the Confederacy's borders, the Tuteloes and Saponis. The former built a village amongst the Cayugas on the southern shore of the lake of that name. Together, they brought another 70 adult males under the League's control. War parties from all these refugee peoples would be found operating from Fort Niagara later in the war.

The Mississaugas of western Quebec Province were considered a dependent rather than an affiliate. This Algonkian nation was not agricultural and therefore was not found in set villages like the Iroquois. The nomadic Mississaugas followed the hunt and were spread across what is now southern Ontario in small groups of temporary communities. The non-Christian Mississaugas were not part of the Canada Indian grouping and appear to have fallen under the control and sponsorship of the Senecas. They were very active participants during the rebellion, always on the side of the Crown. Although numbers were not recorded, they likely contributed close to 100 warriors.

When the Confederacy split, the pro-British faction totalled over 2700 available men and the pro-rebel about 600. Due to the nature of native society, there were individual Mohawks who honorably sided with the rebels and similary Oneidas & Tuscaroras who fought for the Crown, so these totals are by no means pure. In any event, numbers don't signify very much if compared to the strengths of British or American regiments. The Indians could be used tactically like rangers, acting as patrols to provide intelligence or give early warnings, or as a van to protect the advancing army from surprises, or to attack outposts, or to strike deep into enemy territory to deliver blows, crippling to morale and property. Due to their deeply-held traditions, they were unsuitable for building and manning fortifications. Nor did they tolerate set-piece battles with the attendant probability of heavy casualties to which the "European" mind had become adapted. When employed to their best advantage, they were an invaluable military resource and both sides knew this very well.

See: Graymont, Kelsay & Stone, **op.cit.**

★★★

The Canada Indians or, the Seven Nations of Canada

The five original nations of the *Iroquois Confederacy* became a geographical and political buffer between the French and English. Early in the development of this role, the Five Nations completed both the destruction of the Huron, Neutral and Tobacco nations and the absorption of lesser peoples such as the Eries. Simultaneously, there were successful political manoeuvres by the subtle French, and through the inspired and fearless efforts of the Jesuits and other missionaries of Roman Catholic orders, many Iroquoian & Algonkian Indians were led to locate in religious communities amongst the settled areas of *old Quebec.* Three of these towns included a large number of Mohawks, Cayugas, Oneidas and Onondagas. These peripheral settlements of Iroquoian and Algonkian peoples, and a residue of the once great Hurons, constituted sizable villages and became known as the Seven Nations of Canada, or the Canada Indians. These Christian settlements were the physical buffer against English attack and their men provided the French with fearsome allies in the field.

When Britain conquered New France, the Seven Nations of Canada were reluctant to place their faith in the victors, especially the primarily-Protestant, British Americans with whom they had waged a relentless and vicious war for the better part of two centuries. Inevitably, they acknowledged the ascendancy of the English in America. They saw the potential for protection under the wing of the Six Nations, the foremost allies of the victors and they gave recognition to their southern brothers with a bond of native allegiance, accepting their counsel and direction.

The names of these Canadian settlements and their linguistic majority were: the Iroquois of Kahnawake (Caughnawaga), Kanehsatake (Oka) & Akwasasne (St. Regis); the Iroquoian Hurons of Lorette; the Algonkian Algonquins & Nipissings of Lac des Deux-Montagnes and the Algonkian Abenaki of St. Francis. By 1775, only Kahnawake, Kanehsatake and Akwasasne had the strength to contribute strong parties to war — some 500 hatchets in total. While in no way militarily insignificant, the Canada Indians lacked either the infrastructure of the political will developed by the Six Nations.

When the rebels invaded Quebec in 1775, most of Seven Nations remained politically neutral except the Kahnawakes who took a strong pro-rebel stance, greatly alarming the British. When the invaders were driven from Quebec in 1776, the British immediately took a strong hold on the Seven Nations' villages. In 1777, the Canada Indians participated, though many with reluctance, in the Burgoyne campaign. The defeat of Burgoyne's army gave them much pause for thought, but by 1780, large parties of Canada Indians again took to the field in assistance of the British.

The Lakes Nations
This name is given to a loose federation of Algonkian, Souian and Iroquoian nations from the western and south-western Great Lakes region. Prominent amongst them were the Ottawas, Wyandots, Miamis and Potawatamis. They had been under the influence of the Six Nations for over a century, although their white alliance had been with the French. After the conquest, their dependence on the *League of the Iroquois* as mentors deepened and acted as a buffer between them and the British. By the time of the rebellion, this loose federation could field more warriors than the Six Nations and their peoples were feeling their strength and new-found influence. In 1776, they developed a close tie to the nations to the southwards, the Shawnees, Kickapoos, Delaware and Mingos. In combination with these latter nations, the whole are often referred to as the Western Indians.

The British Six Nations' Indian Department
The British Government created Indian Departments which managed the complex relationship of political treaties between the Crown and the various nations in its jurisdiction and the management of payments of good faith which took the form of presents. Complaints from either party were heard and adjudicated in solemn councils and, if beyond the powers vested in the office of superintendent, were referred to the provincial and British governments.

In the north, Sir William Johnson, an Irish immigrant who had taken residence amongst the Mohawks in the *Mohawk Valley,* was appointed in 1755 to have "the Sole Management & direction of the Affairs of the *Six Nations of Indians & their Allies,*" a brief which included the Western Indians (see *Lakes Nations.)* In 1756, he was given the title, "Colonel, Agent and Sole Superintendent of the affairs of the Six Nations, and other Northern Indians" and for his great victory over the French at Lake George the year before, a baronetcy and a very large cash reward.

After the death of his first wife, Sir William married Mary (Molly) Brant, a woman of great family and a clan matron of the Mohawk nation. His reputation amongst the Confederacy was already very strong and this union with a prominent Mohawk wife cemented his influence.

Sir William's department fostered a group of skilled and dedicated men who learned carefully and acted discreetly in the conduct of their functions, fully recognizing the spirit and power of the Confederacy. They learned well the balance of strengths and weaknesses of the Six Nations and their allies, developing key roles as lesser administrators within Sir William's circle. They also recognized the value of the alliance between Britain, her colonies and the Confederacy. They were cognizant of the fighting skills and tactics of the Indian; knowing how these should be best used and maintained for the furtherance of Britain's strategy.

After the conquest of Canada in 1760, Sir William assumed the management of the *Seven Nations of Canada.* He broadened his department's administration by promoting deputy superintendents from his skilled and trusted co-workers — germane to this book, his nephew and son-in-law Guy Johnson acted for the Six Nations and their allies and Daniel Claus, another son-in-law, for the Seven Nations of Canada.

During the rebellion years, 1775-1782, the location of the department's headquarters varied, but for the latter years of the war, it was based at Fort Niagara where Guy Johnson, who had replaced Sir William on his sudden death in 1774, stationed himself after 1779. In 1782, Guy Johnson was the focus of a scandal which resulted in his suspension. He was replaced by *Sir John Johnson.*

A small Six Nations' sub-department under LtCol. Daniel Claus was located at Lachine, Quebec (just west of Montreal) where the Fort Hunter Mohawks had located after fleeing their settlement in the Mohawk Valley in 1777. Claus commanded a small ranger detachment which operated with the Fort Hunter Mohawks on campaign and in intelligence gathering.

It should be recognized that the rebels created a parallel Indian department (Indian Affairs Commission for the Northern Department) in which General Philip Schuyler of New York took a major role. In the early stages of the war, Schuyler was particularly effective in dividing the Iroquois Confederacy. Once the British hatchet had been accepted at Three Rivers, NY, in 1777, the influence of the rebel department waned.

As a mark of respect, it was common to refer to senior war chiefs of the Six Nations and their allies as captains; however the individuals so denoted did not hold British Indian Department commissions in this rank. *Joseph Brant* is an exception to this rule as he was formally commissioned a captain in 1780.

See: Graymont, Kelsay, Stephens, **op.cit.**; Bruce Wilson, "The Struggle for Wealth and Power at Fort Niagara 1775-1783", **Ontario History, Vol.68 (1976); Maryly B. Penrose, Indian Affairs Papers, American Revolution** (Franklin Park, NJ: Liberty Bell Associates, 1981); Robert S. Allen, **His Majesty's Indian Allies, British Indian Policy in the Defence of Canada, 1774-1815** (Toronto & Oxford: Dundurn Press, 1992)

★★★

The Quebec Indian Department

Governor *Guy Carleton* became impatient with the administration of his province's native population being conducted by outside agents from New York province. He distrusted Sir William Johnson, suspecting him of using his position and influence in favour of the New York fur merchants to the detriment of the Montreal trade. In 1773, Carleton had John Campbell appointed as Major-Commandant (later LtCol.) of Indian Affairs for *Quebec Province*. While the Quebec Governor claimed that there was no intent to interfere with Johnson's efforts, Sir William had not been consulted regarding Campbell's appointment and he suspected the very worst of Carleton's manoeuvres. In this, his concerns proved correct.

Campbell had been an accomplished captain in the Black Watch and later the 27th of Foot. When in Canada after the conquest, he married Marie-Anne, eldest daughter of La Corne St. Luc, who was a noted Canadien Indian officer of the old French regime and for whom Carleton had a particularly high regard. Campbell had been named Inspector of Indian Affairs by Governor James Murray in 1768. Sir William forced a cancellation of that appointment. The 1773 appointment by Carleton was an extension of the duties of Campbell's short-lived earlier role and Sir William either didn't have the influence or the energy to have it rescinded. Of course, Campbell could, and did, rely upon his father-in-law to assist him whenever required.

During the rebellion, Campbell was assisted by a number of seconded British officers. Primary amongst them was Captain Alexander

Fraser of the 34th of Foot. Fraser acted as Deputy Superintendent within the Department and in 1780 was stationed at Carleton Island. In addition, a number of Canadien officers were on staff, most of them having a lineage of Indian service that stretched back to the French Regime. These men were mustered as "Messieurs", rather than being given a rank.

The Quebec Department was responsible for the management of both the *Seven Nations of Canada* in the Montreal region and ostensibly for the *Lakes Nations* in the Detroit region. The interplay between the Six Nations and Quebec Departments was extremely complex. For example, sandwiched between the two major jurisdictions of the Quebec Department were the forts at Carleton Island and Fort Niagara. These posts were under the influence of the *Six Nations Department,* although Alexander Fraser being in command at Fort Haldimand on Carleton Island in 1780 strongly suggests an overlap of responsibility. As another example, when the war shifted westwards to the Ohio, Kentucky and Illinois territories in 1781 and 82, companies of Butler's Rangers and Brant's men operated with Lakes Nations Indians which constituted a clear melding of responsibilities.

LtCol. Daniel Claus, who served under Sir William Johnson as Deputy Superintendent of the Canada Indians, was the major victim of Carleton's ploy. When Claus travelled with Guy Johnson to Montreal in 1775, he found himself displaced and without authority or position amongst the Seven Nations, so successful had been Carleton's machinations. Claus travelled to England to obtain a reinstatement of his former position without success. Indeed, Guy Johnson sacrificed his brother-in-law Daniel during his own struggle to have his superintendency officially confirmed. When Guy Johnson returned to America with *Joseph Brant,* Claus remained behind to continue attempts to salvage his livelihood. He managed to obtain a temporary commission as Superintendent of Indians for St. Leger's Expedition and sailed to Quebec, but after the ignominious failure of that operation, he was unable to regain the equal of his former position. From 1778 onwards, he managed a sub-department of the Six Nations from Montreal where his relations with the Quebec Department must have been strained at best. In 1782, Sir John Johnson was appointed Superintendent & Inspector General of Indian Affairs and the two departments were again amalgamated.

The Armies of the Chief Protagonists
The British Forces
The British army in America was composed of several elements. First were regiments of British Regular Infantry, or Foot, which were denoted by numbered battalions. Germane to this book are the 8th, 29th, 34th, 53rd and 84th, elements of which were actively on campaign in

1780 operating from bases in *Quebec* and Fort Niagara as well as men from the 4th Battalion, Royal Artillery, which had detachments across the province.

Many regiments were formed in America of men who chose to remain loyal to the Crown and the established government. Prominent leaders were given warrants, or Beating Orders, to raise these units from defined recruiting areas. These were known as Provincials and were de facto British-American Regulars. A number of these units were based in Quebec and *Indian Territory* in the *Northern, or Canadian Department* under the command of the Quebec Governor who issued Beating Orders for the raising of men from New York. Those which were active in the 1780 campaign were the 1st Battalion, King's Royal Regiment of New York (Royal Yorkers); Butler's Rangers and Leake's & Fraser's Independent Companies.

Several regiments had been raised in 1777 and transferred to the *British Army's Central Department* when General Burgoyne invaded New York. After Burgoyne's surrender, remnants of these units returned to Quebec and, of these, Jessup's King's Loyal Americans were active in October 1780. An embryonic battalion of rangers commanded by Major James Rogers had been sent to Quebec from the Central Department and these men were also on the expedition.

Over 6000 troops from the German principalities, raised to fight in America, were active in Burgoyne's expedition and afterwards continued to garrison Quebec Province. Governor Haldimand assigned a detachment from the Hesse Hanau Jaeger battalion to Sir John Johnson on his October 1780 expedition.

A key element of the military capability in Canada was the *British Six Nations' and Quebec Indian Departments,* both of which came under the command of the Quebec Governor. Large parties of men from the various Indian nations participated in the October 1780 expeditions. The Mohawk chief, Joseph Brant, had raised a body of white and native men known as Brant's Volunteers. This very active unit was ex officio to the army, but represented an important element of Johnson's raid into the *Schoharie and Mohawk Valleys.* A small group of rangers managed by LtCol. Daniel Claus of the Six Nations' Indian Department also participated in the October operations.

The Army of the United States
Each of the American States raised and maintained a number of regiments for Continental service. Pennsylvania at one stage fielded 12 regiments and this contribution was known as the Pennsylvania Line. Together, the whole army was known as the Continental Line and this constituted the United States' "regular" army. The strategic use of the Continental regiments was directed by the Continental Congress

and the brigades, corps and armies created from combinations of these regiments were commanded by General Washington and his General Staff.

Only one Continental regiment is prominent in this book. It is Seth Warner's Additional Regiment, accredited to, and maintained by, New York State. The designation of "additional" to a regiment's title suggested some odd political derivation to its raising. For example, Warner's had been first raised from Green Mountain Boys of *the New Hampshire Grants* area of New York State. By 1780, the composition of the regiment had altered dramatically. See the text and notes for further detail.

As there were never enough Continentals for all the needs of the war, Congress authorized the raising of para-regular regiments of state Levies. The officer corps of these regiments were drawn from supernumerary or retired Continental officers and the men were drafted from the county militias for specified terms of service. In 1780, New York had raised five regiments of Levies specifically for the defence of its frontiers and Massachusetts had raised two regiments of Levies for this same purpose. One Massachusetts and four New York regiments of Levies are prominent in this book.

The largest element of the American military was the militia. All men of military age, if not on active service with the Continental Line or Levies, were expected to be enrolled in a county militia regiment and instantaneously available for duty. These men were called out in time of local emergencies. Very prominent in this book are the militia regiments of Albany and Tryon Counties.

Two nations of the *Iroquois Confederacy,* the Oneidas and Tuscaroras, sided with the rebellion and provided yeoman service to the cause of American independence. By doing so, they broke faith with their brothers of the League. For the Iroquois, the rebellion was as much a civil war as it was to the white Americans.

Both France and Spain were allied to the United States during the war. French troops and the French navy were very significant in the defeat of Cornwallis at Yorktown in 1781, but neither they, nor the Spanish, play direct roles in the events of this book.

★★★

The Central and Northern (Canadian) Departments of the British Army in America

The British administration of the war in America was divided into Departments. The Central, or Main, Department was headquartered in New York City and the commander-in-chief in America took post there. The navy was under entirely separate control and its commanding officer on the American station primarily kept post off New York

City. Cooperation between the two services was complex, difficult and sometimes inefficient.

A wing of the Central Department stretched north to Nova Scotia and Newfoundland. Halifax was a major Naval station and critical to control of the Atlantic. Newfoundland controlled an invaluable resource — the fishery. When operations were conducted in the southern states, the command element, and often the troops, came from headquarters in New York City.

The military affairs of *Quebec Province* were managed by *the Northern*, or *Canadian Department*. This gigantic province bordered two states — Massachusetts (now Maine) and New York; *Indian Territory* and Spanish Louisiana. Its affairs were so complex that the commander-in-chief in New York City left their management to his subordinate, the Governor of Quebec (see *Carleton & Haldimand.*) Coordination between departments was difficult with communications being slow and uncertain, either by sea and the St. Lawrence, or overland by express couriers of the *British Secret Service.*

It should be recognized that the rebel administration also created separate departments to manage the operations of the war. As the New York frontier lay within the rebel's Northern Department and no other zones are discussed, there are no confusing, overlapping references made in the text.

★★★

The Sullivan-Clinton Expedition of 1779

The expedition against the *Indian territories* was planned by *General Washington* and approved by Congress in February 1779. General Horatio Gates, who had accepted the surrender of Burgoyne's army in 1777, was first offered the command, but declined due to age and health. The aggressive John Sullivan readily accepted the task and began preparations. By July 1st, Washington had grown impatient with Sullivan's delays and, in mid-August, the commander-in-chief wrote a scathing report to Congress regarding Sullivan's sluggishness. Nonetheless, Sullivan retained the command and mounted his expedition later that month, achieving the destruction of the majority of the *Six Nations and allied* settlements.

There were four phases to the invasion. The main body was led by General John Sullivan and numbered about 2300 men which were assembled at Easton, Pennsylvania.

An opening gambit of the campaign was commanded by Colonel Goose Van Schaick whose regiment, the 1st New York, was in garrison at Fort Stanwix on the upper Mohawk River. His 558-man force was given the task of destroying the Onondaga villages (see *Six Nations Confederacy.*) A smaller party, which included the rebel Oneidas and Tuscaroras, were sent to raid the British post at Oswegatchie on the St. Lawrence River in a ruse to keep them occupied while Van Schaick fell upon their brothers, the Onondagas. Van Schaick was entirely successful in destroying the Onondaga villages. The Oswegatchie venture was abortive, but had served its purpose.

James Clinton, the older brother of Governor *George Clinton,* had been a militia captain in the Seven Years War and was commissioned the LtCol. of the 3rd New York Continental regiment in 1775. He participated in the invasion of Canada and the next year was promoted to brigadier in the *Continental Army* (see, *Armies, U.S.)* As the post commandant of Fort Clinton, he received a bayonet wound during the heroic, but unsuccessful, defence in 1777. He was posted to Albany in 1778 and in 1779 was given an important task during the expedition against the *Indian Territory,* commanding a wing of 1600 men which operated from the *Mohawk Valley.* His force assembled at Canajoharie and marched south-west, destroying a number of Indian settlements en route, and united with Sullivan at Tioga. Together they marched into the Cayuga and Seneca country where they laid waste to virtually all the castles. At Yorktown, Virginia in 1781, James Clinton's brigade had the honour of receiving the surrendered colours of the British regiments. Like his brother George, James enjoyed a political career and was governor of New York State on two occasions. He was a promoter of the building of the Erie Canal, a water highway that opened the north-west Indian Territory to American commerce.

Colonel Brodhead, from his base at Fort Pitt (modern Pittsburgh, PA), led a third force of 605 men against the settlements of the Alleghany Senecas, Mingos, Delawares and Shawnees. This carefully planned and executed campaign illustrated the growing power, confidence and capability of the United States.

★★★

Rebel Committees and Commissions

To illustrate a process that occurred across settled America — on August 27, 1774 several prominent citizens of Tryon County, who shared the type of political values which later led to open rebellion against the British Parliament, held a meeting to make several resolutions. As well as proclaiming their "Faith and Allegiance" to King George III, this group "conceived it necessary" to have a Committee appointed to correspond with like committees in New York City and Albany so that they may share their "sentiments." This, and similar committees across New York and the other provinces, were known as Committees of Correspondence.

It was not too long before subcommittees were established in each large town and district of the County and, in this manner, a de facto government was created parallel to the established one. Soon these committees were making political decisions in the place of Crown officials. They eased out the established government's sheriffs, magistrates, jailers, clerks, surveyors, etc... in short, in every branch of government, the Committees substituted men who would "safeguard the liberties of America."

It was not too long before the name of these committees was altered to Committees of Safety and the task of questioning suspicious persons became a regular and most important element of their activities. Those who openly espoused loyalty to the established government, so-called "disaffected" folk, received immediate attention. If these intransigent persons could not be intimidated, they would be fined, or pressured to sign "associations" which promised acceptable behaviour, and, if it was thought necessary, would be incarcerated. If they were repeat offenders or particularly active in some "dangerous" activity, loyalists could be sent out of the county to a jail, or even to another province and held in make-shift prisons such as the infamous old copper mine at Simsbury, Connecticut where the disaffected from across the north were confined. In other cases, if a repeated "crime" was considered particularly offensive, the perpetrator could be hanged.

Even persons who took no sides and did everything sensible to remain neutral, could find themselves accused of secreting arms, helping fugitives, uttering damning loyalist phrases, giving secret signals, meeting with suspected persons, etc... Unfortunately, for unprincipled rebels, the Committee of Safety offered an excellent opportunity for imaginative tattling so that old scores which had no bearing on politics might be settled. Vindictive witch hunts were not uncommon.

Obviously, before long serious loyalists took measures of their own. They became far more secretive, held their own meetings and formed their own committees and groups to further their activities. To the rebels, these actions were viewed as conspiracies. In New York State, in order to combat such loyalist machinations, a special body with wide ranging powers, known as the Commission for Detecting and Defeating Conspiracies, was created. Very senior, hard-case proponents of the rebellion sat as members and they swung a heavy hammer. Their brief was to uncover all activities of the *British Secret Service* such as safe houses, intelligence gathering and courier networks. Discovering loyalist recruiting officers was very important, not only because they bled men away to bolster the loyalist regiments in Canada or New York City, but as much for the fact that they reduced morale amongst the populace. This book details some of this commission's activities.

See: Maryly B. Penrose, **Mohawk Valley in the Revolution, Committee of Safety Papers** ... (Franklin Park, NJ: Liberty Bell Associates, 1978)

★★★

The British Secret Service

The gathering of intelligence regarding the rebels was always a vital activity in the *Northern Department.* There were two distinct types of intelligence — political affairs and military matters. To be sure, these often overlapped and a coordination of both types was required. *Carleton* and *Haldimand* employed civilian scouts, Indians and Regular & Provincial soldiers in this role even from the first hints of political unrest. Particularly important in *Quebec Province* was a network of political friends and informants amongst the Canadien population, elements of which had assisted the rebel Americans during their 1775 invasion of the province. Once the French openly entered the war, the Governor feared a renewed sympathy for the rebellion amongst the Canadiens.

Captain Justus Sherwood of the Queen's Loyal Rangers became involved in gathering and analysing intelligence shortly after Burgoyne's defeat and he exhibited such an aptitude for the work that, over the next three years, Governor Haldimand came to rely heavily upon him. When negotiations with the *Republic of Vermont* were to begin in 1780, Sherwood, the past Green Mountain Boy, was an obvious choice for such a dangerous and delicate role. His cover was to be the exchange of prisoners held by both sides and the relief of loyalist families still within the rebel lines. (See Chapter III of this book)

In 1781, Sherwood's role became formalized; his sole duties related to the negotiations with Vermont and the running of agents gathering intelligence. This did not preclude his involvement with prisoner and refugee problems. Sherwood was appointed the Officer Commanding the Secret Service and Dr. George Smyth (see text and notes) became his second-in-command. Sherwood handled intelligence matters relating to Vermont and Smyth that of New York's.

See: Hazel M. Mathews, **Frontier Spies - The British Secret Service, Northern Department, during the Revolutionary War** (Fort Myers, FA: the author, 1971); Mary Beacock Fryer, **Buckskin Pimpernel, the Exploits of Justus Sherwood, Loyalist Spy** (Toronto and Charlottetown: Dundurn Press, 1981); Mary Beacock Fryer, **Loyalist Spy, The Experiences of Captain John Walden Meyers during the American Revolution** (Dundurn Press)

**Lord George Germain,
Secretary of State for
the American Colonies
1775-1782**
Engraving after George Romney,
1780 (from Piers Mackesy, The War
for America 1775-1783)

**Sir Frederick Haldimand, Governor
of Quebec**
(National Archives of Canada)

George Washington, Commander-in-Chief of the Continental Army
For his role as the primary architect of the expedition against the Indian Territories, the Six Nations gave Washington the name, 'Town Destroyer.'
Charles Peale Polk, 18th Century

General John Sullivan of New Hampshire
Leader of the expedition into Indian Territory in 1779.
Richard Morell Stargg, 18th Century (from Barbara Graymont, Iroquois in the American Revolution, 1972)

I

THE BACKGROUND

The large-scale raids into the Hudson, Schoharie and Mohawk Valleys in October 1780 by the forces of the Crown provide excellent examples of the different perspectives found in North American history. The Canadian view of this endeavour is radically opposed to that taken by American popular historians who ignore the military value of the raids, the consummate skill and daring of their leadership and the vigour of the native and white troops who accomplished the deeds. Their emphasis is on the horrors of the native mode of warfare, the sickening revenge taken by the detested Tories and the back-breaking labour of the valiant American Levies and militia.

By 1780, five years into the war, the rebellion had spread far beyond the borders of the thirteen rebelling colonies, indeed far beyond North America. It had taken shape as a major, world-wide conflict involving a number of large and small European powers and, for Britain, a major protagonist, the war had no clear, simple resolution. To modern historians, it is now obvious that America was not about to return to its former role of several dependent colonies. This was not so apparent to the British government which was badly divided along partisan lines in its attempts to subdue its fractious colonists. The administration stumbled on with its halting fight to retain its first empire, for its vast commercial market, if not its prestige.

Britain's traditional enemies had taken advantage of her plight and chosen to support the rebel cause. Their entry was certainly not motivated by any high-minded, egalitarian reasoning, nor any true sympathy for the American rebels' position. France and Spain were themselves monarchies with overseas dependents. As regimes they were considerably more despotic and feudal than the British system. Certainly, the last result that either of the Bourbon monarchies wanted was to find their own colonies fighting to gain independence. No, their motivations were quite simple — the French wanted to punish the British for the humiliations they had suffered in the Seven Years War and the Spanish saw an opportunity for gain at Britain's expense.

Consequently, while Britain fumbled the conduct of the war in America, her supremacy of the seas was contested across the world. As the war ground on, her very highly-valued West Indian colonies were threatened repeatedly by French and Spanish combinations. Making life even more difficult, the Dutch, a traditional ally, were supporting the rebellion through trade, causing the British to feel insecure in their northern, home waters while, at the same time, vulnerable to a Bourbon invasion across the English Channel. In fact, Britain faced the most serious threat of invasion since the Spanish Armada of 1588 and the administration was frequently frozen into indecisiveness in the face of it. All of these diversions led to retrenchment in the war for America.

In Canada, Frederick Haldimand, the Swiss-born Governor of Quebec, was understandably concerned that the French had eyes on regaining their North American empire. He was overseer of a gigantic province which, due to the "Intolerable" Quebec Act of 1774, now extended from the Atlantic on the east, west to the Mississippi and south to the Ohio. Faced with a daunting task and blessed with only sparse resources, he made every effort to prevent a French success. To goad him on, the Marquis de Lafayette, the expatriate French nobleman who had become a close confidant of Washington, would soon cause proclamations regarding a future Franco-American invasion to be posted on many Quebec church doors and agitators were encouraged by rebel agents to stir up the populace.

The rebel invasion of Quebec in 1775 had initially found a significant level of sympathy amongst many Canadiens (ie. French Canadians); however, when the invaders were unable to pay for their food, forage and quarters in hard money, the support evaporated.[1] Memories of this commercial ineptitude lingered and the prospect of rebel Americans again entering the province was uninspiring to the majority. On the other hand, the possibility of France regaining the colony had an immense appeal to virtually all Canadiens, and especially to the middle-aged and older adults who had keen memories of their former glory under the Bourbon banner of the Fleur de Lis.

Haldimand might postulate that the French were not eager to regain their costly American colonies, or that Congress would not wish to have France restored to power in North America. However, he dared not ignore the many threats of French fleets in the St. Lawrence and a Franco-American army assembling in Albany. The Governor was aware that the rebel general, Moses Hazen, who before the war had been a businessman and large land owner in the province, was building a road through the wilderness of north-eastern New York. Certainly, Haldimand, with his tiny army spread across a vast province, had many reasons to be cautious.

In the late summer of 1779, the United States mounted a major expedition against the Governor's native allies — the Six Nations and their dependencies. The affair was led by two rebel generals of experience, John Sullivan and James Clinton. When intelligence reached the Canadian Governor of the rebels' plans, he at first doubted its veracity, no doubt assuming that Congress lacked the wherewithal to fund and mount such a venture. Besides, Haldimand's attentions were focused on his nearer problems. But the rumours persisted and could not be ignored. As the pressure rose and physical evidence of Congress' plans became blatantly obvious, the Six Nations were greatly alarmed and sought assistance from every quarter from which they had every right, by various alliances and treaties, to expect a positive reaction. From Niagara, the Commandant, Colonel Mason Bolton, sent the welcome assistance of Major John Butler and several companies of his famous Rangers with a platoon of the Light Company of the 8th; however, the garrison was sickly and the Commandant had only these few men to spare. No assistance came from the garrison at Fort Detroit, nor the Lakes Nations (Wyandot, Ottawa, Potawatami, etc.), as the rebels' expedition led by George Rogers Clarke held everyone's attention in that region. But worse, and less understandable, from Quebec City came silence.

Finally, when the Continental troops were deep into Iroquoia and the centuries-old settlements were being put to the torch and the native families were being driven into the forests, Haldimand reasoned that the season might be too far advanced for a Franco-American attack on the lower province and he decided to risk the dispatch of an expeditionary force to assist his allies. In reporting his actions to his superior in the British government, Lord George Germain, Secretary of State for the American Colonies, the Governor advised that "about 400 of the best and most active Troops besides a large body of the Seven Nations of Canada [Canada Indians] and some [Fort Hunter] Mohawks, who have resided here since their Country was destroyed [he is referring here to their expulsion in 1777]" had been placed under the command of "Sir John Johnson, whose natural Influence with the Six Nations, joined to the zeal and strong attachment he has upon all occasions manifested for His Majesty's Service, will, I hope, produce a happy effect."[2]

Although Haldimand had reported only 400 troops, the expedition increased so that Johnson had under his command four of his own companies (Captain Samuel Anderson's Light Infantry; Captain Richard Duncan's; Captain-Lieutenant Thomas Gummersall's Colonel's Company and a platoon from Captain John Munro's[3]) totalling 151 all ranks. Captain Robert Leake's large Independent Company of some 80 muskets, which was attached for administration

brigade up the St. Lawrence from the Government's victualling depots in Ireland and Britain.

The third objective was in no way attained. Flick was in error to consider Oswego a target as what was left of that post had been destroyed by American action earlier in the war. The site was only a convenient terminus for the troops coming up the St. Lawrence and over Lake Ontario to meet with forces sent out from Niagara. From Oswego they could gain access to the upper regions of the New York frontier settlements, but there were no storehouses or barracks there.[10] Indeed, its situation was similar to the fort at Crown Point which, although consumed by fire prior to the rebellion, became a major assembly point for British expeditions on Lake Champlain. As to Fort Niagara, no attempt was made against this major post during the expedition, although the rebel troops were within 60 miles of the fort at the time of turning about.

Regarding Flick's fourth objective — as the fort at Niagara was firmly in Crown hands and the site at Oswego lay open to the Indian nations, British shipping & Crown troops until well after the close of the war, it could never be said that the expedition put the area into American possession or domination. The devastated Iroquoian homelands were not occupied by either troops or settlers until well after the war's end. Indeed, in the north, the loyalists and Indians continued to roam the frontier at will as far east as the out-skirts of Schenectady and the south-eastern shores of Lake Champlain, as far south as the Susquehanna River and even into upper Virginia and the new Kentucky territory. The north-western posts at Detroit and Michilimackinac remained British and, of critical importance to Canadian and British commerce, the fur trade contin-ued successfully. The Great Lakes were clearly in combined native and British control.

Another American historian, Archibald Howe, made the fol-lowing sensitive observations — quite unusual for a man writing in the early 20th Century at a time long before white society had awak-ened to the questionable morality of the previous three centuries of unremitting warfare against the natives.

> Sullivan's retaliating expedition of July, 1778 [1779], was as bad in its character and effects as anything ever done on behalf of any cause, good or bad. The destruction of many Indian villages by Sullivan and General James Clinton was no doubt thorough, but of little avail ... [11]

The year 1780 would bring to the United States' northern frontiers due retribution for the destruction of the Six Nations' territories. The Indian war in the northern regions of Pennsylvania and New York was far, far from over and would sputter and flare for years after the official end of the conflict. Indeed, the revolutionary war was never lost in the north; it came undone in the southern theatre, on the high seas, in the West Indies and then finally at the bargaining table where shrewd American negotiators outsmarted an exhausted and dispirited British administration.

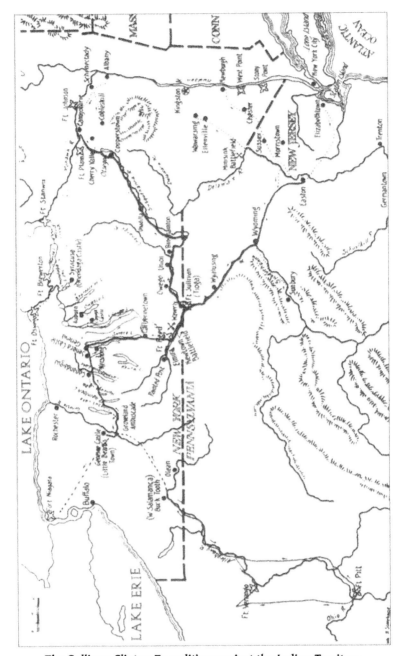

The Sullivan-Clinton Expedition against the Indian Territory

This map illustrates the four prongs of the invasion of the territory of the Iroquois Confederacy and their allies in 1779.

Roger H. Stonehouse, 1929 (from The Sullivan-Clinton Campaign in 1779 (Albany: The University of the State of New York, 1929))

II

1780, THE YEAR OF REVENGE - THE CAMPAIGN OPENS

As the new year of 1780 dawned, there was perhaps a degree of optimism in the settlements and farms in the frontier regions of New York. While the crops had failed in the fall due to bad weather and the winter had been brutal,[1] some folk recalled with pride the great expedition into the Indian Territory that had occurred late the previous summer. It was reported to have destroyed all the Six Nations' towns from Lake Ontario to as far south as the Ohio Country. As a result, not a few must have believed that the Indians were now entirely cowed and driven so far west that the threat against their frontiers was over. Even New York's governor, George Clinton, was expecting "overtures of peace."[2]

To those who were somewhat wiser in these affairs, the fact that so few Indian prisoners had been taken, indeed so few Indian casualties had been reported, suggested that the positive results of the expedition may have been greatly exaggerated. Indeed they were. To use a contemporary metaphor, "the wolves had been driven from their lair" and were maddened by the destruction of their homelands and hunting grounds. The Iroquois saw their families struggling to make a life in refugee villages at Fort Niagara. Their proud hearts shrank from their need to beg for constant charity at the hands of the British Indian Department. They yearned for revenge — that driving motivation of native warfare.[3]

Most of the Onondaga nation, the Keepers of the Grand Council Fire of the League of the Iroquois, had been grievously stricken by disease in 1776 and had maintained a quiet neutrality for the first four years of the rebellion. To be sure, their "hot" young men, who were keen for reputation, had joined with their clansmen of the other nations and gone to war as all junior warriors had done throughout the long history of the Confederacy. But the older Onondagas had chosen to stand aloof from the conflict in the firm belief that the rebellion had nothing to do with Iroquoian affairs. What was their reward for their circumspection? As the opening gambit of the great Sullivan-Clinton expedition, the garrison of Fort Stanwix had fallen upon them and devastated their towns. To the uncommitted of the Confederacy, this treacherous act by the rebels followed by the ruthless desolation of their towns, set their minds upon all-out warfare. Only a few of the Oneidas and their close brethren, the Tuscaroras, held to the rebel cause.

To the folk of the New York frontier it must have been difficult to imagine that the raids and killings could intensify. With eyes wide-open at the outset of the rebellion, they had opted for a conflict with their despised loyalist neighbours whom they viewed as traitors to American ideals. A contest against these conservatives held little fear for them. But the constant threat of an Indian war had been viewed with a particular terror. All of them well knew, either by experience or by stories, its frightful characteristics of instant surprise, ambush, abduction and merciless killing. With some sense of hardened guilt, not a few of them recognized that their open expressions of contempt for the native and a few "clever" land deals of the past would single them out as prime targets for vengeance.

Diplomatic efforts to keep their Indian neighbours from the conflict had been intense. General Philip Schuyler, a man well-respected by the Six Nations, led the American Indian Department and enjoyed substantial success. The Confederacy was deeply split into three factions; those who favoured the rebel cause and those who wished to stand neutral and, despite the best efforts of Schuyler and others, those who saw their best interests being served by the ancient alliance with the Crown. As it transpired, the main strength of the Six Nations sided with the British administration and the war fell upon the Mohawk River region in all its horror.

Making things worse, the loyalists, those conservative pro-government elements of the region's population, proved themselves to be a most effective enemy, as stealthy and robust as the much-feared and equally detested Canadien irregulars of the Seven Years' War. In the words of Franklin Hough, a respected American historian, "Those who had fled to the enemy to bear arms for the king, proved the most dangerous and vindictive of partizans, being thoroughly acquainted with the topography of the country, and familiar with every road and stream and valley, that would favour the movements of an invading party, or of a lurking foe."[4]

The first real battle of the Mohawk region war took place in August 1777. It was a superbly executed ambush in the grand native style fought in the Oriskany ravine some 12 miles from the besieged

Fort Stanwix. As Indian combatants dominated the fight, the action was ferociously hand-to-hand. It was also the first confrontation of the Mohawk region's loyalists and their neighbours and relatives who comprised the Tryon County Militia brigade. The latter had been on the march to reinforce the garrison of the fort when it stumbled headlong into the ambush. The fighting was extremely bitter and, as a result, the battle became known as the bloodiest of the Revolution. Of some 900 militiamen who entered the ravine, about 250 broke and fled. Only 130 finished the battle fit for duty. Amongst the Indians, 70 men were killed, many of these being prominent leaders, and many more were wounded. Of the 200-250 Royal Yorkers and Indian Department rangers who participated,[5] there were only a handful of dead, but a great many wounded. On balance, the battle in the ravine was clearly a Crown Forces' victory; however, this success was followed by a most ineffectual siege of Stanwix. Soon came the threat of another rebel relief column, this time made up of Continental Regulars and led by the masterful Arnold. The Indians were already extremely discouraged because of their many casualties suffered in the ambush and, in the face such a threatening confrontation, they chose to withdraw, abandoning their allies. This defection caused a shameful, precipitate retreat of the Crown's troops from Stanwix before the rebel troops were even in sight.

In revenge for their losses at Oriskany, members of the local rebel militia looted and burned many of the buildings owned by loyalist Mohawks of the Canajoharie Castle and made threats against the Mohawks who had stayed neutral in the lower castle at Fort Hunter. All of this was ill-advised, but of course understandable, for the militia's losses had been truly staggering. For their part, the loyalist Mohawks sought revenge against their Oneida brethren at the Oriska settlement who had openly, under arms, supported the rebels in the ravine. The Confederacy had been struck asunder and war was about to overwhelm the Mohawk region.

The first serious raids occurred in the Susquehanna region with parties of Indians and rangers roaming freely through the woods. Many farms were destroyed and cattle run off. The survivors were forced to flee into small forts, a cycle of destruction and flight that would continue on the frontiers for five long years.

That fall the Six Nations-British alliance was somewhat shaky. The defeat of St. Leger at Stanwix, soon followed by the even more portentous surrender of Burgoyne, gave the Confederacy much to think about regarding their British ally. Over the winter, the Senecas "abstained from molesting" the New York frontier to allow their clansmen and friends who might possibly be the subject of retaliation at the hands of the rebels to come into the safety of their towns, but by the late winter, the Seneca war chiefs, the traditional leaders of the Confederacy, had concluded that the Six Nations must support the British. One major factor preventing siding with the rebels, or even standing neutral, was the rebels' demonstrated inability to provide essential trade goods in sufficient quantities. In addition, the Iroquois continued to desire revenge for the deaths of so many of their principal men at Oriskany. The war chiefs, Old Smoke and Cornplanter,[6] advised Butler that their people meant to "strike as one body."[7]

John Butler, in recognition of his faithful service with the Six Nations at Niagara and his performance with St. Leger, had obtained a beating order from Governor Carleton to raise a regiment of Rangers. He recruited his companies in late 1777 and early 1778 until he judged he had enough strength to conduct his first campaign. In mid-April, Butler left Fort Niagara with two companies of Rangers (likely his own and Captain William Caldwell's),[8] to council with the Senecas at their castle (town) of Canadasaga (Kanadesaga), where the Major was happily reunited with his 25-year-old son Walter who had just escaped from captivity in Albany.[9] After developing their strategy, the Rangers, Senecas and Cayugas set out for Unadilla, a loyalist townsite on the very edge of the Six Nations' Territory in southern New York. They would have the assistance of Joseph Brant, with his white and native Volunteers, who was already operating from Oquaga, a mixed-nation Indian town only a few miles from Unadilla. From Unadilla, the leaders planned to mount their campaign, utilizing the local cattle herds and the two grist mills to supply their rations.

They proceeded with care, first dispatching Brant and Ranger Lieutenant Barent Frey to the Mohawk Valley to bring off all the families from the Canajoharie and Fort Hunter castles. The two men performed this duty with great secrecy and skill, although only those Mohawks who shared Brant's view were willing to leave, the others professed neutrality and believed they could escape becoming embroiled in the war.

The Seneca chiefs & Butler chose as their first major target the settlements in the Wyoming Valley, now in Pennsylvania but at the time a disputed territory between that state and New York. Butler had already drawn a number of recruits from there and he hoped to add a great many more during his campaign. As Frederick Haldimand, the new Governor of Canada, was later to comment, ideal Ranger recruits had little need for arms and foot drill, indeed little need for the military discipline of the garrison; they had "to shoot well, to march well, and to endure privation and fatigue."[10] Butler would oft prove how well his Rangers met those criteria.

As for his strategic purposes in targeting Wyoming: first, he wished to protect the Indian towns by throwing the rebels off-guard with offensive actions against their major frontier settlements and second, he wanted to render assistance to the operations of the British Central Department by creating major disturbances in the enemy's northern frontier areas.[11] On their part, the Senecas had every interest in securing their vulnerable towns along the edge of the Indian territory by beating back the settlements and, in particular, they held a smouldering grudge against the Wyoming settlers who had grasped Seneca lands by a particularly odious method.[12]

Prior to the Senecas and Butler setting out for the Wyoming Valley, the friends, Joseph Brant and Barent Frey, led a party of some 200 muskets into the Mohawk region striking at Cobuskill (Cobleskill, etc.), destroying farms and running off cattle. A handful of Continentals stationed in Schoharie and a force of local militia pursued Brant's force and were cut-off. To the horror of the Schoharie citizens, only four survivors returned. Cherry Valley was on the raider's return route and a senseless killing of two riders outside of the village thoroughly alarmed the community.[13]

The tactical combination of the Senecas, Cayugas and Butler's Rangers proved extremely effective. The Wyoming Valley was devastated; forts were abandoned or surrendered and then destroyed, rebel farms put to ruin and Continental Regulars and local militia roundly defeated. In native fashion, those men found in arms against them were killed outright or taken as hostages, some for ransom, others for adoption. Butler gained his recruits; the rebels were too preoccupied and disorganized to immediately retaliate against the Indian towns and both State and Continental Congresses were extremely alarmed at this success. Cries from the states for assistance on the northwestern frontiers were answered by dispatching scarce Continental regiments, thus bleeding the main efforts in the eastern theatre. The presence of John Johnston, one of two brothers of that surname who fought the war in the British Indian Department operating amongst the Seneca nation, served in rebel minds to place Sir John and his regiment in the battle. Similarly, it was never doubted by the rebels that Brant participated, although he was at Oquaga managing his own campaign at the time.

The raids continued throughout the long summer, perhaps the most extensive being led by Captain Caldwell of Butler's involving four companies of Rangers and 160 Indians. They fell upon the German Flatts, destroying five mills, 120 other buildings and killing or driving off 826 cattle.[14]

In the fall, a large detachment of Regulars sailed south on Lake Champlain aboard vessels of the Provincial Marine to raid the lower regions of the lake and the Connecticut River settlements.[15] The force was under the command of Major Christopher Carleton, 29th Regiment[16] and was composed of four matrosses of the Royal Artillery with two Cohorns and two Mantelets[17] and almost 300 troops drawn from the 29th, 31st & 53rd Regiments. Also included were Captain Alexander Fraser's Ranging Company of British Regulars, an unspecified number of loyalists under Captain Justus Sherwood of the Queens Loyal Rangers and some 100 Kahnawake & Lakes Nations' warriors.

A platoon from the Light Infantry Company, KRR NY commanded by Lieutenant William Byrne and a party of Kanehsatake Mohawks overseen by Lieutenant William Redford Crawford, KRR, accompanied Carleton's force part way and then ventured through the woods to Johnstown to gather intelligence and recover Sir John's family papers.

Carleton reported, "I can venture to assure Your Excellency that we have completely destroyed Four months Provisions for Twelve Thousand men."[18] The daring Royal Yorker force gained information on the health and security of the loyalists in the area; but, the attempt to recover Johnson's papers was foiled as they had been destroyed by moisture seeping into their container while they lay buried for a year at Johnson Hall. Consequently, Sir John estimated his loss as in excess of "twenty thousand pounds."[19]

The action with the most lasting impact occurred in late October, near the close of the normal campaign season, when 200 men from five companies[20] of Butler's Rangers under their now-senior captain, Walter Butler, 50 volunteers from the 8th Regt and a 300-warrior party of Senecas under Old Smoke and Cornplanter moved against the settlement and fort at Cherry Valley. Joseph Brant and his Volunteers of 300 men, mixed white and native, joined the expedition en route; however, after a threatening argument with the younger Butler, who deeply resented his boyhood acquaintance's success in recruiting non-natives for his Volunteers, ninety of Brant's whites took to the woods. Joseph and his clansmen remained with the raid.

The season was so late that the garrison at Fort Alden was lulled into a sense of security and ill-prepared for what was to follow, although there had been prior warning given by an Oneida spy. Sleeping on snow-covered ground and then advancing through sleet, the Crown forces fell upon the village. The Rangers concentrated upon the fort, leaving the settlement to the Senecas who were merciless in their attack on the inhabitants, both rebel and loyal.

Their emotions were inflamed over decades of racial abuse and, once again, their losses of key men at Oriskany. They had been accused of conducting a massacre in the Wyoming Campaign and deeply resented it. As well, they were deeply affronted when a number of Continental officers, who had been given their parole at Wyoming, immediately broke their promise and were again found under arms.

Brant made every attempt to protect the loyalists amongst them, with very little success. It was as if the Senecas decided to create a massacre if that was what they were going to be accused of. The old phrase applied, "if you're going to have the name, you may as well play the game."

These constant raids throughout the frontiers of New York and Pennsylvania had many results. Primarily, the crops couldn't be sown, or the harvests were interrupted, or the collected grains were destroyed in their storage magazines. No matter which of these occurred, the result was the same, the Continental army was in danger of serious privation. A desperately hungry army is not an effective one, then or now. Moreover, the plight of the inhabitants of these frontier zones could not be easily ignored. There was a newly-found sense of possession and national sovereignty that was offended. If succor could not be given, there was the very real danger that the populace would seek British protection with all that might entail. These very real threats set the determination of the Continental Congress and the army command to send an expedition against the Six Nations that would not only punish them for their actions against the settlements, but would virtually knock them out of the war.

As we have reviewed in Chapter One, the timing was fortuitous. With the Canadian Governor fidgeting over a possible Franco-American attack against the settled regions of Quebec, the Continental army proved free to mount a massive expedition against the League of the Iroquois. We have reviewed the results. The Indian Territory was devastated, crops and orchards destroyed, native homes razed, the inhabitants driven off; but, significantly, there were few Indian prisoners or casualties. An enraged people were thrown upon the charity of the British, who, although their great resources were stretched taut with a world war, gathered their strength and, with tremendous energy and no little skill, took full advantage of the occasion.

As the new year of 1780 dawned, the smouldering rage of the Six Nations and their dependents[21] led to an extremely early campaign. Brant readily gathered 230 eager warriors, with the Onondagas, Senecas and Delawares represented, as well as men from the mixed-nations' villages of Oquaga and Owego. A large element were 88 Cayugas and Tuteloes under the Cayuga war captains, Fish Carrier and Tagaais. Karaghqunty and Tekarihogea, two principal men of the Canajoharie Mohawks accompanied Brant as did the Indian Department Captain, Hendrick Nelles. Snowshoes and sleds had been prepared and the party left Niagara on February 11.

Only one day's journey out, Brant's party met four emissaries on their way to Niagara with a message of peace for the Six Nations from General Schuyler. Two were Fort Hunter Mohawks, Little Abraham and White Hans and two were Oneidas, Good Peter and Skenandon. The latter was Brant's father-in-law from his first marriage. These men bore a strangely bogus message of forgiveness from the rebels. Joseph sent a runner back to Niagara to warn Indian Superintendent Guy Johnson of the emissaries' intentions. Johnson, with the compliance of Mohawk Captain Aaron Hill and Old Smoke the senior war chief, deftly snuffed out Schuyler's strange peace mission. The miserable men were uncharitably held as prisoners in dreadful conditions.

Parties, as small as six and as large as 75, departed regularly from Niagara. All of the Six Nations were represented as well as their Algonkian allies such as the Delawares, Mississaugas and Nanticokes. After Brant's departure, there were three more in February, two in March, seven in April, four in May and five in June which left and returned, 495 men in total. These brought in prisoners, horses and cattle and reports of many victims killed and farms destroyed. In addition, another ten parties were out on service during the same period and by the end of June had not yet returned. In total, 33 forays, including Brant's early start, were, or had been, across the frontiers, ranging along the Mohawk and Delaware Rivers, east to the Schoharie Valley and as far south as Virginia.[22] By early June, the activity across the frontier had been so marked that Continental Congressmen noted to each other that "The expedition of General Sullivan against the Six Nations seems by its effects to have exasperated than to have terrified or disabled them."[23]

Governor Haldimand believed his province was more secure from invasion than the year before. His fortifications, from headquarters at Quebec City to Michilimackinac in the far west and south to Île-aux-Noix, had been strengthened; two blockhouses had been built on the Richelieu River approach route from the south to guard that approach and the Provincial Marine had a number of ships afloat on Lake Champlain, the whole of that lake being in their control. Also, the Gulf of St. Lawrence was being regularly patrolled by the Royal Navy and he had frequent intelligence reports regarding the movement of the French fleets. It was not that bad news didn't continue to reach the Governor. For example, he learned that Spain had declared war against Britain, which would obviously serve to broaden an already complex conflict. Haldimand noted that privateers were active against the fishing ports in the Gulf of St. Lawrence, but was pleased to report that the inhabitants had repelled one of the more significant raids. Rebel agents continued to be very active in the province and he employed several artifices to capture them with some success. In short, his house was in order and he could afford to look beyond his immediate borders.[24]

In mid-March, Walter Sutherland, a very active junior officer in Sir John's Royal Yorkers,[25] returned from a scout to Johnstown with the report that the rebels were intending to force all men of military age to enroll in ranging companies for local defence. Those who refused to comply would be sent to the east as prisoners, their homes destroyed and property confiscated by the state.[26] Alarmed by this persecution, Haldimand suggested to Sir John, in his quite new role as director of the Secret Service, that a select body of men should be sent to conduct these loyalists overland to Lake Champlain and thence by ship to Quebec province. Sir John instead offered to lead an expedition to the area with the dual purposes of bringing relief to the loyalists, evacuating those men who were willing to serve and their families and, at the same time, striking a blow at the rebels. The Governor warmly concurred.

Sending two trusty scouts, guided by one of Colonel Daniel Claus' Fort Hunter Mohawks, to forewarn the loyalists in and about Johnstown, the Baronet set about preparing for a fast, decisive thrust deep into the enemy's heartland on the Mohawk River. Haldimand, who had extensive North American experience as the commander of a battalion of the 60th "Royal American" Regiment during the Seven Years' War and later in Florida, offered much useful advice. For example, regarding the carriage of additional black powder, the meticulous Governor recommended, "I have found most Effectual... putting loose Powder into dry Canteens well Corked with a piece of Bladder or oiled Linen tied over it."[27]

He was particularly adamant regarding secrecy and by heeding his many recommendations, the expedition caught the rebels entirely off guard, despite the fact that word had leaked of its coming. Indeed, the whole Mohawk region had been thrown into the greatest alarm when the news arrived that an expedition was in the planning. Colonel Goose Van Schaick in command at Albany wrote to Governor Clinton on May 17, "... I should not be surprised if all the settlements to the Northward of the Mohawk and the Westward of Hudson's River were shortly either destroyed or abandoned... I am incapacitated to draw forth the militia for want of provisions... Drafts from the militia have been made... but being unfurnished with provisions were obligated to disband." Two days later he again wrote, "... the Militia of Tryon County have as good as refused to turn out... the frontier settlements are breaking up fast & if some remedy is not soon applied, Schonectady will be our frontier Settlement... Your Excellency's feelings must daily increase on the account of the distressed situation of our Affairs relative to supplies for the Army & the naked situation of our Western & Northern frontiers for the want of men & provisions."[28]

Remarkably, only three days before Sir John's arrival, a meeting of the officers of Tryon County's Third "Mohawk district" militia regiment was held at Johnstown and the decision was taken to dismiss the militia companies that were assembled at that post to allow the sowing of seed as the scarcity of provisions was so extreme. Colonel John Harper, the commander of a regiment of New York State Levies[29] stationed in the area, was in attendance, with Colonel Frederick Visscher, the Third regiment's commander, LtCol. Volkert Veeder, his second-in-command and his officers, Major John Newkirk, 5 captains, 3 lieutenants and 1 ensign. The decision was made the easier when the regiment's Quartermaster, Abraham Van Horn, quoted Colonel Van Schaick to the effect that, "it was his opinyen that no Body of the Enemy was not yet on this side of Lake Champlen... "[30]

However, the review of these actions taken by the rebels gets well ahead of the raid's planning and mounting. To continue - to ensure the secrecy of the small expedition, Haldimand suggested a subtle artifice. Sir John was to complain, through the regular, quite open channels of correspondence, about the Governor's intention to employ the Royal Yorkers in the menial chore of wood cutting. As the KRR NY comprised the largest element of the small expedition, this tasking would provide a cover for the concentration of the KRR companies and their movement to the staging point of Île-aux-Noix on the southern Richelieu River. Indeed, the Orderly Books of the Royal Yorkers reflected this ruse which ensured that the Officers and men would be in the dark and maintain security through ignorance.

A Brigade Order in an Orderly Book entry written at Chatogue (Chateauguay, Quebec on the south shore of the St. Lawrence opposite the island of Montreal) dated 13 April 1780 reads -

> two Capt Six Subalt 9 Sergt 9 Corpl and one hundred and fifty of Sir Johnstons Reigment to hold theselfs in Rideaness to preesed [proceed] to Ile of aux

in noix aux [Île-aux-Noix] where the[y] are to remain tell further orders for to be a[i]ding and asissting to the Garrison there — to Cut and bring in Timber and furnish partys for the wood Cuting for that place.

William Dunbar Majr Brigade[31]

This same Brigade order sent a subaltern, sergeant and corporal with twenty men of the 84th on a march to Carillon on the Richelieu "to prevent any canoes or Battaux to pass at the river Except such as has passes si[g]ned by the Commander in chief."[32] This was an obvious measure to improve security.

The same day's entry records a Regimental Order stating -

Sir John orders that the party be axcuipt [equipped] with arigml [a regimental] and Blanket Coat[,] two Shirts[,] one wo[ol]len and one linnen pair [of] over halls [overalls, — ie. gaitered trousers,] indian Shoes [one suspects above-the-ankle, laced moccassins similar to mucklucks] and one Blanket.[33]

The Governor allotted smaller detachments from several Regular regiments to Johnson. Captain Thomas Scott, 53rd Regt, a former lieutenant in the Company of Select Marksman, for whom Haldimand held a high regard, was to serve as Sir John's deputy as well as command all Regulars. Assigned were two of the "best" officers and 34 men from each of the 29th, 34th and 53rd Regiments and one officer and 20 Hesse Hanau Jaegers from Von Kreutzburg's battalion.

Of the loyalists, four companies of the KRR NY were chosen; both the flank companies - 29 Grenadiers under Captain John McDonell (Scotus) and 48 Light Bobs under Captain Samuel Anderson. Two Hat companies were nominated, 45 men of Captain Richard Duncan's and 39 from Captain-Lieutenant Thomas Gummersall's Colonel's Company.[34] The men of the latter company appear to have been essential for this service as the majority of them had worked in and about the Johnson estate in Johnstown, the expedition's primary target. Four private men from the Colonel's who were doing temporary duty in the Artificer's Company at Sorel were asked for specifically by Sir John. Obviously, they had important knowledge essential to Sir John's plans. In addition, a company of 50 volunteers was raised from the other loyalist units headquartered at Sorel, one suspects these officers & men were drawn from Jessup's King's Loyal Americans, Peter's Queen's Loyal Rangers and McAlpin's American Volunteers.

As many of the Canada Indians were not thought trustworthy, Sir John chose only Kanehsatake (Lac des Deux-Montagnes) Mohawks to accompany him stating that the force being predominantly of white men and the ever-loyal, Fort Hunter Mohawk warriors, "will prevent the Canada Indians from holding any correspondence with the Oneidas."[35] A measure suggested by Haldimand to control desertion was to, "send the Savages after them and give them a Reward for bringing their Scalps. I believe this to be essential to Your Safety, and therefore should be Executed universally without respect to Corps."[36]

In some confusion, the rebels took action to offset the coming expedition. One half of Brigadier General Ten Broeck's Albany County brigade was ordered out and four regiments were assembled at Saratoga on May 20. Five other regiments were designated for the Mohawk Valley, but were held back awaiting some indication of where they should march.[37]

Nonetheless, the expedition was remarkably successful. The troops and natives, numbering 528 all ranks, were transported by the Provincial Marine on Lake Champlain to below Crown Point where they disembarked and then cut overland to the southwest, skirting around Schroon Lake and entered the Scotch Settlement (Kingsborough Patent) north of Johnstown on May 21. As to relieving the persecuted loyalists, 143, including some women and children and 30 blacks, were brought back from the area. This great influx allowed Sir John to complete his first battalion and begin to build a second which Haldimand had immediately authorized.

As to attacking and alarming the rebels, with the blessing of Sir John, the Indians wounded & killed a number of officers of the Third "Mohawk District" Regiment, Tryon County Militia. Men who had been particularly active in the rebellion or who had been quite offensive to the natives, were primary targets as were their properties. The troops secured the Johnstown area, burnt buildings owned by the more inveterate rebels and took a number of prisoners. Units of the Third Regiment formed up on the southern edge of the town; but, correctly concluded they were too weak to offer any effective resistance. The Crown force took 27 prisoners, of which Sir John released 14 as being too young or too old to withstand the return march. The loyal families who chose to remain behind prevailed upon the Baronet to release two "principal" prisoners in hopes of preventing retaliation. Veeder, a militia captain, was released in promise for the exchange of the highly-valued, Lieutenant George Singleton of the KRR Light Infantry Company who had been wounded at Oriskany and captured at Fort Stanwix on the same day in '77.

Sir John had some personal business to attend to. His silver plate had been buried at Johnson Hall prior to his flight to Canada and he had this dug up and distributed to the men of his companies. A careful record was made of which soldier carried each individual piece of plate so that their collection upon return could be assured. Could this have been the reason for Johnson's request for the temporary transfer from engineering duties of four specific men of the Colonel's Company so they might accompany the expedition? Had they buried the plate in '76? The term "conflict of interest" was unknown in the 18th Century when men of power and influence looked after their personal affairs with impunity. Such behaviour was simply expected and condoned.

The troops and Indians had covered an arc of about four miles south from the town and burnt 120 barns, mills and houses, destroying stores and provisions essential to the rebel cause. Upon their return march, rebel scouting parties dogged their steps for four days as three columns marched to cut them off. Governor Clinton of New York assembled a force of Albany County militia and a combined force of 800 Continentals and Tryon Militia under Continental Colonel Goose Van Schaick were in pursuit. Another force was raised in New Hampshire and sent to intercept them; but, Sir John's force was well-disciplined and easily motivated to keep on the move. Johnson's withdrawal was substantially assisted by his spreading of a rumour that Brant and Butler were about to raid the south side of the Mohawk. Colonel Jacob Klock wrote to Brigadier General Ten Broeck that "spies have been seen on the south side of the River about an hour before night... We momently expect to see all in flames."[38] In consequence, the rebels were torn in two directions. The raiders herded their prisoners and the refugees at a brisk pace and evaded all attempts to overtake them. They embarked at Crown Point just prior to 1700 rebels arriving there.[39] Clinton noted that the loyalists "were much beat out and many of them lamed by their long march... so it is likely their march will be very slow and dilatory."[40] Perhaps the Governor had been relying upon his enemy's fatigue. In the event, it was not the loyalists who were dilatory.

Haldimand expressed great satisfaction to Sir John on the success of the 19-day expedition, sentiments which he repeated in his report to Lord George Germain, making note to the Secretary of State of Johnson's "great Merit" and the "very high sense I have of [Sir John's] Loyalty and Zeal for the Service."[41]

The rebels deluded themselves on the value of the raid as the following letter clearly reveals -

In my last I mentioned to you the accounts we had of the approach of the Enemy & my fears on that occasion; I did not Imagine that Sr. John would have come with so large a force on so trifling an Errand. I am induced to believe his principle object was to carry off his plate. Could the Governor have been Supplied with boats & provision, the plunderers would have lost their Booty. Coll R. Van Rensselaer commanded upwards of Six Hundred of the best Militia I ever saw (two hundred & fifty of them from the Grants at the Request of the Governor). He arrived at the Enemys Encampment near Crownpoint the day after they embarked — Notwithstanding we were so unfortunate as not to overtake them, this pursuit will I hope have its uses.

John Taylor
Albany, 19 June 1780
[To] Philip Schuyler[42]

Such tripe! Governor Clinton wasn't supplied with either boats or provisions, so that comment was pure wishful thinking. Nor did he overtake the raiders, no matter how fine his militia were. What possible benefit could result from this failed pursuit other than to scare off any future attempts? Of course, the destruction of so many farms and mills; the death and capture of many militia officers and men; the heart given to the loyalist families of Tryon County and the blow given to the morale of the Mohawk Valley rebels; the collection of sufficient recruits to allow completion of the 1st Battalion Royal Yorkers and the initiation of a 2nd had no military value whatsoever.

★★★

This civil warfare was by no means exclusive to the white population. Many of the Oneidas and Tuscaroras had held firm to the American cause; however, an Onondaga chief warrior, Wagondenage, had some considerable success when he visited the Tuscarora castle at Ganaghsaraga south of Lake Oneida, a town very significantly left undamaged by the Sullivan expedition when it passed through on its return march. The Onondaga persuaded a number of Tuscaroras, Oneidas, and families of his own nation who had been domiciled there, to join with the Confederacy in the camps about Fort Niagara. His persuasion was not without coercion, which included threatening the complete destruction of the neighbouring castle of Old Oneida (Kanowalohale). The Oneidas in particular were alarmed by this ploy and after Wagondenage's departure with those he had persuaded, they made representations to their white friends for sanctuary which was granted near Fort Stanwix. On June 24, before they were able to flee to safety, a party of Mohawks under the Fort Hunter war chief, Captain David Hill, and a detachment of Butler's Rangers commanded by Captain John McDonell (Aberchalder), arrived at the castle and in a council called for the Oneidas to join their brethren at Niagara. The persuasive force of the lengthy debate that followed was reinforced by the arrival of the Seneca war chief, Spruce Carrier, who came the next day with a war party. Cowed, the Oneidas complied, and leaving some chiefs to care for the families, another 11 men left as a show of faith for Niagara. By July 2, a total of 294 of these Indians had come to Niagara, 184 Onondagas, 78 Tuscaroras and 32 Oneidas. They told Guy Johnson "that their eyes had now been opened and that they were deter- mined to serve the king."[43]

On July 11, Captain Brant and Lieutenant Joseph Clement of the Indian Department set off with 300 warriors, amongst them 59 of the formerly recalcitrant Onondagas, Oneidas & Tuscaroras who had so recently arrived at Niagara. The Oneida chief Skenandon performed penance by accompanying this party, more to escape a harsh impris- onment than due to a changed heart. The party destroyed the empty Oneida and Tuscarora villages and, moving on to Fort Stanwix found many of the Oneidas who had fled their towns encamped outside. Brant had some success in "persuading" a few to move to Niagara. However, some 400 souls managed to flee into the fortress, along with 6 Kahnawake (from Caughnawaga, Quebec) who had been staying with them. What confusion for the garrison with so many new, and likely unwelcome, mouths to feed.

After an unsuccessful blockade of the fort lasting several days, Brant decamped to conduct operations far and wide through the Mohawk region, most likely with his latest "converts" in tow as a test of their resolve. Their activities ranged from Fort Planck below the Mohawk River to Vrooman'sLand in the Schoharie Valley. The latter locale was laid waste by Seth's Henry, and his Schoharie Mohawk party. From across the Mohawk region, the raiders drove off 500 hors- es and cattle and caused great destruction and alarm.[44]

At Canajoharie, Brant and his Volunteers united under the Seneca war chiefs, Old Smoke and Cornplanter. The Tuscarora chief, Sagwarithra, and the Cayuga war chief, Fish Carrier, with men of their own nations, were also in attendance. Fifty three houses, a like number of barns, a gristmill, two small forts and a church were burnt.[45]

In addition, many mixed white and native parties were operating for the Crown in the Susquehanna and Ohio regions; the frontier of Pennsylvania was so overrun that the state offered a substantial bounty for Indian scalps.[46]

The pro-British Iroquois had dealt very harshly with their recalcitrant brethren. Yet, the poor fugitives who held firm to their convictions and fled to the charity of the rebels fared badly. They were sent to terribly inadequate, disease ridden camps outside of Schenectady where, literally abandoned by Congress, they froze and starved. When their closest friends objected to their plight and had them moved to barracks in the town, the natives were abused and vilified by the rebel soldiery, as prejudice reigned supreme over politics.[47]

**Brigadier General George Clinton, Governor of New York State 1777-1794 &
1800-1804**

*unattributed, undated painting (William H. Carr & Richard J. Koke, Twin Forts of the Popolopen, Forts Clinton and
Montgomery, New York 1775-1777 (Bear Mountain, NY: Commissioners Palisades Interstate Park, 1937) Historical
Bulletin Number 1*

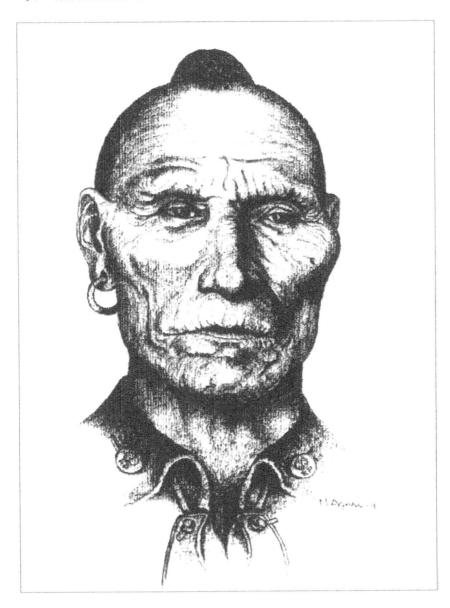

The Seneca, Old Smoke (Sayenqueraghta), Six Nations Confederacy Joint War Chief

No likeness of Old Smoke has survived into this century. Agnew has given his impression of this great leader.

Norman J. Agnew, 1992

The Seneca, Cornplanter (Gayentwahga), Six Nations Confederacy Joint War Chief
Paterson borrows the face from Bartoli and replaces that artist's strange rendition of a pipe axe with an extant Seneca tomahawk, circa 1800, held in the collections of the Museum of Civilization, Hull, Que.
Scott Paterson, 1996 (adapted from a portrait by F. Bartoli, 1796)

Lieutenant Colonel Sir John Johnson (He Who Makes the Roof to Tremble)
Watt borrows Johnson's face from Mare and portrays the baronet in the uniform of
Lieutenant Colonel of the Royal Yorkers. Elements of such a uniform are extant.
The shoulder epaulette, narrow metallic button-hole lace and unique, regimentally
cyphered buttons are found on the coatee of Lieutenant Jeremiah French, 2KRR
NY, in the collections of the Canadian War Museum in Ottawa. The monogrammed
sword belt plate is copied from that worn by Captain John McKenzie, 1&2KRR NY,
on display at the Loyalist-Nor'Wester Museum in Williamstown, Ont.
Gavin Alexander Watt, 1996 (adapted from John Mare, 1772)

Lieutenant Colonel John Butler, Commanding Officer of Butler's Rangers and Deputy Superintendent of the Six Nations Indian Department
The original portrait portrayed Butler in a somewhat fanciful uniform. Paterson has borrowed Butler's face and added known elements of the Butler's Rangers uniform.

Scott Paterson, 1996 (adapted from an unattributed, undated portrait in the John Ross Robertson collection, Toronto Public Libraries)

Joseph Brant (Thayendanegea), a War Chief of the Canajoharie Mohawks and Captain of the Six Nations Indian Department
Paterson has included in his likeness an officer's gorget as worn by Brant in other famous portraits. The chief's face is painted in a typical Mohawk fashion.
Scott Paterson, 1996 (adapted from a portrait by Gilbert Stuart, 1786)

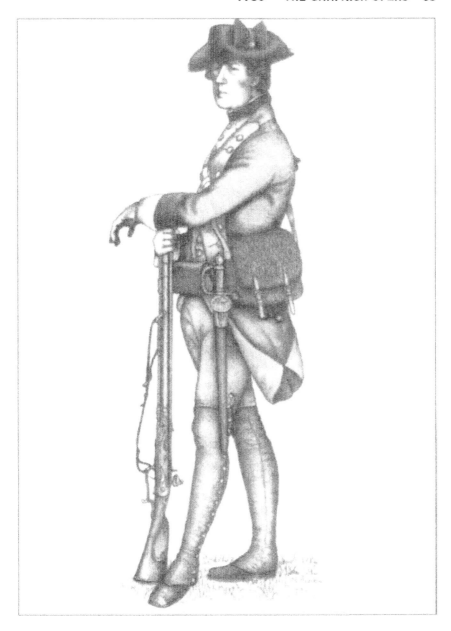

A rifleman of Von Kreutzbourg's Hesse Hanau Jaeger Battalion
The tiny principality of Hesse Hanau dispatched this Jaeger battalion in 1776 to Canada to serve in Brigadier General St. Leger's expedition. Due to bad sailing weather, only one company arrived in time. The regiment remained in Canada throughout the war. Jaegers went on Johnson's two 1780 expeditions.
Norman J. Agnew, 1996

JOHNSON HALL.

A rear view of Johnson Hall
Two barrels of the Johnson family's silver plate were buried in the garden of the Hall prior to Sir John's flight to Canada in 1776. Dug up during the May 1780 raid, the items of plate were carried to Canada in the knapsacks of the Royal Yorkers.
Artist unknown (from Jeptha R. Simms, The Trappers of New York, 1850)

III

THE FALL CAMPAIGN OF 1780 - THE EXPEDITIONS ON LAKE CHAMPLAIN

Without accessing correspondence from the highest levels of the British administration both at home and in America, it is always difficult to understand the broader strategic goals or implications of various military actions. Fortunately, in the case of the October 1780 expeditions against the New York frontier, we have some insights. Governor Haldimand had been contemplating a major, strategic stroke against the frontiers by mounting a double pincer attack of 600 men each, one to set out from Oswego, the other to act on Lake Champlain. Although puny in comparison to the rebels' expedition of 1779, his plans were circumscribed by the limited resources at his disposal in the Canadian Department. These moderately sized expeditions would occur almost simultaneously near the end of the campaign season.[1]

The attacks had several purposes.

> ... to divide the strength that may be brought against Sir H[enry]. Clinton, [Commander-in-Chief in America who was headquarted at New York City] to favor any operations his present situation may enable him to carry out, as well as destroy the enemy's supplies from the late plentiful harvest and to give His Majesty's loyal subjects an opportunity of retiring to this province.[2]

According to the Canadian military historian, Ernest Cruikshank, the plan also fulfilled Haldimand's "settled policy of devastating every advance frontier settlement, which might be used as a base of operations for the invasion of his province [ie. Quebec]."[3]

The Governor in addition thought to bring the remaining rebel Oneidas, estimated at some 300 souls, either "to obedience or to cut them off,"[4] because they had recently interfered with a loyalist scouting party returning from the Mohawk Valley with intelligence and recruits. At the time of these deliberations Haldimand was unaware of the unilateral actions being taken by his allies of the Six Nations in their own political interest against their recalcitrant brothers, the Oneidas & Tuscaroras and faint-hearted Onondagas.

Of significance, negotiations had begun between Sir Henry Clinton and Ethan Allen and his associates from the self-proclaimed Republic of Vermont, previously well-known as the highly-contested region of "the New Hampshire Grants".[5] Allen & his fellow travellers had "quarrelled fiercely with [the Continental] Congress"[6] over their plans for the region's statehood. When rebuffed, Allen was approached by Clinton's agents to discover whether the republic might return to an allegiance to Britain. Allen held out some hope and Sir Henry turned to Haldimand for opinions regarding the Vermont leader and his likely motives. The Canadian Governor replied,

> His character is well known and his Followers or dependents are a Collection of the most abandoned Wretches that ever lived, to be bound by no Laws or Ties.[7]

Although Haldimand had very little faith in a positive outcome to any negotiations with Vermont, he recognized that such discussions would gravely embarrass and discomfit the Continental Congress. In addition, while negotiations proceeded, the British Provinicial Marine might enjoy virtually uncontested control of Lake Champlain, as the Vermont men held no love whatsoever for their political protagonists in New York State and would most likely turn a blind eye to any offensive action directed against New York. The Northern (Canadian) Department became deeply involved in the negotiations. Ironically, the officer chosen to head the talks was Justus Sherwood, an accomplished loyalist Captain of Peter's Queen's Loyal Rangers who prior to the war had been one of Allen's confederates in the Green Mountain Boys. As he was from the Grants, Sherwood put his heart and soul into the talks, although it was apparent to many how futile the efforts were. During the period of negotiation, the Vermont side of Lake Champlain became a haven for escaping loyalist families working their way north to Quebec.

At the time of launching the various expeditions, the Canadian Department's negotiations with the Vermont Republic had just begun.

Haldimand planned to take advantage of this state of affairs by expanding his Crown Point phase to strike at the New York forts at South Bay and the bottom of Lake George, convinced that the Vermonters would shun overt action. Such a blow against the upper Hudson Valley region would serve to damage the rebels as well as illustrate the power of the Crown to Allen and his confederates. He would be proven correct in his assessment. His forces were unopposed by Vermont troops during their attacks against the forts. Soon after the various expeditions had been completed, the Republic of Vermont agreed to remain neutral in the overall conflict while further talks proceeded.

CARLETON ATTACKS THE HUDSON VALLEY

Command of the diversionary thrust against the lower Champlain & upper Hudson Valleys of the New York frontier was given to Major Christopher Carleton.[8] A Regular officer of the 29th Regiment, he had led the Indians during his uncle, Governor Guy Carleton's 1776 campaign on Lake Champlain and under Haldimand had conducted a successful raid in 1778 against that same frontier. He was considered by the Governor to be an active, bold and experienced leader who could be entrusted to achieve substantial results using a mixed corps of Regulars, Provincials and natives. Needless to say, not every old-country British officer possessed that blend of managerial skill.

Christopher Carleton had an interesting background. He was orphaned at the age of four and, being of a military family, entered the army at twelve. On his first tour of duty in Canada, he had visited Johnson Hall and developed "a fondness for frontier life."[9] Doubtless his observations of Sir William Johnson's methods of success with the natives were a lesson to the young Carleton. In the mid 1770's, he resided amongst the natives at Kahnawake, and likely also at Kanehsatake, taking an Indian wife, whom he remembered with great affection even after his marriage of advantage to his uncle Guy's sister-in-law. Christopher became involved in village politics and developed lasting friendships with significant native and Canadien connections. Baroness Von Riedesel wrote of him that "he became so accustomed to the restless but free and merry life that not until after many years and repeated entreaties did he return to his uncle."[10]

Upon his return to Canada with the 31st Regt in 1776, he took a leave of absence to again live amongst the Indians where he readopted their rigorous way of life, their clothing and customs. At some time he had himself tattooed and wore a ring through his nose, as did so many of their men. Clearly, he became completely fluent in one or more dialects. During his Revolutionary War campaigns, he often wore native clothing, paint and ornaments. His sincerity in all of these matters earned him the deepest respect amongst the Indians and when he returned to his duties, he commented, "that the hours spent with them were the happiest of his life."[11]

A German officer from Brunswick, who greatly admired the tremendous endurance and natural skills of navigation and tracking displayed by the natives, wrote of Christopher Carleton in August 1777 that he "continued to command the Indians who constitute our advanced guard, and by whom he is greatly beloved."[12] This same German officer gave further insight into Carleton's personality by describing him as "refined, gentle, friendly, well-mannered" and "unaffected." He noted of Carleton that his "constitution has become wrecked and delicate," an affliction which was to lead to his early death in 1787. The Indian trader, John Long, who campaigned with the Indians in 1776 recorded that the Canada nations "loved him with a Roman friendship; they flew to his standard with alacrity, obeyed him with cheerfulness, and never deserted him."[13] It may be seen that Haldimand had chosen a somewhat eccentric, yet sensible officer who was able to blend the goals and skills of two cultures for strategic purposes.

On Sep. 27th, Carleton's forces assembled at the fort at St. John's (Saint-Jean-sur-Richelieu) where Carleton was post commandant.[14] The expedition was to be divided into two distinct wings with Major Carleton commanding one and John Munro, a half-pay Regular officer and senior captain of the KRR NY, the other. Although Munro's force would be comprised solely of Provincials and Indians, the Royal Yorkers in their redcoats, which had been first issued the year before to loyalist "line" regiments, would have the appearance of British Regulars. With the inclusion of the two Royal Yorker companies under Munro's command, the total number of men rose to 971 all ranks. The following table describes the complement of each and includes some of the officers in attendance:

Officer Commanding: Major Christopher Carleton, 29th Regt

Regulars
29th Regt - Captain Archibald Campbell
    Lieutenants John Enys, James Kirkman & William Farquhar[15]   201
34th Regt - Captain David Forbes, Lieutenant James Roche   113
53rd Regt - Lieutenants Thomas Booker, Robert McFarlane   113
84th Regt - Captain Malcolm Fraser   57
Jaegers[16] (Chasseurs)   34

Provincials (drawn from the several small corps in Quebec)
King's Loyal Americans - Major Edward Jessup,[17] Lieutenant David Jones
King's Rangers - Major James Rogers[18]
    Guide - Volunteer Roger Stevens[19]
total, all loyalist corps   150
Quebec Indian Department - Lieutenant William Johnson, 47th Regt
Kahnawake & Kanehsatake Indians[20]   108

Total, Carleton's men   *776*

Officer Commanding: Captain John Munro, 1st Bn, KRR NY

Provincials
1st Battalion, King's Royal Regiment of New York[21]
    Captain John Munro's Coy   48
    Captain Joseph Anderson's Coy   38
      Subalterns: Lieutenants Archibald McDonell, William Byrne,
      Richard Lipscomb; Ensign Allan McDonell; Adjutant John Valentine
    Subtotal, KRR NY: (includes Officers, Sergeants & Drums)   131
Captain William Fraser's[22] Independent Coy of Rangers -   34
Six Nations Indian Dept - Lieutenant Patrick Langan, KRR NY
Claus' Rangers & Fort Hunter Mohawks - Captain John Deserontyon[23] 30

Total, Munro's men   *195*

On Sep. 28th,[24] the troops of the force embarked in eight ships of the Lake Champlain squadron of the Provincial Marine[25] and 26 bateaux and sailed to Île-aux-Noix in the company of Brigadier General Henry Watson Powell, the district commander. They paraded under arms the next morning for Powell's inspection. Rogers' men were the poorest armed of the force. A few of his Rangers carried their personal fire-locks they had brought with them into the army and 42 of them were armed with "Indian pieces",[26] the ubiquitous trade musket.

As Governor Haldimand lacked confidence that the Provincial corps of Jessup, Peters and McAlpin which had been raised for service with Burgoyne in 1777 would be allowed to remain with him in the Northern Department, he withheld his full support as his limited resources could scant afford to have supplies bled off. He viewed Rogers' men in the same light, as they had been foisted upon him by the Central Department. Consequently, both Jessup's and Rogers' men were short of regimental clothing. Indeed, some of the King's Rangers and likely some of Jessup's that were sent on the expedition had been uniformed in the very unpopular blue coats faced white, the exact same colours so often worn by rebel troops.[27] Needless to say, the wearing of such clothing led, at the least, to many anxious moments and sometimes serious cases of mistaken identity.

Powell's inspection completed, the force reboarded the ships and boats and set sail. That night they stopped at Île-la-Motte after a voyage of 20 miles. The ship *Maria* with Commodore William Chambers, commander of the Champlain squadron, and Major Carleton joined the expedition the next day. Due to contrary winds, little headway was made during the next two days.

On Oct. 2nd, the expedition arrived at Valcour Island, site of the naval battle of 1776, where they were joined by the Fort Hunter Mohawk party and Claus' Rangers. All set sail the next day and along the route, Captain Munro dispatched two mixed parties of Ranger and Indian scouts from Ligonier Bay to seek intelligence at Johnstown and Ballstown.[28] The expedition finished the day at Rivière Bouquet where they camped for the night and most of the next day.

The force embarked at 6:00 PM on the 3rd and travelled to Split Rock Bay where they halted to camp for the night. The next morning, Carleton sent out scouts and one of his parties fell in with two strange Indians. When they were asked if they were on their way to join Major Carleton they replied in the affirmative and they were allowed to continue on their way; however, when the scouts returned to camp and reported the incident, describing the men as being very fatigued and heavily laden, a concern arose as to their true identity. As these mysterious men may have been rebel Oneidas, a party of Fort Hunter men was sent out to track them down, but the effort was unsuccessful. There was now a concern that the expeditions were compromised.

That afternoon Lieutenant William Johnston of the 47th Regt,[29] who was seconded to the Quebec Indian Department, arrived with 108 Canada Indians, said to be principally from the Kahnawake and Kanehsatake towns. He brought word that Lieutenant Richard Houghton,[30] another British officer seconded to the Quebec Department, had taken the majority of the Canada Indians, who had been left at St. John's, on a thrust against the "Head of the Connecticut River." This was good news, as the rebels' attention might be distracted by Houghton's efforts.

On the evening of the 6th, the force departed Split Rock.[31] The boats then travelled to "West [a.k.a. Bullwagga] Bay behind Crown point," arriving about 2:00 AM. "Soon after day light Capt. Monro's detachment" left the expedition and crossed the bay.[32] Munro left behind a pair of Royal Yorker Gentlemen Volunteers,[33] Thomas Smyth and Oliver Church, and two soldiers, to perform the hazardous duty of express runners between the two forces. Both Smyth and Church had much experience of operating in the deep woods as they had been employed in the Secret Service and would earn their commissions by these special duties. Smyth's father, Dr. George, was still serving as a spy amongst the rebels and would soon be spirited away to Canada where he became the deputy leader of all Secret Service activities.

Carleton's men spent the balance of the day "Making up our packs and preparing everything for our March, taking twelve day[s] provisions with us... " The expedition left the shipping here as the lake rapidly narrows below Crown Point making large vessels vulnerable to musket and artillery fire from the shore.

South of Crown Point, the rebels kept out regular scouting parties. That evening, Carleton's force commenced a stealthy approach towards the enemy's country, rowing for Ticonderoga "our Boats all in a line each boat following his leader". In the black of night, just below Ti, Lieutenant Enys' boat got fouled on an underwater obstruction. This snag turned out to be one of the sunken piles of the floating bridge[34] which the rebels had built across the lake between their fortifications on Ti and Mount Independence in 1776 and which had been burnt to the waterline by the British in 1777. The boats that preceded him were quickly out of his sight before Enys' crew could disentangle themselves. Once free, Enys attempted to rejoin the leaders, but soon despaired.

Remarkably, Carleton had set off into the night without sharing any details of his intended route with his boat commanders. Badly worried, Enys rowed back down the line of boats to report the separation to the remaining senior officer, Captain Malcolm Fraser of the 84th. Fraser was equally without information and he asked amongst the boat crews for a man who knew the area well enough to advise a good place to lay over until light. Everyone was aware that small parties blundering about the lake were vulnerable to discovery by rebel scouts in dawn's light. One of the soldiers from the locality advised that the only place to offer sufficient cover would be the narrow connecting waters between Lakes George and Champlain.[35]

Acting upon this advice, the separated boats turned about and made their way back to that entry only to find its mouth blocked by a double row of pickets, which they were unable to negotiate in the dark. The men lay in the bateaux until dawn when a boat sent by Major Carleton came down the narrows looking for them. The Major had entered that same waterway the night before; however, even if Enys had been told that the narrows was the next stop he wouldn't have recognized the opening as he had never "been above Crown point before." Ironically, the mouth to the narrows was immediately beyond the ruins of the bridge and, while Enys was stranded on the piles and preoccupied with getting free, the boats ahead simply disappeared through the hidden opening in the pickets. The force had been fortunate that the separation had been of so little consequence.

They "lay" in that place all the day and in the evening embarked again onto Lake Champlain and rowed into the South River and then into South Bay, these bodies of water constituting the narrow extension of Champlain. They pulled to the bottom of the bay, landing at 2:00 AM to make camp. The hazards of night travel were again illustrated by a gunboat becoming separated en route and entering the branch off the bay which led to Castleton, an important military centre for Vermont's troops. The force's good fortune again prevailed and the craft escaped discovery; the crew had recognized their error and turned about.

The troops lit fires and slept till daylight. That morning, Carleton made two large detachments. Having safely arrived at the bottom of South Bay without meeting any rebel reaction, he sent back Captain Malcolm Fraser, two subalterns and 100 privates of the 53rd & 84th to secure his return route.

Fraser was to take with him a second party commanded by Lieutenant Robert McFarlane of the 53rd with 30 of his men in two large bateaux, each carrying a Cohorn mortar. McFarlane was ordered to enter the narrows to Lake George and row south to join the main force when it came overland to attack Fort George. If required, the mortars would be used to subdue the garrison.[36]

The main body marched shortly after daybreak and continued until 3:00 PM when they stopped for the night at a place the loyalists called Parks Farm. As the force was only 1 1/2 miles from the Fort Ann blockhouse, Carleton was concerned about "Alarming the Country as there were some Setlements preety Near" and he ordered a fireless camp. He then found that he had to bring to bear all of his considerable diplomacy to persuade the Indians to forego fires. They were perfectly confident of their ability to keep their fires low and smokeless; however, the Major recognized that he couldn't indulge the natives while denying his white troops the same comfort.

A scout was sent off to reconnoitre the outlying blockhouse, its companion sawmill and the fort. They chose to scout the fort first, coming so close to its open gate that they observed a man sitting making something like a wooden bowl. As they watched, a sentry called for the sergeant of the guard. They prudently withdrew. On their return route, they investigated the blockhouse and sawmill and discovered both were deserted. Their report gave Carleton reason to be confident; however, he chose to remain cautious and make a night approach.

Enys' recorded in his journal a very clear picture of the hazards of night movements, whether on the water or through the woods. The advance began at 2:00 AM when Carleton sent off Lieutenant Farquhar of the 29th with 30 of his men and a like number of loyalists to cut the road coming north from Fort Edward. This precaution would block a rebel reinforcement.

The rest of the force got underway about 2 1/2 hours later. Almost immediately they found themselves struggling in stygian darkness over broken ground, falling over deadfalls and wading through swamps. To quote Enys, "it was so very dark it was with the utmost difficulty we could see the Man before us." To their surprise, the leading men came up with the rear of Farquhar's detachment. His scouts had taken a turn in the dark and followed a wrong track. Someone in the party had recognized the error and they backtracked to find the correct fork. Not too long after being overhauled by the main body, Farquhar's scouts identified their turnoff and the detachment struck out to perform their mission.

The Indians were in the lead of the main body and were thought to be not very far ahead; however, as first light broke they were out of sight. Carleton then called a short halt for a much-needed rest and, when the march resumed, the head of the column departed without advising the rear of the move. The error was soon discovered and the rear immediately set off, but the force was now divided into three non-supporting elements — not a favourable tactical situation. Again, no harm resulted, and at full light, the front of the troops came upon the Indians and, shortly after, the rear fell-in with the front. The expedition's good fortune had persisted.

A very short march took them to the blockhouse which was still abandoned. A substantial supply of timber was piled nearby for sawing at the mill. Carleton detached a sergeant's party to destroy the buildings and timber, and the main body marched on.

Immediately upon their arrival at Fort Ann, a flag of truce was sent forward to summon the garrison. A discussion ensued between the garrison commander and the flag officer. After considering a description of the strength of the force brought against him and the Crown officer's advice that the communication with Fort Edward was severed, the rebel commandant held a council with his officers and together they decided to surrender the fort with the proviso that the British troops occupy the installation before the Indians to prevent any "outrages." This condition was agreed to and Carleton's troops moved forward to examine their prize.[37]

The little fort was no more than a small wooden house surrounded by a large palisade cut with loopholes which were placed so low that attackers could run up to the pickets and fire into the interior.

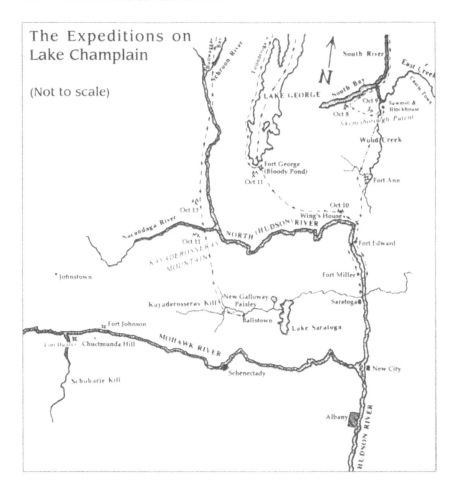

The Expeditions on Lake Champlain

(Not to scale)

Making things worse, the small garrison was supplied with only four rounds of ammunition per man.[38] The well-equipped Crown force observed that the garrison was badly clad in sparse, shabby clothing and most of them were barefoot.[39] Remarkably, the fort's gate had no lock or hinges. When the British erected the gate and barred it into place to prevent the Indians from entering, a mere handful of natives, impatient for plunder, readily pushed it in.[40]

The garrison consisted of a Continental captain named Adiel Sherwood, two militia lieutenants and 72 privates. Sherwood advised that he had been warned of the expedition by some hunters who had seen the boats at South Bay the night before, but he had not expected so large a force. When warned of the invaders' appearance, he was dining with Colonel Henry Livingston at Fort Edward. He immediately returned to Fort Ann and began his preparations, but these were obviously sparse, indicating that he was either beyond caring, or perhaps found it impossible to motivate his Levies and militiamen. Whatever was the case, Governor Clinton took a very dim view of the capitulation and reported to General Washington that the fort "appear[ed] to me to have been surrendered thro' Treachery or Cowardice."[41]

Sherwood had served with merit since 1776 as a lieutenant in Van Schaick's 1st New York Continental Regiment. For a time, he had commanded the Colonel's Company; however, when passed over for promotion the previous May, he had taken mild umbrage and resigned, pleading through the proper channels a very valid concern for the welfare of his family which inhabited the frontier near Fort Edward. However, he was not long at home before he applied to join the Levies, and being highly recommended by Van Schaick, he was given a captaincy in Graham's 3rd Regiment of New York Levies. On Aug. 11th, he led his company to Fort Ann, an installation not far from his family's holdings. The post was a logical location for Sherwood as he had commanded a garrison of the 1st New York there in 1777.[42]

Carleton had no sooner taken possession of the fort than Lieutenant Farquhar arrived with a prisoner, a militia Lieutenant. Farquhar reported that a man accompanying the Lieutenant had attempted to escape, but his detachment had fired upon him; they believed he was killed, although Enys secretly doubted it. The expedition destroyed the fort and all around it; then, herding their prisoners, they took the cart road towards Fort Edward, destroying all the farms along the route except two which belonged to loyalists who came forward to ask the favour.

Seth Sherwood, Adiel's father, the captain of the Exempts' Company of Webster's Charlotte County militia regiment, had ventured out alone from Fort Edward to determine how a relief of Fort Ann could be conducted. An express had come through Fort Edward the night before with "intelligence that the tracks of one hundred and fifty to two hundred of the enemy had been discovered by a scout from Fort Anne, near South Bay. And rather thinking them to be less in number than more, as generally proves in alarms... I rode off for further information." He blundered into Farquhar's men and was taken. He could scarcely credit their word that the fort had been taken and burned, but soon saw for himself the size of Carleton's expedition and their prisoners from the garrison and was "made sensible of the truth."[43]

Carleton's men continued forward, destroying by fire the Kingsbury district, and in the afternoon had come to the turn-off leading to Fort George. Carleton took this turn and by nightfall, after burning the Queensbury district, the force stopped at Abraham Wing's house on the Hudson River about 7 miles east of Fort George.

When darkness fell, having been encouraged by his loyalist officers from the neighbourhood, Carleton detached a party of the King's Loyal Americans under Lieutenant David Jones, a Fort Edward man,[44] and a second officer with 12 King's Rangers.[45] The two parties were to travel down the road towards Fort Edward "to destroy the Country."

The inhabitants, who were warned of the burning at Kingsbury "when the afternoon sun [was] an hour high" had fled at the first alarm, "people rushing down the road." The Bitely family "could scarcely believe the enemy would have the audacity to cross the river and come directly in rear of the fort and burn our buildings and our neighbours' under the very guns of the fort. Still, we deemed it safest to fly... We tied up our beds and most valuable and necessary clothing and tied them onto the horses backs... " After travelling several miles south and spending the night opposite Schuylerville, "[f]ather still supposed it was not probable our house was burned, so he took one of the horses and rode directly back, but on coming in sight he at once perceived all our buildings were in ashes, and all our grain and hay was consumed. They also killed all our cattle and hogs."[46]

When the Jones' detachment returned, they brought a supply of provisions and several prisoners.[47] Jones reported that his detachment had gone 14 miles south of Fort Edward on the west side of the Hudson and destroyed all in their path without opposition, including the village of Fort Edward and Colonel John McRae's new house, just being finished at Fort Miller.[48] Ironically, Colonel McRae was the brother of Jones' fiancee, Jane, who had been tragically killed by the Canada Indians during the Burgoyne campaign. The natives had been leading her to the British camp when, having some disagreement amongst themselves, killed and scalped her. One can only imagine the tumult of Jones' emotions as he watched his men destroy the home of his dead lover's brother.

The King's Rangers' party was ordered to march south and destroy all they found on the east bank as far as Fort Miller and then to cross the Hudson to the west bank and burn the mills and grain barracks east of Saratoga. On their return, the Rangers reported having a brush with a superior body of militia which had caused them to withdraw. Both loyalist detachments were back with Carleton by 7:00 AM on the 11th.[49]

It was supposed by the inhabitants of the Fort Edward area that the Tuttles and George Campbell, notorious local loyalists, were the leaders or instigators of "[a] large company of Tory refugees who volunteered to come down from Canada... and burn our homes." Of course, Jessup's and Rogers' men had been chosen for the expedition because of their knowledge of local conditions and they were undoubtedly glad to do this service. George Campbell had joined the

King's Loyal Americans in June of 1777 and had done duty with Captain Hugh Munro's Bateaux Company as had George Tuttle who had been with the Jessups in Canada over the winter of 1776/77. Campbell had transferred to James Rogers' Company of King's Rangers by Sep. 8th, 1780, whereas George Tuttle seems not to have survived the Burgoyne Campaign. However, many Tuttles were mustered in Jessup's and the KRR after the 1780 campaign, and some of these men may well have joined Carleton in Kingsbury or Queensbury to offer themselves as guides. These activities of the loyalists were to cause the local folk to remember 1780 as the "Year of the Great Burning."[50]

Carleton's reunited force advanced towards Fort George early that morning. Close by the fort, the Indian van discovered a man near Bloody Pond.[51] Unknown to Carleton's men, the garrison at Fort George had been "two Days destitute of provisions"[52] and the commandant, Captain John Chipman,[53] had dispatched an "express" to Fort Edward for supplies and the man fell in with Carleton's van. The Indians gave immediate chase and fired at him without success. The harried "express" got into the fort and told Chipman of the Indians he had encountered. Remarkably, Chipman had received no warning[54] from the neighbouring posts of Carleton's large force, and believing the natives to be no more than one of the many small parties which had been annoying all of the posts over the summer and fall, he decided to send out a sortie under Captain Thomas Sill[55] to deal with them.

Chipman claimed to have provided Sill with the following written order.

> GARRISON ORDERS FORT GEORGE OCTBR 11 1780
> Sir as it is reported to me that their is a small party of savages near Bloddy Pond, you will immediately take Forty Eight men, officers included and Proseed on the main road untill you make discoveries of them, keeping a Suffiscient advance and Flank gards in Such a manner as to prevent being surrounded. if you find a large party you will Emmediately Retreat to the fort except they should be savages only in which case you will attack and immediately Charge upon them —[56]

When Carleton's advance party of King's Rangers arrived at the fort, they sent a report back that they had observed about 50 men exiting the place.[57] All of the Indians immediately dropped their packs and set off after them, but when they failed to make contact, they returned. The Indians had just rejoined Carleton when word came from one of the force's flanking parties that the rebel party had been discovered.[58]

Again, the Indians set off, this time supported by 25 King's Rangers[59] and 50 men of the 34th under Captain Forbes and Lieutenant Roche. The detachment successfully surrounded and defeated the rebels in a very sharp, decisive action.[60] Of Sill's 48 men, 8 were captured and 27 killed; only 13 men were able to escape into the woods.[61] None from the sortie made it back to the fort.

The main body had paused for a time on the road, at a short distance from the action. When the fire became heavy, Carleton committed them as a reinforcement; however, as they pushed through the woods that screened the pond, the reports of musketry stopped. They were soon met by prisoners being brought in by the loyalists and Indians. Carleton was advised that a prisoner, believed to have been a Stockbridge Indian or a black, was killed — conformable to native custom — in a dispute of ownership between two warriors from "different villages."[62] This event illustrates one of the rules of engagement of frontier warfare employing natives. Either Indians or blacks, which were found in the rebel service, could be dealt with by the Crown's Indian allies as they found fit, without recriminations.

The whole force assembled on clear land atop a feature called Gage's Heights. From there they could see the fort, and equally well, the rebel garrison could see them. In response, the garrison fired three solid shot from a six pounder without any success; however, further risk was needless, and Carleton moved his troops into a small hollow under the cover of dead-ground where they formed up for a formal attack. Thus prepared, he sent a flag to summon the fort.[63]

While negotiations were underway in the fort, another prisoner was brought to the main body. At a distance, he was taken to be an Indian, as his head was glistening red; however, when he drew closer, he was seen to have been scalped. The man was very badly knocked about. His scalplock was torn off, an arm was broken by a musket ball and three very deep tomahawk cuts had been made to his head. He was recognized as being a British deserter from an artillery guard detachment which Enys had commanded four years before. At first the man denied this accusation, but eventually he confessed.[64]

Some of the prisoners admitted that there were very few men in the garrison. So, it was not unexpected when Carleton's call for a surrender was accepted and the fort fell into the Crown's hands.[65] Captain John Chipman, previously of the 2nd New York Continental Line, was the fort's commandant. He and the garrison were from Colonel Seth Warner's Additional Continental Regiment credited to New York State. Chipman requested a quite enigmatic condition of surrender, which Carleton chose to accept. This was the paroling of Ensign Barrett allowing him to take south in two wagons his young family, their personal baggage and the regiment's returns and account books.[66]

Whether the regimental paperwork or Barrett's youthful family were considered more important by Chipman remains a mystery.[67] Governor Clinton reported to Washington that Chipman "obtained a very honorable Capitulation before he could be induced to surrender."[68]

The fort was immediately occupied by Forbes' detachment of the 34th. The installation was too small to accommodate all of the force, so a camp was prepared outside of the works. When all the administrative details of the capitulation were complete the garrison was allowed to march out and the Indians entered the fort to plunder the interior, which Enys noted was "a thing they always look upon as their undoubted Right."[69] Indeed, this was the case and the activity represented another accepted practice of native warfare. Carleton was very aware that the natives did not always share the same sensibilities as the British, so while they were occupied looting, the wagons with the paroled officer and his family were sent away.[70]

Of course, the expedition had abandoned the majority of their bateaux at South Bay. Carleton learned that the fort's bateaux had been sunk in the lake for safekeeping and to stop the boards from springing. He dispatched parties around the shoreline to locate and raise them. This task lasted until near dark. The rebel garrison was then put inside the fort under a guard of the 34th & 53rd, a precaution which saved the prisoners from possible native reprisals.

Enys observed that the fort had many advantages which could have allowed a considerable defence, even though the works were commanded by adjoining heights. The walls were constructed of stone with thick earthen parapets; however, an excellent well had been so contaminated with refuse, that the water was undrinkable. The palisades were frail, having been burnt often and not repaired. Only one six-pounder was mounted while another dismounted tube lay in the grass, and was thus useless. A third barrel lay broken outside the works, likely with a fractured trunnion. As at Fort Ann, the garrison had been poorly supplied with small arms ammunition with only 16-18 rounds per man and four day's provisions. In Enys' opinion, undoubtedly one that was discussed amongst his fellow officers, Chipman had gravely weakened his potential for defence by sending out the sortie, as none had been able to return. The despondency, deprivation and apparent incompetence found in these rebel frontier garrisons must have given the British a great sense of confidence, if not one of contempt.

On the 12th,[71] the bateaux were bailed as dry as possible and carefully examined to choose the best craft. The wounded were immediately sent off in the care of the expedition's surgeon. Several families who had decided to "come off" with the expedition were given the balance of the bateaux in which to travel and they departed. Lieutenant

McFarlane had arrived with the two cohorns. The two good six-pounders from the fort were loaded into his boats, as was Captain Chipman who was entrusted to the Lieutenant's care.

After putting the fort to the torch, the force marched north via Rogers' Road, a track named after Major James Rogers' famous brother Robert who had operated extensively in this area during the Seven Years' War.[72] Consistent with custom, the prisoners were heavily laden with the Indians' plunder.[73]

Prior to departing, Major Edward Jessup sent two men of his corps, John McMullen and Volunteer William Moffat, into the country to gather recruits and intelligence. Another man, James Van Dusen (Driesen), said to have been in the late Major McAlpin's corps, requested permission of Major Jessup to take a leave. His request was approved. When Moffat discovered that Van Dusen was going to be abroad in the same area as himself and McMullen, he complained to Major Jessup that he had reasons to distrust the man's loyalty. Jessup withdrew the approval and Van Dusen quietly took his own leave and disappeared. He was quickly taken up by the rebels and immediately proved that Moffat's concerns had been entirely valid.

The rebel militia were not inactive during this time. Private George Fowler recalled that, when the warning was received that the British were in the area, the Cambridge and Hoosic companies of the Charlotte County Militia Regiment were paraded some 300 strong and marched through Union Village (now Greenwich) to Fort Edward and encamped outside the fort. The fort's commandant, Colonel Livingston, attempted to take command of them, but "our officers preferred acting entirely distinct and independent of him." The morning of the 12th, they marched to Glens Falls and discovered that a party, which they supposed had been Indians, "had penetrated down towards Schuylerville and burned some barracks down that way which were filled with wheat." They continued onto Fort George and arrived to find, as did militia units arriving piecemeal from other areas, that the post had been burned and the British "had just gone down the lake." How fortunate they were, for Carleton's disciplined troops would quite likely have thrashed these rashly independent amateurs.

Another Charlotte County militiaman, Austin Wells, recalled this trip to Fort George "to bury the dead and secure any property that might be left." He remembered being accompanied by one of the officers from Warner's Regiment. His record of what they found speaks volumes for the viciousness of native warfare and, although everyone knew its characteristics, the shock of observing its results was never lost. "We found twenty-two slaughtered and mangled men. All had their skulls knocked in, their throats cut and their scalps taken. Their clothes were mostly stripped off. [Warner's officer] recognized Lieutenants Ensign and Eno and cried like a child at beholding them. They laid upon their backs, scalped and with their throats cut. Their stocks had been torn from their necks, the silver buckles taken from them, and the stocks were then laid across their breasts... One man only had not his throat c[ut]; he was a mulatto and was lying on his face — the only one found in this posture. We supposed he was the drummer, and his arms were tied behind him with the cord of his drum, and he had been killed by a spear in his back after he was tied. There were six or eight spear wounds in the middle of his back, on each side of his back bone, and the spear was left in his back. He was scalped. We supposed he had been more obstinate and valiant in withstanding the enemy, and they had therefore bound and tortured him alive... The Negro... had his clothes all on; all the other bodies were stripped more or less..."

From Well's further description, the closing moments of the Bloody Pond combat must have been very severe. "The fighting had been mostly with clubbed muskets, and the fragments of these, split and shivered, were laying around with the bodies. The barrel of one I observed had been bent full six inches from a straight line." While the mangling of the bodies was a distinct characteristic of native warfare, there is no reason to believe that all of the victims had been killed by Indians. The mutilation — scalping and disfiguring — of all of the dead on a battlefield was considered another of the rites of native combat. Wells also advised that the party found a British officer buried at the fort with his clothes on. Who could this have been? A private soldier of the 34th was reported as killed in Carleton's return, but no officers and such occurrences were not ignored in official reports.[74]

★★★

After a difficult march of three days through rugged terrain, Carleton's force arrived at the landing at the north end of Lake George. They found it secured by Lieutenant Thomas Booker of the 53rd with a detachment sent for that purpose by Captain Fraser of the 84th. The force continued its march, with Booker's detachment acting as rearguard, and arrived at Ti late that day, Oct. 15th. There they found the shipping, bateaux and Captain Fraser's detachment safe and sound.

On October 16, the force moved north to Crown Point where they encamped to await word of Munro's expedition. After enjoying the companionship of several of the Crown officers, the rebel prisoner,

Captain Adiel Sherwood, wrote to Colonel Livingston from on board the ship *Carleton* that he had "not had the least reason to complain since [taken] a prisoner, but have be[e]n used with the greatest politeness... "[75]

On the 18th, the Canada Indians decided there would be no further opportunity for action and began their return trip. Some of loyalists were given permission to return with them. That same day, the troops moved north to Mill (Miller's, Mile) Bay. On the evening of Oct. 23rd, word came from Captain Munro that he would be at his boats at Bullwagga Bay the next day. The force moved there to meet him that morning.

When they arrived at Bullwagga, Carleton was concerned that the rebels may have found the resources to mount a pursuit and, as many days had now elapsed, they might be near at hand. Consequently, he employed the troops all the morning in building an abbatis as a defensive work to cover where their boats lay on the shore. Munro arrived at 1:00 PM, bringing several prisoners. He had suffered no losses during his venture.

Having marched overland for the entire 17 days of their mission, Munro's men were much fatigued. In consequence, the recombined force lay over at Bullwagga Bay until the next morning when they embarked in the ships and boats for the voyage to Canada. En route, they were greatly disappointed to meet with an express vessel from Governor Haldimand carrying orders that they were to remain on the lakes[76] as long as the navigation remained open, in order "to draw the attention of the Enemy."[77] Captain Justus Sherwood of the Secret Service[78] had been aboard the express vessel and he transferred ship to join Carleton. Likely the prisoners and wounded were sent to the express vessel for delivery to Canada. The force then turned about and returned to their old camp at Mill Bay.

The brief meeting between Munro and Justus Sherwood could hardly have been cordial. John Munro would have vividly recalled "that upstart Yankee" Sherwood's prewar role in the Green Mountain "banditi". On his part, Sherwood knew Munro as a hard, conservative, uncompromising and vindictive Yorker. The two men typified the two sides of the politics in the Grants and had no use for each other.[79]

Justus was faced with the potential for another awkward incident. The rebel prisoner, Captain Adiel Sherwood, was a close relative.[80] Proper etiquette dictated that at least a greeting be exchanged, albeit a strained one. However, Justus' mission was extremely delicate and the risks were too great to allow such an ardent rebel as Adiel to discover the slightest detail of his whereabouts and activities. Likely Justus took no chances.

Agent Sherwood set off from Mill Bay in a naval cutter carrying a flag of truce to the Republic of Vermont under the guise of negotiating further prisoner exchanges. While this purpose was quite real, his more important goal was to further talks regarding Vermont resuming an allegiance to the Crown. Captain Chipman, the late commander of Fort George, was paroled with Haldimand's consent and went with Sherwood.[81] As Chipman had been a volunteer under Ethan Allen in 1775, it was hoped that his release would assist Sherwood's negotiations for the prisoner exchange. It may be that the parole did assist Sherwood; but, a great price was paid when Chipman broke the promises he had given to secure his release. A great number of Vermont loyalists were ruined by his betrayal.[82]

The Enys journal provides some interesting statistics. At the capture of Fort Ann, 1 captain, 2 lieutenants and 72 private men were taken. At Fort George, 1 captain, 3 subalterns and 23 men of the sortie were killed and one man wounded. One captain, 1 subaltern and 42 men were captured and the one subaltern had been paroled. In all, 148 men were, at least temporarily, taken out of the war. In a material sense, much had been accomplished - 2 forts, 6 saw mills, 1 grist mill, 38 dwellings, 33 barns and 1500 tons of hay were destroyed.

The cost in personnel had been remarkably low. Amongst the Regulars — of the 34th, one man was killed and a sergeant was wounded. Two men had deserted, one from the 84th, the other the pseudo-loyalist Van Dusen. John McMullen had been captured when left behind to recruit, although this was not known when the report was written. Amongst the Indians, one man was killed and two wounded.

AN EPILOGUE TO CARLETON'S EXPEDITION

A tragic epilogue to the Carleton expedition was the capture of John McMullen and James Van Dusen (Driesen.) Both were brought to trial in Albany on Oct. 25th.[83] Corporal Jacob Schell (Shell)[84] of the Royal Yorkers was tried at the same time. He had surrendered, as he himself termed it, as "a prisoner of war." All three men were tried under a New York State law entitled, "An act subjecting all persons who shall come out from the Enemy & secretly lurk in part of this State to Trials by Courts Martial as Spys." If found guilty, the penalty was death by hanging.

Schell was the first examined. Faced with death, many loyalist prisoners would attempt to escape the halter by claiming to be deserters. Schell was either too proud to do so, or felt that his claim to be a prisoner of war would be enough to save him. He pled "not guilty" and then began his story of being taken aside at Lake Onondaga by Sir John Johnson and "granted permission to go and see his Family... and charged... to tell the Inhabitants that if they remained quietly at Home they would not be injured." It had taken him ten days to cross the Valley to Helleburgh. Schell stated that when he had arrived, he called upon Captain Van Aernum to "surrender.. himself as a prisoner of war." Schell obviously recognized that if the Court would accept him as a prisoner of war, he would avoid being found a spy. He finished his testimony by naively stating that "if he might be permitted to remain at Home he would behave himself peaceably & quietly."

Captain Guy Young was called as a witness for the state and his testimony sealed Schell's fate. Young stated that Schell "informed me yesterday, that if the Militia had not been flocking in, he would have got clear and that he intended to return to a place appointed for that purpose; that he thought it was better to surrender himself a prisoner of war than to be killed on the way." Clearly, thoughts of surrendering had been quite secondary. Someone who knew that Schell was a loyalist soldier had either seen him, or heard rumours of his presence in the neighbourhood, and the local militia had been called out to conduct a search. Schell was sentenced "to be hung by the Neck till he be dead."

John McMullen was brought before the Court Martial and entered a plea of "not guilty." The prisoner was not given an opportunity to state his case as he had previously signed a confession before Commissioner Samuel Stringer which was entered as exhibit No. 1 and annexed to the proceedings. McMullen's confession was a complex story. He had been a Continental soldier in "Colonel Sheldon's Corps of Light Horse..." and when on patrol "was captivated by the [British] enemy... " and "enlisted in Colo. Emerick['s] Corps of Light Horse in the British Service." He obtained a release from Emerick's and travelled to Canada with Thomas Mann (Man)[85] and George Gosby, arriving on Aug. 1st, 1780. "[H]e was appointed an ensign in Ebenezer Jessup's Corps" and was engaged recruiting men at St. John's when they came in from the states. McMullen admitted to being with Carleton at Fort George and advised that "Major Jessup gave him permission to leave the party and come into the Country; that he was to return by the first opportunity..." He was "without any written permission or Furlow", not that such paperwork would have assisted him much, unless it stated that he was visiting a sick relative, which the Court may have recognized as a benign purpose if it could be confirmed. His testimony implicated "one [Henry] Tinkey, near Batten Kill" who, in the full knowledge that McMullen had "come from the British Army," had assisted by concealing him for two days and nights and then directing him to a canoe. McMullen used this craft to cross the Hudson and went to visit his mother at Stillwater where he was taken prisoner.

While McMullen's "confession" attempted to make his arrival at Henry Tinkey's appear a simple matter of fate, the fact that an Abraham Tinkey was a soldier in Jessup's KLA in Canada would suggest that the house in Batten Kill was a known "safe-house" for loyalist operatives. However, Abraham's presence in Canada may not have been known to the Court and, in any event, the substantial assistance Henry Tinkey freely gave to McMullen was enough to brand him a Tory sympathizer. He would very soon pay the price. McMullen was found guilty of spying and sentenced to death.

James Van Driesen was next examined. His case was another matter altogether as his name had previously been entered in the minutes of the Commission for Detecting and Defeating Conspiracies at Albany as being suspected of being "in League with the Scouting parties of the Enemy."[86] He also had signed a "confession" for Samuel Stringer on Oct. 23rd. It contained many details of his chequered career. James had taken "an oath of allegiance to the State of New York" in 1777 and then promptly joined with Burgoyne's army at Fort Miller where he then took an oath swearing "to be true to King George." He served the campaign as an artificer in McAlpin's American Volunteers and returned to his home at New Town after the defeat. Since that time he had "worked at different Places" and in May of '80 heard from "McIntosh[,][87] Van De Bergh's Son in Law" that William Moffat was about "to pilot a party to Canada." Van Driesen joined with Moffat, but became separated and made his own way to Quebec where he claimed to have rejoined McAlpin's.[88] He confessed to carrying arms against the state and to being at the Bloody Pond action[89] outside Fort George. Van Driesen had obtained leave from Major Jessup to accompany McMullen. Before the approval was countermanded, due to Moffat's strenuous objections, he must have had time to discover McMullen's plans. As Van Driesen was taken prisoner before McMullen, he was very likely the informant who betrayed the recruiting officer.

Clearly Van Driesen knew that his salvation might lie in offering as much information as possible about Tories — Tory plots, Tory spies, Tory recruiters and Tories living amidst the rebels. He sang like a nightingale, giving out names as free as advice. His detailed account of William Moffat[90] leading a party of men from New York to Canada implicated Captain Joshua Losey [Losee],[91] William Totten, John Ostrander and "old and young" Moore.[92] Another tale mentioned two "young Fellows from the Scotch Patent [who] joined Major Carleton's Party at Fort George", one named Archibald McNeal,[93] the other

Gilchrist.[94] William Vrooman, his wife and James Brisben,[95] who had given him assistance after he deserted at Fort George, were cravenly betrayed. Van Driesen had given a great deal of information and promised that he had much more to offer — would it be enough to save him?

Then came the first announcement. "[T]he Court upon considering the evidence are of opinion that the prisoner is guilty of the Charge exhibited against him... "[96] He was sentenced to be hanged. He must have been struck dumb; his ploy had failed. However, the Court had the measure of their man and were playing him like a fiddle. The announcement of the sentence was followed by their unanimous decision "that as Van Driesen... has intimated to this Court that he can make Discoveries advantageous to the United States it be recommended to his Excellency, the Gov'r to grant a Reprieve to the said Van Driesen, to afford Time to enquire into the Nature & extent of his Discoveries."[97]

The consequences of Van Driesen's testimony were quickly felt throughout the region. The day before Van Driesen's formal "confession" had been recorded before Samuel Stringer, a meeting was held in Albany by the Commission for Detecting and Defeating Conspiracies in the State of New York. A letter from General Philip Schuyler was read into their minutes. He advised that he had forwarded under guard Hans Peter Snyder and James Brisben of the Saratoga District on a charge of "Harbouring[,] concealing and forwarding into the Country Spy's sent from the [British] Enemy."[98] Obviously Van Driesen, at the very moment of being taken into custody, had burbled with information and the names of the various people he implicated travelled quickly to Schuyler who, with characteristic energy, had quickly apprehended the two suspects.

By Oct. 26th, the Court Martial resumed to hear the decisions of Governor Clinton. "Jacob Schell, John McMullen and James Vandriesen charged as Spies" had been "severally sentenced to be hanged by their Necks until they be dead." Clinton's words were next read:

> "His Excellency... approves of the Proceedings of the court and confirms the Sentences." This was immediately followed by the announcement that Shell and McMullen would be hanged "at the Common Place of Execution near the Barracks this afternoon at four O'Clock."[99]

One can readily imagine the pall of silence that fell over the prisoners. The two condemned men stared death in the face while a stunned Van Driesen exulted that his name had not been read. The Governor's second statement followed, "Vandriesen is respited for the Space of fourteen Days."[100] He had won. He now knew for sure which way the wind was blowing and would trim his sails accordingly.

Major Davies, the Field Officer of the Day, was ordered to give directions for the executions. The Governor's instructions stated that "The Continental Troops, Levies and the City Regiment of Militia, are to parade at three O'clock at the Place of Execution."[101] The war was over for John McMullen and Jacob Schell.[102]

On Oct. 28th Peter Jost (Yost) of Johnstown was brought before the conspiracy commissioners. He swore that he had been taken prisoner by the Tories in the May 1780 raid on Caughnawaga. He was believed and discharged, but not before he implicated two persons of whom more will be heard later. Entered into the minutes of Oct. 29th was another letter from General Schuyler advising that William Vrooman and Henry Tinkey, two of the men exposed by the confessions of Van Driesen and McMullen, had been apprehended. Schuyler advised that there were a number of "Tory woemen who are at present at Saragtoga and who are desirous of going to Canada."[103] He wished that the commissioners would bring these nuisances to the attention of the Governor. These were the women whom, we shall see, would unwittingly prevent John Munro from attacking Saratoga.

Van Driesen made a lengthy appearance before another court at Albany on Oct. 31st.[104] To the obvious satisfaction of his examiners, he exceeded his previous performance. Chief Justice Morris and Justice Yates heard his testimony and they were so impressed with his candour and veracity that they recommended a pardon for him to the Governor. James had even succeeded in convincing the justices that he was a genuine deserter. Their belief was developed in the face of much contrary evidence. He had taken an oath to Congress and then to the King and spurned both, all in the same year. He had enlisted and served twice in the same loyalist regiment. Even more remarkable, he had left Fort George only after being refused formal leave by Major Jessup. How he could be trusted as a deserter "with a design not to return to them [the loyalists] again"[105] is a mystery. With his neck on the line, Van Driesen understood that a great volume of information was required. Innuendo, exaggeration and sheer fabrication could have met his purpose equally as well as fact; however, what he reported proved to be remarkably accurate. Obviously, the amount of loose talk and rumour-mongering amongst the loyalist exiles was prodigious.

His most important revelation was about the Vermont negotiations that were under way with Ethan Allen and his confederates. He told of reports "prevailing in Canada, and amongst the Tories" in the State that "Coll. Eaton Allen was making Interest among the Inhabitants of the Grants, to join the Brittish army, and that he has been about this business ever since he was exchanged."[106] This exposure would not come as news to Governor Clinton as there had been a great deal of sober correspondence with General Schuyler and others on the topic, but it did confirm that there was every reason to be greatly alarmed.

Several men were revealed to be regularly in the state recruiting for the loyalist regiments or reaping intelligence. John Twisley, a German who spoke English and Dutch as well, was said to be presently recruiting at Spencertown. Van Driesen again took a shot at William Moffat and stated that he was regularly in the Scotch Patent and to make the cheese even more binding, Van Driesen advised that Henry Tinkey, who had been imprisoned as a result of James' earlier confession, knew the present whereabouts of Moffat. The revelations rolled on. "Old" Defoot (Dafoe) of Hosick[107] was a regular at both recruiting and carrying intelligence. Also from Hosick were John Ruiter, another of the same surname[108] and John Best. These three were often sent out to gain recruits and intelligence, as was James Muckle Miles[109] of Ballstown. James O'Niel[110] was yet another collector of intelligence and recruits. Abraham Ostrander and John Gregs[111] were "sent into the Country by Major Jessup at Cumberland Bay" and John Gibson's wife said that both had been at their homes. Lieutenant Fraser[112] of Ballstown entered the state and visited his home at the same time as Ostrander. David Palmer had been recruiting at Newtown as the sergeant major[113] of Rogers' Corps.

Details of several "safe-houses" were exposed; Joshua Lossee's back of Newtown; John Lantman's[114] and "old Defoots [Dafoe's]" at Hosick; Abraham Hayard's at Ballstown; "old" Hans Snyder's[115] and Hick's,[116] "whose two sons are with the [British]", both at Newtown. David Palmer had visited at Hick's place and at Alexander Brevoort's. Archibald McNiel of the Scotch Patent had offered assistance to Moffat, as had a man named Gillis.[117]

Van Driesen was on a roll. He named a number of persons who were rumoured in Canada to be "Friends of the Brittish King", the very type who might offer intelligence or material assistance to spies and recruiters. His list included a Roff, a Kline,[118] Jotham Beemus and Ezekiel Ensign. Van Driesen stated, "that during this Summer five Persons have at different Times brought dispatches from New York to Canada one of whom was a young man who had served his Time with Dr. Stringer." The thought that a young "traitor" had been deep into the bowels of the Commission for Detecting Conspiracies must have sent a jolt through the commissioners.

The Lansings (Lansinghs) of New City[119] were named, in particular young Philip,[120] the sheriff of Charlotte County. Van Driesen testified that "[W]hen he [Lansing] arrived [in Canada, he] brought a great number of news Papers." This would have been an immediate concern as there were few imposed controls on what was printed in the newspapers and often quite detailed and accurate news of troop movements, promotions, supply shortages, negotiations, mutinies, etc... could be found. The Lansings had been suspected of playing a double game for years. Because of Van Driesen's wandering testimony, the Canadian Department's Secret Service network "in rebellious New York" had been severely compromised. The conspiracy committee had a veritable host of names to feast upon. They would not be long in doing so.

While Van Driesen had exhausted all the names and places that came to his fertile memory, he was not quite through. Perhaps the commissioners gave him the impression that more information was needed if he was ever to receive a full pardon. Perhaps in his panic he simply began to invent. Whatever the case, Van Driesen blurted out a story which reflected terribly on Major Carleton's honour and conduct and nurtured the well-developed prejudices of his audience. This tale received much currency amongst the rebels and led to a bitter exchange between Colonel Peter Gansevoort, 3rd New York Continental Line, Brigadier General Henry Watson Powell and Major Christopher Carleton. The letters were written primarily to arrange the reciprocal movement of civilian and military prisoners. As each man wrote to the other, phrases in the letters referring to the treatment of persons held by each government grew vitriolic. Powell assigned Major Carleton to the task of organizing bateaux for the movement of some loyalist families and when Gansevoort wrote to him, the Van Driesen tale came to the surface. Colonel Gansevoort wrote on Nov. 26th --

> A certain James Van Deusen, who deserted from our service to you, and who, since you were on this side [of] the lake, has stolen back into the country, has been apprehended, and will suffer death as a deserter. He confesses that after the rencontre near Fort George, with some of Colonel Warner's men and your party, in which one of our Indians was killed, your Indians, in cool blood, scalped one of Warner's men alive, tormented him a considerable time, and afterward cut his throat — and all this in your presence. Your character, Sir, suffers greatly on this account.[121]

Needless to say, Major Carleton vehemently denied this charge by a return letter; however, there is little doubt that his reputation had been stained.

Van Driesen's efforts were to be rewarded, but not without some further uncertainty. On Nov. 16th, he was again brought before the board and recommitted to custody. He faced a wait of several months before the Governor wrote to the commissioners requesting his release. His discharge was approved on Feb. 27, 1781.[122]

The loyalist sympathizers unearthed by McMullen's thoughtlessness and Van Driesen's calculations were quite small fish in comparison to two mysterious men revealed by Peter Yost and examined in Albany in early November. On the 6th, Hugh McManus, a Tryon County constable, appeared before the conspiracy commission with Albert Van Der Werken. Albert was a clever fox of the first order. He was under considerable suspicion, but the rebels were unable to prove a case against him. In fact, he was an active recruiting officer[123] for the King's Rangers and had been at large in Tryon County since early September.[124] In this instance, Albert prevailed upon the commission to call two witnesses to his behaviour while he had been in Canada. This request was granted and Peter Sietz and Michael Cannon, "who [had] been Prisoners in Canada and were lately exchanged"[125] were examined and reported that to their knowledge, Van Der Werken had been employed as "a Bar Keeper in a Tavern and they could not learn that he had taken up Arms in the Enemies service." This was an ingenious cover story which the commissioners found acceptable and Albert was released on £400 bail after giving "a Recognizance for his good Behaviour."

★★★

Major James Rogers, whose small corps had mustered only one company of 49 all ranks in early September, 1780, was intent on building its strength so that both he and his officers could receive the pay consistent with their ranks. The King's Rangers had a convoluted history. James' famous and scandalous brother Robert, after abandoning the command of the Queen's Rangers just prior to their famous victory at Brandywine in 1777, had attempted to interest Governor Carleton of Canada in giving him an opportunity to raise a new corps. Carleton had too many problems of his own to seriously consider such a request and declined. Robert turned to Sir Henry Clinton in New York and was rewarded with a Beating Warrant to raise two battalions with two typical provisos. His officers were to be appointed only after they recruited a specific number of men and Clinton himself would confirm their rank. Before raising the prerequisite number, an officer would receive no pay. Robert would not be confirmed as LtCol. until 600 men had been recruited, nor James as major until four companies of 60 men each were completed.[126]

Robert Rogers was recommended to Governor Haldimand, Carleton's replacement, by Clinton's Central Department. Sir Henry's staff explained that, of absolute necessity, the King's Rangers officers were going to locate in Quebec Province. The Rangers' recruits were being raised on the frontiers of New Hampshire and New York and would be able to work their way north more readily than to New York City. Thus, the Rogers brothers came to Quebec. It proved to be a disappointing venue. Robert soon disgraced himself with the Governor and fled the province. James was left on his own, unsupported, with a handful of men and no resources.[127] Haldimand was displeased to have another small unit recruiting in the same regions as his favoured regiments, the 84th RHE, the KRR NY and Butler's. Worse, recruiting from these same areas were the officers of the skeleton battalions commanded by Messrs. Jessup, Peters and McAlpin, who were struggling in the same manner as Rogers to fill out their companies so that they would be confirmed and paid in their ranks. As all of these latter units were nominally part of the Central Department, Haldimand had no interest in them recruiting at the expense of his loyalist regiments of the Northern Department. There simply were not enough men to bring all these corps to full strength and James soon found himself at odds with all the other unit commanders[128] as he crossed into their recruiting zones and employed some "interesting" methods to lure men, eg. Van Der Werken was recruiting in the same area from which the KRR and Butler's drew.

Enter the second mystery man — Van Der Werken wasn't the only recruiting officer that Rogers had in the state. On the first day that Albert was arraigned, the conspiracy commission entered into their minutes a letter from the Poughkeepsie commission giving information that one William Laird (Lord, Leard),[129] a Tryon County citizen, "says he was taken Prisoner last spring by the Enemy and that he has in Sir John's late Expedition made his escape from them." Lord appeared the next day, immediately after Van Der Werken, and in some clever, unrecorded manner convinced the board of his claim to have been captured and then to have escaped. In reality, William Lord had also been at large in the state since early September and was, like Van Der Werken, busily recruiting men for the King's Rangers.[130] As he had been taken up in the Poughkeepsie area, his beat was likely in southern Albany, Ulster and Dutchess counties. How self possessed these two men must have been when they were brought together in the court's ante chamber.

On Dec. 4th, Lord was again a topic of discussion with the commission. They noted —

> that from the Assertions of some Persons at present with the [British] Enemy there is good reason to suppose that William Laird at present residing at Johnstown who some time ago entered into a Recognizance before us... is at present enlisting Men for the service of the enemy with whom he intends to join them as soon as they make a descent into the Country...

Amazingly, this affair stumbled on for the next two months with report after report of Lord's recruiting activities being noted.[131] The matter was resolved the next February when Constable McManus appeared before the board with the information that Lord had "inlisted in the Nine Months's [rebel Levies] Service and [was] offering faithfully to do his duty in future... " The agile and opportunistic John Lord was discharged after paying McManus "the Costs accrued by his Apprehension." He was never seen again in Canada.

As to Albert Van Der Werken, sometime after his release, it was confirmed that he was recruiting. Captain John Zielie of the Palatine Regiment assembled a detachment to apprehend him at Spraker's Tavern, a small house owned by the Tribes Hill Bowens and run by Jacob Van Loan, "whose politices were of a suspicious character."[132] Zielie and his men surrounded the tavern and peered through the windows to see Van Der Werken and Frazee, another suspect character, eating their supper. Somehow the two men sensed their danger and slipped out of the house to hide in a nearby hay barrack. After searching the house, Zielie concluded they were hiding in the barrack and surrounded it to await the dawn. As first light came, the fugitives saw their peril and broke from the barrack at a run. Militiaman Adam Empie thrust his bayonet through Frazee, killing him outright. Resourceful Albert evaded the party amidst a fusillade of musket balls and ran into the woods which covered the hill behind the house.

After such a close call, Van Der Werken must have believed the jig was up. He appears to have used an intermediary to negotiate a surrender[133] and he was in confinement when the conspiracy commission met on Feb. 6, 1781. They examined Melchart (Melgert) Van Dusen,[134] a former Committeeman for Caughnawaga, who himself had been in grief with the County authorities and was confined with Van Der Werken. Melchart advised that "he ha[d] received Information that a certain Albert Van Der Werken is able to prove that Major Jellis Fonda [3rd Battalion, Tryon County Militia] was know[n] to Robert

Snell[135] who lived with the said Jellis Fonda [prior to] going to the [British] Enemy last spring." It would seem that everyone was willing to trade information to save their necks. The next day Albert was brought before the commissioners and he advised them that Fonda had been perfectly aware of Snell's plans to "go off" with the enemy, which tacitly implied that Fonda was in sympathy with Snell's action as he had neither stopped or reported him. If that wasn't enough, Van Der Werken claimed that Peter Boon (Bowen),[136] a declared loyalist who was very likely imprisoned with Van Dusen and Van Der Werken, "is able to give some very material Information respecting sundry disaffected Persons ... " Needless to say, the board resolved to examine Peter Boon. After this, the resourceful Albert Van Der Werken disappeared from view, a smudge on the page of the rebellion.

MUNRO'S EXPEDITION THROUGH THE WOODS AGAINST BALLSTOWN

As mentioned by Enys, Captain John Munro left Carleton's force at Crown Point on Oct. 6th and travelled across Bullwagga Bay to begin his march. This was the same landing place that Sir John had chosen for his May raid into the Valley. Once disembarked, Munro had the troops sink their bateaux for safekeeping in the time-honoured fashion. The Captain reported that only seven miles were covered on the first day's march as the men complained so strenuously about "the great weight of their Provision & Ammunition."[137]

Consequently, he halted to camp and "complete them to 50 Rounds pr. man and 30 days provisions." The remainder of the ammunition and provisions were left in a cache. Munro had obviously been expecting to fight his way through to Sir John as his original ammunition issue per man must have been greater than the 50 rounds the Baronet would issue to his troops the day before they entered the Schoharie.[138] A problem with the quantity of provisions was the likelihood that they would have to be shared, either with loyalists who came off with the raiders, or with prisoners that were taken. It was often not possible to forage for supplies if uninhabited back routes were used for the advance and retreat. If plans were made to be away from base for only 25 days, the troops had to carry additional food to meet those contingencies. Munro's force had been issued with one pound of bread and 10 ounces of pork per day and he halved this daily ration to lighten their burden and keep the troops content.[139] With these reductions, each man then carried over 23 pounds of provisions and over 3 pounds of ammunition, to which was added a 12 pound musket and 40 pounds of clothing, footwear and accoutrements — in all, some 78 pounds (32Kg).[140] Before they were done, the men would regret their complaining which had led to this drastic reduction in foodstuffs.

On Oct. 9, the fourth day of the approach march, one of the men wounded himself with an axe and another fell ill. A third man had to be detached to look after these invalids. At an appointed place on the Sacandaga River[141] on the morning of Oct. 11, the force was rejoined by the four Royal Yorkers who had been left at Crown Point with Major Carleton as express runners — Church, Smyth and two soldiers. They brought news that Carleton had taken Forts Ann and George and then retired to Ticonderoga.

This was both good news and bad in that Hank Bowen[142] and Maybee,[143] who had been detached from Ligonier Bay to travel to Johnstown with two Mohawk Indians to gather intelligence, had ominously not rendezvoused at the Sacandaga River as instructed. In consequence, Munro had no news of Sir John's progress and was very unsure about whether to attempt the planned junction at Schenectady.[144] With Carleton's raid already completed and the whereabouts of Johnson unknown, Munro was certainly "out on a limb." The Captain confessed that this lack of information "gave me a great deal of uneasiness."[145] In fact, the Johnson/Munro timetable was substantially awry with Munro being in position to join with Sir John five days before Johnson arrived at the south end of the Schoharie Valley. Munro had no way of knowing that the Niagara-based troops had arrived eight days later than expected. Perhaps the scouts sent to Johnstown had not rejoined as they simply had no news to report.

Munro's unease was made worse by the fact that his second party of scouts also failed to arrive. Captain William Fraser and a Mohawk had been sent to Ballstown to collect intelligence. That settlement was very close to Saratoga, Munro's primary target. He later reported that he had discovered that a large number of the wives and children of his men were being held in custody in the barracks there. Consequently, he decided not to proceed to Saratoga, as he knew his men and their women would demand that the families join his force. If he risked being saddled with such an impediment, any further military action would be impossible. As well, Major General Schuyler had taken post at Saratoga and his presence implied that a large, alert force was at hand. Munro's troops were already short of provisions and he later protested that their "Shoes, Mockosins, Trowsers, Leggings, &c." were already worn out.[146] He judged that the Ballstown area would make a reasonable secondary target as it was a well developed farming district with a mill, houses and harvests to be destroyed and provisions, clothing and perhaps footwear to be plundered. Besides, there were other scores that might be settled at that place.

Two prominent Ballstown officers were about to receive some rough loyalist justice. LtCol. James Gordon[147] was the district commander of the militia and second-in-command of the 12th (Half Moon & Ballstown) Regiment of Albany County.[148] The captain of his 5th Company was Tyrannis Collins.[149] Zealous partisans of the rebellion, Gordon and Collins had from the outset been active against supporters of the Crown. Daniel McAlpin, a half-pay British officer, owned a large, developed estate in the district and had many fellow Scotsmen in his employ and debt. Early in the conflict, Gordon recognized McAlpin as a man of military talent and a likely source for raising manpower, but his attempts to lure the Scot to side with the rebel cause were quietly and cleverly refused. Eventually, McAlpin was jailed in Albany for his recalcitrance, although he was able to later escape and join Burgoyne's army. In revenge, the rebels apprehended his wife, Mary McAlpin, a mature and dignified lady, and dragged her through the streets of Albany in a cart, clad only in her shift — a punishment usually meted out to a common bawd.[150] Similarly, Gordon was involved in the persecution of another half-pay British officer, Lieutenant Heaveton, who was a local inhabitant. Gordon's leading role in the council that passed the state law for executing loyalists without the benefit of clergy was particularly odious.[151]

One of McAlpin's recruiting officers, the future Captain William Fraser, experienced similar difficulties with Gordon and Collins. In May 1777, he and 40 other loyalists were taken by Collins from their lair in the woods near Schroon Lake where they had been hiding to escape rebel persecution and, at the same time, watching for an opportunity to join the British army. The Ballstown militia triumphantly marched them into Albany where they were held in irons.

In court, Fraser's men were only sentenced to a $15.00 fine, but William himself was assessed a term of one year in prison. All of them were returned in irons to the cellar of the Albany Town Hall while the authorities awaited payment of the fines. William's brother Thomas was amongst the men. Being very slight of frame, he was able to slip his irons and utilize a file which had been artfully secreted by his wife in the rations she supplied daily to the men. The whole party was soon free and many of them, including the Fraser brothers, were able to join with Burgoyne to serve under McAlpin in the American Volunteers. Not quite two years after that disastrous campaign of 1777, Daniel McAlpin died an untimely death due to the hardships he had undergone while hiding over the winter in the bush and campaigning with Burgoyne. Indeed, Gordon and Collins were well remembered by the Fraser brothers and many other loyalists from the Ballstown region.[152] These men were ideal targets for capture or, if needs be, death.[153]

Fraser was obviously a natural choice for the scout to Ballstown as he knew the area intimately and had family and friends who would be trustworthy and of willing assistance. His Mohawk companion could guide and safe-keep him through the trails of the upper country if necessary, although Fraser knew the area quite well as the Sacandaga River region was where he had secreted his party in 1777. Fraser's failure to arrive at the rendezvous meant that Munro had no word of the rebels' reaction to the Carleton strike. Information regarding the volume of troops that had been drawn off from headquarters at Albany and in what directions they had been sent was of critical importance to him.

Weighing his options, Munro made his decision and set the force on the track to Ballstown the next morning, the 12th. To Munro's relief, Fraser rejoined along the route. He advised that there had been no news of Sir John amongst their loyalist friends and that the whole Ballstown area was alarmed by the testimony of a deserter from Rogers' corps who had told of Munro's strength and likely destinations.[154] In consequence, 200 men of the Schenectady militia had been called out and sent to guard the town and 100 men of the local militia were on instant call. Munro was not deterred.

His resolve may have been strengthened by information that 2nd Major Andrew Mitchell, a Ballstown resident had been ordered on Oct. 11th by Colonel Jacobus Van Schoonhoven, the commanding officer of the 12th Albany, to rush the two companies of Ballstown militia to the relief of Fort Edward as the presence of Carleton's force was reported in that quarter.[155] Mitchell and his men made the march and returned home once they discovered Carleton's bateaux leaving Fort George.[156] Munro could take some satisfaction in the knowledge that they would certainly be wearied by their efforts.

Munro was determined to get his men as close to the settlement as possible without detection. Within ten miles of the town, he took the precaution of detaching groups of Indians and Rangers to close off three roads leading to the town. They had orders to secure all persons they found. Not long after, one of the groups brought in the noted hunter, Isaac Palmatier, and another man as prisoners. Munro was unable to glean any new information from either of them. The captives did confirm that a blow was expected against the town, that the Schenectady militia were in garrison and that "all the men in Town were in Arms."[157]

Not being satisfied with this information, Munro sent Oliver Church and two Rangers to some friends' houses giving Church instructions to meet the force on its way to Ballstown. The party set off express while the expedition "proceeded along the highway." The force had marched for about two miles when "the Rangers and Indians fell in with and took one Sue [Shew], a Rifleman and Hunter who had been out to discover any tracks of an Enemy".[158]

John Shew had previously been captured in June of 1778 by a mixed detachment led by Grenadier Lieutenant John Ross of the 34th Regt. (later the major-commandant of the 2Bn, KRR NY) which was operating in the area east of Johnstown. One of the purposes of the foray was to bring off a number of loyalist families. When these people had been collected, the group withdrew to the Sacandaga River where the Shews inhabited a farm of some 100 acres near Sir John's Fish House. John Shew, with his father, brothers and many others, was captured by the raiders. Amongst Ross' men were several Fort Hunter Mohawks, including the famous war captains, the brothers Aaron and David Hill, and a party of Kahnawake men with five loyalists, including William Bowen. The Mohawk warriors knew the Shew family and were very well disposed towards them. As an offer of native friendship, John and several others were adopted and taken to the exiles' village at Lachine. Being a superb hunter, Shew was given the relative freedom to travel and hunt. On one of his trips, he met with another of the prisoners who was enjoying similar liberties. The two men contrived a plan for what was to be a later successful escape to the Mohawk Valley.[159] Now, two years later, John Shew was forced to confront his former adoptive relatives.[160] They possessed absolutely no forgiveness for his breach of their trust. In Munro's words, "this man being a Prisoner before in Canada, and making his escape from the Indians; soon determined his Fate, for he was instantly put to Death."[161] His close friend Isaac Palmatier, a fellow marksman and hunter who had been captured shortly before, must have been in great shock.

A little time after, Church rejoined the force with James McDonald,[162] a local loyalist, who had agreed to serve as a guide. McDonald told of 150 men "in Arms in the Town, and... a Hundred more [who] were to be raised on the first certain Alarm!"[163] This was only confirmation of the intelligence brought earlier by Captain Fraser, but for some reason Munro reported that the news "staggered me much." Perhaps Fraser's information had been drawn from doubtful sources and was thought to have been exaggerated. Now it was confirmed by a local, fellow Scot with whom Munro was face to face. He wrote that "I flatter'd myself shou'd they have such a number that by surprising them in the night I wou'd be able to carry my party off safe, and procure them some Provision which they stood in very great need of."

On the southwest corner of the town square in Ballstown there stood the house of one Weed, built of oak logs and surrounded by a stout palisade pierced with loopholes.[164] A church was being erected adjacent to these works.[165] The Schenectady militia of the 2nd

Battalion of Albany County had been stationed there under the command of their 1st Major, Abraham Switts.[166] Not trusting the Schenectady "Dutchmen" to have the resolve to do their duty, the local militia had taken post at Pearson's (Pierson's) Hill on the outskirts of the town about two miles from the fort. The position overlooked the raiders' expected route. They built a small outwork and kept vigil there for several nights. Quite convinced the alarm had been false, they dispersed and returned to their homes two nights before the arrival of Munro's force.[167]

From his report, it appears that Munro called a council of his officers and the principal Mohawk chiefs. Amongst them was the campaign-hardened, Captain John Deserontyon. A decision was made as to the route of advance and they proceeded on the road leading through Paisley and New Galloway, two hamlets close by Ballstown. At about dusk, the force stopped at the house of Angus McDiarmid on the Paisley road. Some of Munro's force assembled inside, the natives amongst them being delighted by Mrs. McDiarmid's spinning wheel. Word of the marvel passed amongst the Indians and soon the house became so full of people taking turns spinning the wheel that the floor collapsed dumping everyone into the cellar.[168] All of the raiders escaped without harm, but the McDiarmid's had great cause to regret their hospitality.

Munro later advised that they had enjoyed ten miles of a secure advance as their route led them past "Friendly Inhabitants" many of whom came out to act as guides.[169] He stated that the roads were "the worst I ever traveled and the night being very dark; the Detachment was several times scattered," even though they had the benefit of local guides. The expertise of the Indians, who themselves were lost, repeatedly drew the force together again without incident. "[A]t about 11 o'Clock the moon appeared, by which means we got the party together. We passed several houses pointed out by Mr. Fraser as Friends.

"[B]etween 12 and one o'Clock in the morning, I arrived at Colonel Gordon's House."[170] The locale was known as Gordon's Mills, as the Colonel operated a grist mill on his farm on the Mourning Kill. Munro dispatched Fraser and his company to the nearby home of Captain Tyrannis Collins with orders to secure him.[171] The more influential prey he saved for his Royal Yorkers and Langan's men.

Here Munro proved himself to be an excellent tactician who clearly understood the use of psychology. Not wanting to offer Gordon the least hope of defence or chance of escaping, he surrounded the house with his two companies of red-coated Royal Yorkers, each man drawn up at two paces apart and standing at "shouldered Arms & fixed Bayonets, the moon shining so bright upon the mens arms, &

forming the Line so large[, that] a Person not Acquainted with our numbers wou'd imagine them much greater than they realy were... "[172] "I ordered Lieut. Langan with the Rangers and Indians to rush in at once on the House... "

Gordon was asleep in bed with his wife Mary and young daughter Melinda. He was rudely awakened by his windows being broken in by the hatchets and spontoons of the Indians. He rushed to the hallway which was choked with his enemies. Opening a door, he was met by a gigantic Mohawk who raised his tomahawk to strike. With great presence of mind, the man's arm was held back by Munro,[173] thus saving Gordon's life. At that very moment, the clock in the hallway began to strike the hour of twelve. Startled, a Mohawk shattered the face, supposedly uttering the words, "You never speak again!" The Gordons were led from the house, the Colonel with his daughter in his arms. The native women who had followed the war party rushed in to join their men in plundering and they soon emerged heavily laden with loot. Mrs. Mary Gordon, her son James Jr. and their servant John Parlow,[174] the son of a loyalist who had been captured by Oneida Indians, were all taken.[175] Three black slaves, Nero, Jacob and Ann, and a friend, or hired man, named Jack Galbraith also became prisoners. The two black men had been taken while trying to escape through a window.[176] Another black woman named Liz ran away and successfully hid in a cornfield in the rear of the house. The family dog ran up to her and began barking. She tore a strip from her petticoat and muzzled the beast.[177]

Munro immediately released Mary and Melinda Gordon and the pair took refuge in the woods overnight. Gordon's house and barn were left standing,[178] a strange favour in view of the enmity felt towards him; however, this was explained by the rebels as a deliberate artiface on the part of Munro to avoid alerting the militia.

Gordon had been captured in his nightshirt and he stood shivering in the bitterly cold October night air. He requested of Munro to be allowed to recover some of his clothing, but a quick search of the house was to no avail as the Indians had taken everything. In sympathy for the captive's plight, Langan stripped his own capote from his knapsack and gave it to him.[179]

Fraser's party was not quite so successful. Collins had barred entry and as the party attempted to break in, the rebel Captain put his back to the door as a reenforcement. He held this post until one of the tomahawk blows came through the door and struck him on the back. He then unbarred the door and the loyalists broke into the house and secured him, although his measure had delayed them sufficiently to allow his son Mannassah to escape through a small square hole in the upper story wall. Mannassah ran to the home of his uncles, John and

Stephen Ball where he gave warning. Mann and John then took to the woods to hide while Stephen mounted a horse and rode to the house of the 12th Regiment's second major, Andrew Mitchell, to offer warning. Mitchell gathered his family and took to the fields and woods. Ball rode on to the fort and alerted the Schenectady militia.[180]

A vivid description of a house being broken into was recorded by Josiah Hollister, one of the Ballstown victims.[181] Awakened from his sleep as his doors were burst open and thinking the intruders were Indians, he shouted the greeting, "Sago! Sago!" He was gruffly answered, "There are no Indians here. You needn't 'Sago' Damme you. Get up and leave the house before the Indians come."

Hollister was confused; were these men from the Schenectady militia who had come to warn him that Indians were near? He asked them and received an abrupt reply, "Damn you we will show you who we are. We are King's men." Hollister asked them why they troubled him; he truthfully told them he'd moved a hundred miles to get clear of the fighting; however, he was a trifle disingenuous, as he was an active soldier in the 12th Albany. They replied, "We know who are King's men, who are friends and who are not. Leave the house immediately, or it will be the worse for you."

He attempted to retrieve a pair of breeches and a jacket that hung behind his bed. A loyalist tore these from his hands and barked, "God damn you, you must not think to take everything." Struggling into a pair of linen trousers, he was hurried from the house clutching his young son and leading his wife with another child. Outside, he was told to give his son to his wife and when he protested that she couldn't be expected to look after two children, a soldier presented his musket to his chest and swore he wouldn't "be plagued with me any longer." His wife pled for his life and another soldier, pushing up the muzzle, led him off to the guard.

He was herded away; behind him the flames rose from his house and his loved ones stood half naked beside the road. He found that his neighbour, Issac Stowe, had been taken as well. He was the miller working at Gordon's mill. When Stowe recognized his employer approaching, he failed to see that he was also a captive, and he broke away to offer a warning. Hollister watched in horror as the fleeing man ran, shouting to Gordon to beware of Indians. An alert Mohawk guard hurled his spontoon at the runner which struck him in the back. Leaping forward and grasping the shaft, the warrior slammed his tomahawk into Stowe's skull. His scalp was quickly lifted and the warrior flourished it over his head and then struck the dead man's head repeatedly with his axe — a sad reward for such a brave display of loyalty.[182] Stowe's wife and infant child were able to escape. The mother waded a creek up to her neck and hid in the woods.[183]

Having witnessed the brutal death of his miller, Colonel Gordon became worried that some stragglers would murder his wife and daughter. He obtained permission to have one of the black servants return under guard with the message for his wife that she should go to her father's home to stay overnight. Mary Gordon had reentered the house to find a burning brand stuck into a straw ticking. She extracted the brand and extinguished the flames just as the servant and guard came through the door with the black woman Liz who had been spotted in the cornfield. The guard ordered Liz to come with him and Mrs. Gordon protested that surely they weren't "so barbarious as to take a naked woman along."[184] Chastised, the guard ordered the slave to gather some clothes. Liz again saw an opportunity and left the room to hide. The message delivered, the guard grew impatient of waiting for the woman and with the messenger returned to the raiders.

Now that the two arch rebels had been secured, Munro was faced with either attacking "the Militia in the Church, (which was a mile out of my course) or proceed on the plan laid down from my former intelligence." He judged it most prudent "not to risk my men but to make the best of my time in burning & destroying all the Rebel Houses & property in the centre of the Town."[185]

Consequently, the raiders continued taking prisoners, most of them active militiamen, and burning their buildings. All the time that this was underway, Munro made sure to "keep a sharp look out at my rear which was illuminated by the Houses and Barns set on fire." Thirty prisoners would be collected before the night was over including three officers, four sergeants and 13 soldiers of the 12th Albany; amongst them were Elisha Benedict,[186] his three sons and his slave, Dublin who was able to escape later. Elisha had been a captain in the 2nd New York Continental Line in the 1775 Canadian campaign and his son Caleb was an ensign in the 12th Albany.

Jonathon Filer woke up to see burning buildings south of his home and roused his family. They all ran to the woods and successfully hid. His house was pillaged and his mother-in-law, Granny Leake, had the presence of mind to rush into the building as soon as the raiders left to find the beginnings of a fire which she readily extinguished. This building has survived into the late 20th Century, as has a remnant of a braided, corn-husk, Indian torch which Granny had smothered. Next door, Anste Wilcox, who was at home alone as her husband was away in the army, awoke to the noise of raiders. She rushed from the house and ran across a clearing to hide in the woods. She was immediately pursued by a "stalwart Indian carrying a burning torch in his hand." The warrior had glimpsed "the glitter of a string of gold beads" hanging around her neck. He stopped her and "with a stroke of his scalping knife he severed the chain" and ran off to join his party. The terrified woman sank to the ground with no more injury than a small cut on her neck.[187]

A detachment was sent under Fraser to take George Scott, a former personal friend and Gordon's brother-in-law. Scott had been aroused by the barking of his dog which he thought was warning of some wolves which had been bothering his calves. As he reached for his "English musket"[188] his wife warned, "George, don't take the gun, it may be Indians." Scott retorted that it was a wolf and with his firelock in hand, opened his front door. A voice shouted, "Scott, throw down your gun, or you are a dead man." Stunned, Scott did not immediately comply.

The rules of engagement were quite clear to the Mohawk warriors and obviously had been to Jane Scott as well. If they were opposed by men under arms, they were free to attack. Three tomahawks flew through the air and struck the immobile Scott. He collapsed like a sack of potatoes in his doorway. The warriors rushed forward to take his scalp, but were prevented from doing so by Fraser and a Ranger named Staats Springsteen[189] who had formerly been Scott's hired man.

At the same time, the dog "Watch" threw himself at one of the Indians and took him to the ground. Another warrior struck the dog with a thrown tomahawk and a third rushed forward to plunge his knife into its body. Young James Scott heard the dog's wail inside the house.[190] While the Indians pillaged the house, James ran off to the woods. He remembered the faces of the Indians being "painted with alternate stripes of red and blacke" and that "they had bells in their caps and wore Dutch blanket coats.[191]

The Indians removed some silver dishes, but, in the light of day, when they discovered them to be pewter, they abandoned them along the withdrawal route. One native attempted to ascend to the upper floor and was forcefully prevented by Captain Fraser who took hold of him and threw him to the floor. As plunder belonged by rights to the Indians, it was a rash deed by Fraser who could have suffered a swift, quiet revenge along the trail. Fraser couldn't prevent all of the pillaging and the Indians successfully removed an entire suit of clothes, a beaver hat, a watch, several pairs of stockings, some wigs and Scott's musket. A young lad named John Oxby had been staying overnight in the house and awoke amongst the tumult letting cry a scream. An Indian brandished a knife in his face and stamped on the floor exclaiming a warning "UGH!"[192]

The looting finished, the unharmed Mrs. Scott was left behind at the side of her husband who was presumed dying with "a deep perpendicular gash by the side of his nose."[193] After the raiders had disappeared, she called out to James and was greatly relieved to have him appear out of the woods. The boy lived to recall his stricken father's face covered in blood that night. Their home had been saved from the torch, one supposes due to the past friendships. Amazingly, George Scott survived his wounds.[194]

When the raiders struck at George Kennedy's home, his wife, the daughter of John Higby, one of Munro's prisoners, ran in terror. She was very advanced in pregnancy and fled only in her night-shift, stumbling through the darkened woods in bitter weather. By daylight she had waded through three streams before she stumbled exhausted into a neighbour's clearing.[195]

Understandably, the prisoner Hollister held a very dim view of the men who had captured him, put his family at risk, destroyed his property and the community. He wrote, "Such a company of men I never saw before or since. They were the offscourings of the earth; a parcel of torys and thieves who had left their county to escape the halter. I thought I had heard swearing before, but I never heard anything to compare with them. The horrid oaths and blasphemy were enuf to make one shudder."[196]

He recalled, "It was a very cold, frosty morning. The mud puddles were skimmed over with ice. I was barefooted; the ice cut my feet so that they bled, and to add to our misery, we were insulted by the torys and called "damned rebels"; that we might be thankful they had spared our lives."

By the time the raiders reassembled it was first light on the 13th. They emerged unscathed except for Lieutenant Richard Lipscomb of the Royal Yorkers who had somehow hurt his foot. A horse was found and the troops "got him along with some trouble." As they withdrew, Nero, Gordon's black servant, attempted an escape by jumping down a ravine. As he plunged down the slope his head jammed into a sapling and he was easily retaken.[197]

Fillmore, a hired man of Enoch Wood who was also a prisoner, found himself guarded by an Irish redcoated "Regular" of the Royal Yorkers in front with a young 'German' (Palatine?) recruit following behind. As he came abreast of a familiar cow path, Fillmore sprang down the track, running for his life. He heard the youngster ask, "Shall I shoot?" The Irishman responded, "Yes, you damned fool." Both men fired and one ball struck a lock of hair hanging over Fillmore's ear. The fugitive kept running and took shelter under a fallen hemlock tree that blocked the path. By the time his pursuers had caught up, he had wormed well into the blow-down's branches and they soon gave up their search.[198]

Neither the Schenectady men from the 2nd Albany nor any men from the local companies of the 12th Albany had made any effort to stop the incursion. Munro found that his men "were not at all pleas'd that they had not more satisfaction of the Rebels...", but he reasoned that staying any longer would seriously put the whole detachment at risk as he was only 25 miles from Albany and nine from Schenectady. There were still no "certain accounts" of Sir John and it was now several days since the appointed time of joining.[199] Sir John's appearance might be sensibly expected to create a major diversion, but without that assistance, Munro realized he could be faced with serious retaliation if he lingered. The local guides led the raiders as far as the woods where they took their leave after refusing any payment for their assistance.[200]

The force marched on for ten miles, crossed Kayaderosseras Creek[201] and continued to the foot of the mountain of the same name before halting. Munro then ordered the slaughter of the cattle and hogs which they had driven off as he had found they were going to seriously impede his retreat. With the flour that had been taken from the mill, the hungry men prepared a solid meal of biscuit with fresh beef and pork.[202]

★★★

The Schenectady and Ballstown militia assembled that same morning and began a pursuit. No historian has recorded the reasons why the militia had taken no action against the raiders while they were occupied taking prisoners and destroying the housing, mills and farms. Perhaps the report from Stephen Ball had exaggerated Munro's strength. Perhaps the Schenectady men were lacking in courage as the Ballstown militiamen had suspected. Certainly, if the two bodies of militia had been able to assemble at the fort that night, they would have constitued a force the equal of Munro's. They could have harried the loyalists in detail rather than attacking the whole on its retreat. At the very least, a demonstration of resistance would have disrupted, if not halted, the destruction. Perhaps they had more confidence in bringing on an action in daylight rather than in the dark of night. For the Ballstown men, having the raiders out of the community and no longer threatening their families would have been a consideration. Whatever the case, the militia did not pursue very far before they came across some locals who "exaggerating gleefully, told of having seen 500 tories and Indians. Gravely they cautioned the rebels to turn back."[203] The militia did not recognize that their informants were the very men who had assisted and guided the raiders the night before. The irresolute militia quickly turned about. On their return to the fort, they sent off an express rider to inform the command in Albany of this great force. Their account thoroughly alarmed an already over-stretched headquarters.[204] Later that same afternoon, a party of volunteers,[205] made up of relatives and friends of the prisoners, set out to make a second attempt at a rescue.

Munro's men finished their meal and took a brief rest. Before they started, Munro made sure each man was loaded with joints of raw meat. They got underway that same afternoon and made the slow, tiring ascent up the slopes of Kayaderosseras Mountain. When over the mountain's ridge, they began a tedious descent. Reaching the bottom, they took a well-beaten Indian trail to the Sacandaga River which, without delay, they immediately crossed. They continued marching till just before sunset when they halted and made camp two miles northeast of Lake Desolation.[206] The last yoke of oxen was killed and the meat shared out amongst the force and the prisoners. With the earlier distribution, each man now carried three days raw provisions.[207]

According to rebel accounts, on the morning of Oct. 14th, Munro is said to have told his men to instantly kill the prisoners if any of them made an attempt to assist the expected pursuit. Each prisoner had his hands tied. Many were barefoot and poorly clothed, most of them having been taken in the night from their beds. In the bitter cold, they were in understandable discomfort. On the march, they were intermixed amongst the Mohawks and soldiers so that a guard was immediately in front and behind each of them. Munro indicated that should a pursuit draw near and discharge so much as a single firelock, all of the prisoners were to be instantaneously dispatched. Such precautions put the fear of death strongly upon the captives and, coupled with their physical distress, ensured their very best behaviour.[208]

Colonel Gordon was told by an old "German" soldier of Munro's that he had been through many wars in Europe and had never been party to "such bloody orders." The soldier assured Gordon that he had nothing to fear from him, but warned that the Indian marching behind him was "thirsting for Gordon's blood and the moment a gun is fired, Gordon is a dead man."[209] Gordon also observed one Indian wearing George Scott's wig caused him to believe Scott to be dead. With wry, macabre humour, the queue of the wig hung over the forehead of its new owner.[210]

Munro found that four of the prisoners could not continue. In the worst condition was George Kennedy, who had cut his foot a few days prior to his capture. He had endured the hard march and cold night wrapped in a sheet and now his foot was badly inflamed. Kennedy was in such extreme pain, he pled to be killed rather than suffer the march. Of the others, two were old men who were terribly fatigued and one a very young boy.[211] Munro decided that these men should be allowed to return, but he found his Mohawk allies were strongly opposed to such a measure. This disagreement led to much discussion.

Native honour and well-being was at stake and Munro, besides drawing upon his own considerable experience, was fortunate in having the advice of Langan and Claus' men who were particularly knowledgable in these matters. The chiefs and warriors expected to receive rewards for prisoners that were brought to Canada and they knew that to allow the return home of any of them would forfeit their claim. However, scalps were another form of achieving honour, if not a reward, and killing the four men who could no longer keep up was an acceptable alternative. Munro would not hear of this proposition and another solution was negotiated. Captain John was allowed to choose from the captives a number of men for adoption. These would be taken to the Mohawk refugee village at Lachine when the party arrived in Canada. They would serve as replacements for those Mohawk men who had been recently lost on campaign. This ancient native custom was recognized as a time-honoured agreement of the native and white alliances in wartime. The four Benedicts,[212] Thomas Barnum, Isaac Palmatier, John Higby and his son Lewis, Elijah Sprague and Gordon's "negro man Nero" were chosen by Captain Deserontyon.[213] They would have the fate of John Shew to remind them of what was expected of them.

Munro was warned that some of the Mohawks, likely the young warriors in the party, were not satisfied by this adoption arrangement and they planned to drop out of the column and fall upon the liberated men to take their scalps. He arranged that his rear guard would release the men "5 or 6 miles farther behind than the place proposed, which saved their lives... "[214]

★★★

Advancing to rescue the captives, the volunteers saw figures on the trail ahead and, fearing that some of Munro's raiders were returning, set an ambush. Before their trap was sprung, they recognized the approaching group as some of their friends, the three lame men and the boy. The released captives brought a message from Colonel Gordon warning the rescuers not to continue because of Munro's "brutal" order.[215]

There is another account which claims that the disgruntled Mohawk warriors, who were intent on taking the released men's scalps, had seen through Munro's gambit and had been trailing them. They were just about to attack when they spied the volunteers lying in wait. The warriors quietly withdrew.[216]

★★★

Munro had considered staying "in the Country" to join with Sir John, but due to his lack of firm intelligence, he concluded he was offering no real assistance to Johnson by lurking in the woods. Rather than "endanger the whole Party" he decided to rejoin Carleton. He set out with purpose and wasting no time arrived at Crown Point at 2:00 PM "without the loss of a man."[217] Remembering the forced march, the captive Hollister wrote, "We had to wade all of the branches of the North [Hudson] river. The main branch was fifty or sixty rods wide, waist deep, the current very strong, the stones very slippery, which made it very difficult to wade."

In Munro's report to Haldimand written on Tuesday, Oct. 24 he advised that his three men, left behind at the outset, were on their way to join him and he expected them "in every hour." His force had been in extremis as the provisions, which they had cached in the woods on the first day of their mission, had been in part spoiled by vermin and in part used by other parties.[218] Hollister recalled

> We were eight days marching through the wilderness, and having provisions for only three days, there were five days that the chief we had to support nature was to boil hemlock boughs and drink the tea. On the way we came to where we [obviously he means Munro's force] had left some provisions. One Joseph Bonner,[219] having got his, I asked him if he would give me a piece of his bisquit. He answered: 'No, by the Lord Jesus Christ, if God Almighty should come in the shape of my father, I would not give him any.'[220]

The trek had proven arduous for all of the prisoners. Thomas Barnum, a sergeant in the 12th Albany, later recalled that he had been "suffering from the fever and ague" yet he "was forced to carry his own looking glass [mirror,] naked and a pack on his back so heavy that when he sat upon a log he could not rise without help."[221]

Munro proved himself to be as prone to praise his subordinates as was Sir John. He reported

> I have the pleasure to Acquaint your Excellency that both the Officers and men went thro' this hard & disagreeable march with great spirit, particularly Lieut. Langan who was foremost upon every occasion, and I

also beg leave to recommend Adjt. Valentine to your Excellency's notice.[222]

As we have seen, the united force under Major Carleton was ordered to stay on Lake Champlain and continue to alarm the frontier in that quarter. Lieutenant Langan wrote to LtCol. Claus from aboard the Commodore's vessel at Crown Point on Oct. 31. He advised that he had been the day before at "Mile" (Mill) Bay, en route to Canada with the Fort Hunter men and their prisoners, when he was overtaken by an express messenger sent by Carleton. The Major had been warned that the rebels were in large numbers only four miles from Crown Point and he wanted Langan to return as a reinforcement.[223] At the time that Langan was writing, it was 9:00 PM of the following day. He could see the rebels' camp fires which were "very plain at the Narrows, on both sides of the Lake, within a Mile to half of the Old Works." Langan reported, "I don't believe we shall come to blows with them, as I fancy their intention was to fire on the Boats at the Narrows[;] however if this was their Scheme, it has been frustrated by our arrival here at One oClock this Morning, from a Bay about Seven Miles above Mount Independence where we went to make a Diversion — "[224]

Bowen, Maybee and the two Mohawks had by this time come in from Johnstown with two recruits named Gasper and Peter Bower.[225] One of the Bowers brought detailed, second-hand information about Sir John's actions at Stone Arabia and at Klock's Field. He reported to Langan that the rebel militia opposing Johnson at Klock's had numbered 2000 men, although research would suggest that this number more likely applied to the total of the Levies and militia which was assembled at Fort Herkimer under Governor Clinton two days later.

Langan gave detailed information about the troops the state had brought against Sir John telling Claus that men had been called out from as far south as thirty miles below Albany. He noted that the Schoharie had been reinforced by some of these men before Johnson arrived and that 700 "New England Men which were under Colo. Brown.. went up there in the Spring." Langan laid the blame for this rush of preparation at the feet of

a rascal of Rodger's, which deserted from Major Carleton at Fort George and gave Intelligence of all our Number, & Intentions! [B]esides[,] a recruiting Captn. of Roger's, one Laird [Lord], which came in with Sir John last Spring had given himself up to Congress, and consequently gave all the Information he cou'd, and one Mr. Van Dervarkin, a recruiting Lieut. of his, is now parlaying at Johns Town, and will give himself up if they accept of him, and wou'd you suppose the honest Peter Yost,[226] who went out with me, has done the same, and was very near having Young Helmer[227] which I sent in to Johns Town made Prisoner, and Peter Sarvis[228] was actually made prisoner thro' his means, but afterwards got away.

He wrote Claus that he was going ashore to see to the men "who have behaved extra well on every alarm, and I have taken the liberty of drawing on Mr. Dobie for some Rum I purchased for them here since our arrival from Balls Town, which I hope you wont be displeased at."

In closing, he advised that a Flag of Truce had just returned from "Brig. Genl. Athen Allen of the [New Hampshire] Grants in answer to one sent by Major Carleton: with assurances from the Brig. that no Hostilities shall be commenced from his Quarter." Haldimand's strategy of negotiating with Vermont to take them, at least temporarily, out of the war was working. The consternation in the rebel Congress might be imagined when word of this arrangement filtered through. The emotions of the earnest Justus Sherwood would be an unintentional sacrifice to the duplicity of both parties.

History has not dealt well with the character of Daniel Claus, painting him as a stiff, stubborn and vindictive German-American. The affectionate closing of Langan's letter indicates his very warm relationship with this austere figure which was apparently reciprocated –

Adieu – May God bless you – please to give my best respects to Mrs. Claus, & remember me to my Dear Billy,[229] & all the Family,
I am Dear Colo.
yours very Sincerely
P. Langan

Upon his arrival at Crown Point, Munro visited the sutler Sutherland, who, like Dobie, had come to meet the expeditions. He purchased some "Gills of Rum And Soap" for his men as an indulgence as they had been so terribly deprived due to the lack of provisions. They had given part of their own rations to the prisoners on the march, only to find that their cache had been spoiled.

LtCol. Gordon later wrote in his reminiscences that on the return of Langan with the prisoners to Bullwagga Bay, he was invited to breakfast with Captain Munro and some of the other officers. That same day at noon, Captain William Fraser came to find Gordon to invite him to a meal at his fire. As Gordon walked with Fraser to his camp, he was met by his "old acquaintance"[230] James Rogers who invited him to have a grog. That afternoon, the rebel prisoners were sent to a desolate island as a security measure. Towards evening they were all taken aboard Commodore Chamber's ship, the *Carleton,* for shipment to Canada. Chambers called the senior rebel officers to his cabin and advised them that they were to remain there and enjoy the same fare as the ship's officers "provided we made no bad use of the indulgence."[231] It may be seen from Gordon's and Adiel Sherwood's comments that the rebel officers were treated with the utmost civility.

In Captain Munro's report, he theorized that Major General Schuyler had assembled a large body of militia with the intent to cut off his retreat "back of Lake George", but had been dissuaded from doing so upon hearing the inflated reports of the size of his force which had been spread by Munro's guides.[232]

Munro further reported that his guides had told him of "a Combination" of 400 blacks in the Schenectady and Albany region "wanting to Join the King's Troops, and that they were certain had I sent a person before my Arrival there to inform them that all about Schenectady would have been able to Join; six or seven of said Negroes are Come in since, and confirm the same report."[233] Nothing more was done about this opportunity to raise such a substantial number of recruits.

The Captain, who prior to the war had served as a sheriff for the Province of New York in the contested New Hampshire Grants, closed his second report with dire warnings about the perfidy of his old political enemies. "There is no Faith or Confidence to be put in those Gentlemen Called the Green Mountain Boys, I have been at open War with them these Sixteen years past — they have been a pest to the government of New York since the last war, they are a Collection of Malefactors... " Many of the King's "reduced Officers and Soldiers" were "tied to the Trees, Flog[g]ed" and driven from their lands, their houses burnt in defiance of the government. "[W]ell meaning People who Settled amongst them under the Government of New York were Harrassed and are so still."[234] One senses Munro's very real feelings of horror to find that the British administration was even considering treating with these bandits from the New Hampshire Grants.

Captain Robert Mathews, Haldimand's military secretary, later wrote to Munro that the Governor "fully approved his conduct and the good behaviour of his officers and soldiers."[235] There is no record of whether this approbation assuaged Munro's guilt over his failure to come to grips with the rebels.

THE CANADA INDIANS AGAINST THE WHITE RIVER REGION

In answer to the summons for warriors to assist Major Carleton, about 300 Canada Indians arrived at Fort St. John's under LtCol. John Campbell, the superintendant of the Quebec Indian Department. Carleton selected 108 Kahnawake & Kanehsatake men for his force. Captain Munro, who already enjoyed the assistance of the Fort Hunter Mohawk band, had received many blandishments from Sir John and LtCol. Claus about the unreliability of Canada Indians on operations where rebel Oneida scouts might be employed against him. He accepted no other assistance. As a result, two thirds of those who had volunteered were left behind.

Brigadier General Powell decided to send these unwanted men, who "insisted upon being employed," on a smaller expedition up the Onion (Winooski or Ouinouschick) River under the direction of an experienced Canadien officer named Joseph Marie La Motte [LaMothe][236] and Lieutenant Richard Houghton, a British regular officer seconded to the Quebec Indian Department. This decision was clearly prompted as much to mollify and reward the obvious willingness of the Canada Indians as it was to annoy the rebels; however, one must not discount the strategic impact of operating on the eastern borders of the New Hampshire Grants at the same time as demonstrating British naval and land power on Lakes Champlain & George and in the Hudson and Mohawk Valleys.[237]

Considering the substantial reluctance of the Seven Nations of Canada to campaign for the Crown in the earlier years of the conflict, a force of 300 men in the field was nothing short of remarkable. It is tempting to ascribe noble motives to the warriors who were so eager for this campaign. Perhaps their zeal was a show of solidarity with their "older" brothers of the Iroquois Confederacy who had lost so much the year before. More probable was their desire to indulge in the fruits of frontier terrorism — captives to exchange for currency, scalps to prove their prowess in war and plentiful plunder to keep or sell — all at little risk to themselves. No matter what the motivation, Houghton was able to achieve some material success for the Crown's 1780 campaign.

Leaving their bateaux at the mouth of the Onion River, his party followed the river inland and penetrated the Green Mountains. They were piloted by a Tory named Hamilton,[238] whom the captive Zadock Steele described as "a despicable villain, who had been made prisoner by the Americans at the taking of Burgoyn, in 1777."[239] Hamilton had been at Newbury and Royalton the previous summer while on a parole. He was noted as having left Royalton with a group of men, ostensibly to survey lands in the northern reaches of New York State, but in reality to take them to Canada to enlist for the King, thus defaulting on his personal guarantee of good behaviour. Now he was back with a quite different mission.

A 19th Century American historian[240] gives another reason for Houghton's mission, that being to attempt the capture Major Benjamin

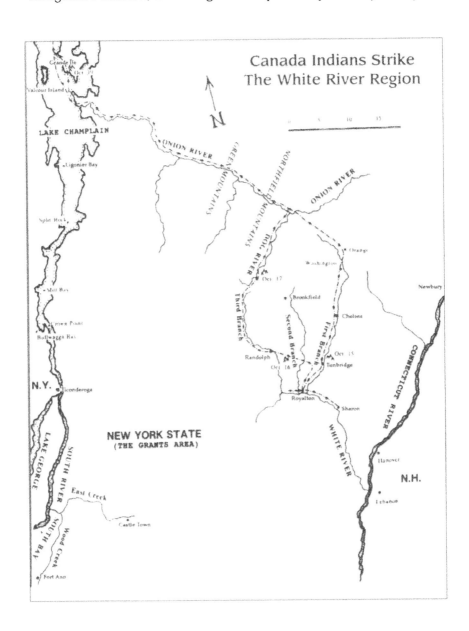

Canada Indians Strike
The White River Region

Whitcomb, an active rebel partizan who had gained considerable notoriety during the 1776 campaign in Canada. While on a scout, he lay under cover in the woods from where he sniped and mortally wounded British Brigadier General Patrick Gordon.[241] This act was viewed very dimly by all the British officers, and in particular by Governor Carleton, who saw it as a brutal assassination, as Gordon had been unarmed and could easily have been taken prisoner. Carleton's general order regarding the affair in part said, "The Rebel Runaways not having dared shew their Faces as Soldiers, have now taken the part of the vilest Assassins, and are lurking in small parties to Murder, if possible, any single or unarmed officer, or soldier, who may be passing the Roads near a Wood side. B.G. Gordon was danger-ously wounded yesterday by one of these infamous skulkers."[242] A description of Whitcomb followed and soldiers were counselled to take the sniper prisoner so that he could receive "due punishment, which can only be inflicted by the Hangman." The British were not alone in decrying the deed and many rebel officers referred to the Connecticut Lieutenant as an assassin, perhaps worrying that Whitcomb had blazed a new trail of conduct and fearing similar Tory retribution upon themselves. It might be supposed that Whitcomb was thought to be stationed along the expedition's route and Hamilton had promised Houghton the opportunity to bring him in. However, the British accounts of the expedition make no mention of a planned attempt against Whitcomb.

On the march, about 20 miles west of their first target, the settle-ment of Newbury, the force captured a party of hunters. These Newbury men were questioned about the defences of their settlement and naturally they claimed that a large force was garrisoned there. Their bogus report dissuaded Houghton from attacking that place.

The party then set course down the Onion for Wildersburgh, crossing a second mountain range. They proceeded along the banks of the First Branch of the White River and advanced secretly through Orange, Washington and Chelsea to Tunbridge. There is no report why those small settlements were left untouched or why their inhabitants did not observe and report their advance. The force encamped at Tunbridge on Sunday, Oct. 15 and planned their next movements.

They were afoot before first light on Monday and, just as dawn broke, struck at the home of John Hutchinson, which lay halfway between Tunbridge and Royalton. Hutchinson, and his brother Abijah, were taken prisoners and their house plundered. From there, the force struck quickly and often, taking male prisoners and leaving behind females and very young children. If a man resisted capture, he was dispatched. If he attempted escape, he was chased down and killed. The corpses were scalped.

The Indians' tactics were their own — simple and terribly effective. The party moved in a dense, herd-like body, travelling from one target to the next with great rapidity. All of the men carried the axe and knife. In the van were warriors called "runners" who were armed with spontoons. Their task was to pursue and kill anyone who broke and ran. Most of the main body were armed with firelocks and these warriors were called "gunners"; these second wave men would scalp any of the victims who had been bypassed, gather in and guard the captives, destroy or take the livestock, plunder and destroy the buildings. Such a dense mass of men would have been an ideal target for any disciplined form of resistance, but there was none, either expected or encountered. The Indians understood that speed would give them surprise, which in turn would ensure the taking of captives. Surprise also prevented the hiding of family treasures, so the plunder would be of the best quality. Also, there was no time to release the livestock into the woods, so it was easily destroyed or collected and driven to the rear as victuals.

The captive Steele wrote how one man described his warning of the Indians' approach. Before he could see the advancing mass, there was a noise of sheep or cattle running at full speed through water. This fluid-like sound of their running must refer to the dull jangling of the small metal cones with which the Indians decorated the outside edges of their garments. When moving stealthily, even the smallest sound from the cones warned the wearer that he might be heard. When moving at speed, the cones struck together making this distinctive, water-like rushing noise. Contrary to what one might expect, there was great discipline in this attack and the advancing band "kept a profound silence" as they ran forward. Prisoners who were taken were warned to keep utterly silent on pain of death. The terrifying war halloo and the triumphant scalp call were held until a predetermined signal.

Steele reports many frightening accounts of the raid. One lad who ran from a building was pursued and brought to ground by a thrown spontoon which pierced his torso. He continued to run, dragging the haft behind him, until he fainted from loss of blood. The following warriors closed and thrust their spears into the dying youth, then scalped him. Soon after, another unsuspecting youngster came from out of the woods into the roadway to find the Indians rushing upon him. He fled and shared the identical fate of the first. Remarkably, a few men were able to gain cover in sufficient time to hide successfully, often under a deadfall. The Indians showed great exasperation when this happened and the fugitive, with bated breath, could hear their angry exclamations. They, however, did not spend much time in their search. They either achieved a quick success, or they moved on.

Unresisting women and little children were generally unharmed; however, their treatment was by no means gentle. One woman had just arisen from her bed to begin dressing when her door was broken down and Indians rushed in. A warrior sprang at her flourishing a large knife which he laid against her bare throat. She was convinced she was as good as dead when the man spied a string of gold beads hanging around her neck. His passions instantly cooled; he removed the beads and strode away.

The Indians' lightning attack had taken them to Morgan's mills at the junction of the First and Second Branches of the White River. Houghton chose to halt, making the mills the rendezvous point for the next phase of the attack. He divided the force into two wings, one was sent down White River, the other up the Second Branch, while a guard remained at the mills. Some horses had been taken and a few of the Indians thought that being mounted would increase the speed of their attack, however they found the animals were so skittish, because of the riders' strange scent and dress, that the attempt failed.

As on all frontier raids, there were numerous men out of their homes at dawn tending to the usual farming chores. Some of these saw the Indians before they themselves were discovered. If their foe was close at hand, these men faced the terrible decision of whether to save themselves or their families who in some cases were still abed or had just arisen in supposed safety. What guilt and anguish must have settled on those who chose the former! Lucky were those who made the discovery early enough to rush to their homes and rouse their families and then their friends. Not a few found that the position of the Indians blocked their way home. To save their skins, they had to turn away from their families. In many cases, they gave warning and help to others.

One young fellow emerged from the woods and seeing the Indians at his father's door turned to flee. As he turned, the first shot heard in the raid was fired and the ball entered his back, ran around his body just under his skin and lodged below his ribs. He spurred his mount and rode the 16 miles to Lebanon in New Hampshire, the whole of the way holding the bullet between his fingers in morbid curiosity and fear.

Those who received warning of the Indians were sometimes so panic stricken that reason abandoned them in their attempts to flee. Only a few took to the woods, the majority instead ran and stumbled down the road. As the settlement had already been warned by the gunshot, the previous silence of the Indians was abandoned and, closing fast upon the fleeing folk, they gave voice to their discordant war halloos. There was now more value in creating terror than attempting surprise.

The women were particularly vulnerable surrounded by swarms of young children, either held in their arms or clutching at their petticoats. In desperation, they ran for their lives, sobbing tears of frustration and anguish. When overtaken, the older male children were torn from them for removal to Canada. The women were left as they were found in the roadways and fields with babies in their arms and little ones clinging to them. About them, parties of the Indians emptied houses and barns of everything of use or trade value. Feather mattresses were stripped from the beds and taken outside; their ends slashed open and feathers strewn to the wind with naive, maniacal delight. Plunder such as kettles, pans, plates, chains, tongs, sickles, shovels, scythes, iron spiders, irons, hooks, trammels, mirrors, clothing, footwear, boxes, chests and saddles was shoved inside these make-shift packs which the prisoners were forced to carry.

The eastern detachment of Indians travelled down the White to as far as Sharon where they turned about with their prisoners, scalps & plunder. As they returned to Morgan's mills, they set fire to all the buildings containing hordes of winter supplies and furnishings. Seven yoke of oxen, herds of cows, sheep and hogs were all killed; they left a trail of woeful destruction in their wake.

The western group set about the same errands. Some men were found at a local smithy, but most were captured at home or in their fields. One women had her young son ripped from her. She begged the Indians to tell what would become of her child; they gave her cold comfort by replying that a soldier would be made of him.

Hannah Hendee (Handy)[243] had suffered a similar outrage and was determined to have her only son released. Amidst the scenes of destruction, this 27 year old hero strode downriver to find the force's commander with her terrified, blubbering daughter clinging to her skirts. She was unable to get any answers to her questions from the Indians, but she encountered several Tories who heartlessly responded to her questions of what would happen to the boys with the answer that they would all be killed. This only stiffened her resolve; she continued to search for someone who was clearly in charge. She discovered a large group of Indians on the opposite shore and, assuming that the leader would be with them, made to cross. An older Indian had just made a crossing and seeing her, he made signs asking her intentions. She indicated her wish and he offered to carry her and the child across on his back, which favour she declined. The Indian then insisted on helping by carrying the daughter. The little girl cried her fear, but the Indian scooped her up and together the pair began the crossing. Coming to deep water, the old fellow signed for Mrs. Hendee to sit on a rock while he took the child to the bank. He then returned and carried her across. What the Indian's motivation was for such kindness is unknown; perhaps he thought the mother was a loyalist in distress, as the folk they encountered usually fled, rather than remain to mingle amongst the raiders.

Mrs. Hendee found Lieutenant Houghton and boldly asked what was intended for the youngsters. He advised that it was specifically against orders to harm either women or children and further, that "Such boys as should be taken would be trained for soldiers, and would not be hurt" — native soldiers, loyalist soldiers, British soldiers, he didn't say. She persisted by telling him the obvious: such young boys were not going to survive the rigours of the return march. She argued persuasively that the attempt to take them through the wilderness was to consign them to sure death for once they faltered and slowed the pace, they would have to be killed. She argued with conviction that Houghton could not possibly understand the feelings of a mother whose first-born had been taken from her. He argued pragmatically that the Indians would never surrender what they saw as their property by right of war. She countered that he was the commander; they must, and would, obey him. She knew nothing of his role as coordinator and the conventions she was asking him to break in retrieving her son. Face to face with such a spirited and reasoned argument he acquiesed, promising to restore the boy when the Indians brought him in.

Hannah waited impatiently. When the party with her boy appeared, Houghton, with much difficulty, prevailed upon the Indians to surrender the lad. Grasping him with one hand and her little girl in the other, she then set off, but had scarcely gone 50 yards before Houghton overtook her and told her to return lest a different band of Indians take the boy. She concurred and waited amongst the Indians until all of them were assembled to start northwards.

During the wait, a number of other young boys had been brought in and Hendee courageously chanced her previous good fortune to successfully argue the same case for them. Sitting on a pile of boards, she was surrounded by a group of huddled, bleary-eyed boys when an older Indian came forward and taking her son by a hand made to lead him off. She held fast to his other and refused to release him. The Indian registered his rage in words and waved a hanger over her head while the stretched and frightened youngster screamed and wailed, joined by all the others. The fracas attracted other Indians and Hendee soon recognized that the lives of all of the boys as well as her own were in grave danger as the "tigers were clearly excited by the bleating of the lambs." She gave up her son and sought out Houghton to plea again for his release. Through much persuasion and argument, the boy was again returned to his mother. When Hannah Hendee finally left the mills, she had her daughter and eight small boys in tow. In addition, she had the guarantee of the release of a ninth youngster who was being held at the Haven's house.

After leaving Morgan's mills in flames, the force stopped at Haven's farm. Haven himself had lain all day under a log. Many times, parties of Indians had passed nearby, some had even stood on the log and he had clearly heard their voices planning their next moves. After releasing the ninth boy who was lame, they set fire to Haven's buildings and withdrew up the First Branch towards the hills west of Tunbridge where they turned west and travelled towards Randolph beyond the Second Branch. They encamped for the night with their captives, 26 men and boys and 30 horses. Houghton then released an aged prisoner, a Mr. Kneeland, who after a day's travel was considered too frail to make the trip. Letters were given to him to pass on to the militia advising that "if they were not followed, the prisoners should be used well — but should they be pursued, every one of them would be put to death."[244]

The word of the incursion had spread far and wide and about 300 militiamen gathered at Evans' house in Randolph where they selected Colonel John House of Hanover, New Hampshire as their commander. They had intelligence that the Indians were camped at Brookfield, about ten miles to the north. After some rudimentary organization, they set off at midnight, hoping to fall upon the Indians before light and make them prisoners. As the Brookfield settlement was 10 miles off, they likely were careless in the early stages of their advance. To their complete surprise, they had travelled only two miles when they came against an outguard of the Indian encampment which met them with a very warm fire. The militia advanced, firing several volleys, and receiving a great deal of musketry in return. When one of the militiamen was wounded, Colonel House ordered them to halt and cease fire. Probably he wanted to organize a concerted attack rather than a pell mell rush; however, the delay allowed Houghton's force to retreat precipitately, after abandoning much of their plunder and the horses.

As daylight broke, the militia entered the abandoned camp to find their enemy gone. The Indians had killed and scalped Joseph Kneeland, perhaps because it was his father who had carried the message which was either ignored or not received by the militia. Giles Gibbs had also been killed; he was found with a tomahawk left in his skull that probably couldn't be extracted. Steele claims that the militia had been disgusted with Colonel House's order to halt and his account is very derisive of the Colonel's decision to wait for dawn before entering the Indians' camp. Steele probably would have been amongst the first to accuse House of rashness if the attack had been made in the dark and resulted in serious casualties. Steele also ignored the known fact that the pressing of an attack could lead to the wholesale slaughter of the prisoners. Such an act would be conformable with the native custom whereby prisoners were killed rather than given up to a rescue.

As this mixed force of militia were not under any rigid military discipline and had chosen House to lead them, they could simply have ignored him and followed another, bolder leader. Likely it was a relief to all concerned that House showed such circumspection and only later did the weight of their collective guilt force them to recognize that more could have been done to effect a rescue.

Leaving the abandoned encampment, Colonel House marched the militia north to Brookfield where it was expected the Indians would be found. Their fixation about the Indians targeting Brookfield suggests that their loyalist guide, the mysterious Hamilton, had some scores to settle there and everyone was aware of it. Either the firm belief that Brookfield was the next target blinded them to the Indians' tracks, or no one amongst the militia had the skills to read sign. Obviously, no matter how clever and adept the Indians were, when they retreated in haste in the dead of night, herding a large body of prisoners, they could hardly have obliterated all traces of their route. In fact, Houghton's force had not gone north, but had struck off due west over the hills to the western edge of the Randolph settlement on the Third Branch of the White. When the militia arrived in Brookfield and were unable to find any evidence of the Indians, House disbanded them and they returned to their homes.

On the previous day, the 16th, word had been received at Randolph that Indians were pillaging Royalton. The inhabitants spent the day removing valuables and children from their farms and hiding them in the woods. Zadock Steele had assisted in this task and when finished at the close of the day, he suggested sending a party to Brookfield to alert the people there of the danger. No one would agree to go, so he decided to conduct the mission himself. As there were only blazed trees to mark the way, and these could be easily missed in the dark, he stopped for the night at his farmstead. At dawn he set out on his self-appointed mission, but soon encountered such a severe snowstorm that he turned about for home. He was no sooner in his cabin than he heard "a shocking cry in the surrounding woods; and trembling for my own safety — I ran to the door, when, to my utter astonishment, I beheld a company of Indians, consisting of not less than three hundred in number, not ten rods [50m] distant, approaching with hideous cries and frightful yells!"

Steele had no escape. A chief came up to him and in good English asked if other persons or any cattle were nearby. Steele answered in the negative, but a thorough search was made anyway.

His captors loaded their packs with booty, destroyed everything else that the flames might not and then set his buildings afire. Steele was stripped of all his outer clothing which was distributed amongst a few of the Indians and he was given a blanket to spare him from the bitter cold. Later, he somehow managed to obtain a coat.

In a strange gesture, one of the Indians took a sack of grass seed, poked a hole in it and threw it over his shoulder. The seed scattered as he strode along and a trail of grass was seen in later years to mark the events of that day. They had not gone far beyond Steele's farm when the Chief, who had claimed Steele as his personal captive, noticed he was wearing a pair of silver buckles on his shoes. The Indian made to remove them, but Steele was able to dissuade him by promising to surrender the buckles when they had finished the journey. Not long after, another Indian spied the fine buckles and, paying no attention to Steele's protestations, took them, giving him some strings as substitutes to hold the shoes in place.

As Oct. 17th drew to a close, the force stopped to camp on the Dog River, some 20 miles from the smouldering ruins of Steele's buildings. A fire of several rods in length was made and everyone was brought close by it. Sentinels were posted all around the perimeter of the group so that any movement would be silhouetted against the glow of the fire's embers. As a further precaution, a rope was passed around the body of each captive and Indians lay between each prisoner to prevent any concerted attempts to escape. Steele had been told that if a pursuit caught up with the force, all of the prisoners were to be put to death. In the face of such a threat, he felt compelled to get away and avoid such a fate. He was able to slip out of the rope loop, but found that everytime he raised his torso, he was confronted by Indians sitting nearby who were either preparing their clothing and equipment for the next day or were augmenting the guard. He had a very restless night expecting that at any moment a militia force would arrive and the slaughter would begin. He need not have worried. All attempts at rescue had been abandoned and, as noted above, the burden of guilt had already been successfully transferred onto Colonel House's shoulders.

The next day, many of the prisoners were again compelled to carry the enormous packs. The captives took some wry pleasure in roughly handling their burdens and breaking the looking glasses to deny the looters any future use. A particularly surprising feature of captivity noted by Steele was the insistence by all of the Indians that their captives not go hungry. Indeed, the prisoners were urged to share in the Indians' food which many of them found most unpalatable due to its preparation. Even the best portions which Steele was offered included hair and offal, items that white society always discarded. Even so, this charity greatly puzzled the captors who could not decide whether it was motivated by true concern for their welfare or the knowledge that starving captives brought less reward. A prisoner could not even reach out to pick a berry without an Indian offering him something to eat.

The force travelled alongside the Dog to its junction with the Onion and then followed that river to the north-west, finishing the day's march atop a mountain where a supply of fine flour had been cached on the inbound trip. Steele was amazed to see the Indians making fire-biscuit by preparing dough and winding it screw-like around sticks which were stuck into the earth to hang over a low fire to bake. He found this bread to be most wholesome.

Several days had now gone by without any sign of pursuit and the Indians were less apprehensive of being overtaken. The prisoners sensed their growing safety from instant death, although fear was never entirely absent because of their captors' sudden and fierce reactions to even the slightest cause for alarm. As the captives drew nearer to Canada, they had many reasons to dread the next phases of their captivity. All of them knew of the native practice of entertaining their villagers by having prisoners run the gauntlet, an ordeal that frequently led to maiming and sometimes death. Another chilling prospect was the possibility of native adoption with a grim future of years of living in unaccustomed deprivation. A few could hope to escape with the risk of a return trip through hostile country. For the majority, their very best hope would be to endure a long captivity in a British prison guarded by embittered Tory exiles.

The force arrived at the shores of Lake Champlain on Oct. 19th. When their secreted bateaux were recovered the Indians "gave a shout of exultation, and laughter, manifesting their joy and triumph."[245]

Before they set off on the lake, Steele's captor decided to purloin his coat, reasoning that some other Indian would only take it and he at least was offering a blanket in exchange which another might not. The force travelled the lake to Grande Île and encamped. The next morning they embarked and worked their way north to Île-aux-Noix where the Indians traded a part of their plunder for a large supply of rum. As the natives became deeply drunk, their emotions gave way to "savage yells, and shrill outcries... and death seemed to stare every captive full in the face."[246] Not all the Indians drank; the prisoners were guarded by a number who dutifully avoided intoxication. As well, there were some British soldiers from the garrison who watched over them. Soon the drinkers were rendered insensible from an excess of rum and the danger had abated; however, escape was impossible.

The following day the force travelled to St. John's and again the Indians "found a plenty of ardent spirits" which they made free use of and "became more enraged, if possible, than before." Those captives who had not had their faces painted as a sign of adoption were threatened with death. Although adoption had been promised to Steele, he had for some reason been left undecorated. He was approached by an Indian, who "under the influence of intoxication, like many white people, more sagacious than humane, came up to me, and pointing a gun directly at my head, cocked it, and was about to fire... " when Steele's new master, the chief, "knocked it aside, pushed him backwards upon the ground, and took a bottle of rum, turned down his throat a considerable quantity, left him and went on." Soon, some Indians came to paint Steele's face and hands on behalf of the chief and instantly, almost magically, he was made safe. Now he received signs of friendship from those who only minutes before seemed intent on killing him. It was made clear that he would now be adopted and become one of them.

Steele was indeed fortunate, as were his companions who received this blessing. Most of the others were led through the villages and underwent trials of strength and courage; however, we only know the experiences of Steele and his fellow adoptees. He was taken to "Caghnewaga" (Kahnawake) and soon an older white man named Philips came to see him. He was an interpreter, and an important political figure, who had been captured on the western frontier of New York in the previous war. Philips had been adopted and had chosen to remain with his new relatives where he was given the name Santorese. Over time, he received and returned their closest friendship which grew into esteem.[247]

Philips advised Steele that he would be adopted into a family to replace a man who had been killed during the recent campaign. A fellow captive from Randolph, Simeon Belknap, and a few others were to be given this same privilege. After the ceremonies, Steele was conducted to the home of an old woman who gave him as much as her very meagre larder allowed. However, by many small and clever artifices, he and his fellow adoptees proved so uncooperative as new members of the community that the Indians soon despaired of them. They were taken to Montreal and sold to the British. Steele fetched a "half Joe." For many of the captives, this event marked the end of the Houghton raid, although it is very likely that the young boys, who would not have possessed the cunning to defy their captors, did not escape adoption so easily.[248]

★★★

On Oct. 25th, Governor Haldimand reported to Lord George Germain the results of Houghton's activities. The Indians had burned the old towns of Tunbridge and Randolph and in the process destroyed two mills, 32 barns loaded with grain and an equal number of houses and other buildings as well as many of the inhabitants' cattle. They had taken 32 prisoners and although they were pursued by a superior detachment of troops, the rebels were thought to have lost a number in the effort without being able to inflict any casualties.[249] Haldimand was clearly pleased that such a last-minute venture was able to accomplish so much destruction of rebel property for so little expenditure of his scarce resources.

Rebel accountings indicated that 21 houses and 16 barns were destroyed in Royalton alone and noted that the raiders ran off 30 horses, 150 cattle and many hogs & sheep. Contrary to Haldimand's assertions, which were doubtlessly drawn from Houghton's report, Steele's account mentioned no militia fatalities and only one wounding, although the American historian, W.L. Stone, recorded decades after the events that several militiamen had been killed.[250]

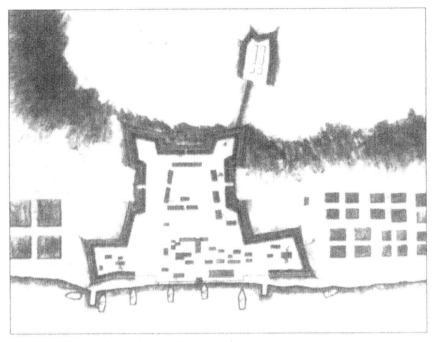

Fort St. Johns on the Richelieu River, Quebec Province
Haldimand considered this fort to be the key defence to the province's southern approaches and ordered substantial improvements. The two 'shoreside' redoubts had lain outside the main perimeter during the siege of 1775; these were incorporated into the works. The Lake Champlain Provincial Marine was headquartered here.
Gother Mann, 1791 (from André Charbonneau, The Fortifications of Île-aux-Noix (Parks Canada, 1994))

A Silhouette of Captain John Enys, aged 26, 1783
As a Lieutenant of the 29th Regiment, Enys served under Major Christopher Carleton in operations on Lake Champlain in 1778 and 1780.
Artist unknown. Original in the possession of the Enys family (from Elizabeth Cometti, Ed., The American Journals of Lt John Enys)

A view of His Majesty's armed vessels on Lake Champlain, October 11, 1776.
Some of these vessels were employed by Major Carleton in 1780. Commodore
Chambers' flagship, the 14 gun schooner, *Maria*, is the third from the right.
C. Randle, 1776 (National Archives of Canada)

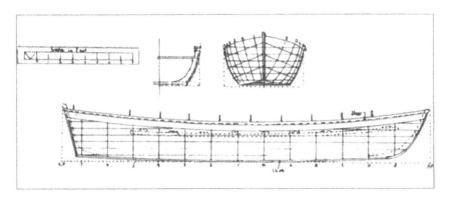

A Plan of the 1776 Pattern Admiralty Bateau
Thousands of these craft were employed by the military on the rivers and lakes of
North America to transport troops and provisions. This pattern measures 30 feet in
length, a beam of 6μ feet and drew 6 inches of water. Bateaux were powered by
oars and, in favorable winds, square sails.
Howard I. Chapelle, ca 1930 (courtesy Parks Canada, Niagara-on-the-Lake)

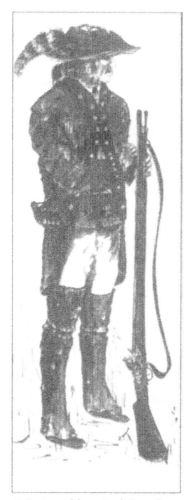

A late-war British Regular
Cut-down red coat, slouched hat and leggings were favoured in the woods. He wears shoulder wings indicating he serves in a flank company.
George R.P. Howse, 1995 (on trek at Hoffman's Notch, Adirondacks, NY)

Private soldier, 2nd Battalion, King's Rangers
In 1780, James Rogers' led about 50 King's Rangers on Carleton's expedition. David Johnson's representation shows a King's Ranger of the late war uniformed in a regimental coatee, green faced red, slouched hat, leggings and a regulation, Short Land Pattern musket.
David Johnson, 1992 (courtesy of the recreated company of Captain Henry Ruiter, King's Rangers)

One of Jessup's Men
This recreator is uniformed in the early-war, full-length red coat with green facings provided to the King's Loyal Americans & Peter's Queen's Loyal Rangers in 1777. He has flopped and cut the brim of his hat and uses a belly box stamped with the King's cypher.
Janice Lang, 1993 (at Schroon Lake, NY)

The Blockhouse & Sawmill on Fort Ann Creek
Planks from this mill were used by Arnold to build the rebel fleet on Lake Champlain which the British overwhelmed at Valcour Island in 1776. Major Carleton's scouts found the buildings empty on Oct. 9, 1780 and they were destroyed the next day.
unattributed, undated engraving (from Thomas Anburey, Travels Through the Interior Parts of America, 1789)

A Sutler's Tent
Sutlers, Sutherland and Dobie, travelled to Crown Point to meet the expeditions on Lake Champlain. These specialized traders sold liquors, soap, candles, fruits, cheese and bread. Sutlers were licensed by the Army and sometimes regimental women were granted this commerical privilege.
Janice Lang, 1995 (at site of the Lower Fort, Schoharie, NY)

LtCol. James Gordon, 12th Albany County Militia Regiment

Gavin Alexander Watt, 1996 (from an unattributed undated portrait in New York History, Vol XVII, No 3 [1936])

Captain John Munro, 1st Bn, KRR NY

Gavin Alexander Watt, 1996 (from an undated, unattributed engraving in George F. Jowett, The Hon. John Munro Pioneer in Upper Canada)

Battalion Company men, King's Royal Regiment of New York
A section of reenactors uniformed in post-1779 red coatees faced in royal blue, slouched hats and gaitered trousers.
George R.P. Howse, 1995 (at Cherry Valley, NY)

An Indian Department Officer
While it is a matter for conjecture what such officers wore in the woods, their clothing and equipment undoubtedly reflected their duties. This reenactor carries a custom-made rifle, tomahawk, beaded ball bag and powder horn and wears a red coatee with green facings.
Janice Lang, 1996 (at Schroon Lake, NY)

The Lurking Presence

Body paint was meant to strike terror in an enemy and was commonly used by all Indian nations. It could be an effective camouflage in the deep shadows of the woods, as was the darker skin of the natives. Indians discarded all encumbrances such as packs and blankets as soon as combat was imminent. Their highly developed capabilities to track, stalk and conceal themselves, made Indians fearsome foes.
Janice Lang, 1996 (at Schroon Lake, NY)

Indians see to their firelocks

Before going into action, these recreated warriors see to their flints and priming. Tattoos and nose rings can be observed.
Janice Lang, 1990 (at the original battle site in Stone Arabia, NY)

IV

THE EXPEDITION FROM OSWEGO - THE "INFAMOUS BANDITTIE"[1] ATTACK THE SCHOHARIE VALLEY

Haldimand gave command of the expedition from Oswego to LtCol. Sir John Johnson. In a letter dated Aug. 24, the Governor advised Johnson that "from hence [lower Quebec] you can have the Detachment you last Commanded with some additions... "[2] By this, Haldimand referred to the force of four and a half companies of British Regulars and four companies of the KRR NY which Sir John had led on the May expedition against Johnstown plus an augmentation from the Regular regiments brigaded in lower Quebec. The Governor also noted that two light infantry companies of Regulars, 200 of Butler's Rangers and "a large Body of Indians" would join Johnson from Niagara. In total, Sir John could look forward to a command of 720 troops and at least 200 Indians. In terms of the Canadian department, this was a substantial force. Haldimand noted,

> This is a Critical period to detach Troops but to effect so essential a Service, I would risk it. I must therefore desire you will by the next Post give me your ideas upon the most Eligible means to carry it into immediate Execution, for if it is to be done there is no time to lose as the Corn [a general term used in the old country to mean grain] will be hurried away the moment it is fit to Transport.[3]

Haldimand's instructions were sent express from Quebec to Montreal and arrived there on Aug. 27, taking three long days. Sir John replied the next day. He had a number of interesting recommendations to make to Haldimand.

> ... but from the lateness of the season and the uncer-
> tainty of the Troops and Indians from Niagara Co-
> operating, I would wish the whole to Rendezvous at
> Oswego and that no time may be lost the Troops &c.
> [etcetera] from Niagara would be transported there in
> the Shipping, from thence to proceed by the shortest
> Route through the Indian Country to Schoharie, from
> thence to Duanesborough or Schenectady as circum-
> stances may admit, returning up the Mohawk River
> and through Oneida &c. to Oswego, or the
> Detachment from this [quarter] may return by the
> shortest Route to Oswegatchie. Two Royals and the
> Grass Hopper might be found serviceable and can be
> easily conveyed on Horses for which there are good
> Roads all the way. I shall be happy with the assistance
> of Capt Scott and the same Detachments as I had
> before, but think that British in lieu of the Chasseurs
> [Jaegers] will answer better as they are not accus-
> tomed to Wood Marches or carrying large Packs...[4]
> From the nature of the Service the Troops destroy their
> Cloaths surprisingly. The Indian Shoes they received
> for the last Expedition were scarcely worth accepting.
> Blankets, overalls, and Shoes are necessary.[5]

Before the Governor had received Sir John's thoughts, he wrote again, altering his approach. His letter of Aug. 31 advised Johnson that, "the uncertain situation of affairs here and the better to Conceal this Enterprise, determined me not to send a man from the [British] Regiments here... " He offered Sir John the solacing explanation that this elimination from the expedition of British troops from the lower garrisons "will likewise accelerate your march."[6]

The question arises, what possibly could have changed in "affairs" in six days? A search of published documentation reveals nothing of particular note although the evidence of plotting by Canadien rebels hoping for a French invasion of Canada had been recently uncovered and may have given the Governor unusual cause for concern.[7] Might it be that Haldimand's restructuring of the force suggests more than a concern for secrecy, or speed or political turmoil? Might he have warned the British regiments that detachments would be required for another expedition led by Sir John and received a clear message of protest in return? This is not to suggest that the British Regulars were snobbishly offended by the thought that a Provincial officer would be in command over them. Rather, they may have been unwilling to accompany "this bold partisan, whose energy insured enormous hardship, labor and suffering to his followers, to which regulars, more particularly German mercenaries, were especially averse."[8] His driving command of the May expedition had already signalled an appetite for activity not shared by many professional soldiers. The German historian, Von Eelking, writes that an incipient mutiny amongst the British regiments was just prevented in 1781 when word was received that Haldimand was about to send a large force under Sir John deep into Pennsylvania against Pittsburgh.[9]

The removal of the Regulars from his force meant that Sir John might have to increase the number from his own regiment to at least 300 men. A return of the KRR NY dated Sep. 1st indicated that only 314 rank & file were readily available and fit for duty, 139 were on special duties and the balance sick in quarters and hospital.[10] Sir John likely wondered how the effective strength of his whole battalion could be simultaneously taken from its various duties without causing a great stir in the various posts and garrisons. Surely a wholesale removal would cause tongues to wag and endanger the enterprise! The Governor's answer to this tacit question was not long in coming.

On the same day that the return was prepared, Haldimand wrote another letter to Sir John giving more detail concerning the troops for the expedition. He noted, "Since my letter of yesterday, I have reflected upon the Circumstances of its contents and am strengthened in the opinion that the fewer men you take from this part of the Province, the more likely you are to conceal your views, and the fewer will be your difficulties."[11] He continued by recommending that -

> ... 150 of your own Corps added to the Troops from Niagara, will be sufficient to execute the purpose of your Expedition. You will have 600 Troops exclusive of Commissioned Officers, and no doubt will be joined by a considerable number of Loyalists. A larger body could not be moved with the dispatch that is necessary and would be very unwieldy by the Route you are to take — at Carleton Island you will take Captain Leake and as many of the Company as you may think fit, leaving a like number of your Corps in lieu of them, but I must desire that you will not take men who are essentially employed in the works, particularly at Coteau du Lac, as forwarding the buildings there is of the utmost consequence to the Transport to the upper Country.[12]

As Sir John's own company, the Colonel's, were in garrison at Coteau-du-Lac, they were eliminated from the expedition. They deserved the rest as the men had been on campaign at Stanwix in 1777, at Johnstown in 1778, to the upper country in 1779 and again to Johnstown in May of 1780. But they were seasoned campaigners and would be missed from the expedition. On the other hand, Leake's company was also composed of veterans — picked men of known high quality and zealous for the cause. They were a most welcome addition.

That same day, Haldimand wrote a letter to Colonel Mason Bolton who commanded at Fort Niagara and Colonel Guy Johnson who commanded the Six Nations Indian Department headquartered at that post. He sent the letters via Sir John and left them open for his perusal. Bolton was instructed to supply a detachment of 140 men from the 8th (The King's) and 80 from the 34th. John Butler was to supply 200 Rangers. A 3pr Grasshopper and two Royals with "a *necessary* proportion of ammunition will be wanted with ten expert artillery men and twelve serviceable horses."[13] Guy Johnson was to encourage the maximum participation by the Six Nations and their dependents and the Governor indicated his good opinion of Brant and his Volunteers by writing, "I hope Joseph is returned as I would by all means have him imployed on this service."

To Bolton the Governor wrote, "I would by no means have you send a single man who is not a good marcher and capable of bearing fatigue. The same must be observed in your choice of officers, without paying attention to the rosters [ie. seniority], as success will entirely depend upon your Dispatch and Vigour; those whose personal Abilities are not equal to those Efforts would rather weaken than give strength to the Detachment, for with every man that falls sick[,] one or two must be left behind... The troops are to be provided with a blanket, leggings, and a pair of moccasins."[14]

Scouts were sent out from Montreal and Forts Haldimand and Niagara on a regular basis to determine the state of the defences in the target areas and, more importantly, to prepare local loyalists who continued to occupy farms along the proposed routes to assist the raiders with current intelligence and depots of provisions. As many of those people had reason to fear retaliation for their efforts, they were also advised to prepare for removal to Canada in the company of the invaders.

As noted above, Sir John had recommended a route for the advance of the expedition. As the strongest element of his force was to be drawn from Niagara in the north-west, he could not expect to use the eastern approach route from Crown Point which he had employed in May. In any event, a key target was the grain-rich Schoharie Valley and to attempt an advance through areas which were strongly posted by the rebels could prevent him from reaching that valley. An alternate had to be chosen.

It was well known that the southern regions of Tryon County bordering on Pennsylvania still contained a strong loyalist element. Many of the Royal Yorkers, Butler's Rangers & Brant's native & white volunteers came from the area. In addition, the Mohawks from the Schoharie and Canajoharie castles would gladly accompany an expedition and render invaluable assistance. With the rebel Oneidas and Tuscaroras driven off their lands, it was expected that a march southwards through the desolated eastern margins of the Indian country would evade rebel patrols. This would be followed by an eastwards march through loyalist-dominated country to the southern end of the Schoharie Valley putting the force deep into the guts of the region. A surprise penetration would be virtually ensured.

Once into the Schoharie, the destruction of the barns and grain magazines would have to proceed at an extremely rapid pace. When the presence of the raiders became known, a strong reaction could be expected from Albany as well as the intervention of local militia companies and the detachments of State Levies in the many posts in the Schoharie and along the Mohawk River. Johnson would have to be wary of the rapid deployment of rebel forces to the junction of the Mohawk River and Schoharie Creek which would block his entry into the Mohawk Valley and prevent the destruction of the grains held in that quarter. Such a reaction could also necessitate a more difficult, and certainly much less fruitful, route through Cobuskill and Cherry Valley.

Haldimand had foreseen just such a concentration of forces against his raiders and planned a diversionary strike to confuse the rebels and divide their reaction. He visualized a raid mounted from the Richelieu River route which would send its strongest element deep into the upper Hudson River area to reduce Forts Ann and George. A strong secondary force would head to Saratoga, north of Albany, attack that settlement, and then join with Johnson in the Mohawk Valley. If all of this activity could be coordinated successfully, the New York State command would be pulled every which-way.

The planning of Sir John's expedition was implemented with great secrecy, so much so that the district's brigadier, Allan Maclean of the 84th "Royal Highland Emigrants", was not informed of the true purposes behind the troop movements. Well before the troops had set out for Oswego the cat was out of the bag, when several officers of different regiments, including some whose units were not even involved in the expedition, spoke quite openly of the venture. Maclean was truly incensed and in a somewhat irrational spate of anger widened the circle of revelation by discussing details with a number of officers.

Haldimand wrote to warn Sir John that the expedition had been exposed, which advice reached him en route at The Cedars. The Governor wrote, "The Enclosed Extract will shew you how difficult it is to conceal anything of the Kind, and how discouraging it is to attempt them under such circumstances. I should not wonder if the Rebels are apprized of your march and prepared to Receive you before you can possibly make your way into the Country. So cautious have I been that there are but two of my [military] Family to whom the design is breathed."[15] To Maclean, he sent a letter taking all blame for the secrecy upon himself and reprimanding the Scot for his intemperate behaviour.[16] In fact, so loose had the talk been of the planned expedition, as it had been before Sir John's May venture, that it was not long before news of it reached rebel ears in the target regions, confirming rumours which had been rife since August.[17] Additional preparations for the rebel defence were immediately instituted; however, their resources were lean and they did not foresee the attack route which had been so carefully and wisely chosen.

Sir John had suggested a strike against Schenectady or Duanesburgh in his August response to Haldimand's request for thoughts on the expedition. Upon reflection, the idea of attacking Schenectady was embraced by the Governor, as the strategic impact of successfully reducing that place would be enormous for it lay only a day's march from Albany, the hub of the rebel's northern operations. Destroying Duanesburgh, simply another farming district, did not hold the same allure and could be, and was, left for another opportunity. It was decided to assign a secondary force of Royal Yorkers, Rangers and Mohawk warriors under the command of Captain John Munro to penetrate the country by the Lake Champlain route. It was thought that Major Carleton's diversionary attack against Forts Ann and George would distract the rebels from both Johnson's and Munro's efforts. Captain Munro was given orders to first attack the town of Saratoga and then march to Schenectady, where he would join with Sir John's main column. The combined forces would then destroy that town and other targets of opportunity before withdrawing up the Mohawk River to Lake Oneida and/or overland to Fort Oswegatchie on the St. Lawrence River.[18]

A glance at a map reveals the supreme confidence of the Governor and his subordinates in even attempting such a bold stroke. An attack on Saratoga would expose Munro to the risk of being cut off by a reactionary force out of Albany as he marched from there to Schenectady. To achieve success, the timing of Munro's movements would have to mesh carefully with Sir John's. As long as the threat of Johnson's force held the attention of the rebels, Munro stood a chance. If the timing went wrong, Munro would be extremely vulnerable.

With the addition of the force under Munro, the 1st Battalion KRR NY was about to mount its greatest active service commitment. With one company on special duties at Coteau-du-Lac, one company assigned to garrison Fort Haldimand on Carleton Island and the equivalent of another company on furlough, sick or prisoners with the rebels, the battalion would put elements of seven companies, over 60% of its total strength, on expeditions deep into rebel territory.

Sir John had arrived at Fort Haldimand, Carleton Island, with his Montreal-based contingent on Sep. 20th, after the usual exhausting battle up the rapids of the St. Lawrence. At the fort he was joined by Captain Leake's Company, leaving Captain Alexander McDonell's Company as a replacement.[19] Simultaneously, at Albany, the senior Continental officer wrote to Governor Clinton that he had received notice that Sir John had left Canada.[20] Both sides had their spies hard at work.

No time was wasted. The force immediately took sail for Oswego which was reached the next day.[21] Disappointingly, the men from Fort Niagara, who had been expected two days later,[22] did not arrive until month's end because they had encountered severe storms which blew them substantially off course. On the day that Johnson expected to see the Niagara force, General Washington was apprised of the Baronet leaving Canada for the New York frontiers with a force of 500 men.[23]

John Butler's craft, with his Rangers aboard, was the first to arrive on Sep. 29th, followed by the second ship on Oct. 1st containing Brant, his Volunteers and the Regulars.[24] Sir John knew that his timetable was badly off the mark and cooperation with Munro's force had been already rendered unlikely. Impatient and active as the war had made him, Johnson began his advance the next day.

The senior officers from Niagara had brought Johnson the very disappointing news that the number and quality of their men was less than planned. The garrison at Niagara had been terribly weakened by disease. Bolton was to explain in a letter to the Governor that he had never seen so many men sick at once.[25] To make up his numbers, LtCol. Butler advised Johnson that he had taken every Ranger "who can be of the least service, even some convalescents are gone in order to send as many men as possible."[26] So, the Governor's sensible instructions about taking only men who were "capable of bearing fatigue" had, of necessity, been ignored. Considering the gruelling march and timetable which were planned, it is remarkable that any but the most robust of men could be expected to survive, let alone do duty.

Bolton also wrote "The number of Indians Colonel [Guy] Johnson collected in so little time astonished me, considering the short notice he has had and the many parties that have been sent out, one of which amounting to near one hundred warriors left Carleton Island not many days before Sir John arrived and are gone towards the Mohawk River. These will certainly join him... A great number of Indians are come in too late to go on the expedition, but as Colonel Johnson intends to send out a large body of them towards Fort Pitt, I hope it will be of some service, as I hear a considerable body of enemy marched lately from that place against the Shawnee."[27] This dramatic native response indicated their eagerness to avenge the destruction of their homelands. Bolton's report concluded with the erroneous and optimistic intelligence that "every militiaman... has been called even from their forts, a few excepted"; however, the sentiment which followed was genuine enough. "This will give Sir John Johnson the most favourable opportunity of returning Mr Sullivan's visit to the Six Nations."[28]

Although an official return of the men brought from Niagara has not been found, the following table shows the likely composition of the expedition.[29]

Officer Commanding - LtCol. Sir John Johnson

From Niagara and the Indian Country:
Regulars: Officer Commanding - Captain Thomas Scott, 53rd Regt

8th Regt: Captain Andrew Parke	
Light Infantry Coy	35
34th Regt Light Infantry Coy	35
'Hat'[30] Coys of 8th & 34th, Lieutenants Coote & Armstrong picked men	80
Artillery Detachment	
1 X Cohorn[31] Mortar & 1 X 3pr 'Grasshopper' Fieldpiece[32]	10

Provincials:

Butler's Rangers, Officer Commanding - LtCol. John Butler[33]	
Companies of Captains John McDonell (Aberchalder), George Dame, Andrew Thompson & Barent Frey[34]	206[35]
Indian Department: Lieutenants George McGinness (McGinn),[36] Adam Crysler[37] & Hendrick Nelles[38]	
Six Nations:	
War Captains/Principal Warriors: Old Smoke & Cornplanter, Seneca; Joseph Brant, Oquaga Mohawk; Hung Face, Cayuga; Sagwarithra, Tuscarora; Seth's Henry, Schoharie — Warriors	265
Subtotal - from Niagara & the Indian Country	*631*[40]

From Montreal & Carleton Island
Regulars

Von Kreutzbourg's Hesse Hanau Jaegers	25

Provincials:

1st Battalion, King's Royal Regiment of New York: Major James Gray	
Grenadier Coy, Captain John McDonell (Scotus)	36
Light Coy, Captain Samuel Anderson	49
Major's Coy, Lieutenant & QM William Morison[41]	39
Captain Angus McDonell's Coy, Lieutenant James McDonell[42]	26
Captain Richard Duncan's Coy	42
KRR NY subtotal (includes Officers, Serjts & Drums):	*227*[43]
Leake's Independent Coy,[44] Captain Robert Leake,	
1st Lieutenant William McKay; 2nd Lieutenant Henry Young	60
Subtotal - from Montreal & Carleton Is.	*312*

Grand Total - The Expedition: all ranks	*943*[45]

The artillery and provisions were carried in a brigade of 18 bateaux, guarded by a strong detachment, down the Oswego River to the Three Rivers junction, then southwards on the Onondaga River to Lake Onondaga. At the south end of the lake lay the devastated Onondaga castle and the brigade was met there by the main column of the men and horses who had marched overland.[46] A cache of provisions were prudently concealed for the return march and an issue of rations for a ten day's march was given to each man. The first reverse to the expedition occurred here. Captain Robert Leake became very ill and he, with 10 sick soldiers and 5 Indians, was sent back to rest at Oswego. Johnson would miss Leake's activity and experience.

Prior to beginning the march, Sir John set in motion a daring Secret Service mission. Corporal Jacob Schell (Shell), a 1777 veteran of Duncan's Coy, had volunteered to travel across the Mohawk Valley to his home at the Helleburgh, a settlement lying about 15 miles southwest of Albany. He was to investigate an intelligence report brought to Quebec by Volunteer Thomas Smyth. Smyth had collected the information during a Secret Service scout to Albany in early August. Supposedly "three or four hundred men at the Hellbaragh" had taken cause for the Crown "and beat off all parties sent to apprehend them and Wore Red Cockades in their Hatts."[47] With Schell's intimate knowledge of the area and the people there, Johnson hoped that he would be able to assemble a large number of these loyalists as recruits and bring them to meet the expedition when it arrived in the Schoharie. Schell's mission was a risky venture at best. All of the many men who accepted such tasks over the years of the war understood the danger. One of the temptations which prompted men to volunteer for such assignments was the opportunity to visit with relatives and friends, albeit in great secrecy. Schell had agreed to take the risk. He was to pay the supreme price for his temerity.[48]

Sir John also appointed 1st Lieutenant William McKay[49] of Leake's Company to lead a scout into the Valley to gain intelligence. After assessing various factors suggested by Johnson, McKay was to secret his party in the area of Stone Arabia. In this manner, he would be able to bring Sir John fresh intelligence before the Baronet led his troops against that community.[50] With Leake having fallen ill and McKay sent on a scout, command of the Independent Company would probably have devolved upon 2nd Lieutenant Henry Young,[51] an accomplished "old" soldier of the Seven Years War.

Crude sleds were built to drag the three guns and the march continued to the ruins of the Old Oneida castle (Kanowalohale) where, upon arrival on Oct. 8th, the raiders were rejoined by a party of 15 Indian scouts. They brought in four prisoners, from whom Sir John learned that his expedition was expected. The captives told the story about two Oneida men, supposed converts to the King's cause, who had gone from Niagara to Albany with intelligence of Butler and Brant leaving on campaign "for some part of the Mohawk River" with 800 men.[52] Surprisingly, he also learned that his expedition was anticipated to follow the Schroon Lake-Sacandaga River route used the previous May and a large force had been posted there to intercept them. A second force was being held at Canajoharie,[53] perhaps because of the news about Butler and Brant. The former information was of no surprise considering the many security leaks, but the latter report offered some satisfaction, as Sacandaga was a long march from the Schoharie — although the force at Canajoharie could prove a nuisance during a withdrawal if he chose to return up the Valley.

A day later, on the march southwards, one of the expedition's Oneida warriors (likely another of those recent converts to loyalty) deserted, taking an empty mortar shell with him as proof of his word. It was expected he would travel to Fort Stanwix with a report of their route and strength. This must have caused some anxiety. Their supposition proved correct. By Oct. 11th word had been received by Colonel Malcom in Albany from Major Hughes at Stanwix that the Oneida deserter had brought word of the expedition, advising that Johnson, Butler and Brant were on the march, that the column was very strong and possessed artillery — indeed Malcom advised Governor Clinton that "a 5 inch Shell [was] in every Mans pack."[54]

On October 12, a second scouting party rejoined the march with four prisoners from the German Flats. The Baronet heard the story repeated of the two Oneidas who had left Niagara and also had word that "the Enemy had not the least Knowledge of our being so near them."[55]

While the exact route traversed by the column through the deserted Oneida territory has not been found, it was likely southwards, inside the western boundary of the Fort Stanwix Treaty line of 1768, past the Brothertown settlement and down the Unadilla River. This track would pass close to the small, deserted white settlement known as the Butternuts and take the expedition to the junction with the Susquehanna River near Unadilla, the mixed-nations' Indian town which had been destroyed by the rebels in 1778. At this point, the force would be about thirty miles north of the Pennsylvania border. They then likely turned east-northeast into the Mohawk nation's country, marching up the Susquehanna to its junction with the Charlotte River. Then, they followed the Charlotte eastwards, almost to its source, and cut east, up and over a height of land, to Kennanagara Creek.[56] As that creek flows into the Schoharie Kill, they were positioned to issue into the Valley below the major farming district.

The latter stages of this arduous route took the column past Captain John McDonell's (Scotus) land on the Charlotte. The column's final stage of the advance closely followed the route McDonell had taken in August, 1777 when he marched into the Schoharie with his newly raised company and joined with Adam Crysler to bring the valley into open conflict.

On the 13th, when they were in the Unadilla area, the expedition's provisions were close to exhaustion and a party was sent forward "to a Scotch settlement within Twenty miles of Schoharie [likely associates of Captain McDonell's] to bring us some Cattle."[57] That same day, 20 Cayugas left the column, deciding there was more profit and less risk to be found in attacking German Flats. It was "with difficulty [that] the whole [of the Indians] were prevented from following their example as they did not like going so low down into the Country where it was whispered we would meet two Thousand men to oppose us."[58]

The lack of food necessitated the sacrificing of many of the horses ridden by the officers; even the mount of the septuagenarian, Old Smoke, was butchered. "The fastest of the young hunters were sent out to kill ducks, partridges, rabbits... "[59] and brought in quantities of ducks, but never enough to satisfy the strong appetites that developed with the exertions of the march. The Seneca, Blacksnake, was later to recollect that the Schoharie-Mohawk Valleys' expedition was "the severest campaign the Senecas were ever engaged on from the provision given out".[60] Coming from a hardened warrior representing a race of men who were utterly inured to the hardships of warfare, this was a significant comment.

The leaders were pushing the column on at the fastest possible rate. The need to take advantage of the furor which would be caused by Carleton's efforts on Lake Champlain was very apparent. While the opportunity to join with Munro had been lost, there was still the hope that the Captain's activities in the Saratoga area would provide a further diversion of rebel resources. This assistance would only be effective if Sir John's expedition could maintain its forward momentum and arrive in the Schoharie close to the time that Carleton and Munro were conducting their operations. Johnson knew they were already late.

The Seneca Blacksnake recalls that six rebel scouts were discovered, probably on the 13th or 14th. A party of ten of the swiftest Senecas were dispatched to capture them.

> Just as the army was encamping at sun down to go supperless to rest before the campfires, they heard the well-known hallos resounding through the air, and repeated six times in succession, indicating that all the whites had been taken alive. They were delivered up

to the British officers, who chastened them as to the distance to Schoharie, strength of the garrison, &c. They replied that it was a day's journey there, that there were 100 Americans in the first fort, four miles from Schoharie Village, 50 in the fort at the further end of the village, and a large stone house in the village well-filled with men, and did not exactly know how many were in the fort 6 miles beyond the town, but thought there were over fifty.[61]

Without any food,[62] they continued their relentless advance on the 15th, apparently using the captured scouts as pilots. They were met by the forward party returning with 11 head of cattle. The column halted[63] and immediately butchered the animals, distributing shares to the famished men who had been three days with very little sustenance. A number of local inhabitants joined the expedition,[64] many of whom had provided the cattle. These men may also have supplied a wagon, as the gun was later carried in one rather than dragged on the crude sled. Of course, those who had assisted feared the retaliation that would follow the raid; many of them had been imprisoned previously for such demonstrations of loyalty.[65] They had much to fear, as incorrigible offenders were sometimes hanged.

The next day, the 16th, the raiders halted their march, camping at the junction of the Schoharie Kill and Kennanagara (Panther) Creek just north of Ottegus-berg Mountain;[66] they were now at their first target, after a gruelling march of over 250 miles along narrow Indian trails. Regimental Returns note that 24 men were enlisted on this date.

Amongst these recruits was a Jacob Merckley, said to have come from Stone Arabia, north of the Mohawk River. He was undoubtedly related to the large concentration of Merckleys that lived at New Dorlach, a settlement due south of the river and about 15 miles west of the Lower Fort in the Schoharie. Folk from that settlement who practised the Dutch Reform faith had attended services in the limestone church which now formed the structural core of the Schoharie's Lower Fort. A number of Merckleys were already serving in the KRR NY. Another Jacob and his brother Michael were in Duncan's Company; their brother Henry and, possibly cousins, John & Frederick Merckley were serving in Samuel Anderson's Light Infantry Company. All of these men were most likely with their companies on the expedition.

Michael Merckley had left New Dorlach the previous month and travelled to Canada to join the Royal Yorkers. He would have brought news that a great many of the inhabitants there continued to favour the Crown. The other Merckleys in the KRR NY had joined at Fort Stanwix in 1777. They were part of an 85-man militia company from the New Dorlach area which had marched to Stanwix to join St. Leger's expedition. Forty-nine of these men enlisted in the KRR and the Indian Department and 36 of them mysteriously returned home. Now, as Michael would have reported, many of these returnees were willing to re-join the British army. The newly-enlisted Jacob was sent to assemble these recruits and march them to meet the expedition in the Schoharie Valley.[67]

Sir John reported that his column encamped within three miles of the "Upper End of the Settlement of Schoharie." (The Schoharie Kill, or Creek, runs south to north, thus the upper end of the settlement is in the south.) This lush farming valley was protected by three forts. These were of the frontier style, not like the elaborate and complex, stone fortresses of European design such as those at Quebec and Niagara. The expedition would first encounter the Upper Fort. It was said to have been the strongest of the three and erected around the house and barn of Johannes Feeck which acted as the centrepiece of the installation. Two-and-a-half acres of ground were regularly surrounded by four walls. The ground sloped down on the south side where there was a strong picket of stout timber fronted by a friezed breastwork of earth and timber some 8-10 feet high and wide enough to accommodate a wagon. It faced a ditch or moat and in the corners were fortified blockhouses, the one in the southwest corner mounting a cannon. The other three sides were strongly picketed. A redoubt of earth and logs was in the northwest corner and in the northeast stood a sentry box. A soldiers' barrack and log huts for civilians were inside the works arrayed along the eastern pickets.[68] The strength of the Upper Fort's garrison was between 75-100 men drawn from the locally-raised 2nd Company, 15th Albany Regiment under the command of Captain Jacob Hager[69] augmented by a detachment from Captain Foord's Company of Brown's Massachusetts Levies.[70]

The Middle Fort was located just to the north of Middleburgh. It was the headquarters for the Schoharie Military District, a region which stretched from the Harpersfield settlement in the southwest, between the Charlotte River and the west branch of the Delaware, to the Duanesborough region in the northeast, several miles below Schenectady. The Middle Fort enclosed three acres and was the largest of the Schoharie forts. The old, two-storey stone house of Johannes Becker, which had been christened "Fort Defyance"[71] during the "uprising" of 1777, formed the core of the works. Becker's barn became a barrack for the troops and another frame building had been built for the same purpose. Soldiers' huts were erected along the eastern and western sides of the fort, their slanted shed-rooves making ideal parapets for the defenders to stand on to fire over the stockade. A large oven was built inside the works in which 40 loaves could be baked at once and a well was dug to secure an internal water supply. Almost

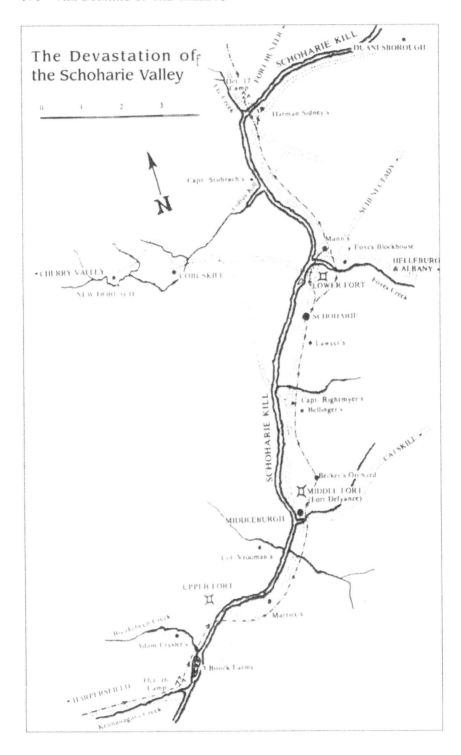

The Devastation of
the Schoharie Valley

2000 logs, approximately one foot in diameter were cut and drawn by teams of oxen to build the stockade. These were erected to rise 10 feet above the ground and were pierced for loopholes. Outside the walls was a deep ditch. This fort also had two blockhouses, one in the northeast corner, the other in the southwest. Each blockhouse mounted a threepounder cannon, one of bronze, the other iron.[72]

The garrison of the Middle Fort was strongly reinforced with quasi-regulars as befitted a headquarters. Elements of four regiments of Levies were represented, Graham's & Harper's from New York and Brown's & Jacobs' from Massachusetts. The detachment from Harper's included a small number of riflemen from Captain Bogart's company.[73] The garrison's senior officer was the New York major, Melancton Woolsey,[74] of Graham's. Woolsey had two companies of his own regiment totalling 106 men, one of which was commanded by Captain Jacob John Lansing, the other by Captain Christopher Muller, whose men were on a three month term. Of Massachusetts men, there was a company of Colonel Brown's under Captain William Foord which, less a detachment on duty at the Upper Fort, comprised some 60 muskets[75] and 30 of Colonel Jacobs' under Captain Pool. Colonel Peter Vrooman, the commander of the 15th Albany County Militia Regiment, with his lieutenant colonel and 1st major centred their command at the fort. Local militia captain George Rightmyer, and his 3rd Company was part of the garrison which therefore totalled about 250 all ranks.[76]

At Schoharie town, the key element of the Lower Fort was the limestone church erected in 1772 by the High Dutch Reformed faith. A stockade was built in 1777 to surround the church and about an acre of ground. Again, two blockhouses were erected in offsetting corners and a cannon was placed in each. Small huts lined the west side of the stockade to house the troops and families who sought shelter. A tavern was placed outside of the northeast blockhouse owned by Jacob Snyder. The fort's powder magazine was placed under the church pulpit. In the church belfry a timber parapet was erected to protect a section of sharpshooters of five riflemen. From that vantage point, they could protect all approaches to the fort.[77] Lieutenant Colonel Volkert Veeder[78] of the 5th Albany County Regiment was in command with a detachment of his regiment which had been sent as a reinforcement a few days before.[79] Lieutenant Colonel Barent J. Statts, 3rd Albany, was also in garrison, but his responsibilities have not been recorded; however, both colonels appeared to take an active role in the fort's management and the area's defence.[80] The 15th Albany's 2nd major, Jost Becker, and the adjutant, Lawrance Schoolcraft Sr., with the 1st Company commanded by Captain Christian Stubrach formed the local element of the garrison.[81] One source advises that a company of Normans Kill militia were also on duty as were some of the 15th Albany's company of Associated

Exempts under 1st Lieutenant Peter Snyder.[82] The Exempts were older or crippled men, and frequently those with occupations considered essential, who were only called out to meet emergencies. The total number of men on duty lay between 150-200.

For the invaders, the Schoharie Valley represented a highly concentrated target. The distance between the three forts was not even 15 miles and the majority of the farms with their barns and barracks of grain were within easy marching distance on either flank of the main highway. An important factor of such concentration was that it allowed Sir John to keep his force tightly organized and mutually supporting. Johnson was very clear that his main goal was to destroy the grain harvest, but there is no doubt that he was greatly attracted to the thought of destroying the focal point of rebel resistance in the valley — the Middle Fort.

It was known in the valley that a large raid was coming. In preparation for the worst, Marcus Bellinger, a local Committeeman, had travelled to Albany and returned on October 16 with a wagonload of ammunition.[83] However, just how close the raiders lay and from where and when they would debouch into the valley remained a mystery.[84]

The expedition's camp was less than a mile from three farms owned by Bouck families. Although the Bouck surname was commonly found in the area and a number of that name served in the rebel forces, quite a few were loyal. There was a Christian Sr., David and three Fredericks serving in the Royal Yorkers, all recruited by McDonell in August 1777, and a John Bouck Sr. & Jr. were mustered in Leake's Company. Thus, it may have been no coincidence that the Oct. 16th camp was located so close to these Bouck homes and, from Sir John's comments, it is likely that assistance with current intelligence and some foodstuffs was received there by the raiders.[85]

The column was underway before dawn the next morning. Hoping not to "give the alarm too soon," the troops bypassed the "Upper Fort and a few houses mostly the property of Friends";[86] however, just as the tail of the column passed the fort,[87] the roar of three cannon discharges alarmed the valley. Oddly enough, it was not an alert sentry who espied the raiders, but one of the garrison, Peter Feeck, who was out searching for some cows. Feeck saw the column and, unseen, ran to warn the duty sentry who fired his musket causing the guard to be turned out. The agreed signal of three cannon rounds was then fired.[88] Immediately upon hearing the alarm guns, Sir John gave the order to begin destroying all houses, barns, grain barracks and livestock, save only the homes of known friends. The sad burning and slaughter of livestock began and Frederick Mattice's barn, on the Clauverwie road south of Middleburgh, was the first building to receive the torch.[89]

Those at the Upper Fort were by no means convinced that they had escaped the attentions of the expedition. Captain Hager ordered all of the refugees into the long cellar under the Feeck house while the garrison mounted the parapets and manned the loopholes. Mary Haggidorn, a robust and fearless young lady, confronted Hager and argued that she was as good as any man and was not about to hide in a cellar when she might take a pike and defend the fort. The Captain was more than happy to have this unexpected reinforcement and told the woman to get a pike and stand ready at the pickets.[90]

However, the Upper Fort had no cause for fear. Sir John's column had moved on and was advancing against Middleburgh. As the Senecas approached the first fortified house, six of them ran up to beat down the door. They were fired at from within and one of their men was killed. They abandoned the attempt and ran off to join in the plundering of the deserted houses. The village[91] had habitations down one side of the road and orchards on the other. The men looted the abandoned houses of food and valuables, then set them afire. Some warriors approached the second fortified stone house through the orchards and were repulsed. A loyal Oneida was wounded in the side and a Seneca, Old Head, was ironically struck in the forehead by a spent ball which had been deflected by a branch of an apple tree.[92]

Of course, some folk stayed with their homes and took their chances. After all, there had been many raids in the valley and they had survived; however, even loyalist families knew the risks of staying behind. Raiders were frequently undiscerning; all too often the musket and axe claimed King George's friends.

Blacksnake recalled entering one house with Cornplanter, Conne-di-yeu, the half-brother of the chief and five others. An abandoned breakfast lay uneaten upon the table and soon eight very hungry warriors tucked in. When they emerged, greatly refreshed, they felt so strong and bold that the eight men attacked one of the fortified houses, found the door unfastened and entered without opposition. The occupants, likely terrorized by the numbers of Indians and troops entering the village, had taken refuge in the upper floor of the house and were easily gathered in by the warriors.

A party of soldiers and Indians forced the door of another house with their hatchets and captured the inmates. Much time was spent gathering in all the provisions that could be found before the buildings were torched.[93]

Just ahead of the raiders lay the Middle Fort, described by Sir John as "a Square Work of Picquets and Earth."[94] When the fort prepared to relay the Upper Fort's alarm signal, the Artillery commander was caught unprepared. One of the fort's women, Susannah Vrooman, rushed to bring him a live coal from the hearth which he used to light the slow-match.[95] A scouting party was required to find the cause of the alarm and 1st Major Thomas Eckerson, 15th Albany, called for some volunteers to accompany him. His call drew a mixed detachment of 19 men from the militia and Levies. It is recorded that because of the gale-like wind, the men left behind their hats and tied kerchiefs about their heads.

Amongst the volunteers was the ranger, Timothy Murphy, a noted marksman in Bogart's rifle unit in Harper's Levies. He was a Virginian who had served with Daniel Morgan's Rifle battalion against Burgoyne in 1777. During that service, he had sniped and killed the very popular Scottish brigadier, Simon Fraser.[96]

It was a cold, bleak and overcast day with patches of sleet driven on a harsh wind from out of the northwest.[97] One can readily imagine the fear and anger of those scouts as they observed the evidence of the approaching raiders rising above the horizon in ever-multiplying, dense clouds of smoke, whipped by the gale-like blast. They may have suspected that the rumoured large-scale raid was upon them, but small forces had caused such havoc before. The scouts were approaching the Dutch Reform's brick church, when suddenly, the Indians were amongst them and they retired towards the fort skirmishing on the way. The scouts took temporary cover behind a board fence from where Murphy spotted troops attempting to outflank their position. He advised the Major and Eckerson ordered a retreat just as the advancing company levelled and fired. Murphy had hung back to get a better shot at the advancing foe. The fence boards were riddled with ball and a few of the men had their linen, riflemen's frocks punctured, but all of them escaped without harm.[98]

Back at the Upper Fort, Captain Hager sent out a three-man party, including his son Henry, Lawrence Bouck and Isaac Vrooman, to harass the rear of Johnson's column and take a prisoner for questioning. The men discovered several of Sir John's force on the opposite side of the river and crossing over soon came up to an Indian who was lagging behind his fellows. Discovering their presence, the warrior levelled his firelock and his ball struck Isaac Vrooman's powder horn. The Indian took cover behind a large tree. The three militiamen returned his fire and three balls hammered into the trunk. Seeing his chance, the warrior took to his heels, abandoning a poor mare which was carrying his pack loaded with plunder.[99]

Early that same morning, 2nd Major Jost Becker at the Lower Fort, aware that the Middle Fort was low on gunpowder, sent a couple of bags in the care of two men. They were well along their way when they heard the firing of the alarm guns "walking" up the valley and, spurred on by the discharges, they were fortunate to arrive just before the raiders appeared.[100]

As Sir John's companies deployed into the clearings surrounding the fort, a sortie, led by Levies' Captain Jacob Lansing,[101] was sent from the fort to meet the advance. The sally exchanged a few volleys before retiring with the loss of Private Amesiah Lyons.[102] David Ellerson, one of the fort's rangers who had sallied under Lansing, had been hiding behind a board fence when he saw a red-coated officer advance out the British ranks to give orders. Ellerson levelled and sniped at the man. His rifle shot was answered by several company volleys. Ellerson scooted back to the fort and claimed that "seven hundred fired at him in this flight."[103] As had happened to his friend Murphy earlier in the morning, the fence behind which he had hidden was peppered with holes. Colonel Vrooman watched Ellerson's precipitate retreat with some concern. Another officer thoughtlessly called upon the rifleman's wife to observe his run for safety as if it was nothing more than an innocent entertainment. Whatever could she have done if she had seen him struck down? One of the fort's guns assisted his flight by discharging at some companies of the red-coated Royal Yorkers as they marched past the exposed flank of the fortress. This created some confusion in their ranks, but caused no execution amongst them.

Parties of Rangers and Indians spread around the small fort and commenced a brisk fire at the loopholes and parapet while Johnson ordered the 3 pr Fieldpiece and a Cohorn[104] forward. Although surprise had been lost, Sir John still had hopes of forcing a capitulation. The two artillery pieces took up a position in Peter Becker's[105] orchard and commenced firing. Some infantry companies were also posted in the orchard and were firing at the fort to prevent snipers from bothering the artillery crews.[106] Sir John reported that "I soon had the mortification to see [the guns] were of no use, the men not understanding their business sufficiently to do the Enemy any Injury."[107]

Johnson was not simply observing inaccurate gunnery. The small shot and shell lacked effect. The garrison recorded that the initial three mortar shells fell into the fort, the first, "sung in the air like a pigeon"[108] and exploded directly over Becker's stone house. An invalid elderly lady, who was bedridden in an upper room, leapt from her bed and stumbled down the stairs to shelter on the lower floors. The ordeal claimed her a few days after. The second shell landed inside the pickets near the well. As the shell, with fuse sputtering, "danced" in a mud-hole, all who were nearby had time to take shelter. Neither of these shells did any harm. The third crashed through the roof of the house exploding mattresses and setting the beds on fire. An old fellow chanced to be in the room at the time and was badly frightened. He emerged from the room spitting feathers and exclaimed that the devil was loose in the chamber. The blaze was brought under control by the quick action of a water brigade. Many solid shot were fired from the bronze three-pounder "with less precision." Private Asahel Foote of Captain Foord's Company of Massachusetts Levies was in the garrison and he recalled over a dozen mortar shells being fired into the post and the fort's magazine being set on fire three times.[109]

Being disappointed with the results of the artillery fire, Johnson decided on a different course of action. Ordering the cease-fire of his guns and muskets, he sent Captain Andrew Thompson of Butler's forward with two men under a flag of truce to summon the fort to surrender. One man carried the white flag aloft, while the green-coated Thompson strode to one flank and a fifer on the other played Yankee Doodle.[110] One might be sure that the choice of such an air to signal a truce either entertained or infuriated the Massachusetts men in the garrison, but it would not have gone unnoticed. This offer was made three times and on every occasion the courageous Thompson and his two men were met by a lead ball snapping over their heads.

What Sir John could not have known was that discord raged within the little fort. Woolsey wanted to admit the flag and hear what terms were going to be offered. None of his officers, either of the Levies or militia, agreed.[111] While this discussion proceeded, Murphy, abetted by Ellerson, both of whom had reason to fear a summary execution if taken by the raiders, took it upon himself to fire at the advancing Captain. Woolsey was understandably incensed and demanded to know who had the temerity to fire upon a flag of truce. One colourful account records that Murphy retorted he would sooner send a ball into the Major's heart than see a flag enter the fort. A postwar pension application by a participant in the fort noted that Woolsey ordered the arrest of Murphy and the officer who was about to comply was prevented from doing so by the rifleman's friends.[112] Finding insufficient support amongst his fellow officers, Woolsey is said to have abdicated command to his junior, Colonel Vrooman.[113] Once the truce had so obviously and firmly been refused, Sir John ordered the artillery to recommence their firing, but it proved no more effective than previously. Colonel Vrooman on several occasions went to the powder magazine to draw ammunition for the men and he later admitted that his hair stood on end each time, as the supply came closer and closer to exhaustion. He feared Sir John's men would soon notice the slackening of their fire and storm the works.[114] How useful the two bags of powder from the Lower Fort must have been!

Sir John abandoned all attempts against the fort and ordered his raiders to complete the destruction of the area's buildings. From the walls of the fort, the garrison and refugees could see the Indians and "tories" spread far and wide with their torches.[115] At some risk, the buildings near to the fort also received their attention. In response to these attempts, several small sorties were made during the day to harass the raiders and to try to save specific structures. When John Becker's barn, a very inviting target with many stacks of hay still clustered about it, was approached by a party of Indians, a sortie was made to save the building. A brisk exchange of fire between the two groups resulted in Sergeant Cooper of the garrison being wounded in the leg. As he was carried off by two men, he was hit again in the body and died soon after being brought into the fort. Another soldier was shot in the head as he reentered the fort and two men were wounded.[116] While costly, this effort did save the barn and stacks.

One of the parties sent out from the fort under Murphy's command captured a Butler's Ranger named Benjamin Burton (Butts) who upon being questioned advised that he had been looking for the opportunity to desert since he joined Butler in Canada.[117] Another party under 2nd Lieutenant Martinus Zielie of the 15th Albany captured a "French" Indian who was attempting to steal a horse. He was reported to have been an interpreter for the "British" Indian Department. As Zielie led him into the Middle Fort, he was speaking extremely haughtily, perhaps believing himself safe from being understood. Doubtless, he was most surprised to find himself struck to the ground for his impertinence by Lewis Denny, a Canada Indian of the garrison who had allied himself with the rebels.[118]

The ranger, David Ellerson, led out another party. One of his rangers, John Wilbur, came across a man leading a horse. As the man was undistinguished by a uniform or special cockade and was a stranger to Wilbur, the ranger asked him to what party he belonged; the man answered "the Indian party." The ranger wasted no more words and shot the man dead — judge, jury and executioner. The man was later found to have come from the Albany area; he was likely one of those "loyalist" opportunists who frequently joined the expeditions to settle some scores and help themselves to booty. Ellerson himself discovered an Indian about to set fire to the hay stacks around Becker's barn and fired at him, apparently without effect. The warrior bounded off into the woods where his body was found the next spring. It was believed that he had been fatally wounded by Ellerson's rifle shot. He was discovered sitting against a tree trunk with his firelock upright between his knees and resting against his folded arms. The man must have been vigilant to the last, his eyes ever watchful, for when he was found, they had been plucked out by birds.[119]

Finding the day well advanced to 3:00 PM,[120] Sir John assembled his forces and pushed the column northwards, "Killing and destroying everything within fifty yards of their Forts."[121] They were pursued by a small party from the Middle Fort[122] who were only able to annoy the stragglers and thereby found no mention in the Baronet's report.

Captain Hager at the Upper Fort had become very worried when the firing at the Middle Fort ceased for the second time. Doubtless, he had been concerned when Sir John had called for the cease-fire; however, the fighting soon resumed and he was reassured. Now the silence went on for much longer and fearing the worst, Hager dispatched a scout under Ensign Peter Swart. The three men travelled to the fort, discovered the defenders were still in possession and Johnson's raiders had marched to the north. The scouts returned to advise Hager that all was well. In celebration, three cheers were raised by the small garrison.[123] Mary Haggidorn could now lay aside her pike.

To the north at the town of Schoharie, many of the inhabitants had taken refuge in the Lower Fort and the small garrison was well prepared to receive the raiders. A scout was dispatched by Major Becker to discover the cause of the alarm guns and the three men visited two houses where local women had stayed behind and were going about the work of preparing food. They were bravely, and perhaps foolishly, intent on continuing their lives as if all was normal and protecting their property as best they could while their men were under arms in the fort. Of course, many of the local women had gone to the fort for safety and some of them were as determined to defend the structure as their men. Armed with pikes, pitchforks and scythes, they stood guard at the pickets to repel any attackers who attempted to gain the interior.

When the Lower Fort scouts arrived at Bellinger's about two miles north of the Middle Fort, they saw Sir John's troops about a mile off. While intently observing these, the scouts were overtaken by an advance guard of seven Schoharie Mohawks, led by Seth's Henry. The Indians immediately gave fire and their balls struck all around the men, one of them shattering a fence and driving a splinter into the arm of a scout. The scouts bolted, running to the next farm. They discovered that the Indians had fallen behind to reload and they stopped to draw the splinter. The wound was so painful, the wounded scout could hardly credit the cause. That was no sooner done than the Indians were on to them and the men split up to confuse the pursuit, two of them running off together while the wounded man successfully hid in a hollow tree trunk.

Understandably, the officers at the Lower Fort became very nervous as the sounds of artillery and musketry built up to the southwards. When the firing ceased and no report had been heard from the scouts, the tension became too much to bear. Becker sent off a second scouting party and these soon fell in with the two men of the first who were being hotly pursued by the Mohawks. All of the scouts took flight to the fort. The tactic of scattering was again chosen and proved effective. Several of the men made it into the Lower Fort ahead of the the Indians, although John Van Wart, a member of the second party, yielded to a foolish temptation and stopped to steal a pie that he had seen cooling on an outside shelf at Lawyer's house just south of the town of Schoharie. He was caught in the act of devouring the pie and, scrambling to escape, was shot down and his body much mutilated.

Westhoft, Schoharie town's German school teacher, who had warned Van Wart of the Indians' arrival, was inside Lawyer's house. As one of the Indians entered, he saw the teacher and raised his tomahawk to kill him when Mrs. Lawyer interceded. Her pleas saved him, a very lucky man indeed considering the passion that had been released over the killing of Van Wart.[124]

Sir John's main body arrived at the Lower Fort at 4:00 PM to be greeted by a discharge of canister from a small cannon, which was mounted outside of the palisades.[125] Captain Stubrach's crew of artillerists were considerably cheered to see their target fall to the ground; but, then were quite chagrined to see them all rise to a man on command. One of the targeted Royal Yorkers had a ball from the discharge hit his knapsack and lodge against the soles of his spare pair of shoes. He was much alarmed when he felt the impact. Unaware, he carried the ball back to Canada where it was found when he emptied his pack. As the gun was being run out, Sir John is said to have taken out a telescope to examine it. Observing only a small piece, he lowered his glass, made some derisive comment, then ordered the men to press on.[126]

Having wasted much time attempting to coerce the Middle Fort, the raiders spent little effort on the Lower. Johnson, who recognized that his work had just begun, knew that he must move rapidly to avoid giving the rebels time to concentrate a large body to oppose him. His line troops passed by the fort to the westwards while the Indians moved on the eastern flank, crossing Foxes Creek en masse. Some parties were ordered to stay behind to burn local buildings and Brant's men worked in close enough to the installation to destroy Jacob Snyder's outbuildings and tavern, lying near the northeast blockhouse. This likely proved as disappointing to the garrison as it did to Snyder. And, to make things worse, Swart's tavern, which was situated at a short walk from the fort, was also burned, all of its woodwork being consumed.

A section of five militia marksmen under Ensign Jacob Lawyer was posted in the bell tower and, while they were doing their best to dissuade the raiders from burning buildings close to the fort, a very strange incident occurred. Ensign Lawyer's brother Peter, a fellow militiaman, approached the fort from the direction of the Schoharie Kill and entered. He mounted the belfry to find his brother, whereupon the two men held a brief, private conference. Then, the pair climbed down from the tower and left the fort without leave or explanation. Command of this important post was taken over by 1st Lieutenant Peter Snyder who successfully kept the section at their work.[127]

At the same time as Swart's tavern was in flames, the marksmen in the belfry observed an Indian stealing through an orchard towards a house about 30 rods southeast of the fort. In his hand was a firebrand.

When he stopped to take cover behind a stout apple tree, the five rifles in the tower barked. All five balls struck the tree and, abandoning his purpose, the Indian took to his heels rather than risk an attempt on the house.[128]

Once the expedition had crossed to the north side of Foxes Creek, the three-pounder Fieldpiece was quickly taken from its wagon and assembled on the roadway where the crew had a good view of the stone church. The rebels, watching the men manhandling the piece, were convinced that the whole action was a sham as the glinting bronze tube had the appearance of a peeled log. They wondered if this was a ploy to scare them and force a surrender. Their suspicions were all the greater when the linstock was brought to the vent of the piece three times before the gun fired; however, at the third try, when the gun's mouth roared, spurting flame and smoke, and a solid shot resoundingly smacked into the stone wall of the church, they knew the fieldpiece was quite real. The gunners' second shot punched through the roof and lodged in a heavy rafter, sending a second shock through the whole building. A third round struck a horizontal beam in the tower,[129] causing the building to "tremble like a leaf in the wind"[130] and, undoubtedly, giving the marksmen in the belfry something to think about. Likely the Royal Artillerymen hoped to collapse the roof or belfry into the inner fort, causing disorder and casualties.

The fort's defenders had stood up well to being surrounded by columns of troops and Indians. They had grieved and raged as all around them their own, and their friends', work of a lifetime was put to the torch. Now, when the Crown artillery started to beat against their "castle keep" a pail of "rum sweetened with gun-powder" was brought around by Mrs. Snyder. The contemporary theory was that the liquor would "embolden, while the powder maddened the warrior."[131] The woman remembered later how the hands of some of the men at the pickets trembled so badly that they could scarcely take hold of the container she was serving from.

Having completed the burning, the two wings of Sir John's force reassembled on the high ground above the large brick house of the faint-hearted loyalist, Captain George Mann, a building which had figured so prominently in the "Tory uprising" of 1777. The riflemen in the church tower commenced a hot fire at such an inviting target, but the range was extreme. More of a threat came from the blockhouse in the north-east corner of the works which fired repeated rounds of canister; however, neither form of retaliation caused any casualties.

Sir John's had little patience with his artillery, and as the day was growing short, he ordered the gun to be disassembled and loaded onto the wagon; then, the column marched off. Several of the garrison were immediately dispatched from the fort and succeeded in extinguishing some of the nearer fires. One militiaman pursued a straggling Indian who, finding he was followed, lightened his load by ditching his pack and a dead goose. Upon examination, the pack was found to contain no less than eight pairs of moccasins, a marvel to the poorly-shod militiamen.[132]

The raiders continued for another six miles, destroying many buildings en route and then halted to camp near the junction of Fly and Schoharie Creeks[133] near Harman Sidney's mills, which were soon in flames. They had marched over 12 miles, fought several skirmishes, invested a fort and created a conflagration beyond imagination. For men who had already traversed a wilderness over rough trails and on very short rations, it had been exhausting. For their pains, a region capable of producing 80,000 bushels of grain per annum had been totally laid waste.[134]

Some of the Indians had found a supply of flour in barrels and carried it off in bags to make fire-cakes that evening. To the looters' surprise the dough crumbled in the heat and fell off the sticks into the coals. Their comrades inspected the flour and with much merriment found it to be slaked lime.[135]

Returning to the Middle Fort — Benjamin Burton (Button), the Butler's Rangers deserter, was carefully questioned and his sworn testimony put to paper. He confessed to having been a Continental soldier who was captured on the Susquehanna by a mixed party which conveyed him to Canada. He enlisted under Captain Butler on "4th June 1778,"[136] telling his inquisitors that his reason for joining his Majesty's forces was that he had "been confined 13 days & inlisted to have an Opportunity of making my escape." He gave useful evidence regarding the raiders' strength and composition and some information regarding the expedition's goals. Burton reported that the number of troops at Sir John's disposal were 335 whites and 150 Indians. If this had been true, such a number would certainly have been very far beneath the Baronet's expectations. Burton advised that 150 Regulars of the 8th & 34th were present. The raiders had a 3 pr "Grass hopper" and "one 4 inch Cohorn."

Burton testified that Colonel Butler was present with only 80 Rangers, strangely referred to as "N. Levies"[137] in the transcript of his interrogation. He said they were commanded by Captains McDonald, Dame and Thompson. Burton reported the presence of a scant 60 Royal Yorkers and 20 Loyalists (those who had joined on Oct. 16?) The number of KRR was so clearly incorrect that it suggests the column was so long that Burton had no means of making a true count. He advised Major Woolsey that Sir John's force included 25 "Green

Yagers" [Jaegers], a detachment which had not been part of any of Sir John's plans, nor would they be mentioned in his subsequent report, although their presence is acknowledged in Johnson's return of casuals.[138]

When asked about the Indians, Burton advised that, "They are chiefly Mohawks, some Onadaga & a few delawares." He was then questioned about the Senecas and answered, "... there may be one or two but not more[.] [T]he Cayugas went back without leave." How very strange! Surely Burton would have known the aged Old Smoke if he saw him, even if only by reputation? That great chief, and the equally prominent Cornplanter, with their followers were certainly more than "one or two."

Burton reported that the troops had been issued 50 cartridges that morning, which he believed was the entire supply. He advised that the cannon had "70 case Shott." There was "one Cask of Powder" for the Cohorn, but he was unaware of how many shells were available as these were being carried by the Indians, which explained how easy it was for the Oneida to defect with an example. The deserter made it clear that the column had been in great need, having "no bread for ten days and have eat[en] horses." He mentioned that the "Scotch people from Harpers Bush" had brought in "12 head of fat Cattle the night before last", but had not supplied any flour.

Of greatest importance, Burton named Stone Arabia as the next target after Schoharie and he gave the route of retreat for the Rangers as across country "via Onadaga Lake where the Batteaus and provisions are left." According to Burton, Sir John with the Royal Yorkers, Jaegers and 34th would "go across to Canada... but what Route I know not... "

While John Butler could hardly have known it, Lieutenant Joseph Ferris of the Indian Department, who had been sent on a scout to the frontiers, was lurking near Schoharie with a few recruits. He intended to join the column, but it moved off too quickly for him to accomplish his design. Upon his return to Niagara in early December, he advised that "the friends to Government are in high spirits, more so than ever they have been since General Burgoyne's misfortune. Had [the column] remained at Schoharie one day more, he would have joined us with a number of men, but they finding us gone were discouraged following... "[139]

Henry Haines, a private in Major Gray's Company of the Royal Yorkers, who had badly burnt his feet while plundering a burning house, had to surrender himself at the Lower Fort. Luckily for him, he was able to surreptitiously make contact with his half brother, John Rickard, who was a private in the 15th Albany serving in the garrison.

Rickard took pity and locked him in a soldier's hut for several days as a safeguard against the anger of the outraged populace.[140]

By noon of October 17, Governor Clinton had arrived in Albany and had been apprised of the raiders' arrival in the Schoharie. As units of Brigadier General Abraham Ten Broeck's First Brigade were already called-out and had been sent up the Hudson to the areas which had been overrun by Major Carleton's expedition, the Governor turned to the second brigade.

In 1778, Governor Clinton had merged the remnants of the Tryon Brigade, which had been so badly mauled at Oriskany the year before, into the Albany County Brigade. Finding this combination to be unwieldy, a second Albany brigade had been created in 1779 in which the Tryon regiments served under Robert Van Rensselaerl[141] as their brigadier. Van Rensselaer had already been alerted to muster 800 men of his Second Brigade in the face of the multiple raids from Canada, and he was now ordered by Clinton into the Mohawk Valley against Sir John's column. The 1st, city of Albany, regiment and some others were immediately dispatched to Schenectady; the General and some of his personal suite following shortly thereafter. Governor Clinton remained behind to organize additional assistance in the form of men and provisions.

That same day Colonel Malcom, the senior Continental officer commanding at Albany, had put pen to paper and written to Henry Glen, Acting/Quartermaster, at Schenectady,

> It is a most disagreeable situation — our country burning on every side & no means of preventing it — It is almost impossible to get the militia to turn out — at least not in time... The [Van Rensselaer's] militia from below [Albany] only crossed the River [Hudson] this morning & are now on their way to your city — for which I have even apprehensions... I have sent on 8000 cartridges to you, not knowing what may be wanted... If genl. Rensselaer shall want any ammuntion be so kind as to spare what he shall want... [142]

Upon arriving at Schenectady, Van Rensselaer was disappointed to find that the town's Commissary had no supplies of meat whatsoever and very little prepared bread. To offset these alarming shortages, some beeves which were being held for transportation to

Fort Stanwix were ordered to be slaughtered overnight and the ovens in the town were given over to baking bread for the troops, most likely with appropriated flour. Orders were also sent to Colonel Abraham Van Alstyne, who had failed to join the brigade, to speed the march of his 7th regiment so that it would arrive at Schenectady by daybreak.[143]

That same evening, Aid-Major John Lansing recalled General Van Rensselaer sending orders to LtCol. Veeder at the Lower Fort instructing him to organize a pursuit of Sir John's column which would "hange on their Rear." Veeder was ordered to "communicate this to Major Woolsey and request him to Join you with all the Force he can spare without exposing his Garrison too much." The officer commanding the immediate pursuit was to avoid an engagement and was regularly to send messages to the General giving details of the enemy's numbers, route of march and general situation.[144] It appears that Woolsey detailed the energetic Colonel Vrooman to perform this duty. Overnight, Vrooman collected detachments from the three small garrisons and set off early the next morning. Other parties moved through the smoking, devastated landscape vengefully putting the torch to the homes of loyalists, which had been spared by the raiders.[145] This was an odd and thoughtless reaction, as the buildings would have been very useful to the "well-affected" inhabitants who could have simply turned the loyalists out.

While Sir John's men slept profoundly, rolled in their capotes and blankets on the cold damp ground and guarded by a watchful cordon of rotating posts and patrols, General Van Rensselaer at Schenectady called upon Quartermaster Henry Glen to discuss methods of speeding his brigade's advance. A suggestion was made to call a meeting of the town's principal citizens to consult upon such means. Glen arranged for the gathering, to which Van Rensselaer voiced his first hope, which was to procure 400-500 horses, probably so that an advance guard could be sent forward. This measure was said to be impossible, so it was decided instead to organize a large supply of wagons to carry the men forward, thereby saving them for the expected battle ahead. Even this plan had to be abandoned by morning as insufficient wagons could be found.[146]

While at Glen's, Van Rensselaer was joined by his second Aid-Major Lewis R. Morris, who had volunteered for this duty.[147] Glen received intelligence sometime during the night from LtCol. Veeder of the 5th Albany County Regiment, who was commanding at the Lower Fort, advising that Sir John's force was encamped at "Harmen Sitneys" [Sidney's] some 15 miles below Fort Hunter. Veeder reported that Sir John's strength was "between 5 or 600, mostly regulars &

Tories."[148] Schenectady was about 20 miles from this same fort; the proximity of the Crown forces must have encouraged Van Rensselaer.

As the slaughtering and apportioning took so much time, the brigade, between 4 to 500 strong,[149] was unable to draw provisions until 8:00 o'clock the next morning. They marched without being able to cook a meal. One might imagine the grumbling as Brigade Major LeRoy and Major Morris set the troops in motion that morning of October 18. The scene of action was about to shift to the Mohawk Valley.

The Forts of the Schoharie Valley
A Plan of the The Upper Fort
This fort was bypassed by Sir John's column early in the morning of October 16th. The fort's garrison fired the first alarm-gun warning the valley.
Rufus A. Grider, 1888

A View of the Middle Fort at Middleburgh
The Middle Fort was laid under a brief siege on the 16th. Three pounder and mortar fire was brought to bear on the works with minimal effect.
O.J. Thiede, 1905 (Lester E. & Anne Whitbeck Hendrix, Sloughter's Instant History of Schoharie County, 1988)

A View of the Lower Fort above Schoharie Town
The Stone Church is the focal point of this post. Solid shot from the 3 pdr rocked the church, but Sir John was too impatient to await the outcome.
Unattributed, undated engraving (Lester E. & Anne Whitbeck Hendrix, Sloughter's Instant History of Schoharie County, 1988)

Captain Samuel Anderson's Light Infantry Company, Royal Yorkers
A Serjeant awaits orders while his section kneels in extended order.
George R.P. Howse, 1995 (at Black Creek Pioneer Village, North York, Ont)

Rebel Militia retreat behind a fence
15th Albany and 3rd & 4th Tryon militia take cover behind a rail fence. These reenactors exhibit the militia's wide variety of clothing and accoutrements.
Janice Lang, 1993 (at Black Creek Pioneer Village, North York, Ont)

Militia Scouts

Reenactor militiamen run forward to scout the enemy. The third man wears a neckerchief about his head as was done in the Schoharie in the stiff, blustery wind of October 17th.

Janice Lang, 1995 (on Borst's Heights, above the site of the Lower Fort, Schoharie, NY)

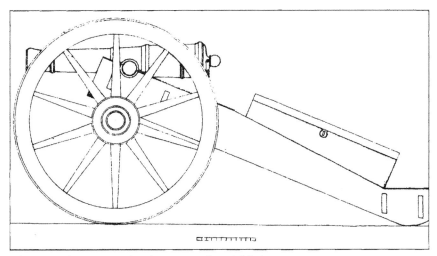

The `Grasshopper' Light Three Pounder Fieldpiece
The gun mounted on its travelling carriage. It could be readily disassembled for carriage by pack animals or a wagon. The scale below the gun is 1 foot (305mm.)

William Congreve, 1783 (from Adrian B. Caruana, Grasshoppers and Butterflies: The Light 3 Pounders of Pattison and Townshend (Bloomfield, Ont: Museum Restoration Service, 1979))

British and Loyalist Officers
A Light Company Officer, 34th, wears a cut-down felt hat and a late-war, cut coat trimmed in yellow. He confers with an officer of McDonell's Grenadiers, KRR NY. The Royal Yorker spares his regimental coat and wears a ranker's coatee. His rank is indicated by a sash, gorget & sword belt plate.

Janice Lang, 1995 (at the site of Lower Fort, Schoharie)

Colonel William Malcom, 1732-1791
A supernumerary Continental Colonel, Malcom commanded the 1st Regiment of New York Levies in 1780 and, from Albany, acted as brigade commander for the Levies. Elements of his regiment were commanded by Major Elias Van Benschoten at Klock's Field. In 1781, Malcom was appointed Continental Adjutant-General of the American Northern Department
Unattributed, undated engraving (courtesy Fort Ticonderoga Museum)

John Lansing Jr., 1754-1827
Lansing had seen Continental and militia service in 1776&79. He was Military Secretary to General Philip Schuyler in 1776&77. Lansing was an Aid-Major to General Robert Van Rennselaer during the pursuit of Sir John Johnson in October 1780.
Max Roish, 1831 (courtesy, Fort Ticonderoga Museum)

V

THE EXPEDITION FROM OSWEGO - "JOHNSON AND HIS BLOOD-HOUNDS"[1] ATTACK THE MOHAWK VALLEY

Johnson's troops arose early on October 18 and set off for the Mohawk using the roadway on the west side of Schoharie Creek which followed some old Mohawk trails. They soon passed by the cairn of rocks placed to mark the trail by Indians in ancient times. The expedition found the road almost impassable[2] for wagons and consequently Johnson ordered the Cohorn slung across the back of a horse; however, when the rear of the column became alarmed, thinking that the rebel pursuit was close and threatening, Major Gray ordered the sinking of the mortar and shells[3] in a nearby swamp. Thus, Vrooman's efforts of dogging their rear were well rewarded by causing Gray to jettison a piece of ordnance; however, the more useful three-pounder Fieldpiece was continued forward with considerable difficulty, an effort which was to prove rewarding later.

About half way to the Mohawk River, likely near Mill Brook, the Indians intercepted a rebel scout of five men, capturing two and killing one. They had been bound for the Schoharie, the "great smoak occasioned by the burning of the Settlement" having been observed. These men yielded no useful intelligence. Shortly thereafter, Johnson detached Brant and his Volunteers with Captain Thompson and 150 Rangers to destroy the settlement around Fort Hunter[4] which lay east of the junction of the Schoharie Kill and the Mohawk. The main column continued along the road putting the torch to many dwellings and barns.[5] A detachment was also sent some 4 miles to the west of the Schoharie Kill and several remote farms were destroyed.[6]

The destruction of the straggling Fort Hunter settlement was accomplished without opposition, the populace having taken refuge in either the woods or the fort with its small garrison. Brant's and Thompson's men spent considerable time plundering homes and out-buildings of food & valuables. John Newkirk, a Major in Tryon's Mohawk District Regiment, lost his farm during this action. The Newkirks and Putmans took refuge in the woods and, while hidden there, the huddled people were completely covered in ashes drifting down from the burning of Newkirk's barn. The concealed families observed that most of the Indians were mounted and correctly sup-posed the horses to have been plundered in the valley below. Gerritt Putman told of watching one of the raiders loot his tobacco. The war-rior exited his house with his arms full of the leaf; he then calmly twist-ed them into hanks and when each was completed, he thrust it into his blanket which he wore over his body secured by a belt at his waist. Several times Putman brought his musket to his shoulder, but on each occasion he lowered the gun knowing that to shoot could mean the death of himself and his family. Other Indians brought a quantity of eggs from his cellar, entered his kitchen and boiled and ate them. Some drew honey from his hives and sat down to leisurely devour the sweet.

Soon after, a gunshot signal was given and the raiders com-menced burning the buildings. Putman observed the Indians' methods of setting the fires, "... one of the party... after swinging a fire-brand several times over his head until it blazed, applied it to the well-filled barns which were soon in flames... several of the party fired their guns into a number of stacks and barracks of grain... " When the raiders had gone, Putman inspected his neighbours' farm. He found seven large, fat hogs lying dead in their pen. Each had been killed by a blow between the eyes with a pitchfork that had been taken from his barn.[7]

When finished their mission of destruction, Thompson & Brant recrossed the Schoharie a mile south of the Fort[8] and rejoined the main column on the banks of the Mohawk near Schrembling's,[9] who was a known friend of the King. Ironically, he had been found outside of his house, was not recognized, and was killed.[10]

Sir John's exact method of forming detachments from his body of troops and Indians for specific duties has not been found. For exam-ple, were these ad-hoc as the circumstances dictated, or did he set upon a more formal division by creating several mini-brigades, each with a detachment of line troops, Rangers and Indians? There is some flimsy evidence to support each possibility. Certainly, there would be no value in having all of the light troops in one location, or all of the Indians in another. Somehow, the disposition of the various elements

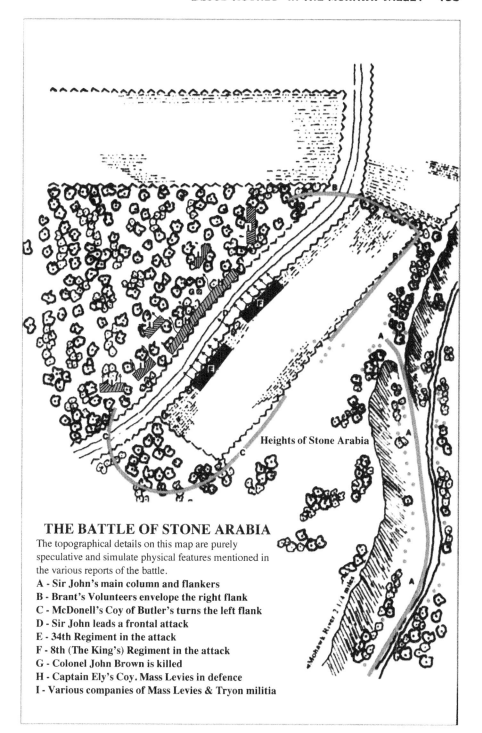

Heights of Stone Arabia

THE BATTLE OF STONE ARABIA

The topographical details on this map are purely speculative and simulate physical features mentioned in the various reports of the battle.

A - Sir John's main column and flankers
B - Brant's Volunteers envelope the right flank
C - McDonell's Coy of Butler's turns the left flank
D - Sir John leads a frontal attack
E - 34th Regiment in the attack
F - 8th (The King's) Regiment in the attack
G - Colonel John Brown is killed
H - Captain Ely's Coy. Mass Levies in defence
I - Various companies of Mass Levies & Tryon militia

Mohawk River 2 1/4 miles

The Battle of Klock's Field – The Setting

A - Sir John's Main Column
B - Brant's Volunteers & Jaegers detached
C - Small Indian Party attacks Fort Hess
D - Van Rensselaer's HQ & Whiting's Centre Column
E - DuBois' Right Column
F - Cuyler's Left Column
G - Militia & Oneida Advance Corps
Scale: Caroga Creek
to Ft. Nellis - 2 miles

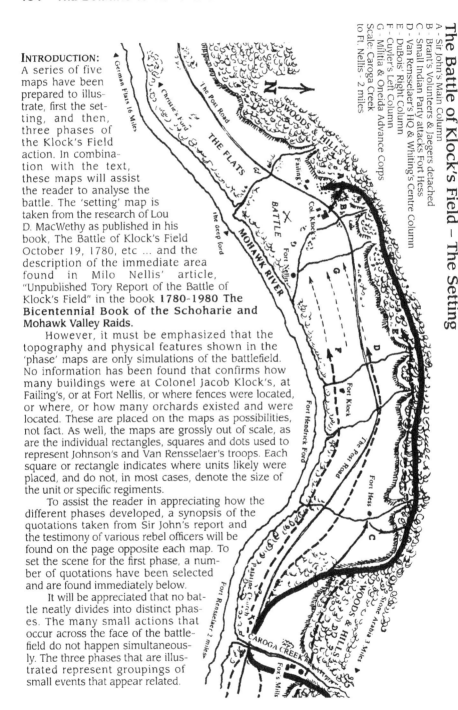

INTRODUCTION:
A series of five maps have been prepared to illustrate, first the setting, and then, three phases of the Klock's Field action. In combination with the text, these maps will assist the reader to analyse the battle. The 'setting' map is taken from the research of Lou D. MacWethy as published in his book, The Battle of Klock's Field October 19, 1780, etc ... and the description of the immediate area found in Milo Nellis' article, "Unpublished Tory Report of the Battle of Klock's Field" in the book **1780-1980 The Bicentennial Book of the Schoharie and Mohawk Valley Raids.**

However, it must be emphasized that the topography and physical features shown in the 'phase' maps are only simulations of the battlefield. No information has been found that confirms how many buildings were at Colonel Jacob Klock's, at Failing's, or at Fort Nellis, or where fences were located, or where, or how many orchards existed and were located. These are placed on the maps as possibilities, not fact. As well, the maps are grossly out of scale, as are the individual rectangles, squares and dots used to represent Johnson's and Van Rensselaer's troops. Each square or rectangle indicates where units likely were placed, and do not, in most cases, denote the size of the unit or specific regiments.

To assist the reader in appreciating how the different phases developed, a synopsis of the quotations taken from Sir John's report and the testimony of various rebel officers will be found on the page opposite each map. To set the scene for the first phase, a number of quotations have been selected and are found immediately below.

It will be appreciated that no battle neatly divides into distinct phases. The many small actions that occur across the face of the battlefield do not happen simultaneously. The three phases that are illustrated represent groupings of small events that appear related.

THE BATTLE OPENS (NO MAP)

REBEL DISPOSITIONS:

The two *advance corps* were in front of the centre and left militia columns. The advance corps "fell in ... and began to skirmish with the enemy's rear guard ... " "The firing on the enemy from the *advance party of the centre* then commenced about two hundred yards distance ... "

Dubois' *right flank column* advanced in the wooded hills above the road.

"The *centre and left columns* were then subdivided ... "

The *centre and left* were "ordered to subdivide in sections and so marched on till they came in sight of the enemy."

The *left column* was "marching on without observing any order."

Cuyler's men began to fire at about 400 yards distance and then inclined towards the river.

CROWN DISPOSITIONS:

"We found ourselves opposed in going down to the High Road by the [rebels] from behind fences, houses and Orchards."

"About sunset ... the [British] came down out of the woods to [Failing's] orchard, when a skirmishing began between [the rebel] left and the [British] in the lowlands."

"I immediately ordered a strong Detachment [*Brant's Volunteers & Jaegers*] to a h[e]ight upon our left which Commanded the Road."

" ... the *Indians and Jaegers* on the left ... "

The rest of the column [*8th, 34th, KRR NY, BR's & Leake's*] "pushed down the hill, crossed the Road and formed in the open Field."

The Crown's forces "were drawn up in order ... " "the *regular troops* in the centre on the flatts in column ... "

Dubois observed that the "*Rangers* were on their right, on the bank of the river"

PHASE ONE (MAP ONE)

REBEL DISPOSITIONS:

The Indians (of the *Advance Guard*) in front opened fire.

"That the rear of our *left* was about five hundred yards from the [British] when the front began their firing at about two hundred and fifty yards and the whole kept up a brisk fire towards the enemy."

"Our *left*, not being pressed, fired irregularly, and were beat back, but advanced again and continued firing irregularly."

"*Colo Cuyler's regt* began to fire upon the enemy, and rushed on a few paces, which broke the line or order they were in."

"Our *left* was much disordered, and fired very irregularly and never were in order after the firing commenced."

"I came to *Van Alstyne's regiment* which was broke. I assisted in rallying it, which was partly effected. I then went to *Colonel Cuyler's* and endeavored to assist the officers in rallying that regiment, which was also partly rallied."

"The Enemy [rebel militia] firing and Retreating to some distance under their Fort at [Nellis'?]"

" ... the rear of two regiments in the low grounds, were strung along a hundred and fifty or two hundred yards behind the front, and kept up a warm fire, but the direction of the fire seemed to be up in the air."

General Van Rensselaer ordered "them to cease firing, and advance towards the enemy," whereupon *Cuyler's* men inclined towards the river.

The *left and centre* "in the low ground had commenced a firing at a long shot from the enemy, broke and some ran."

Dubois' *right column* continued its advance through the wooded high ground.

CROWN DISPOSITIONS:

Sir John's *screen and skirmishers* were fired upon by the [rebels'] advance guard and they gave " ... a warm one in return."

Johnson's *right wing* "changed their front, came down the river and engaged our left, and commenced a regular and heavy platoon firing on them."

When the rebels "formed in some force" at Fort [Nellis?], "the *Indians* who were all on horseback were panic-struck and crossed the River."

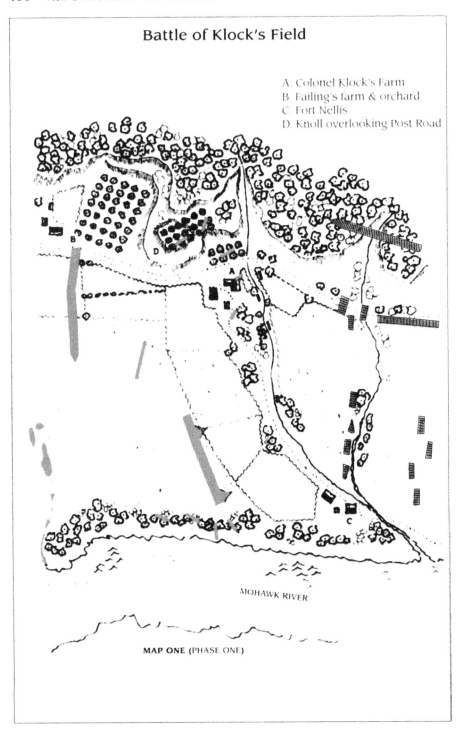

Battle of Klock's Field

A. Colonel Klock's Farm
B. Failing's farm & orchard
C. Fort Nellis
D. Knoll overlooking Post Road

MOHAWK RIVER

MAP ONE (PHASE ONE)

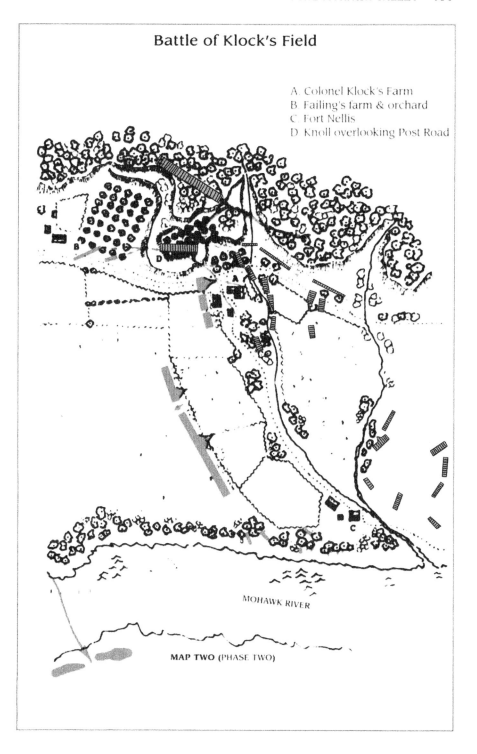

Battle of Klock's Field

A. Colonel Klock's Farm
B. Failing's farm & orchard
C. Fort Nellis
D. Knoll overlooking Post Road

MOHAWK RIVER

MAP TWO (PHASE TWO)

PHASE TWO (MAP TWO)

REBEL DISPOSITIONS:
The *advance guard* of Oneidas and elements of Whiting's militia "file[d] off to the right from the centre and marched very near the right column." *McKinstry* and *Col. Louis' Oneidas* moved forward between Whiting's column on the low lands and Dubois' on the higher ground, they approached Col. Klock's buildings and orchard ... "

" ... five of the *Indians"* continued to advance with the centre.

Hearing the war-halloo of the Mohawks, the Oneidas gave answer.

Advancing into the woods, using the fence lines, the *advance guard* began a crisp fire.

"Part of the *centre column*, filed off to the right and joined Colo. Dubois detachment ...

" "the remainder continued, with five of the Indians, advancing in the *centre* ... "

Whiting's and *Col. Van Rensselaer's regiments* marched forward against the enemy positioned at Klock's farm.

Sir John observed that the enemy "advance[d] upon our left under cover of Woods, houses & fences, and began a heavy fire upon us from all Quarters especially upon our left ... "

Col. Van Rensselaer's companies got into one of Klock's orchards and engaged, but *Whiting's* was prevented from advancing by heavy enemy fire.

After a very heavy firing by the enemy [34th & KRR NY], *Van Rensselaer's* and *Whiting's* regiment had fallen into "the greatest disorder and confusion, and ... the Genl did exert himself to get them in order again."

"Colo. Dubois' detachmt ... attempted to gain the enemy's right flank."

Having got well above Sir John's left flank on the high-ground, *Dubois* detached "two companies" of *Levies & Tryon militia* under Major Van Benschoten and Col. Clyde "to raise the summit of the hill and fire on the enemy in flank ... "

"The detachment [catching the 34th & KRR in enfilade] fired six or seven platoons when the enemy fled." (map shows Levies & militia on high ground behind the left flank of the advanced companies of the 34th & KRR)

Sir John reported the rebels "gave three cheers."

The detached companies of *Levies & Tryon militia* then returned to *Dubois' column.*

CROWN DISPOSITIONS:
McKinstry and the Oneidas approached Col. Klock's buildings and orchard where *Brant's Volunteers* and the *Jaegers* were posted ... As they approached, *Brant's men* gave the war-halloo.

Heavily opposed by fire from the rebel advance guard and centre column, *Brant's men* and the *Jaegers* give ground.

Sir John observed that Brant was pressed and the exposed high ground on his left flank was endangered. He ordered companies of the *34th* and the *KRR NY* forward to take possession of "[Klock's] House, Barn, &c ... "

A rebel officer observed that "the firing on the part of the enemy [34th, KRR NY] was so warm, as to prevent troops under Colo Whiting from advancing."

The *34th* and the *KRR NY* had been slow off the mark and were either unable to seize the cover around Klock's buildings or had relied upon heavy, disciplined firing to force the militia to retire. Sir John reported that his order to take possession of Klock's "had not been attended to in time [and] the enemy [Levies & Tryon militia] took advantage of it and threw in a very heavy fire which forced the *34th* and a *part of my Regiment* to give way ... " (see Map Three for this movement)

What they hadn't counted on was being outflanked to their left rear. When Bunschoten's detachment fired "six or seven platoons," the *34th & KRR NY* "broke.. and ... ran off." (see Map Three)

PHASE THREE (MAP THREE)

REBEL DISPOSITIONS:

Leaving *Clyde's militia companies* on the high ground above Klock's, *Dubois* marched his *Levies* to outflank Sir John's main line and found he "had gained the flank of the [British] main body ... "

Cuyler's regiment had been partly rallied when, "part of another regiment (*Van Alystne's* I think) fire[d] at *Cuyler's* [and] they again broke, and could not be rallied."

Col. Clyde observed from the high ground, "a cross fire upon the right, from the low lands.. from *our own troops.*"

"The troops [*Albany County militia*] were in such confusion that it would be easy for a small party of the enemy to cut them to pieces."

Dubois, realizing he "had got into the [British] rear ... [He] faced the men about, and marched in a line down to the enemy undiscovered [and] gave orders for firing platoons from left to right, when the enemy broke and ran ... [H]e advanced and continued firing upon the enemy till he discovered a firing on the rear of his left. ... it came from some part of our own militia."

In the gathering dusk and smoke, mistaking Dubois' Levies for a body of the enemy, *Whiting's column of Albany County militia* fired upon them.

CROWN DISPOSITIONS:

The companies of the 34th and KRR which had fled from Klock's buildings were reformed into the line.

To stabilize the situation, Sir John "immediately ordered the *three pounder* to be fired with Grape shott which was also followed by a [general] discharge of small arms which totally silenced [the rebels] ... "

PHASE FOUR (NO MAP)

REBEL DISPOSITIONS:

At about dusk, *Dubois*, "had got into the [Sir John's] rear ... and [he] faced his men about, and marched in a line down to the enemy undiscovered [and] gave orders for firing platoons from right to left, when the enemy broke and ran ... "

Dubois "advanced and continued firing upon the enemy till he discovered a firing on the rear of his left."

" ... finding it came from some part of our own militia, *Dubois* halted his men and rode up ... to General Rensselaer on the left of the centre column, where he found the militia had given way."

Dubois advised the *General* "that the right of the centre line were firing on the levies." *Van Rensselaer* stated that " ... the firing should be ordered to cease, least our men should kill each other."

Dubois was ordered by *General Van Rensselaer* to personally ride to the head of the retreating militia and bring them to a halt. As they had retreated so far, he was not able to do so.

Colonel Clyde recollected "that it was so dark as to render it difficult to enter into action with safety ... The enemy could just be discerned and part of them were then heard crossing the river."

CROWN DISPOSITIONS:

Sir John was concerned about it being dark and that his *troops* were "in a good deal of confusion."

While the subaltern officers and NCO's brought about order, the senior officers met in a council of war. Some were for a capitulation, most were not. Johnson ordered a withdrawal.

The *expedition* was organized for a forced night march to the ford at Christie's. The *fieldpiece* was spiked and abandoned with much of the plunder and many of the prisoners.

Some companies, likely of *Butler's Rangers*, crossed the river at 'the deep ford.'

A *rearguard* composed of the *Major's and other companies, KRR NY*, were heavily fired upon by Dubois' Levies and in consequence retired to Christie's ford in some disorder. On reaching the south shore and being unable to locate the expedition in the dark woods, thirteen of the *rear guard* were taken by militiamen. Sir John's servant was amongst these prisoners.

The majority of the expedition was met by *Indians* on the south shore and were led into the woods. A large group of the *8th, Butler's and KRR* became separated in the dark.

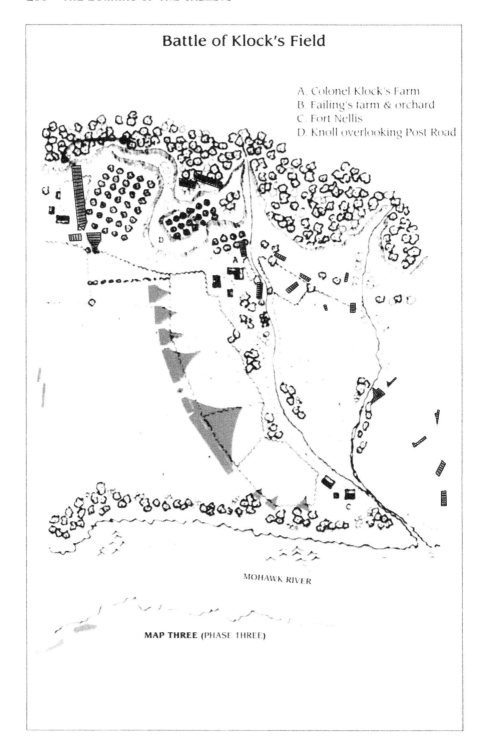

Battle of Klock's Field

A. Colonel Klock's Farm
B. Failing's farm & orchard
C. Fort Nellis
D. Knoll overlooking Post Road

MOHAWK RIVER

MAP THREE (PHASE THREE)

of the force, each with its specialized military skills and many with an intimate knowledge of topography, roads, fortified homes, etc... had to be balanced for maximum effectiveness. As will become abundantly obvious, these skills and knowledge were harnessed most effectively.

While at Schrembling's, Sir John again subdivided his force. Captain Richard Duncan was detached with his own and two other companies of Royal Yorkers and a body of Indians[11] to the north side of the river. The raiders then proceeded westwards destroying everything in their path on both sides of the river as far as Anthony's Nose, a.k.a. the Noses, where headlands on either bank narrowed the roadway and allowed for a ready defence. The fatigued raiders halted there at midnight. They had marched some 24 miles,[12] and while not being opposed in any serious manner, many of the roads were primitive and the men had to be constantly vigilant against retaliation. Although able to forage and plunder the farmsteads, they often had little time to halt, rest and prepare food.

With vindictive pleasure, the officers took the opportunity of the halt to mark their successes by holding a celebration in one Van Vacten's [Van Veghten] house, likely Anthony Van Veghten, the adjutant of the Klock's Second, or Palatine District, Regiment.[13] A report of the affair stated, "... they all Revel'd there that Night, and Crown'd it in the Morning by seting fire to the House."[14]

Many of the men had marched past very familiar scenes, farms where their families, relatives and friends had worked and lived in harmony, in some cases for decades. Not a few had put the torch to buildings that they had known from their youth or had helped to build. In some cases, they must have felt a surge of luxuriant revenge when a detested rebel's holdings were sent up in flames; but, in many instances there would only be a grim sense of satisfaction when their own, a brother's or a friend's property, which had been sequestered by the rebel state, was put to the torch.

Richard Duncan, a resident of Schenectady and a man well acquainted with the area,[15] diligently destroyed the farms which had been missed during the May raid. Many of the distressed inhabitants observed these proceedings while hiding in the woods. His men ignored the stone church in Caughnawaga which had been built under the patronage of Sir William Johnson, although the fact that it constituted an ideal fortification and likely housed a number of rebel militiamen may have had more to do with its salvation.[16] The troops burned a number of pathetic, temporary huts which had been constructed by refugees who had lost their homes in the May raid, yet had found the courage and willpower to work their fields.[17]

★★★

General Van Rensselaer's militia had marched throughout the daylight hours with a few rests and halted at nightfall opposite Fort Johnson.[18] Since leaving Schenectady they had come about 17 hard miles along roads which were in similarly atrocious condition to those experienced by Sir John's men in the northern Schoharie Valley. At this juncture Van Rensselaer held a council to discuss the next phase of the march. It was decided "to refresh the men till moon rise" before attempting to pass Chuctinunda Hill, a notorious landmark, "very bad, miry and deep."[19] The General sent an express rider to the Governor advising of this decision. During the council Van Rensselaer had impressed upon the officers the necessity of obtaining more intelligence and recommended the dispatch of an advance guard to secure the line of march. The latter appears to have been selected from the 8th and 9th Albany County Regiments under the dual command of LtCol. David Pratt, 9th, and Major John McKinstry, 8th.[20] Aid-Major Morris "attended the advanced corps", doubtlessly acting as Van Rensselaer's eyes & ears. Sampson Dykman, a Volunteer of the 8th,[21] recalled that between 10 or 11 PM, just before the moon had fully risen, the General ordered the men to move and within five minutes they were on the road.

As to gaining intelligence, the restless and impatient William Harper, who had been with the General since Schenectady, was sent off as a scout to Fort Hunter to discover the truth of what was happening.[22] William, and his younger brother John, who would also play an active role in the coming events, had removed from their Susquehanna-area land patent of Harpersfield in justifiable fear of loyalist reprisals. Ironically, and defiantly, they had chosen to occupy Colonel Daniel Claus' abandoned home[23] on the north shore of the Mohawk just east of Fort Hunter. This act was quite typical of the brash and aggressive Harpers. Claus, a devout loyalist, was the son-in-law of Sir William Johnson and was in exile in Canada, commanding a group of Tory rangers employed in the collection of intelligence from the Valley. Claus also had under his management his close friends and fellow bitter exiles, the Fort Hunter Mohawks.[24] The Harpers' actions were a clear invitation to be "burned in your beds"!

As William intimately knew the area through which the militia were to advance, he was an excellent choice as a scout. The next morning Harper discovered that the raiders were burning farms a scant two miles below Fort Hunter and he sent an express rider to the General with this news. In the meantime, the militia had negotiated the infamous Chuctinunda Hill, manhandling their two 9 pounder Fieldpieces[25] and ammunition wagon through the mire.

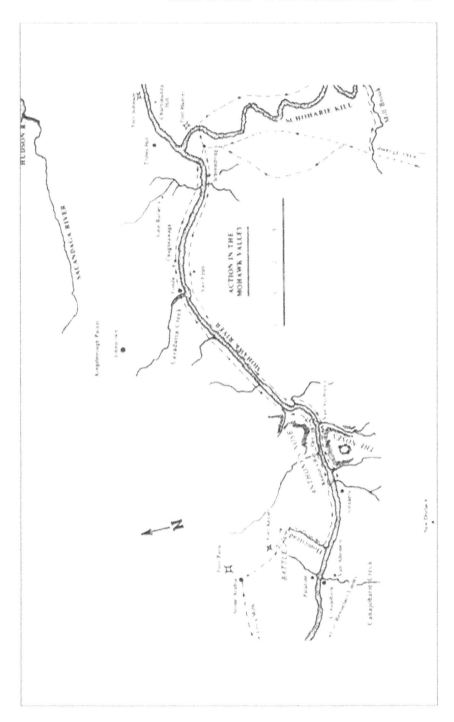

After waiting to gain more intelligence, Harper rode to rejoin Van Rensselaer whom he found halted with the column "at Elliott's at the Old Farms." Harper was requested to obtain even more information and, with Sergeant William Wood and a party of seven men of the 8th Albany,[26] he returned to Fort Hunter. Harper, and one other man, continued on to the Noses where they discovered Sir John's force encamped.

The militia pressed on, arriving at Fort Hunter about midnight. From there to the Noses was only another 11 miles! The General was very clear about his goal, he wanted to close with the Sir John as quickly as possible. The Schoharie Kill had to be crossed and by using a scow and having other men pulled across in relays in the baggage wagons, the procedure was soon underway. Meanwhile, the General with Aid-Major Lansing questioned two enemy prisoners in the fort. Once all the troops were across to the west side, there was a delay while the fieldpieces and ammunition wagon were brought across.[27]

Just before light on October 19, Sir John received an unpleasant shock when he was advised that two men, who had deserted the rebels from the garrison at Fort Stanwix in the Spring and joined the Royal Yorkers, had "left us and went over to the Enemy [in the middle of the night] at Stone Arabia and informed Colonel Brown, who commanded there[,] that the Detachment [Duncan's] on that side of the River was very weak, which induced him [Brown] to march out the next morning with three Hundred and sixty men to attack them."[28] The desertion of the two men, assuming their stories had an influence on Colonel Brown, proved to be quite fortuitous.

John Brown was an experienced, bold and successful commander. As a Continental officer he had been deeply involved in the rebel campaign against Canada in 1775 where he was a primary actor in the capture of Fort Chambly.[29] In 1777, he led a large detachment in a concerted attack on Burgoyne's lines of communication in the Ticonderoga area and achieved a significant victory, seizing the landing, mills and blockhouse at Lake George.[30] A distant relative by marriage of Benedict Arnold,[31] Brown had earned considerable notoriety by openly criticizing that darling of the rebellion.[32] Once Arnold betrayed the American cause, Brown took some understandable pleasure in having "been right".

There are some unanswered questions about Brown's decision to advance against the column. For example, did he believe that he was complying with Van Rensselaer's orders which he had received that very morning? Or, did he instead act on what appeared, according to the two deserters, to be an excellent opportunity to cut off part of Sir John's force and punish it severely? One can be quite sure that the deserters knew the next target would be the grain-bowl of Stone Arabia, as had Burton, the deserter from Butler's Rangers. Obviously, they were counting on earning forgiveness for their earlier desertion by bringing an advance warning.

On the other hand, perhaps Brown reacted to the following message from Colonel Lewis Dubois -

> Fort Ranssalear Oct. 18th 1780
> Night twelve O'clock
> Dr Sir
> I have just received Your Note In answer to which I would inform you that I have Ordered Capt. Wright [White][33] with all the troops belonging to your Regt. over. Have Likewise sent two Expresses to Genl Ransalear. I expect to March the rest of the troops over by break of Day beside Leaving Enough for the Defence of the Garrison. You will Acquaint me with all the Enemies Movement
>
> > and I am Oblige your
> > Humble Sevt
> > By Order of Col. Duboy
> > Jacob Bockee M[ajor]B[rigade]
> > [To] Coll Brown[34]

Did Brown believe his better defence lay in an attack - that he had a good chance of delaying Sir John's column and thus allow Van Rensselaer and DuBois to join together while he pinned the Crown forces down? By taking the offensive, he might spare the community he was mandated to defend. Whatever his reasoning, his plans failed and if the two unidentified deserters survived, they must have been hard pressed to explain the outcome.

There were two forts in Stone Arabia.[35] The larger and better known was Fort Paris, an installation with stone blockhouses and wooden palisade large enough to house a garrison of 200 men.[36] The fort had been named after a local firebrand of the rebellion, Isaac Paris, who had been taken prisoner and subsequently killed at Oriskany in 1777. The other was Fort Keyser, named after the original owner of the house which formed the core of the position.[37] Fort Paris was garrisoned by some 153 Massachusetts State Levies,[38] a detachment of Captain Thomas Lee's Company of Dubois' Regiment of Levies[39] and 22 men of Captain John Casselman's Tryon County Ranger company. It appears that detachments of three companies of the Palatine Regiment, the 3rd, 4th and 5th,[40] which were raised from the communities of Stone Arabia and the hamlet of Palatine itself, were also in the two forts. Fort Keyser was held by a platoon of the 5th Company and some rangers. On the evening of Oct. 18th, Wright's Company and part of Warner's under Lieutenant Norton, both of Brown's regiment, arrived from south of the Mohawk with their companies, totalling 152 all ranks.[41] The garrison at Fort Paris was virtually stripped to provide Brown's force and Ensign George Getman joined with 20 men from Fort Keyser. Brown's column was composed of about 300 Massachusetts men with perhaps 80 militiamen and rangers. When all were assembled, Brown prayed for them, "the tears rolling down his cheeks."[42]

Sir John had wished to combine his whole force on the north bank the evening of the 18th,[43] but he found the men "too much fatigued to attempt it." After setting Van Veghten's house and outbuildings afire, the raiders were on the march before dawn on the 19th and the majority of the southern element forded the Mohawk at sunrise in a thick fog at Keator's Rift not far from Sprakers,[44] a well-known landmark on the south shore of the river.

Somewhere nearby, Lieutenant McKay of Leake's and his scouting party were lying under cover. They had collected the requested intelligence and attempted to arrive at the appointed rendezvous on Oct. 8th as directed, but bad weather had prevented their travel. Instead, they arrived on Oct. 13th, well ahead of Sir John and the column, and they remained in the neighbourhood until the 19th. In the words of McKay's later report, they were —

> ... without hearing any tidings of [Sir John]. On that day they were discovered by three Oneidas one of whom they wounded but he escaped into the Fort of Conadeary [Canajoharie?] where there were twenty two more of that Nation & [rebel] Mohawks. The Scout then came off after having burnt seven houses and a considerable quantity of grain & a Potashery.[45]

How odd! McKay and his men must have just missed meeting with Sir John. They set out over the uninhabited lands to the north to follow Indian trails to Carleton Island.

The main column continued westwards, some of the Indians and light troops paralleling the advance on the south bank where they remained to burn any farms that had hitherto escaped on that side. Several horseman on the high ground were observed to be shadowing the column. They soon rode off towards Stone Arabia and the column turned northwards (likely the small, south-bank element crossed to the north at this time) following the path taken by the horsemen up the deep ravine through which Homestead Creek flowed.[46]

As the trail was very narrow, the men must have advanced in one very long Indian file with flanking parties. Sir John advises that the leading companies were considerably in advance of the main body of troops. The column's frontal screen was composed of some 50 men of Brant's who soon collided with Brown's advance guard of Massachusetts men led by Major Oliver Root.[47] The Volunteers quickly drove these men back onto Brown's main body. At the sound of firing, the companies in Sir John's van pushed forward and "gained the heights of Stone Arabia", where they came against Brown's main body. Sir John, who was with the van, supported the screen of Indians with "part of" the 8th and 34th (likely their Light Coys) and McDonell's (Aberchalder) Company of Butler's. Sir John was able to deploy about 160 men against 170 of Brown's leading units — a very even match.

When his vanguard was contacted by Brant's men, Brown's main body had taken position in a woods behind a stone fence which bordered the roadway.[48] It was not an ideal defensive position as it lay in a hollow. The far side of the road was also lined by a stone fence with open fields beyond it. Following Brant's men, Johnson and his leading companies advanced through these open fields and, upon coming up with the fence, a brisk skirmish commenced in which Colonel Brown, who was prominent atop his black horse, was killed. His death occurred on the exact date of his thirty sixth birthday.[49] Command of the rebels devolved upon Major Root.

Sir John observed that Brant's men were working around the rebel's right flank and sending McDonell to turn the left, the Baronet decisively led the 8th and 34th, leapt over the fencing and drove the rebels out of the woods. They fell back in disorder. The Massachusetts company of Captain Levi Ely received the brunt of the charge, Ely being killed with 15 of his men and five Oneida warriors[50] who had been serving as guides. Veterans of the company recalled that some 26 of the 40 men who had marched from Fort Paris fell in the engagement.[51] Most rebel accounts conclude that Brown's small force of 380 was overwhelmed by Sir John's army of 900. That Sir John only deployed the three companies of troops, some 120 all ranks, and 50 of Brant's Volunteers, that were in his van is simply ignored. It was not numbers that won, it was nerve, skill and decisive leadership.

The routed rebels either fled towards the Stone Arabia forts or took to the woods heading south towards the Mohawk River. Both groups were pursued and some were run down and killed. Six of the fugitives took shelter behind one of those strange, very large, random boulders[52] that often appear around the country. They made a stance there and fired several shots at their pursuers, but were soon out-flanked and "all cut off."[53] A few individuals who were on the way from their farms as reinforcements were driven off by the Indians.

Samuel Woolworth, one of Captain Ely's men, took to his heels. He had loaded and fired his musket repeatedly and, in his anxiety, had seen the pan flash, but had not recognized that the main charge had failed to ignite. Pursued by three Indians, Woolworth turned and fired again and then found himself sprawling on the ground with his musket lying several feet away. He reached for his firelock and saw he had wounded one of his pursuers who was supported by his fellows. He again took flight and was chased by other Indians with whom he exchanged fire, loading on the run. The fleet Woolworth was able to outstrip his foe and gain the protection of Fort Paris.[54]

Sir John claimed that about "one hundred Officers and men were slain" including Colonel Brown.[55] This was an exaggeration. The rebels, who had the task of collecting and burying the dead, reported a loss of 40 men amongst the Levies, militia and Oneidas. Johnson report particularly praised Captains McDonell and Brant for their exertion and leadership in this action. As to his own losses, he reported that Brant had received a flesh wound in his foot and a private of the 8th and three Indians were killed and three Rangers were wounded. Lieutenant McGinnes of the Indian Department was grievously wounded in the leg.

Papers found in Colonel Brown's pocket[56] included the message from Dubois and a letter from which Sir John "learnt that General Ranslaer with six Hundred Militia and three field pieces was at Fort Hunter the day before and of course then could not be very distant." Had Johnson retained any thoughts of attempting a junction with Munro, he could easily march to Johnstown from Stone Arabia and gamble that he would meet with the Captain's messengers. Those men could be sent to Munro with word of his arrival and an instruction to advance against Schenectady; however, the finding of the papers which offered intelligence of Van Rensselaer's proximity and numbers would have dissuaded him. He pushed his troops forward to destroy the settlement of Stone Arabia.

Major Root and many of the men from the battlefield had managed to gain refuge in Fort Paris. A 4 pounder cannon was fired at Johnson's men to dissuade them from any thoughts of attack. The first round was the fort's only solid shot. A second discharge was made up of horse chains and they whipped through the air on their way at the enemy. Root had some men break up a huge iron kettle and the pieces consti-tuted the third firing. The chunks howled and screamed through the air and the Indians who had been annoying the defenders thought better of it and pulled away. Root's efforts produced the desired result and the attackers left the fort alone to concentrate on the farms. Unknown to the raiders, there had been no more powder for the cannon and only small arms would have been employed against an assault.[57]

The settlement was relatively concentrated and soon all of the farms, dwellings and its two churches, one Lutheran the other Dutch Reformed, were in flames. Years later an old man was to recall as a boy peeking out of an upper window of Fort Keyser and seeing the flames of some neighbours' houses and at a distance a file of redcoats[58] passing to the west. A handful of militiamen stood to the loopholes on the first floor of the building, their hats filled with cartridges lying beside them, but no attempt was made on Fort Keyser and the tiny garrison soon heard the sound of a bugle nearby followed by a number of "tin horns." Sir John was assembling his forces. He had decided upon his route — a withdrawal to his boats at Lake Onondaga.

★★★

Van Rensselaer had reached Gardinier's Flatts, some 4 1/2 miles west of Fort Hunter when he was met by William Harper with intelligence of Sir John's column. The march continued and the General arrived with his dog-tired militia at Van Epp's where they halted. This was about 6 1/2 miles east of the Noses on the south bank opposite the settlement of Caughnawaga. They had marched with only a few stops for all of the day and night of the 18th and it was then near daybreak at 4 AM of the 19th.[59] They halted here for about an hour while the General was attended by Lieutenant William Wallace,[60] a Fonda resident then serving in Captain Demuth's Company of Dubois' Levies. Lansing recalled that Wallace brought intelligence of Johnson's men and some details of their camps at the Noses. The General had Lansing, write two dispatches. One was to an officer of considerable experience, Colonel Lewis Dubois, former commander of the 5th New York Continental Regiment. He was presently commanding at Fort Rensselaer, (formerly Fort Plain.) His, Colonel Malcom's and Colonel Harper's regiments of New York State Levies, were garrisoning various posts in the Valley.[61] This letter read:

> Van Eps, Caghnawago, 19th Octo. 1780.
> Sir: We are here, with a force sufficient to cope with the enemy, but if you can possibly cooperate with us, it will in all probability tend to insure us success. General Rensselaer commands here, therefore advises you to march down along the south side of the river, with all the men you have, with as much expedition as possible.

> He intends to attack the enemy as soon as day appears.
> It depends on your exertions to favor this enterprize.
> I am Sir, yours, J. Lansing, Junr.[62]

While the second dispatch to Brown at Stone Arabia has not survived, it was very likely similar in its wording. Lansing later stated that the letters were "advising them of his [Van Rensselaer's] situation and his intentions to pursue the enemy closely, and to attack them at break of day."[63] Lieutenant William Wallace rode "express" to Colonel Dubois and Serjeant Richard Young, Van Rensselaer's waiter, to Colonel Brown."[64]

In view of his nearness to Johnson's encampment at the Noses, an obvious question arises. What prompted Van Rensselaer not to drive his troops forward to fall on Johnson's column before the Baronet got it underway? He might have pinned the force there and held them while Brown closed from the north and Dubois from the west. Indeed, Mohawk Valley residents believed the General's closing with Sir John's army was slow and irresolute. They believed that Brown and his men had been sacrificed, that too many opportunities had been missed while the Crown forces were free to kill and burn. So infuriated were many of the region's officers that Governor Clinton felt compelled to hold hearings the next year to investigate.

All of this aside, an obvious answer was that Van Rensselaer's militiamen were worn out. They had not even had time to cook the fresh beef they had drawn at Schenectady some twenty hours before. Fatigued though Johnson's men must have been, their condition had to have been better than the militiamen who had little sleep and perhaps only chunks of bread snatched from their haversacks. The General was concerned about an insufficiency of troops as neither Dubois nor Brown had yet joined with him. He could have gambled that his messages had got through to both those officers and that they would march to meet him; but, that was quite a gamble. Although never stated by any of the original actors, the General must have been worried about his preponderance of militia versus Sir John's British and Provincial regulars and rangers,[65] let alone the vaunted and feared warriors of the Six Nations and their allies. He must have reasoned that once Dubois and Brown joined with their New York and Massachusetts Levies, these longer-term, quasi-regulars would offer some stiffening to his brigade. Anthony's Nose was a notorious, "very dangerous defile",[66] which was precisely why Johnson had chosen it as a camp site, and Van Rensselaer was not about to stick his hand into that hornet's nest.

In addition to Harper's intelligence and the questioning of the two prisoners at Fort Hunter, Van Rensselaer may have had the benefit of information sent to Governor Clinton from LtCol. Barent Staats at the Lower Fort. Staats advised that two Prisoners from Sir John's army" had been brought in and they told that at "Eight O'Clock this morning, Johnson, Butler and Brant, movd with their army from Sidnyes sawmill down the Mohawk Road to the said River, where they where to joyne the Party of the enemy from the Norward [Munro], of which their strenght by the acco'nt of the Prisoners, is one thousand men, of which where 2 hundred Indians; the Rest Rigular Troops and Torys; another Party of 150 where gone to Katskill [did the prisoners mean Thompson & Brant whom they had seen detached, but they knew not where to?]; the Posts at this Place are safe.[67]

If he did receive this news from the Governor by express from Albany, he must have been jolted to hear of a potential reinforcement from the northward.

Dawn was breaking as Lieutenant Wallace rode off with Van Rensselaer's letters and the militia were put onto "the very bad roads" continuing their march while complaining of their fatigue. After another 4 miles, they halted at the ruins of Peter Lewis' farm for about 10 minutes while a prisoner brought in by the advance guard was examined.[68] The march then resumed for another three miles to a field on Putnam's Lands just short of the Noses and was halted. William Harper met with the General and urged him to march the troops to close with Sir John, but Van Rensselaer pointed out that their ammunition required checking. Aid-Major Lansing recalled that this inspection soon followed and additional quantities, likely that forwarded by Colonel Malcom, were distributed from the ammunition wagons.

The militia had been joined on the road by 50 Oneida warriors under the Kahnawake, LtCol. Louis Atayataghronghta, (Colonel Louis)[69] who was the highest ranking native in the rebel service. While the ammunition inspection and distribution was underway, Colonel Louis was sent off to scout the Noses, using his native skills to determine if an ambush was in place. He soon returned with the information that Johnson's force had decamped and the way was clear. The cartridge issues were completed after the delay of an hour and the militia again marched.[70]

The rebel advanced corps under LtCol. Pratt, augmented by a fieldpiece under Lieutenant Joseph Driskill,[71] had been held just east of the Noses and once Colonel Louis pronounced the defile clear of the enemy, it pushed forward. At the property of "lame Cornelius Van Alstyne", the advance discovered a party of 40 of Sir John's men on the north side "bending their course towards the river." Aid-Major Morris was ordered to take the news of this discovery to Van Rensselaer, who was riding at the head of the main body only 1/4 mile to the rear.

After hearing and considering this message, the General sent Aid-Major Lansing forward with orders for LtCol. Pratt "to make proper dispositions to intercept the enemy, should they cross a ford, which it was said was in our front."

Lieutenant Driskill, observing Sir John's men so close to hand, requested of Lansing, that when he returned to Van Rensselaer, he would, "beg the general to [allow the gun to] give the enemy's party a shot or two"; however, Van Rensselaer reckoned that the small Crown detachment was moving to join his advance corps in the belief that they were friends. He declined Driskill's request, observing to Lansing that such a response would only warn the main party of the raiders that the pursuit was upon them in force.[72] Although there is some suggestion that Sir John had left this detachment as a rearguard to dispute the ford, no firing seems to have occurred and Morris recalled that the company, which was beyond musket range, soon disappeared from view when they saw the artillery taking up position.

Harper recollected that the advance party waited an hour before the main party of the militia column joined them at Cornelius Van Alstyne's. The post road through the Noses had been particularly difficult for the passage of the second fieldpiece and the ammunition wagon. The horses, which had already been "frequently halted on account of the badness of the roads", caused further delays by "being very much fatigued."[73] One can imagine the flogging the animals were suffering.

If indeed there was a ford to which the Crown detachment had been marching, it is difficult to understand why Van Rensselaer did not utilize it to cross his brigade, as he was only a few more miles into the march before he sought information about suitable fords from William Harper. Of course, all officers mull over their options and often develop quite conflicting thoughts while doing so. Perhaps the ford, to which Sir John's men appear to have been moving, did not exist, or, like some others, it was examined and found unsuitable.

Harper stated that the march resumed for another hour, the column halting at another Van Alstyne's property "opposite Major Fry's [John Frey's?]"[74] at about 9 AM when firing was heard to the north.[75] Aid-Major Morris believed that Van Rensselaer wished to cross at this place, but "found it impossible." Spurred by the sounds of musketry, the advance corps was sent on with dispatch. The Aid-Major noted that the two fieldpieces and ammunition wagon marched with the main party and the baggage wagons were in the rear.

Van Rensselaer sent a dispatch to Governor Clinton at this time. The letter was headed, "Canajoharie opposite Frey's 11 A.M."

> Sir, This Morning about nine I arrived so near the Enemy's Rear as to afford me a prospect of engaging

them before Noon. They have, however, by the Celerity of their Movements affected their Escape to Stone Arabia, part of which is now in Flames & the whole will probably share the same Fate, before I can possibly support the distressed Inhabitants. I intend to ford the River immediately and march in quest of them, but harrassed and fatigued as my Force is by a long March, I am apprehensive I shall not be able to pursue them with that Dispatch which is necessary to overtake them. No Exertion, however, shall be wanting on my part to effect it.[76]

His letter continued with some interesting intelligence which offers a further explanation for the hesitation being exhibited in the pursuit of Sir John's expedition.

Two prisoners who were brought in at Fort Hunter informed Mr. Cuyler that Sir John intended to return by the way of Crown Point; that he had left his Boats in the Onondaga Lake but had since altered his intended Rout[e] to Crown Point by the way of Stone Arabia... Dubois will join me at Walradth's [Walrath] about a Mile above this. I am this Moment informed that Colonel Brown who with a party opposed the Enemy was defeated. His Loss is not ascertained. The Enemy are it is said between 600 & 1000 strong.[77]

Soon after the main column got underway, Volunteer Sampson Dykman was sent forward to Van Rensselaer on behalf of a Major Schuyler[78] and other field officers of the militia to advise that if the troops were continued at such a pace they "would not be fit for action." The General answered with the obvious, "... the enemy were ahead destroying the country, and the men must be marched fast at all events, to come up with them." As predicted, a number of the militiamen soon fell out from fatigue and were loaded onto the baggage wagons and others were mounted on horses.

William Harper was now consulted by the General regarding a suitable ford so the militia could cross to the north side. Harper suggested a location at Major Yates'[79] which was tried and found impractical. The march continued to Adam Countryman's about one mile below Fort Rensselaer where another party was sent forward to reconnoitre while the hungry troops were given leave to prepare a meal. Alarmingly, tall billowing spires of smoke were seen rising above the high ground to the north.[80]

Upriver at Fort Rensselaer, Colonel Dubois had been extremely busy that morning. As requested by Brown, he had dispatched all the Massachusetts Levies from south of the river and a detachment from one of his own companies to Stone Arabia. He had assembled those companies of his and Malcom's regiment that were at hand, leaving small garrisons at the fort and other local posts within his responsibilty. He had ordered the local militia battalion's acting commander, LtCol. Samuel Clyde, to muster his Canajoharie District Regiment and this had been done. Clyde similarly must have left small detachments for local defence at the many fortified houses within his precinct. Colonel John Harper, a Tryon county man who spoke Iroquoian dialects,[81] was at this time at Fort Rensselaer, perhaps returning to duty, supposedly from a bout of illness,[82] and he volunteered to serve under Dubois in the "direction" of a party of rebel Indians. At about 10 AM, the three field officers and their men marched a quarter mile downriver to Walrath's (Wolrod's) Ferry on the south bank of the river near the hamlet of Fort Plain where they heard an ominous heavy firing towards the north.

Dubois decided to send his Levies and Harper's Indians over to the north bank. Two small ferries operated at this crossing and the process was just underway when 1st Lieutenant Samuel Van Etten[83] of the Palatine militia and some other refugees from the Stone Arabia battle arrived, closely pursued by Indians, who gave up the chase when they saw Dubois' troops. The fugitives met with Harper and told him of the defeat of Brown's men. Harper informed Dubois of the tragedy. Advice had just arrived that Van Rensselaer's column was a mile below and Dubois gave orders to those troops which were on the north bank to recross to the south. He requested that Colonel Harper ride to the General with the alarming news of Brown's failure.[84]

Harper rode "express" to Van Rensselaer with this intelligence. When asked about local fords, he informed the General that there was one at hand, "about knee deep", and he urged Van Rensselaer to immediately cross the river and march to meet the enemy. The General demurred stating that he "did not know the enemy's numbers, nor the route they intended to take," whereupon Harper made some sarcastic observations. The General then stated that he would "go to Colo. Dubois and advise with him";[85] however, he was saved the travel as Dubois rode up to confirm the destruction of Brown's forces.

Out of the hearing of Colonel Harper,[86] Van Rensselaer asked Dubois' opinion about the best place to meet Sir John's force. Exactly what was suggested by Dubois has not been found; however, he did confirm the location of the nearby ford, pointing out that it would be a far more expedient place to cross than using the two small ferry boats upriver at Walrath's. The General decided that the militia would cross after completing their meal and ordered Brigade Major LeRoy and Aid-

Major Morris to see that this was accomplished "with all possible dispatch." He then ordered Lieutenant Driskill to move the artillery up-river to Fort Rensselaer,[87] as it must have been determined that the ford's bottom would not admit the crossing of this heavy equipment.

Dubois courteously enquired if the General had eaten dinner to which Van Rensselaer replied in the negative. So, at the Colonel's suggestion, he, the General and Aid-Major Lansing rode to the fort to "take dinner." Dubois forwarded orders to his Levies and the Canajoharie militia at the ferries to cross to the north bank and remain there awaiting the arrival of the militia from below. They began this immediately and by 1:00 PM were on the far shore.[88]

At Countryman's the weary militia spent about an hour preparing their meal and, when finished, peremptorily refused to ford the river.[89] Some attempt was made to cross them in wagons, but it was found the time taken to travel back and forth was excessive. Aid-Major Lansing had returned from the fort with orders from the General to expedite the crossing. He found the militia were proceeding across "very tardily, complaining of being too much harrassed by a forced march and many appeared much dispirited on account of Brown's defeat which was generally known among them."

Lansing then suggested to the field officers the idea of building a crude bridge by driving the baggage wagons into the river, end to end, so that the militia could climb their way across on the beds and tongues. The officers readily agreed, but again trouble was experienced. Lansing recalled that "the orders given for the execution of this service, were executed with such reluctance, that at least two hours elapsed before the militia had crossed." During this time, two further messages were sent by Van Rensselaer urging the men on and the Aid-Major conveyed these to the officers commanding the various regiments. Again, "an attempt was made to induce them to ford the river, but proved unavailing."

After a dinner, which must have been filled with anxious discussion, the General ordered Lieutenant Driskill to "leave his men in Fort Rensselaer, to work the artillery in case the enemy should attack it."[90] After ordering some local militia who remained in the fort to march to the ferry, the General and Dubois set off for there. Upon arrival, they discovered that the Albany militia column from downriver was still not in sight and express riders were sent off with messages, as has been noted from Aid-Major Lansing's recollections.

Van Rensselaer observed that some of the local militia had still not crossed and he ordered them to do so immediately. As at least 2 1/2 hours had elapsed since the Levies, Clyde's militia and the Indian party had crossed, Colonel Harper was very impatient of the delay. Observing Van Rennselaer at the water's edge, he hailed across the river, "for God's sake... cross." One suspects that General Van Rensselaer had experienced quite enough from the testy Colonel Harper. The imprudence of advancing against a strong enemy without the main body of his troops having joined was obvious, at least to him. He made no reply. It is suggested by some historians that other officers spoke disapprovingly to the General of the sluggish militia column. This is quite believable, and one can be sure that no one was more concerned than Robert Van Rensselaer.

As soon as the lagging militia were across, he and Dubois followed. While this was underway they could hear firing near at hand and concluded that "the enemy were coming down out the woods towards the river, at or near Fox's Mills."

A momentary digression - while Johnson's combination with Captain John Munro had been foiled by the earlier delays incurred at Oswego, the efforts of both Carleton in the Hudson Valley and Munro at Ballstown had severe consequences for the rebel command as the inhabitants in those areas continued to be seriously alarmed and saw Tories and Indians behind every tree. The New York leadership had grave doubts about their opposite numbers in the Grants (Vermont), as of course, they had every reason to. This distrust was particularly encouraged by the fact that Carleton's force had passed by the Grants' settlements in his travel up South Bay for the strike against Fort Ann. The New York leaders were incredulous that the Vermonters had failed to report the raiders' presence. Clinton and his associates were unaware that the Vermonters turned out their troops in substantial numbers in reaction to Carleton's passing, General Ethan Allen assembling units at Castleton and even requesting aid from Berkshire County, Massachusetts. Haldimand's aim of overawing Vermont had been achieved.

Long after Carleton had retired north to Crown Point, Major General Schuyler reported the appearance of a British party near White Creek east of Fort Edward. While Major Carleton had been ordered to remain on Lake Champlain after his burning of Forts Ann and George, it is doubtful that he had sent a probe as deep as White Creek. Schuyler's alarm simply illustrates how Carleton's presence and his cruising about on the Lake formed the catalyst for many bogus sightings. On the same day as Stone Arabia was being burned and Van Rensselaer was pursuing Sir John, Governor Clinton wrote Schuyler from Albany advising that Sir John's column had yesterday destroyed Schoharie and he was therefore obliged to "divide the small Force that could be raised immediately from the lower Parts of this County to oppose the Enemy at Balls Town and Schohary." Nonetheless, to assuage concerns to the northeast, he detached Colonel Stephen Schuyler's 6th regiment of Albany County militia to reinforce the troops in and about Saratoga. He also promised General Schuyler that Brigadier General Ten Broeck would dispatch further units of militia from Albany when they were assembled. Haldimand's plan to confuse and distress the rebels on many fronts with his multi-pronged thrusts was clearly working well, as was his unpopular order to Carleton which kept the Major's force on Lake Champlain in terrible weather.[91]

★★★

When at Stone Arabia, Johnson's men had been about 2 1/2 miles north of the river and as they moved westwards they followed the slowly descending heights to the Caroga Creek bed. The column's descent met the creek near Fox's Mills where Philip Fox had his house fortified. It was "shunned, but [the raiders] burnt everything else about it" including the mills.[92] They were then slightly north of the Mohawk and by turning south, they followed the creek to the river. There was some firing from Fox's, and perhaps skirmishing against small parties, which was heard by the rebel troops at Walrath's Ferry. Coming to the Mohawk, the raiders turned westwards and resumed their destruction. They bypassed the Palatine Church, which legend maintains was saved from being burned by Indians through the intervention of Lieutenant Hendrick Nelles of the Indian Department. His family had a strong connection with the building and parish. Sir John reported, "we burned everything else... all the way up to George Klock's near the Fort Hendrick Ford, there again we were obliged to take to "the Woods to avoid three or four fortified houses [Forts Hess, Klock & Nellis[93]] that entirely commanded the Roads & flatts."[94] A party of Indians hung back to attack Fort Hess; however, they enjoyed no success and one of them was wounded and had to be carried off by his fellows.[95] The warriors then moved on to Fort Klock and spent some time firing at the building. The widow Haner was standing at an upper window "when a bullet, nearly spent, struck her head, and she sat down stunned but not seriously hurt." Leonard Crouse, John Klock's grandson, "shot a British soldier and went out from Fort Klock to take the soldier's horse and baggage." No more harm was done and the party moved on.[96]

★★★

Once the Albany militia had formed up on the north shore, they marched off with dispatch,[97] but it was almost 4:00 PM before they arrived at the ferry where the impatient, and likely thoroughly disgusted, Levies, Indians and Canajoharie companies "remained paraded."[98]

There was no further delay.[99] Van Rensselaer, who took command of the whole,[100] consulted with Dubois on the method of approaching Johnson's force and dispositions were quickly effected.

The whole was divided into three columns, likely to facilitate rapid movement forward while covering a broad frontage and to allow a response against Sir John's troops by three forward units rather than just one. Governor Clinton later reported that Van Rensselaer's 400-500 Albany militia had been joined by 300-400 Levies under Dubois and some 60 Oneidas. He neglected to include the Tryon County militia of whom he said, "not much could be expected from the militia of the Country, through which the Enemy passed, their whole attention being engaged in the preservation of their Families... "[101] This judgment was quite unfair as Colonel Clyde's men, who were joined by elements from other Tryon battalions, Casselman's Ranger Company and Gray's Company of Boatmen, the latter two coming down from Stone Arabia,[102] were to perform some very good work in the coming action, for which they received little recognition. The Tryon men must have contributed another 200-300 firelocks. Van Rensselaer therefore deployed between 900-1200 men. The following is a table of how the three columns were possibly constituted.[103]

LEFT COLUMN	CENTRE COLUMN	RIGHT COLUMN
OC Col Abraham Cuyler	OC Col William Whiting	OC Col Lewis Dubois
elements of —	elements of —	elements of —
Cuyler's 1st Albany	Whiting's 17th Albany	Dubois' NY Regt of Levies
Van Alstyne's 7th Albany	Van Rensselaer's 8th	Malcom's NY Regt of
Schuyler's 3rd Albany	Albany	Levies
Wemple's 2nd Albany	Van Ness' 9th Albany	1st, 2nd & 3rd Tryon
		Militia
		LtCol Clyde; LtCol Veeder

The Albany County militia were divided into two columns. Militia Colonel Abraham Cuyler, of the County's 1st Regiment commanded the left column[104] which was to advance on the low lands along the river's edge. Colonel William Whiting, the officer commanding Albany County's 17th Regiment took the centre. His column would have marched along, or close to, the post road. General Van Rensselaer and his two aid-majors rode at the head of the centre. The advance corps under Major McKinstry and Colonel Louis' Oneidas were in front of the two militia columns, although Aid-Major Morris noted that the Indians "sometimes changed their situation,"[105] presumably as the ground dictated. John Harper's small party of Indians were directly ahead of the centre column.

Dubois' Levies, Clyde's Canajoharie, and likely Veeder's Mohawk militia,[106] composed the right flank column and operated in the wooded hills above the post road. As the columns moved off, Aid-Major Lansing estimated the raiders were about two miles ahead as he could see the smoke of burning buildings rising above the western horizon.[107]

Sometime later, the General asked Lansing to write a letter to Governor Clinton, who was coming upriver with reinforcements. While Lansing stopped to write, he noted that "the disposition of the troops was made for an attack." The letter to Clinton follows:

> Sir: The enemy are by the best intelligence I can col-
> lect and from their burnings about a mile in advance
> of my brigade. I have about 900 men including about
> 50 (?) Indians. I shall pursue with as much dispatch as
> is consistent with the safety to the troops under my
> command. I am, your excellency's obedient servant.
> A deserter who arrived this afternoon advises that the
> enemy's force does not exceed 500 men.
> Mohawk River about 2 miles above Fort Rensselaer,
> north side of the river one half after five P.M.[108]

Perhaps the alterations to the dispositions noticed by Lansing were those recalled by Aid-Major Morris who noted that "the centre and left columns were then subdivided, and continued on their march." In Dubois' words, "it was found inconvenient to march in columns and they were ordered to subdivide into sections and so marched on till they came in sight of the enemy."

Having sent off the message, Lansing rejoined the General who was observing that the left column "were marching on without observing any order." He was dispatched to "order them to march more compactly." Lansing rode to "Col Cuyler and some other officers" giving them the General's order.

Meanwhile, to the front of the centre, one of John Harper's Oneidas came to inform the Colonel that "the enemy were near at hand, and that [their] force were about four hundred white men, and but few Indians." Harper immediately rode back to Van Rensselaer "at the head of the centre column" with this intelligence. Morris then rode forward to observe and saw, "[Sir John's troops] drawn up in order." He returned with this news and was dispatched by the General to spread the word to the right, and Lansing was sent to the left.

Receiving no new orders from the General, John Harper returned to his charges. They had advanced about one half mile when they "fell in... and began to skirmish with the enemy's rear guard, who were then retreating up the river. Harper's Oneidas may have bumped into the Crown Indians who had diverted from the main column to annoy Forts Hess and Klock. The testimony continued noting "that part [ie.

the advance corps] of the centre column also fell in with that party of the enemy." Aid-Major Morris recalled that "the firing on the enemy from the advance party of the centre then commenced about two hundred yards distance. That about the same time, Colo Cuyler's Regiment of the left column began to fire on the enemy at about four hundred yards distance." Morris was then sent by Van Rensselaer to the left to "order them to cease firing, and advance towards the enemy," but he recalled "it was a considerable time before [he] could effect it" and after delivering the order he saw that Cuyler's men inclined towards the river.

Morris must have crossed Lansing's path as he rode back to his station with Van Rensselaer. Arriving at the centre, Lansing could not see the General and observing a number of men ahead, rode directly towards them. On getting closer, he discovered they were Indians. He spoke to one man, asking him if he had seen the General. He was misunderstood and as he attempted to explain, the Indians in front opened fire. Lansing reported that they "received a warm one in return." Startled, Lansing's mount faltered and fell with him.

Sir John reported that the day had worn on to "near sunset when we found ourselves opposed in going down [in column from the wooded hills] to the High Road by the [rebels] Enemy from behind fences, houses and Orchards." Dominating the post road on Johnson's left was a height of land on which Colonel Klock had one of his orchards[109] and "I immediately ordered a strong Detachment to a h[e]ight upon our left which Commanded the Road." The rest of the column "pushed down the hill, crossed the Road and formed in the open Field."[110]

Once the action was joined, the participants' memories of the sequence of key occurrences seem somewhat confusing and contradictory. This is typical of all battles. Each man's memory is constricted by his personal view and experiences. There is no question that certain significant phases took place, but to piece them together into a clear chronology is difficult. This is particularly the case when attempting to blend Johnson's after-action report with the recollections of the rebel officers recorded at General Robert Van Rensselaer's hearings.

In counterpoint to Sir John's statement immediately above, William Harper recollected that, "About sunset or after, the [Sir John's army] came down out of the woods to Philan's [Failing's[111]] orchard, when a skirmishing began between our left and the enemy in the lowlands." At the time of this observation, Harper was likely with Van Rensselaer's suite in Whiting's centre column. His recollection possibly meant to convey that the raiders came down from the wooded high ground and debouched through Failing's orchard into the low grounds where they began to engage Cuyler's column.

From Dubois' vantage point, where his right hand column was advancing on the height above the post road, he observed the forming-up of Sir John's force and he rode down to advise Van Rensselaer who, being on lower ground, perhaps had not been able to see this for himself. Finding the General with Whiting's centre column, he informed him that Johnson's "rangers were on their right, on the bank of the river, the regular troops[112] in the centre on the flatts in column, and the Indians and Jaegers[113] on the left, about 150 yards advanced of the other troops in an orchard near Klock's house.[114]

In the act of "pushing" their way down the hill, Sir John's troops reacted against the advancing militia. John Harper observed that the leading elements of Johnson's line troops, "changed their front, came down the river and engaged our left, and commenced a regular and heavy platoon firing on them: But that our left, not being pressed, fired irregularly, and were beat back, but advanced again and continued firing irregularly."

Again, Sir John's specific dispositions are unknown. Assuming that he had the expectation that the rebels were close at hand and about to make contact, he would have followed accepted practice and placed his flank companies at the head and rear of his column so that he could face (or wheel) to the left and form a line of battle. This would have presented a balanced front, his "hat" companies in the centre of the line and his flank companies protecting the left and right. His line would have been divided into a right and left wing. His deputy, Captain Thomas Scott, 53rd Regt, may have commanded the right and Major James Gray, KRR NY, the left. From a later occurrence in the battle, it appears that the British and loyalist companies were interspersed. This "changing of front, marching and engaging" witnessed by John Harper was perhaps Sir John's right wing advancing to meet the left and centre militia columns. The "platoon firing" in a "regular", or sustained system of firing by Sir John's men that was mentioned by Harper was a tactic for which British-trained infantry were justly famous. (Dubois' column would employ this same tactic with effect later in the battle) The firing could be accomplished by having the companies of the wing fire in a sequence, either from left to right, or the reverse, or alternating left side to right.[115] When Sir John's right wing was advanced in this manner, its right flank would have been well protected by the Rangers in the woods along the river bank where topography and Ranger skill and grit would anchor that flank. Johnson, or either of his wing commanders, could have protected the advanced, and exposed, left by pushing forward one of their flank companies as skirmishers.

Unfortunately, when specific details are unknown the possibilities are legion. Another equally plausible explanation for Harper's observation is that as the column's leading companies of line troops "pushed" down the hill through Failing's orchard, they were deployed to the left to confront the advancing rebel militia. While the Rangers passed to the rear of them to seize the woods along the river, the balance of the line companies may then have formed in the field behind the cover of their fellows who were engaging the rebels.

★★★

As noted, John Harper, from his position in the lead of the centre column, observed that the left fired irregularly, were beat back, but "advanced again and continued firing irregularly." Other officers' recollections indicate that the left's response was considerably more complicated. Garrett W. Van Schaick, a subaltern in Captain Jacob Roseboom's Company of the 1st Albany[116] recalled, "when Colo Cuyler's Regiment, and the other troops were advancing towards the enemy then yet out of the reach of musket shot, Colo Cuyler's regt began to fire upon the enemy, and rushed on a few paces, which broke the line or order they were in. That soon after, they were in great disorder and confusion and [I] saw Genl Rensselaer with them, endeavoring to form them. That the Genl exerted himself greatly on this occasion, but his efforts were fruitless."[117] William Harper recalled, "That our left was much disordered, and fired very irregularly and never were in order after the firing commenced." He continued, "That the rear of our left was about five hundred yards from the enemy when the front began their firing at about two hundred and fifty and the whole kept up a brisk fire towards the enemy. That he saw several officers (and particularly Adj[utan]t [Henry[118]] Van Veghten of Colo Cuyler's [1st] [R]egiment) exert themselves to bring on the troops, and to prevent their running away, but that they were not able to bring up the men so close to action as to annoy the enemy."

Pulling himself up from under his fallen horse, Aid-Major Lansing regained his feet. He had been aware that "the troops in the low ground had commenced a firing at a long shot from the enemy, broke, and some ran. I again made an attempt to mount my horse, but finding that he would not stand fire, I ran down towards the left, one of the militia attending me and leading my horse, till I came to Van Alstyne's regiment [Colonel Abraham Van Alstyne's 7th Albany[119]] which was broke. I assisted in rallying it, which was partly effected. I then went to Colonel Cuyler's and endeavored to assist the officers in rallying that regiment, which was also partly rallied... " The Aid-Major also recalled that when the militia had commenced firing, "the rear of two regiments in the low grounds, were strung along a hundred and fifty or two hundred yards behind the front, and kept up a warm fire, but the direction of the fire seemed to be up in the air."

Sir John, from his position at the head of his line troops in the open field, observed "the Enemy firing and [then] Retreating to some distance under their Fort at Klock's... " This comment may refer to the militia regiments of the left column breaking under fire and withdrawing before their officers could rally them. Fort Klock lay beyond Sir John's view, so he must have been referring to Fort Nelles which lay just to the east of Klock's farm. It was stated that the broken troops rallied there and this must have been what Johnson observed.[120] Johnson reported that the rebels "formed [there] in some force" whereupon, "the Indians who were all on horseback were panic-struck and crossed the River... ,"[121] as they had seen the large number of opponents arrayed against them.

Now that his Indian allies were gone, excepting Brant's native and white Volunteers who were deployed on the heights above Klock's farm with the Jaegers, Sir John had about 620 men. Although Sir John had no way of knowing it, Van Rensselaer brought against him in excess of 900 men; 5-700 Albany and Tryon militia and 3-400 New York and Massachusett's Levies — a possible 1 1/2 to 1 ratio. Still, if his men would be resolute, Johnson might yet give the rebels sufficient cause to delay and then he could continue his withdrawal.

Dubois was still with the General when he saw that Major McKinstry and his advance corps with Colonel Louis' Oneidas were ordered by General Van Rensselaer to "file off to the right from the centre and marched very near the right column." Colonel John Harper similarly recalled that, "part of the centre column, filed off to the right and joined Colo. Dubois' detachm[']t who attempted to gain the enemy's right flank, and the remainder continued, with five of the Indians, advancing in the centre." As McKinstry's advance corps and Colonel Louis' Oneidas warriors moved forward between Whiting's column on the low lands and Dubois' on the higher ground, they approached Colonel Jacob Klock's buildings and orchard where Brant's Volunteers and the Jaegers were posted about 150 yards ahead of Sir John's line. As they approached, Brant's men gave the war-halloo which was immediately answered by the Oneidas on the lower ground.[122]

The regiments in Whiting's column,[123] had also marched forward against Johnson's men positioned at Jacob Klock's farm and they commenced to engage. Sir John observed that the rebels had seen the retreat of the mounted Indians and "were encouraged to advance upon our left under cover of Woods, houses & fences, and began a heavy fire upon us from all Quarters especially upon our left... " The attack by McKinstry and the Oneidas in conjunction with the two militia regiments acted like a pincer against the farm. It seems that Brant's men occupied the lower orchard and fence lines in front of the house and the Jaegers were in another orchard above and slightly west of the house. The combination of McKinstry and the Oneidas likely matched Brant's strength. Faced with this force and the two militia regiments coming up on his flank, Brant's men retreated. Johnson preceived this particular threat to his front left, "... where I ordered a House, Barn, &c., to be taken possession of... "[124] sending a detachment of the 34th and KRR forward to accomplish the task.

Colonel Henry Van Rensselaer's regiment had advanced to close with Johnson's men at the orchard in front of Klock's house. Their movement was probably first opposed by Brant's men in amongst the trees and fences and then, with more impact, by the companies of troops sent forward by Sir John. Dubois noted that "the firing on the part of the enemy was so warm, as to prevent troops under Colo Whiting from advancing." Morris observed that after this exchange of fire, both Colonel Van Rensselaer's and Whiting's regiments had fallen into "the greatest disorder and confusion, and ... the Genl did exert himself to get them in order again."

This confusion amongst the centre column's regiments would likely not have been apparent to Dubois when he found his column behind Sir John's key left-forward position. He ordered Major Elias Benschoten of Malcom's Levies[125] to detach two companies "to raise the summit of the hill and fire on the enemy in flank, which broke them and they ran off." Colonel Clyde, whose militia companies were with Dubois, recalled this slightly differently. "[T]he troops marched... till they had got above Colo. Klock's... [I] then heard a firing near Klock's house; but, that [we] continued [our] march with design to out flank the enemy. That upon finding that [we] had got above the enemy, two or three platoons of levies and militia were detached [by Major Benschoten] from the rear [of the column], to attack a body of the enemy who were posted about one hundred rods [550yds, 500m] above Klock's. That that detachment fired six or seven platoons when the enemy fled, and the troops returned to their post."

★★★

The order which Sir John had given to the detachment to seize the "House, Barn, &c." was "not... attended to in time [and] the [rebels] took advantage of it and threw in a very heavy fire which forced the 34th and a part of my Regiment to give way, upon which [the rebels] gave three cheers."[126] The 34th and Royal Yorkers, who had been slow off the mark, had been unable to seize good defensive positions before Dubois' companies gained the high ground above their left rear. Perhaps, instead of driving forward into the cover around Klock's buildings, they had concentrated on beating back Whiting's and Van Rensselaer's regiments with an intense volume of fire delivered from the farm's fields. After all, they had observed that that same tactic had earlier stymied Cuyler's column on the left.

While Sir John did not report upon the disposition of his earlier "strong detachment" of Jaegers & Brant's which he had posted to the height upon his left front, one suspects that they withdrew at the same time as the 34th & KRR. Out on a limb to the left front, they had been faced with McKinstry's and Colonel Louis' men to their front, two militia regiments to their right flank and two or three platoons of troops firing volleys above their left rear. They were outgunned and, not sufficiently supported by the 34th and KRR NY, would have felt overwhelmed. In consequence, the dominating feature on its forward left flank of Johnson's line of battle was now lost to the rebels.

Meanwhile, unknown to Sir John, Colonel Dubois, after being rejoined by his detached platoons, continued his advance until he "had gained the flank of the enemy's main body, pursuant to the General's order." On the low grounds, Sir John, who was just as unaware of the great confusion amongst the militia regiments to his centre and left fronts as he was to Dubois threat to his left rear, took action to stabilize the situation. He reported, "I immediately ordered the three pounder to be fired with Grape shott which was also followed by a discharge of small arms which totally silenced them... "[127]

Sir John flattered himself that this tactic subdued the rebels. The discharge of canister and the general firing of his line troops receives absolutely no mention - not so much as a hint - in the recollections of the many rebel officers who recorded the evening's events. While it may not have done any serious execution, this thunderous climax could have resulted in the final collapse of the militia. In any event, their extreme confusion and fear had brought the action to an abrupt close.

★★★

Some thirty minutes had expired since the commencement of the firing and it was very close to being dark, a condition greatly intensified by smoke from the burning buildings.[128] The militiamen were beyond themselves with anxiety. Aid-Major Lansing noted that once Cuyler's had been partly rallied, "part of another regiment (Van Alstyne's I think) fir[ed] at Cuyler's [and] they again broke, and could not be rallied." Colonel Clyde, on the high ground above Klock's, observed "a cross fire upon the right, from the low lands, which [I] supposed to have come from the enemy," but he was later informed by Dubois "that it proceeded from our own troops." This firing upon each other must have come before Sir John's dramatic artillery discharge and general volley.

Van Rensselaer was understandably deeply concerned. Both of the Albany militia columns were in general confusion and in the dark, could not be reorganized. Aid-Major Morris recalled the worry that "the troops was in such confusion that it would be easy for a small party of the enemy to cut them to pieces." In fact, Aid-Major Lansing had overheard "several exclamations at different times, by the militia on the low grounds, that they were in danger to be cut to pieces and surrounded by the enemy and many of them expressed a great disposition to run off." The General was soon to conclude that there was no option but to withdraw from the field.

Above the post road, Dubois had successfully continued his right flank penetration with his Levies. At about dusk, he realized that the front of his column "had got into the enemy's rear... [He] faced his men about, and marched in a line down to the enemy undiscovered [and] gave orders for firing platoons from right to left, when the enemy broke and ran... [H]e advanced and continued firing upon the enemy till he discovered a firing on the rear of his left. That finding it came from some part of our own militia, he halted his men and rode up to the militia, and met with General Rensselaer on the left of the centre column, where he found the militia had given way." Dubois recalled, "[t]hat it was so dark that he could not discover Genl Rensselaer at the distance of five paces, nor know him but from his voice, and that when he came up to the Genl he found his efforts in vain... [H]e informed the Genl that the right of the centre line were firing on the levies, who were advancing against the enemy... [I]t was then proposed by either the Genl or [myself] that the firing should be ordered to cease, least our men should kill each other."

William Harper had become aware that some of Sir John's force was fording the river and he rode to meet with General Van

Rensselaer who was with Cuyler's troops. Harper was told about the decision to cease firing due to the danger of the "troops kill[ing] each other" and of the General's decision to "order the troops out of action." Harper "pressed the Genl to push the enemy while they were crossing the river, but the Genl declined it." Van Rensselaer explained his concern that "the enemy would surround our troops" and sent Harper to see if Johnson's men were attempting such a manoeuvre. Harper repeated that the enemy were crossing the river, intimating that they had no intention to attack. This remonstrance unavailing, he rode down to see what he could find.

Colonel Clyde, whose companies of militia had been left behind by Dubois during his deep penetration around Sir John's flank, recollected "that it was so dark as to render it difficult to enter into action with safety; as it was hardly possible to distinguish our troops and the enemy from one another... [T]he enemy could just be discerned and part of them were then heard crossing the river."

★★★

Johnson had similarly been concerned about it being dark and also that his troops were "in a good deal of confusion... " He reported "[I had] every reason to think the Enemy were Collecting from all the Forts" and, oddly, "that Rensalaer must be at hand if not with them ... "[129] From the latter phrase, he obviously had been unaware that he had been opposed by virtually all the troops the rebels could readily assemble. Of course, how could he have known? - but, his observation begs the question of whether his stand at Klock's Field could, or would, have been even more even resolute or venturesome had he known this information?

Years later, Captain Richard Duncan recalled that a council of officers was held in the smokey darkness of the field at Klock's. He said that the British officers in that group agreed it would be best to surrender as prisoners of war.[130] While the second-hand recounting of Duncan's story only mentions that Van Rensselaer had not given them an opportunity to seek terms, it is very likely that Duncan meant that the "old-country" British officers were willing to treat and the loyalist British officers were not. Amongst the latter, not a few of the captains and all the field officers were proscribed by either the State or the Continental Congress and some would have been tried as traitors subject to the death penalty. Whatever rebel officer agreed to offer them "prisoners of war" terms would have considerably exceeded his authority. They all bitterly remembered the decision of the Continental Congress to reverse the favourable terms of capitulation agreed to by General Gates with Burgoyne in 1777. Clearly, once such negotiations had been opened, all opportunity for a successful withdrawal would have been lost. In the event, Van Rensselaer did not give them the opportunity, as he promptly withdrew the majority of his army from the field.

Sir John, who must have been astounded at the rebel's sudden silence, determined to make the best of his success by using the darkness as cover for an immediate withdrawal. He reported, "I thought it best for the good of His Majesty's Service to cross the River without loss of time which was soon effected without any interruption... "

Before departing, the artillerymen spiked and abandoned the three-pounder cannon with its implements and ammunition. Much of the cattle and other plunder was cut loose or thrown aside. While some of the troops were withdrawing across the river near the field of action, remembered by Colonel Dubois as having a bank "breast high" with deep water, the majority of the raiders commenced a rapid night march, travelling west about two miles to the regular ford at Christie's Rift,[131] where they crossed to the south bank. Sir John likely crossed the ford before his rearguard was confronted and driven off by Dubois' Levies firing platoons; however, he obviously heard the firing. Perhaps there was little reason to think much about it, or possibly he decided that his report would read more favourably if there was no appearance of his column being forced off the field. Whatever the case, a handful of dispirited soldiers from his Royal Yorker rearguard were easily taken prisoner later that night.

As the raiders crossed the river they were met by "the Indians [who] led us immediately into the Woods... " In their fatigue and the stygian darkness of the tall trees, the force became somewhat separated[132] before the men slumped exhausted to the ground. Of course, those who had crossed downriver through the deeper water were on their own, although the Indians could be relied upon to bring them in. While the raiders were bone weary and many must have been near the end of their tether, the promptness by which the "confused" troops were brought to order and the speed & resolution with which they withdrew from the field, marched to the ford and crossed the river speaks volumes for their officers' leadership and their individual discipline and courage.

★★★

To return to Klock's Field, General Van Rensselaer requested that Colonel Dubois "ride to the rear of the troops and stop their retreating, and inform them that the enemy had retired over the river". Dubois rode for some distance and then, despairing, returned to the General informing him that he had been unable to get to the front of the retreating men. Van Rensselaer inquired if Dubois knew of "a good piece of ground to encamp on that night". The Colonel "recommended a hill near [Col. Jacob] Klock's house, and an order was sent [via John Harper] to Major Benschoten... to return to the ground near Klock's house." While Dubois continued to ride beside his commander, the General confessed some apprehensions regarding provisioning the militia the next morning as he was sure they would not march without. He also spoke of a concern that his anxious militia might be subjected to a surprise attack by a detachment of Sir John's troops. Dubois recommended a place near Fox's where the troops could be "secure from surprise" and where provisions could be brought to them from the baggage wagons at Fort Rensselaer. Lansing recalled the General giving orders to have this happen early the next morning, however, in the event, it was not accomplished until after sunrise.

As Colonel Harper rode to find Major Benschoten he came across many men who told him that Johnson's men had crossed the river. Continuing, he found "some Tryon militia and levies, plundering... [and] he forbid it." Concerned by what he saw as evidence of poor discipline amongst the troops, he "ordered the [Oneida] Indians to remain in close quarters, least some accident might happen to them."

Colonel Clyde recalled that after dark the order came to march and his companies returned to Klock's house where they halted. About an hour after dark, the "groanings of a man that lay wounded in the field of action... " were heard and Clyde "detached six men to bring him in. ... these men with some others, brought in the artillery waggons and artillery which had been deserted by the enemy." A report was sent off to the General. Clyde and Benschoten, who had brought the Levies to Klock's, decided to remain there. Soon after Dubois joined them and confirmed their decision. Dubois informed them that "the Genl would be with them in the morning, and that they [Levies & Tryon militia] were to march in pursuit of the enemy."

The pursuit accordingly marched about an hour after sunrise before Van Rensselaer had joined. They crossed the river at Christie's and marched towards Fort Herkimer.[133] The main body of militia left their camp at Fox's about two hours after sunrise after obtaining their provisions and cooking a quick meal. While on the march, the General called for a detachment of "light troops from the regiments of militia who were best able to march, to go as volunteers to overtake Colonel Dubois" who was reported to be very near Sir John's column. About thirty such men were dispatched with Aid-Major Morris.

★★★

On the morning of October 20, Johnson's men were again up early. A large party, which had become separated from the main column, was under the command of Captain Parke of the 8th. They moved along the river road in the direction of Fort Herkimer while the main group under Sir John was taking an alternate road passing well inland to the south. Parke's party included some soldiers of the 8th, some Royal Yorkers and some Rangers under Captain John McDonell (Aberchalder). On the road, their scouts came up with a body of rebels marching to join Van Rensselaer. Not being sure of their numbers, Parke ordered the whole of his party into the woods with instructions to move towards the southern route. Ever the bold partisan, McDonell saw things differently and with his Rangers and Royal Yorkers immediately attacked the oncoming rebels, whom they soon discovered numbered about 60 muskets. McDonell's group drove them into Fort Herkimer, killing ten and taking two prisoners at no cost to themselves. Now McDonell's small party was separated from Parke's, so they went their separate way.[134]

★★★

At about 9:00 o'clock the next morning, as Van Rensselaer's army was crossing the river at Christie's, some of Captain Robert M'Kean's[135] men of Harper's Levies chanced across a small blockhouse containing nine, unarmed loyalist soldiers who had been taken the night before by a party of seven militiamen from nearby Fort Windecker. The venturers had also taken four others, thirteen in total. One of the captives was Thomas Vrooman, a black servant of Sir John's, who had participated with McDonell (Scotus) & Crysler in the 1777 Schoharie "uprising" and then joined the Royal Yorkers. Vrooman carried in his saddle bags Sir John's personal baggage of "fine shirts, silk handerchiefs, watches, pistols and other things." One of his captors successfully laid claim to Vrooman's horse and musket.[136]

Another of the prisoners was Peter Cass, a "near neighbour in Johnstown" of Sammons who was a Volunteer with M'Kean's. Cass was ashamed to relate how the group had been easily taken prisoner by the militiamen who, as voices emanating from the dark, had simply told them to, "lay down your arms." The dispirited group of Royal Yorkers had readily complied and were chagrined to find they outnumbered their captors. Cass said he had been part of a large rearguard of Royal Yorkers, stumbling about in the black night, banging into each other. The prisoners suggested that Sir John's force had been on the point of capitulating,[137] which certainly may have been the talk amongst many of their fellows. In guilt over their own fate, the downcast men couldn't understand why the rebels had failed to take the whole of the expedition.

Dubois' pursuit arrived at Fort Herkimer about two o'clock. From there he penned a report to Governor Clinton.

Fort Harkerman 1 O'Clock

D'r Sir, I am here; pursued the Enemy so close that I prevented them from Burning or Doing the Least Damage to the Inhabitants; from what I can Learn by the Inhabitants, the Enemy is not above four miles in front of us; my men much Fatigued, without Provisions. I must here make a halt, untill I can get some provisions to Refresh them.

The Enemy is very much fatigued. They travelled almost all night, without any Refreshment; they must make a halt.

This moment, I Rec'd Information that the Enemy is at a place Call'd Shoemaker's Land, about four miles from here; Genl. Ransler this moment appears in Sight with the Militia.

The enemy are Bending their Course for Buck [Carleton] Island. I am your

Lewis Duboys.

P.S. My men have agred to march without eiting [eating]. I exspect to catch them in 3 [h]ours time.[138]

Dubois certainly flattered himself as to the worth of his efforts. Just whom had he and his men been pursuing? The main body of Sir John's force had taken the southern route, well below the post/river road to Fort Herkimer. Was he pushing hard against Parke's men of the 8th? Doubtful, as they were heading south to find the lower route. Was Dubois hot on the tail of McDonell and his mixed party of Rangers and Royal Yorkers? Perhaps... However, if the enterprising McDonell had known that Dubois was close on his heels, it would not have been out of character for the Ranger Captain to stop long enough to rattle his pursuers. It appears that Dubois was chasing thin air.

Dubois had been at Fort Herkimer for about an hour when the General arrived "with a party of horse", soon followed by Aid-Major Morris and his 30 volunteers from the main army. Dubois must have been disturbed that the whole of the Albany militia were far behind. Undoubtedly the General heard of McDonell's exploit on the road only a few hours before. If nothing else, the incident proved that the raiders still had some teeth and soon enough there would be additional evidence.

While awaiting the arrival of the main army, Van Rensselaer was briefed by Dubois regarding the intelligence that Sir John's force was concentrated at Shoemaker's. About 4:00 PM the main body came up and the whole marched for Shoemaker's where they stayed until nightfall. As there was no sign of Sir John's white and native troops having passed that way, three Indians and some whites were sent out to scout the area. During their wait, a council of officers was held at which there was some disagreement over Sir John's probable route of retreat. The scouts returned without finding any trace of the raiders, and with night upon them, the army returned to Fort Herkimer. From the lack of "spoor", and the advice of some officers, the General concluded that Sir John was using the route south of the fort.[139]

Governor George Clinton arrived at Fort Herkimer that night.[140] He had collected a sizeable reinforcement which included additional troops of Colonel Malcom's Regiment and detachments of the Levies and militia from Schoharie. While on the march in the dark of early morning, he had Colonel Malcom dispatch letters to Henry Glen and General Schuyler.

> 6 miles above Fort Hunter 2 O'clock AM Oct 20 1780
> Dr Sir
> This moment we have received the following account That the Enemy got to Stone Arabia yesterday morning - the small party of Levys posted there attak'd them but were too weak to make any impression - In the afternoon the Different detachments under General Ranslaer, Co Dubois, & Major Bunscoten formed a junction near the Enemy - attacked, and drove them over the River, leaving plunder prisoners & baggage behind them -
> We expect to reach Fort Ranslaer by 8 O'clock in the morning with a considerable reinforcement as Major Woolsey from Scoherie found us last evening and are determined to pursue with the greatest rapidity - The Governor requests that you communicate this agreeable information to Genl Tenbroeck [BGen Abraham Ten Broeck, OC 1st Bde, Albany County Militia] as we do not [have] time to write - push on provisions with the greatest dispatch - it is uncertain how far we may be obliged to pursue ere we catch the infamous bandittie - every thing except the soil [is] destroyed from Fort Hunter to Stone Arabia -
> your W Malcom
> let the Governors letter to Genl Scuyler be sent on by the nearest & best rout - seal it -
> [To] Henry Glen Esqr
>   Q M Genl
>   Schenectady[141]

When Major Woolsey joined with a contingent of Levies and militia from the Schoharie, he brought with him his highly detailed record of the interrogation of the Butler's Rangers deserter, Benjamin Burton. The Governor was quick to seize on Burton's information about the raiders' bateaux and provisions being left at Lake Onondaga. From the following written instructions it appears that the deserter, or one of the other prisoners, described the boats' specific location.

> Fort Renselaer 11 O Clock 20th Octobr
>
> Sir
>
> It is proposed to send a small Party across the Country to destroy the Enemy's Boats which we are well informed are sunk at this End of Onondaga Lake - I think you told me that you was well acquainted with the nearest and best Route to that Place and that you would be willing to conduct a Party for that Purpose - I therefore wish you to wait on Genl Renselaer & Colo DuBois with the Bearer Major Woolsey & inform on this subject that a proper Party may be dispatched without loss of Time for this Service
>
> I am Your
> Most Obdt Servt
> Geo. Clinton
>
> [To] Major Newkerk[142]

Of course, if the boats could be found and destroyed, the rebel column would have a much better chance of once again closing with the raiders and forcing them into a surrender.

At Fort Herkimer on the morning of October 21, Governor George Clinton assumed command[143] of the army of some 1500 men and the direction of the pursuit of Sir John Johnson's raiders. Colonel Louis and Captain M'Kean were sent ahead to discover Johnson's exact route and soon fell in with an obvious track. A Crown Indian was taken prisoner and a halt was called during his questioning. Colonel Dubois came to the head of the column and urged the advance corps forward. Not too far on they came upon a deserted encampment with the fires still burning lowly. Colonel Louis insisted upon a halt while the main body of the army came up. The advance corps waited for some time before a Doctor Allen arrived with the information that the pursuit had been abandoned and the army had turned about to make its return march.[144] An article published in the Pennsylvania Gazette stated -

The pursuit was continued by the militia and levies, headed by his excellency the Governor, till within about 15 miles of that place (Lake Oneida), when their provisions being entirely exhausted, many of them having been near two days without any, and no prospect of the supplies, which were to follow them, on so rapid a march, arriving in time, they were oblig- ed to return; or, in all probability, the whole would have fallen into our hands.[145]

After what Sir John's men had endured, what might their reaction have been to the Gazette article?

A party carrying Clinton's orders to destroy Sir John's boats arrived at Stanwix on the 21st. Major James Hughes of Harper's Levies, who commanded a garrison of about 300 men from his regiment[146] aug- mented by Tryon County militia, issued the following order -

With the Detachment of Harpers Corps[147] of C[apt] 1 S[ubtns] 2 S[jts] 4 C[pls] 4[&] 50 Rank and file [61 all ranks], which you are to consider under your Command, Proceed by the nearest Rout to old Oneida or the directest Course to gain the front of the Enemy, retiring to Onondaga. Take prisoners, gain Intelligence of their Number and Disyns [designs]. Interrupt their March by harrassing their Rear, Flank or Front. Taking care at the same time that you do not expose Your Party to surprise; or endanger them by being surrounded. Should you gain Certain knowledge of their not having detached any Body to secure their Boats at Onondaga, you are then with the greatest Expedition [to] proceed to that Place and destroy all their Boats, Baggage and Provision. That you be authenticated of this, before the Attempt is made. If your Prisoner afford you any material Intelligence dispatch a Messenger to me with haste. It is probable you will fall in with a large Body of Militia &c. who are persuing them, provide yourself and Party with Red Boughs,[148] as they have the same. Shew your orders to the Commanding Officer and take further Directions from him. If you do not fall in with the Militia or their is no probability of you proceeding to Onondaga so on to effect the Destruction of their Boats &c. you are to return to this Garrison with all Dispatch.

Given at Fort Schuyler [Stanwix]
22d of October 1780
James M. Hughes
   Major Commt
[To] Capt. Vrooman[149]

A partial list[150] of the men assigned to Captain Walter Vrooman reveals that they were drawn from six different companies of Harper's and included some militiamen from Clyde's Canajoharie regiment. The latter may have been on garrison or pioneering duties at Stanwix, or perhaps were the party that had brought the Governor's orders from Fort Herkimer.

It seems strange that men had to be drawn from so many different companies. Perhaps they were volunteers, rather than men ordered to do the task. The calling for volunteers might have been necessary as the morale amongst Harper's Levies was anything but strong. Two prisoners taken by McKay of Leake's Company had advised that "the Soldiers in that garrison on hearing that news [of Sir John's column] declared if they came to attack the place they would not fight, and told their officers they would lay down their Arms as soon as they would make their appearance." This intelligence is confirmed in a letter from Colonel Malcom to Governor Clinton which advised that LtCol. John Harper "is not a proper person" to command at Fort Stanwix. Further, Colonel John Brown had advised Malcom that some of Harper's regiment of Levies had "mutinyed on receiving the orders of march" and that their officers were the abbettors, in short, Malcom claimed that Harper's were "not a Corps to be trusted in the Garrison [at Stanwix]."[151]

A letter written by Colonel Malcom dated at Fort Rensselear on Sep. 25th to Governor Clinton provides a picture of failed leadership on the part of Harper and clearly indicates how little use the brigade commander had for him. To quote, "I might as well ask Col Harpur about the Day of Judgement as about his Regiment — I really have not patience to mention instances of his Un officer like cond[uc]t. To Accomodate Dadys, Mamys[,] Wifes &c I have Transferred Major Hughs — [Capts] Drake & Lawrence wh some Good Sub[altern]s to Harpurs Corps — this will make them Respectable, and Major Hughs will Conduct the Garrison, perhaps as well as those who have been longer accustomed to separate Command— He has more Understanding, & I am Convinced more Industry than any that I can assign for that Command. He will for the future be returned As of Harpur's Regt & Commanding at Fort Schuyler — I have given Harpur a furlough — any time & place... "[152]

★★★

On the same day that Vrooman received his written orders and led his party from Stanwix, the separated parties of Captains Parke and McDonell (Aberchalder) rejoined with Johnson's main body. Except for Captain Dame of Butler's and 52 missing men, all were now accounted for.

The march continued the next day when a great piece of good fortune befell the hurried column. Upon arriving at the site of Old Oneida (Kanowalohale), they took a prisoner. He was Private George Staring of Captain Putnam's Company of Harper's Levies, a member of Vrooman's party sent out from Fort Stanwix to destroy their boats. Staring had fallen, or feigned, sick that morning and had somehow travelled a remarkable eight miles towards Stanwix before being found by the raiders.[153]

Sir John reported to Governor Haldimand that the whole column "immediately pushed on with all Expedition intending to detach a Party to march all night untill they overtook them[,] but falling in with them on their Return at Canaghsioraga (Ganaghsaraga), we took and Killed the whole Party except two who made their escape."

Fifty four years later an old veteran loyalist soldier recalled this significant event. He had served in Leake's Coy on the 1780 expedition and his vivid recollection five decades later of the surprise of Vrooman's party suggests their capture was accomplished by that unit.[154]

Johnson's report can be interpreted that a large number of rebels were killed in this affair; however, that was not the case. Even after receiving such explicit instructions to be on guard against being surrounded and surprised, the party was easily taken while eating a meal.[155] Of their number, two escaped and 52 were captured,[156] which, by computation, indicates that six were killed.

From the interrogation of the prisoners it was found that Vrooman had sent off two Oneidas to find and destroy the boats and provisions. Sir John immediately dispatched six mounted Rangers to intercept the Indians. They rode directly to where the boats were secured and found their cache intact and unharmed.[157]

Needless to say, the rebels viewed the loss of Vrooman's force in quite a different light. When Governor Clinton wrote a report on the devastation in the Mohawk Valley on Oct. 29th to James Duane, a New York Congressional delegate, he added the following —

> ... I am informed, tho' not officially, that a Detachm't of Sixty men who were ordered to march from the Garrison of Fort Schuyler [Stanwix] to hang on the enemy's flank in their Retreat, unfortunately before

they discovered [them,] the Enemy, fell in with their
main body & the whole of them two excepted, are
made Prisoners. I am in great Hopes, however, that
this Account is not true as the Orders given to the
Party by Maj'r Hughes was couched in the most cautious Terms; they were to proceed with the greatest
Circumspection & not to hazard any Thing that might
endanger their Retreat.[158]

As Johnson's main column continued its rapid march to Lake
Onondaga, the prisoner, Captain Vrooman, "a large muscular man",
was forced to carry a huge, cumbersome Indian pack made of stripped
petticoats. It was bulging full of plunder taken at Stone Arabia and its
owner had tired of carrying it. When Sir John discovered the Captain
being used as a porter, he permitted him to cast the pack aside. The
owner, who was marching further back in the column, came across
his abandoned treasures at the side of the trail and, retrieving them,
strode forward in great anger to find Vrooman. With many threats, he
again secured it on his back. Sometime later, Johnson spied the pack
on Vrooman's back. This time, Sir John ordered some soldiers to make
sure the pack stayed off Vrooman's back.[159]

Lieutenant George McGinness of the Indian Department had been
gravely wounded by a ball through his knee at Stone Arabia. With great
difficulty, and undoubtedly even greater pain, he was led through the
woods "upwards of seventy miles over little-used Indian trails"[160] until
he and his helpers arrived at New Oneida, a settlement just north of
Kanowalohale, the "old" castle. Perhaps one of his helpers sought out
the main body. In any event, a party of nine men were sent to assist
McGinness and they took him some seven miles off the main trail, likely
to foil pursuit, whereupon they became alarmed and left the Lieutenant
in the care of a man named Mannerly. The two men survived in the
extreme cold for eleven days without anything but the crudest of shelter, eating a handful of hickory nuts each day, when they were fortu-
itously discovered by a band of Senecas returning from the expedition.

In this, the two men were doubly fortunate, as McGinness' famous
mother, Sarah Kast McGinness, was well loved, indeed had been
adopted, by the Seneca nation. Sarah's father, and her husband
Timothy McGinness, known far and wide as Teady McGinn, conducted
the Indian trade at German Flats before the Seven Years War. When
Teady went to Lake George in 1755 to serve under Sir William
Johnson, he was killed alongside the famous Mohawk, King Hendrick,
at Bloody Pond. The widow Sarah firmly grasped the family's business,
and with her sons-in-law, the Thompsons, became a prominent figure
in the trade. During the difficult winter of 1777/78, she, and her

youngest son George, lived amongst the Senecas and helped to keep them faithful to the Crown, to the great satisfaction of Old Smoke himself.

With the care and reverence due his mother, the Seneca party carefully moved Lieutenant McGinness to their castle at Genesee. He lay close to death for two months before he regained enough strength to be moved to Fort Niagara.[161]

With understandably great relief, the main body of the column arrived at Lake Onondaga on the 25th and found all was well. The expedition embarked in the bateaux and pushed on to Oswego, arriving there the next day.[162] Sir John spent no time in resting from the ordeal. After thanking his remaining Six Nations' allies and seeing to the myriad small details of administration involved in the dispersing of his expedition, he boarded the sloop *Caldwell* with 64 prisoners and their guard and sailed for Carleton Island, at which he arrived the same evening. He left from there at 2:00 AM on the 26th to travel by small boat through the St. Lawrence rapids and landed in Montreal late at night on the 30th. The next day, he wrote his carefully detailed report to Governor Haldimand. He mentioned that he expected Major Gray with the Montreal-based detachment either the next or the day following. His reported loss at the time of his writing was "nine men killed, two wounded, and fifty-two missing, of whom several were known to have been disabled by wounds." Regarding Captain Dame and the absent men Sir John wrote, "I fear [they] are mostly taken, tho' there were many Indians missing who may bring them in."[163]

In a second report written on Nov. 8, he wrote, "I have the pleasure to acquaint your Excellency that, Captain Dame of the Rangers, with Eighteen of the Men that were missing and thirty Indians, arrived at Oswego, soon after we left it, where they found three Boats and some provisions I ordered to be left for them, five, or six men left him in the woods, taking a different Rout; they may also soon be expected, and two of them were Wounded."[164] A report sent to Haldimand three days earlier from Captain Alexander Fraser of the Quebec Indian Department stationed at Carleton Island stated that Dame returned with 10 soldiers, including himself, and in excess of 20 Indians.[165] Assuming that Fraser, who was closer to the scene, possessed a more accurate appraisal, this welcome news gave good reason to expect that the number of missing would be reduced to 43-44 with the promise of five or six to follow.

In his first report, written the morning after his return, he apologized to his commander-in-chief for not appearing at Head Quarters in Quebec City in person --

... from the great fatigue I have undergone I am induced to hope Your Excellency will excuse my not waiting upon you on this occasion being really much wore down, the amazing loss the Enemy have sustained will I hope more than compensate for the loss of the few brave fellows who are missing, many of whom I still expect will make their appearance — Captain McDonell [Aberchalder] of the Rangers obtained Colonel Butler's leave to come down with me on account of his bad state of health, he hopes your Excellency will permit him to remain here for the winter, he really merits every indulgence.[166]

These words speak for themselves. Sir John's concern for his officers and men is made manifestly clear throughout his report, especially in these last few words.

The raid against the Valleys had been a remarkable achievement. In thirty gruelling days his troops had travelled on water and land on a round trip of close to 900 miles. They had met with great privation on their approach march and, in the days of hectic action, had shown tremendous discipline and fortitude. They had faced several skirmishes and fought two serious actions. Their retreat was marked by endurance, bursts of energy and eternal vigilance, which rewarded them with a surprising dividend.

For the natives who played such an essential role in the expedition, the sight of the smoke-filled wasteland that had been created from the bottom end of the Schoharie Valley to the far end of the Mohawk, must have given them great satisfaction. Were these not the homes and farmlands of the men who had devastated their homelands of Iroquoia? They perhaps reflected that their own farms and orchards had been the work of centuries, not a few puny decades. Revenge must have indeed been sweet, but it was not yet enough. There was more to come. The next campaign would again start early and last long - very, very long.

AN EPILOGUE TO THE OSWEGO EXPEDITION

The fate of the prisoners taken by both sides provides interesting stories. Prisoners from loyalist regiments who were taken in combat or while performing their duty under arms could expect to be treated as prisoners of war. As such, they faced imprisonment under conditions of considerable privation and severe discomfort.

They might also choose to do service in the Continental army. However, both of these outcomes were preferable to that which awaited those men who were captured while hiding in the countryside or on farms, especially if they were found with their families, friends or known loyalist sympathizers. If seriously wounded or sick, they might be accepted as prisoners of war; however, healthy men were usually accused of spying and, if proven guilty, their fate could be death by hanging. The following are some scant details of the loyalist soldiers who had been captured during the expedition.

It seems that loyalist prisoners, who claimed to be rebels at heart, had their cases reviewed by the Commission for Detecting and Defeating Conspiracies to assess their veracity. The board met on Oct. 22nd in Albany[167] and two men, Thomas Griffiths and Robert Reynolds, of "Sir John Johnson's party" were examined. Although unstated in the minutes, both men were from Butler's Rangers. They claimed to be deserters and were held until the commission might be "better satisfied as to their Characters." They were further examined the next day, but unfortunately their examinations have not been published. Neither man settled in Canada after the war, which is an indication that their plea was accepted and they were allowed to remain at large in the States.

The conspiracy commission again met in Albany on Oct. 27th. Two new suspects were examined. The first was Christian Frihart, who had been with "Sir John's Johnson's party." Likely Frihart is the man returned as Christian Frish on three Second Battalion, KRR NY lists. Having been born in Germany, he may have retained such a strong accent that this strange interpretation of his name resulted. Frihart is marked as enlisting on Oct. 16, 1780, the night before the expedition entered the Schoharie Valley. He would have been taken out of uniform and this may have led to him being hanged as a spy; however, his fate is unknown.

Benjamin Burton (Benton) of Butler's Rangers was reviewed next. His extensive cooperation with the rebels has been noted earlier and the minutes of the commission reveal nothing more; however, his claim to have been a deserter would seem to have been accepted. The next day, Major Newkirk from Tryon County visited the board in favour of an unnamed man who had been taken prisoner from Sir John's force. Newkirk stated that he "has been reputed a Friend to the American Cause, that he was last Spring taken Prisoner by the Enemy and joined Sir John for no other Purpose than that he might have an Oppertunity of making his Escape."[168] Orders were given that the mystery man be detained by Colonel Malcom for further examination.

On Oct. 30th, Isaac Aerse (Austin,Awson) and Adam Hoofer (Hoober,Huber) of "Sir John's Party" were brought forward. Both men had been taken in the raid on the Schoharie, one from the Major's Company of the Royal Yorkers and the other from Duncan's. They were never exchanged, nor did they settle in Canada after the war.

John Leslie (Lessley,Lassly) was brought before the conspiracy commission on Oct. 31st. He was a private soldier in Major Gray's Company in the Royal Yorkers, was interviewed and claimed to be a deserter. He requested "to go to his Excellency the Governor" which the commissioners decided to grant. What treacherous promises had Leslie made?

Adam Shades was an interesting case. There were no suspicious circumstances to his capture and he was "sent down" with the rest of the prisoners of war. Somehow his presence amongst the prisoners became known to Captain Leonard Bleeker of the 3rd New York Continental Line and Bleeker interceded directly with Governor Clinton on Nov. 2nd on Shade's behalf.[169] The Captain explained that Shades had enlisted in his company for the duration of the war and then was taken prisoner by Indians at Fort Stanwix on July 3rd, 1777. Shades had joined the Royal Yorkers just over a month later on Aug. 5th. He was in arms for the Crown when captured on Oct. 19th in the Mohawk Valley. Bleeker requested that Shades be returned to duty in his company. The exact details of the Governor's response to this request are unknown; however, Shades name is found in a return of Colonel Marinus Willett's New York State Levies in 1781. Ironically, he was noted as a deserter from Willett's later that year.[170]

As we have seen from the above thin accounts, a few men claimed that they had enlisted in a loyalist regiment with the sole purpose of deserting as soon as the first opportunity to return to the States arose. There is little doubt that this was true in many cases. A distressing story arises from the enlistment in the Royal Yorkers by a group of men principally drawn from Vrooman's detachment which was captured at Ganaghsaraga. They, and many other recruits for the 2nd Battalion, KRR NY, were sent for training to the small, 1st Battalion garrison at Coteau-du-Lac. The intention was that by observation and application, they would learn the procedures and discipline of the British Provincial military. The post at Coteau-du-Lac was a key forwarding station for the transportation of supplies to the Upper Posts, but it held another purpose as well. To quote a British officer's journal [John Enys] entry of 1785 -

> Near this place in the middle of the River is a small Island so surrounded by Rapids that it is exceedingly difficult to get either off or on it. Its situation had dur-

> ing the Disturbances [the rebellion] pointed it as a
> proper place to keep the most Violent of the American
> Prisoners... and the Barrackes being built there for that
> purpose it was called prison Island.[171]

The small garrison provided guard details for Prison Island which may
have had some bearing on the events which followed.

If these new recruits found themselves augmenting the guard
details on the Island, they may have been confronted by some of their
fellows from Vrooman's detachment who had shunned the relative
comforts offered by the loyal Provincial army. If not influenced or
goaded by their past associates, there were certainly many hard cases
to be found amongst the other prisoners who could have tempted the
newly-minted loyalists. Whether these 2nd Battalion men smarted
under such provocations, or simply developed their ideas from their
own fertile minds, is a moot point.

Eight of them "formed and agreed upon a Conspiracy", a particularly bloody mutiny. It would unfold as follows. First, they would "kill
the Commanding Officer," who at the time was Captain John Munro.
Then, they would kill "all other Officers and Soldiers... who should
oppose their proceedings, which were to lay that Post in Ashes, to
desert the Service, and join the [Rebels]."[172] The mutineers may have
also thought to release the prisoners on the island.

An essential part of their plot[173] was an approach to a Canada
Indian present at the post with a bribe to conduct them over the
Adirondacks to the Mohawk Valley. Either motivated by loyalty to the
British, or by the thought of a greater, risk-free reward, the Indian
turned them in. Nine suspected men were arraigned before a Court
Martial assembled at Montreal on June 6th, 1781. They were: William
Edwards, John Garter (Gasler), Peter House, Seth Jacque (Jacquay),
Nathanial Miller, Peter Sharpe, Nicholas Smith, Sefferenus Tigert
(Dygert) and Andrew Van Waggoner (Wagner.)

Edwards, House, Sharpe, Smith, Tigert and Van Waggoner were all
of Vrooman's detachment of Harper's Levies and are shown as enlisting
in the KRR on Oct. 25, 1780. Seth Jacque had enlisted at the same time,
but is not found on Harper's rolls. John Garter had enlisted a month
later on Nov. 25th; he had been captured at Rheimensnyder's Bush by
an Indian party on Apr. 3rd, 1780 as a private in the 2nd Battalion of the
Tryon County Militia. It had taken him some time to enlist, likely with
an eye cocked towards desertion. Nathanial Miller was a very recent
conversion to loyalism having enlisted on Feb. 10, 1781.

A number of notables sat on the Court Martial. Major John
Adolphus Harris of the 84th, RHE, was president. Major James Gray of
the Royal Yorkers, Captain Alexander Fraser of the Quebec Indian

Department and Captain Thomas Scott of the 53rd, who had commanded the Regulars under Sir John during the October 1780 expedition, were members. Nine other officers also sat. The case obviously had some terrible implications and was of great moment. The decisions of the Court were given on June 25th.

There was one fortunate man amongst them. House was found not guilty and was acquitted of all charges. Jacque, Garter and Sharpe were found guilty of "exciting and concealing a mutiny" under Section II, Articles 3 & 4 of the Articles of War. They were each sentenced to 1000 lashes upon their bare backs at the head of their regiment. This was the equivalent of a death sentence of the most gruesome variety and the irony of their secondary punishment would not be lost on the members of the Court, or the prisoners. These three men were "to serve His Majesty in foreign parts for life."

Tigert, Van Waggoner and Edwards were awarded 1000 lashes each in breach of Section XX, Article 3 - a variation on the theme of mutiny. Miller and Smith were each awarded 500 lashes for a lesser commission of the same crime. All of the sentences were to be put into execution except that of Smith whom the commander-in-chief was willing to forgive "in consequence of an application by the Court in his behalf." He had possibly been a witness for the Crown and given evidence against his fellows.

The guilty men were "to be sent down to Quebec in Irons in a Batteau as soon as they c[oul]d undertake the Journey after the Infliction of their Corporal Punishments." John Garter died as a result of his punishment.[174] The others, if not dead, were most likely crippled for life.[175]

Fort Johnson on the Mohawk River
Van Rensselaer halted the Albany militia opposite Fort Johnson the night of October 16th. This was Sir William Johnson's second home in the Mohawk Valley and Sir John's first.
unattribued, undated engraving (from Jeptha R. Simms, The History of Schoharie County, 1895)

Fort Hunter
This sketch is of the Queen Anne's Chapel Parsonage, the home of Reverend John Stuart, the Anglican priest to the natives of the Mohawk Castle and the white settlement and Chaplain to the Second Battalion, KRR, NY. Surrounded by a heavy palisade, the parsonage became the core of the Fort Hunter post. Thompson and Brant avoided this fort during their destruction of the Fort Hunter community.
J. Fraser, 1850 (from Jeptha R. Simms, The History of Schoharie County, 1895)

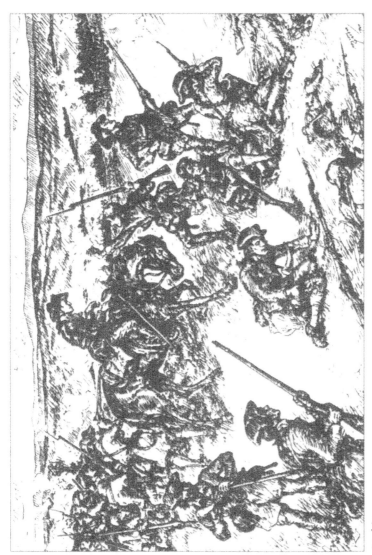

Battle of Stone Arabia
Greene portrays Colonel John Brown at the moment of his death at the head of his Massachusetts Levies. Greene has accepted the hypothesis that Brown's men were in an open field and Sir John's men behind a fence. Sir John's eyewitness report states that the Levies were in a woods behind a fence line and his troops attacked across open fields and vaulted the fences to make their assault.
Nelson Greene, 1907

Light Infantry of the 8th (King's) Regiment
This interpretation of the 8th Lights has the men wearing boiled-leather caps emblazoned with King George's white horse of Hanover and red coatees with shoulder wings and blue facings.
Janice Lang, 1990 (at the site of the Middle Fort, Schoharie Valley, NY)

McDonell's Company, Butler's Rangers in the Attack
A Serjeant commands his section to flank right with bayonets fixed for an assault. The heavy, canvas knapsacks worn by all troops on campaign can be seen on both Rangers.
Janice Lang, 1995 (at the original battle site in Stone Arabia, NY

Fort Keyser, Stone Arabia

Built for Johannes and Margaretta Kayser (Keyser) in 1750, the house became the core of Fort Keyser, one of two stockaded installations intended to shelter the populace of that grain-rich settlement. Johnson's raiders ignored Fort Keyser during the destruction of the community.

Rufus A. Grider, 1886 (Montgomery County Department of History and Archives, Fonda, NY)

"Shall we leave this one?" — Palatine Barn at Stone Arabia

The barn of Conrad Kiltz of Stone Arabia, a militiaman who fought in the battle of Oct. 19th. It was painstakingly restored in the 1970's and 80's by Willis Barshied, a local historian and craftsman. Its design is typical of the hundreds of Palatine barns destroyed throughout the Mohawk region.

Peter W. Johnson U.E., 1996

Fort Rensselaer

In 1780, this post on the Mohawk River at the settlement of Fort Plain served as the Headquarters for Colonel Lewis Dubois. Greene portrays General Washington being greeted by a detachment under the command of Lieutenant Colonel Samuel Clyde of the Tryon County militia in 1783. Whether or not Greene's structural details of the fort are accurate is unknown.

Nelson Greene. 1944 (from a calender printed by the Courier-Standard Print of Fort Plain, NY)

Fort Klock

Built in 1750 by Johannes Klock, the house served as a fort in two wars. Often mistaken for the location of the October 19th battle, Fort Klock lies about two miles east of the action. In 1973, the restored building was designated a National Historic Landmark "of exceptional value in commemorating or illustrating the history of the United States."

Nelson Greene, 1900

Receiving Orders

Royal Yorker officer issues instructions to a Serjeant and his squad.

Janice Lang, 1996 (at the site of the Battle of Johnstown, Johnson Hall, Johnstown, NY)

Rebel Militia Volleying

Albany and Tryon militia animators elevate their muskets as a safety measure; their appearance must resemble the wild volleying of the badly rattled Albany County regiments at Klock's Field.

Allan Fitzpatrick, 1995 (at the site of the Lower Fort, Schoharie, NY)

The 'Grasshopper' being deployed
Reenactors wheel up a reproduction 3 pounder Grasshopper. Just such a gun with its implements and ammunition were abandoned on the field at Klock's as Sir John's army rapidly withdrew into the gloom.
Janice Lang, 1989 (at Black Creek Pioneer Village, North York, Ont)

Skirmishers Advance
Royal Yorkers, advancing through their own smoke and working in files, drive in rebel pickets.
Janice Lang, 1996 (at the site of the Battle of Johnstown, Johnson Hall, Johnstown, NY))

REFLECTIONS AND CONSIDERATIONS

A MYSTERY

It seems to be a wonder that so many parties of Crown troops and allied Indians were able to penetrate the frontier defences of New York, spend days deep inside rebel territory fighting skirmishes, marching and destroying buildings, livestock & grain magazines — ever on guard against retaliation — and, when at the very end of their supplies of provisions, ammunition and shoe leather, withdraw virtually intact to their bases.

Of course, small war parties of 30-50 men allowed for ease of movement and concealment. For such little groups, the vast wilderness lent itself to cut and run tactics. In such extensive and sparsely populated regions, even the movement of flotillas of a hundred or more bateaux and long marching columns of 500-1000 men were readily concealable. When a column retired for the night, one thousand men could be hidden in a small valley and the terrain abounded with just such opportunities. Movement on the water proved more difficult to hide; but, the bodies of water were vast and there was no such thing as aerial reconnaissance to concern the raiders.

A most remarkable consideration regarding the movement of the larger bodies of men was their fragile supply arrangements. It may readily be appreciated that a man can carry only so much food on his back. The wilderness was no source for volumes of foodstuffs and was in no way supportive of large pack trains of animals. There had to be meticulous preparation before an expedition left its bases. While on the march, scouts were often sent ahead to warn trusted friends of the coming troops so that provisions, such as fresh beef, could be organized. Once into the settlements, the raiders relied upon looting to sustain them; but, always they faced a harrowing withdrawal through the neutral wilderness where military and individual discipline were crucial for survival. The repeated mentions of privation on the march, of men searching for food in the farms they were about to destroy, and the care taken by the leadership to leave caches along the trails emphasize the importance of this essential, controlling factor. That great fortitude and courage was required to conduct these deep-penetration raids cannot be doubted or denied.

As remarkable as the discipline required to face the uncertainty of sustenance was the organizational cohesiveness exhibited by the raiders. That they could be broken into small detachments for specific duties, and then reassemble on the march, was a considerable feat worthy of admiration. There are recurring stories of men, unavoidably separated from the main body, who had the tenacity to group together, fight and evade the rebels, battle the wilderness and return to their bases

It has been noted that the rebels were invariably warned of the coming of every large raid in 1780, and yet, they were patently unable to prevent the Crown forces either from assembling their troops at forward staging points, from advancing to, and penetrating into, the frontier, or from completing their missions of destruction and then returning, virtually unscathed, to their home bases. Popular American historians, confronted by this fact, have chosen to denigrate the military value of the raids, thus diverting attention away from their superb execution and the attendant accomplishments.

To find answers to this mystery, it must first be recognized that the New York frontier was in many ways as open to penetration as a sieve. To be sure, there were only a handful of staging areas from which to mount the raids, but the routes of advance and entry options were numerous. The British alliance with the native nations, whose warriors knew the waterways and trails so intimately, and the employment of the American loyalists, who often knew the roads and waterways equally well, and in addition, possessed an in-depth knowledge of the communities and their inhabitants, was a combination that was virtually impossible to defend against.

Yet, it was not only topographical and demographic knowledge that these two elements contributed; of equal importance was their high degree of motivation. The native nations harboured a desire to revenge the centuries of rapacious encroachment and the racial and religious bigotry which clearly threatened the very survival of their way of life. The British monarchy and government, their representatives and supporters, were viewed by the majority of the nations as their best hope for the establishment of an equilibrium between the two societies. This somewhat naive conclusion was deeply reinforced by the early bankruptcy of the rebels' frontier trade, followed soon after by the Sullivan expedition in 1779, which utterly destroyed the homelands of the Iroquois Confederacy. The irony that neither the funds nor the will could be found to sustain the Indian trade, but that both were in evidence aplenty when the decision was made to mount Sullivan's grand, punitive expedition against their homelands, was not lost on the keen native observer.

As to the loyalists — their relationship with their rebel brethren had begun as merely strident political debate, soon followed by the overt taking of sides by the protagonists, on somewhat noble terms. But, as the uncompromising British Government argued and took action to maintain its rights, the scene degenerated into violence against the King's representatives and all those proponents of British rule, whether strangers, neighbours, friends or relatives. When open conflict began, the antipathy was greatly fueled by the persecution of loyalist families left behind in rebel territory; the sequestration of their lands, buildings and chattels by the rebel governments, not only as punishment, but also to finance the war; and, in some cases, the proscribing of their senior leadership with a sentence of death. The loyalists' anger and distrust of the rebels soon grew to the deepest detestation & enmity and often — a controlled, determined rage. In war, there can be no greater motivation.

WITH CONSUMMATE DARING — THE QUESTION OF LEADERSHIP

Certainly the matter of courage, military skill and application should not be overlooked. There is much evidence of these characteristics in the expeditions. Some examples amongst the junior leaders — the elan of John McDonell (Aberchalder) at Stone Arabia and Fort Herkimer; similarly, Joseph Brant's forceful driving-in of Brown's van and immediate outflanking of his main body at Stone Arabia; John Munro's rapid night advance and equally rapid withdrawal at Ballstown and his "bayonets in the moonlight" tactic; the rapid, and obviously skillful, attack led by Forbes and Roche of the 34th, and the unnamed officers (very likely James Rogers) of the King's Rangers and Canada Indians at Bloody Pond; the forceful, disciplined response against the rebels' left and centre columns at Klock's Field by Sir John's unnamed right wing commander; Andrew Thompson's coolly courageous, second and third advance with the flag of truce at the Middle Fort in the face of Murphy's sniping.

Of the two senior commanders — we follow Major Christopher Carleton's disciplined advance deep into hostile territory. His care to secure his route of retreat, his fireless camp, his night marches to avoid discovery by rebel patrols and his sure-footed successes over a rather pathetic opposition. That he exhibits a strong hand on the reins is not doubted, nor is his skill in managing a disparate force. He had little to fear from the rebels, although, to his credit, there is no indication that he had any prior knowledge of how little retaliation would confront his efforts and his careful dispositions to his flanks and rear confirm this. That Carleton was skillful and deserving of commendation is amply illustrated.

The more daring expedition is Johnson's. His tremendous drive and energy lays like a cloak over the account of the raid. Of course, for him to be successful, his officers and men had to mirror these same characteristics; however, the mastery of such hazardous missions requires the primary leader to possess self-assurance, mental & physical toughness, a measure of charisma and a strong dose of tactical cunning. Sir John's character fits this bill.

John Johnson was a remarkable man, whose accomplishments lie in the shadow of those of his even more remarkable father, Sir William. The father's American reputation was saved by his death preceding the rebellion, while the son's received the victor's wrath. Sir John's great service to the Crown was acknowledged repeatedly by Haldimand and Carleton. He carried the burden of so many overlapping military roles and administrative portfolios, it is a wonder that his health held throughout the rebellion. His strong leadership, both strategic and tactical, is graphically demonstrated in the planning and execution of his expeditions against the Mohawk and Schoharie Valleys, in particular, that of October 1780. His personal courage, so often called into question by his rebel enemies, is confirmed without doubt in his personally-led, short, sharp, frontal attack at Stone Arabia. Exactly when Sir John received his native warrior's name has not been found. It was a fitting name, one that rang with his military accomplishments — Owassighsishon, or He Who Makes The Roof To Tremble.[1]

His capacity to be daring, that essential characteristic of the outstanding leader, dominates the study of his two 1780 raids as does his possession of that other critical requirement — the need to be fortunate. Johnson was obviously thus blessed and, while his timing has every appearance of being impeccable, a closer look oft reveals that he was simply fortunate. Coupled with his amazing personal drive, his luck yielded great dividends.

One other characteristic, with which so many of the British, loyalist and native leaders and their troops were imbued, was boundless energy. In the accounts of the October raids, recall how often it is recorded that the Crown Forces are up before the crack of dawn and on the march? Recall how often they march throughout the night, skirmish, fight and destroy through the day, and then set off in a brisk withdrawal with only the briefest of stops to eat and rest?

By comparison, the rebel troops, militia and Levies, are never quite so energetic, never quite so capable of endurance. Governor Clinton observed of the Crown's forces that "their Troops [were] more enured to march'g."[2] Van Rensselaer mentioned the "Celerity of their Movements"[3] which prevented him from catching Sir John at the Noses and from stopping his advance against Stone Arabia. The energetic Dubois reported how closely he hounded Sir John's withdrawing force; he emphasizes "The Enemy is much fatigued, They travelled almost all the night, without any Refreshment; they must make a halt."[4] He reports how much his Levies drove themselves to overtake the raiders - yet he failed.

Examples of exceptional activity abound in all of the raids. When Johnson was fortunate in the capture of the sick rebel soldier at Old Oneida, he spurred forward the whole of his force to catch Vrooman's detachment, and, that accomplished, he sent mounted Rangers ahead "express" to prevent the Oneidas from destroying their bateaux.

In Carleton's raid, the parties from Jessup's and the King's Rangers, who burned the farms around Fort Edward and Fort Miller, had without significant rest began to march at 2:00 AM the night previous, the next morning had been part of the investment of Fort Ann, and that afternoon had destroyed the habitations of two districts. To accomplish their raid against the lower settlements, they were on the move from dusk the same day throughout the dark hours of night along both banks of the Hudson River and had returned to Carleton by 7:00 AM the morning of the following day, after which they took part in the capture of Fort George; all of this without a period of rest of more than 2-3 hours.

When Munro withdrew from Ballstown, his men had already marched the better part of the day before, had been employed without rest for the whole of the night, and yet he marched them at speed for a few hours before stopping to kill the livestock and eat a brief meal. He then set them on their feet again to march over a mountain and across a river before halting to rest overnight.

Houghton and the Canada Indians, when surprised by the militia in the dead of night, made a fighting withdrawal, herded their prisoners with them and entirely evaded their pursuers. These are only three examples of a great number of energetic — well organized, forceful and immediate — actions taken on the raids.

WASHINGTON'S OPINION OF THE EFFECT OF TERMS OF ENLISTMENT

Of the British Regulars and loyalist volunteers, there is little to say about enlistment terms that has not already been noted. A Regular soldier signed on for life[5] and could only escape the service by loss of health or desertion. Similarly, the loyalist enlisted for the duration of the conflict. He had forfeited his property by his exile and knew he had to fight to regain it. In the Regular battalions, individual military experience amongst the Commissioned and Non-Commissioned Officers' corps was substantial.[6] Amongst the private soldiers it was quite varied; however, there was always a thread of long service woven throughout the rank structure upon which a habit of discipline could be founded. Given a competent and dedicated officer and NCO corps, a regiment could be brought, and held, to a high degree of efficiency when there was stability in personnel. The rebels lacked this discipline of continuous service. Of course, the inexplicable, contemporary practice of breaking up regiments into company-sized packets and assigning them to widely spread posts, did not help either the Crown or the Congressional forces to attain, and maintain, a high degree of professionalism, but the Crown's forces had longevity of service on their side to offset this strange procedure.

Comparing the American loyalist regiments to their rebel counterparts, a key factor in favour of the former was the great number of veteran officers who became battalion and company commanders. These Provincial regiments were not as amateurish as is so often painted, particularly in British and Canadian accounts wherein a mild contempt for their proficiency is often found that is not matched in the American works. Many senior loyalist lieutenants had more experience of army life and active military operations than some rebel brigadiers.[7] While the loyalist troops might not perform well on the parade at the Quebec citadel, they were outstanding in the conditions of forest warfare where physical and mental toughness, good musketry, common sense tactics and high morale won the day.

To contrast enlistment terms — the rebel militiamen, who still had farms and businesses to operate, were called out for periods of short term service, a few days or at most weeks, to fulfill a specific duty or meet a local emergency. The Levies were signed on for longer terms, such as 3, 6 or 9-months, but not beyond. A great number of men in the Continental service were also taken under short-term enlistments. General Washington's words best describe the effects of enlistment practices in the Continental Line. The following are excerpts from a lengthy letter of Oct. 18, 1780,[8] written to Governor Clinton concerning the New York regiments in particular, but reflecting the state of affairs across the Continental army. (note, how contemporary this letter is to the events on the New York frontier in the same month)

> ... the present state of the troops of your Line [ie. New York's agreed contribution to the Continental army], by which you will preceive how few men you will have left after the 1st January next. When I inform you also that the troops of the other lines will be in general as much reduced as yours, you will be able to judge how exceedingly weak the army will be at that period, and how essential it is the states should make the most vigorous exertions to replace the discharged men as early as possible...
>
> I am religiously persuaded that the duration of the War and the greatest part of the misfortunes and perplexities we have hitherto experienced are chiefly to be attributed to the System of temporary inlistments. Had we in the commencement, raised an army for the War [like the Crown Forces], such as was within the reach of the abilities of these States to raise and maintain, we should not have suffered those military Checks which have so frequently shaken our cause, nor should we have incurred such enormous expenditures as have destroyed our paper Currency and with it all public credit. A moderate compact force on a permanent establishment capable of acquiring the discipline essential to military operations would have been able to make head ag't the enemy without comparison better than the throngs of militia which at certain periods have been, not in the feild, but in their way to and from the Feild; for from that want of perseverance which characterises all militia, and of that coercion which cannot be exercised upon them, it has always been found impracticable to detain the greatest part of them in service even for the term for which they have been called out, and this has been commonly so short, that we have had a great proportion of the time, two sets of men to feed and pay, one coming to the army and the other going from it. From this circumstance, and from the extraordinary waste and consumption of provisions, Stores, Camp equipage, arms, Cloathes and every other article incident to irregular troops, it is easy to conceive what an immense increase of public

expence has been produced from the source of which I am speaking...

... I mention Cloathes. It may be objected that the terms of engagement of the levies [it appears that a uniform was not supplied, but that any clothing item received on service became the man's property] do not include this; but if we want service from the men particularly in the cold Season we are obliged to supply them notwithstanding, and they leave us before the Cloaths are half worn out.

But there are evils more striking that have befallen us. The intervals between the dismission of one army and the collection of another have more than once threatened us with ruin.[9]

I am convinced our system of temporary inlistments has prolonged the War and encouraged the enemy to persevere... Nothing will tend so much to make the Court of London reasonable as the prospect of a permanent army in this Country, and a spirit of exertion to support it.

'Tis time we should get rid of an error which the experience of all mankind has exploded, and which our own experience has dearly taught us to reject — the carrying on a War with militia, or, which is nearly the same thing, temporary levies against a regular permanent and disciplined force. The Idea is chimerical, and that we have so long persisted in it, is a reflection on the judgment of a nation so enlightened as we are, as well as a strong proof of the empire of prejudice over Reason. If we continue in the infatuation, we shall deserve to lose the object we are contending for.

... I solemnly declare I never was witness to a single instance that can countenance an opinion of militia or raw troops being fit for the real business of fighting. I have found them useful as light parties to skirmish in the Woods, but incapable of making or sustaining a serious attack. This firmness is only acquired by habit of discipline and service... we must not expect from any [militia], services for which Regulars alone are fit.

An ill effect of short inlistments which I have not yet taken notice of, is that the constant fluctuation of their men is one of the sources of disgust to the officers. Just when, by great trouble fatigue and vexation (with which the training of Recruits is attended) they have brought their men to some kind of order; they have the mortification to see them go home, and to know that the drudgery is to recommence the next Campaign. In regiments so constituted, an officer has neither satisfaction nor credit in his command.

The army is not only dwindling into nothing, but the discontents of the officers as well as the men have matured to a degree that threatens but too general a renunciation of the service, at the end of the campaign. Since January last we have had registered at Head Quarters more than one hundred and sixty resignations, besides a number of others that never were regularly reported... We have frequently in the course of this Campaign experienced an extremity of want. Our officers are in general indecently defective in Cloathing. Our men are almost naked, totally unprepared for the inclemency of the approaching season. We have no magazines for the winter; the mode of procuring our supplies is precarious, and all the reports of the officers employed in collecting them are gloomy.

On the subject of enlistment terms, no more need be said.

THE DESTRUCTION OF GRAIN & LIVESTOCK AS A MILITARY STRATEGY[10]

The destruction of grain, forage and livestock as a military strategy has sometimes been called into question. Critics reason — surely the burning of a few hundred barns and magazines and the razing of a handful of grist mills could have no impact on a war as complex and far ranging as the revolutionary conflict. Surely a young, vibrant nation, as rich and well developed as the United States, could easily have shaken off the effects of such predatory attacks. If such doubts as these can be nurtured in an investigator's mind, then the raids of 1780 can be readily dismissed as malevolent and savage acts of British and Tory war criminals and their native allies. Certainly, many popular American historians have drawn this conclusion.

The following review of correspondence in the year 1780 between rebel military commanders and government authorities indicates otherwise. These letters reveal the perilous state of: the New York State defence system; the ability of the new country to continue the war and the state of the Continental army. The immense frustration, distress and alarm contained in this correspondence confirms how harmful, to both the rebels' morale and their capability to wage war, such extensive damage to the harvest and livestock would prove to be.

Earlier in this text, a report of May 17, 1780 from Colonel Goose Van Schaick to Governor Clinton was quoted. It is important to review his words again.

> ... I should not be surprised if all the settlements to the Northward of the Mohawk and the Westward of Hudson's River were shortly either destroyed or abandoned... I am incapacitated to draw forth the militia for want of provisions... Drafts from the militia have been made... but being unfurnished with provisions were obligated to disband.

Two days later he again wrote -

> ... the Militia of Tryon County have as good as refused to turn out... the frontier settlements are breaking up fast & if some remedy is not soon applied, Schonectady will be our frontier Settlement... Your Excellency's feelings must daily increase on the account of the distressed situation of our Affairs relative to supplies for the Army & the naked situation of our Western & Northern frontiers for the want of men & provisions.[11]

After several months had elapsed, the situation had in no way improved, as is illustrated in a letter from Colonel William Malcom, the recently-arrived, senior Continental officer at Albany in command of a brigade of Levies raised for defence of the frontiers, to Colonel Jacob Cuyler, Deputy Commissary of Purchases.

> Albany Sept. 8, 1780
> The public Service requires that a very considerable Quantity of Provisions should be instantly provided at this Place or Schenectady — I have called upon the State Agent — but have no Prospect of obtaining the least Supply from him — Considering you as a Continental Officer and unconnected in your Purchases with this or any other state, I apply to you and request to know whether you can supply me with any or with what quantity of flour, Beef, Pork and Salt... I ought at least to have 20,000 Rations in 10 Days — I beg your immediate answer which I shall communicate to his Excellency the

General [Washington], and therefore request that you explain and account for the Difficulties which arrise at present in the Commissary Department...[12]

The aggressive, even threatening, tone of this letter reflects Malcom's frustration over his discovery of a lack of proper stores in Albany and the effect this insufficiency was having on his new command.

In another letter of the same day written to the New York Governor, George Clinton, Malcom again exhibits his frustration over the lack of supplies and with the citizens of Albany -

But Sir — no provisions here; nor no one to get it — Mr Lush [his A.D.C.] can give me no encouragement nor thinks it proper to make any written report... the people here do not seem to care a farthing what comes of any thing but their scalps — Brant is their best Doctor. I pray you Sir, urge the State Agents to send us a supply. The supply ought to be now here & forwarded one in several convoys for the western subsistence of Fort Schuyler [Stanwix] — I want hard bread for my own Troops that go into the woods — no flour to bake it — 500 & odd Rations drawn here — in the City dayly — the Lord knows what they do for it...[13]

On Sep. 9th, Malcom wrote to the Governor -

... for prov[isio]ns my dependence I find is entirely on the lower Countys — ie. for Beef particularly.

He continues with some other administrative details and then closes with -

The Commanding officer at Fort George [Captain Chipman] has this day given notice that he has not a ration — & must evacuate the Post — he called for waggons to bring them off — this among other things evinces the necessity of Sending us provisions — the Frontiers here are of consequence... [14]

One of the State Agents, Udny Hay, the exiled Scottish-Canadian, wrote to Governor Clinton from Albany on Sep. 13th.

Sir, Upon my arrival here, I found an allmost total want of every supply necessary for the army; flour,

> however, will soon be obtained, at least the prospect
> is such as gives me reason to think so; but as to beef,
> without some much more coercive mode is adopted
> than what the law has yett pointed out, I am sure we
> shall not be able to furnish the necessary supply.
>
> I this day saw a small drove of Cattle from Ulster
> County... they were eight in number, not one of them
> really fit to kill, and two of them so poor they could
> scarce walk... therefore, beg your Excellency would
> represent to the Legislature the necessity of empower-
> ing the Assessors not only to determine the weight
> each Creature shall be[,] but that the persons assessed
> shall be oblidged, under some certain Penalty, to deliv-
> er their quantity in such Cattle as by proper judges
> shall be deemed fit for the knife.
>
> ... upon my return shall go to the westward [into
> the Mohawk Valley] where I have already taken the
> best steps in my power to have the people sounded
> respecting making voluntary sales of their grain upon
> the security of the State.[15]

It can be readily seen from Hay's letter that the problems were not simply a lack of supply. There was a lack of will, both within the government and the citizenry — might it be said amongst the latter — a lack of
patriotism? The cattle and grain were available, but due to the deva-
luation of Continental currency and the General bankruptcy of the State,
most citizens could not be persuaded to sell and, those who did, took
advantage of the situation to rid themselves of substandard animals.

After Sir John's raid of May, Governor Haldimand wrote to Lord
George Germain about Johnson's observations of conditions in the
lower Mohawk Valley.

> Sir John assures me that however the Colonies may be
> distressed for Public Resources, no Private Wants
> could be experienced in the Part of that Country where
> He was, the Houses and Farms being well stocked with
> Provisions, and a Prospect of a plentiful Harvest.[16]

This commentary is worthy of note, not only as it reveals an attitude
amongst the rebel populace, but as it reveals an early warning of the
prospect of a superb grain yield which obviously did not escape
Haldimand's notice.

Malcom wrote to Governor Clinton on Sep. 14th from Albany.
Amongst many military details and concerns, the Colonel adds - "Things

begin to brighten up — I get acquainted & the people begin to find out that they must either give up their sup[p]er or Rations... "[17] A definitely threatening tone to his observation is detectable, again reflecting his impatience, now bordering on disgust. He was understandably eager to execute his orders which were to secure all posts on the north and western frontiers of the state and to relieve the 1st New York Continental Line at Fort Stanwix with one of his regiments of Levies.

Two days later, and still in Albany, Malcom wrote to Clinton that he expected to have accumulated 100-150 barrels of flour and 50 cattle, the latter from New England. Thereafter, he would move into the Mohawk Valley to fulfill his duties. He also observed "There is a large body of Indians & French refugees [likely families of Canadiens serving in Congress's Own Canadian Regiment] at Schenectady [who] yet consume a world of provisions — the latter have a good claim to our bounty, but the former are a pack of scoundralls."[18] Typical of officers from the lower country, Malcom characterized the Oneidas as cunning rascals not deserving of the country's support, yet their adherence to the rebel cause had split the ancient Iroquois Confederacy and caused their people to sacrifice their towns and all their material goods. As we have seen earlier in the text, their subsequent service in Van Rensselaer's advance guard proved their great value to the rebels, as did the constant concern being shown in Canada regarding their activities, indeed their very existence.

On Sep. 20th, Malcom reported to Clinton that he was departing Albany "at last... Setting out for Fort Schuyler... but no Cattle [the New England commissaries had failed] unless Major Woolsey shall suceed in a scheme of Collecting a parcell between Schoharie & the Indian Country — I really am at a loss to know how to feed the troops — if there is not some Exertions among the Comyrs [Commissaries,] Magestrates and indeed every body it is certain there will not be a soldier beyond Albany in a Month (Fort Schuyler excepted)... " On another coercive note, he states that Colonel Udny Hay "went to [Shemenden?] yesterday & expects to sweat something out of them."

Smarting over how difficult it had been to find a resolution to his provisions problems, Malcom again found a party of refugees who, in his opinion, did not warrant rations. He said "There is a parcell of creatures called Shakers — prisoners of war & the devil knows who all — Eating our provisions... " Ominously, he added "I am sure they might be thin'd... "[19]

Two days later, Malcom wrote to General Washington advising that he had been "dissapointed in provissions from every Quarter."[20] On Oct. 3rd, while at Fort Rensselaer, he wrote to Governor Clinton recommending that Fort Schuyler (Stanwix) be abandoned,[21] as it was proving ineffective as a block to incursions from Niagara and Canada, and was very difficult to garrison and service. He suggested as an alternative "establishing the Garrison thirty miles lower down the River" where about half the number of troops as required at Stanwix would better serve to protect the populace and their habitations and farms. He commented "for so low are the inhabitants" that he feared "this fine Country which is able to furnish bread to the Army will be depopulated."[22]

All of the above correspondence relates to Albany and Tryon Counties; however, the problem persisted across the state. The key installation at West Point on the Hudson River had narrowly escaped being taken by the British the month before through the machinations of the newly-varnished loyalist, Benedict Arnold. Its commandant, General Nathanael Greene, wrote on Oct. 10th to Governor Clinton, "The garrison this night is without an ounce of flour; nor have we any certain account of any coming to our relief."[23]

The next day, Colonel Malcom wrote to Governor Clinton advising of Carleton's attack on Fort Ann and the burning of the farms about Fort Edward. He advised that the militia were ordered out, but their colonel "thinks the men would desert." He continued, "If we had men[,] we have[not,] nor can get[,] Provisions — but Genl. Ten Broeck thinks it will be difficult to get the Militia out on this Acct... Provisions must be sent on or we are... "[24]

Colonel Stephen Lush's letter of Oct. 12th to Governor Clinton offered more details of Carleton's activities and included this paragraph -

> The Scarcity of Provisions and the total uncertainty of obtaining Supplies is truly alarming. If any means can be fallen upon to supply the Troops now ordered out and those already on the Frontiers, Colo. Malcolm requests your Excellency's Interposition, as without Supplies the Militia must disband as soon as they take the Field. And if Reinforcements of men can be obtained from any other Quarter than those already mentioned, Colo. Malcolm conceives they will be wanted provided they come with sufficient Supplies of Provisions.[25]

On Oct. 13th, the news that Fort George had also fallen reached Albany as did intelligence from Fort Stanwix where the Oneida deserter had been questioned and revealed details of the column under Johnson, Butler and Brant. In response, Colonel-Commandant Malcom, in his role as senior Continental officer at Albany, ordered a call-out of 800 men of the militia brigade of Brigadier General Robert Van Rensselaer. Just the day before he had requested only 500, but this was before he had an "idea of so formidible a [Crown] force being out."[26] In his order of the 13th, he advised Van Rensselaer -

> ... beg, therefore, that you will be pleased to give your orders accordingly; unless we have reinforcements immediately, no doubt but Fort Schuyler [Stanwix] and all that remains of the fine Country, the Mohawk River, particularly Stone Arabia will be destroyed. It is also necessary that Cattle and flour come forward not only for your subsistence but for the Troops already here. It is a fact that we have no Beef, nor is there either wheat or flour collected notwithstanding my consent and most pressing Solicitations.[27]

It is interesting to note that Malcom was concerned about Stone Arabia four days before the deserter, Benjamin Burton, revealed it to be a prime target for destruction.

On the same day, Van Rensselaer wrote to Governor Clinton from Claverack, on the east side of the Hudson below Albany. He included a copy of Malcom's order and advised that he had "requested the agents of the State in this Quarter to forward on all the Cattle and flour they can collect."[28] He had clearly taken Macolm's warnings very seriously.

On Oct. 14th, LtCol. Ezra Badlam of the 2nd Massachusetts Continental Line, who was doing duty with his regiment in Totoway, New York, wrote to Governor Clinton requesting permission to export eight barrels of flour to his home state.[29] While Massachusetts had beef, it would seem they lacked flour. Clinton was being besieged from every quarter.

That same day, Governor Clinton wrote to General Washington apprizing him of the Crown Forces' activities on the frontiers of New York and asking for the assistance of Continental troops.

> If it was possible for your Excellency to spare some Continental Troops on this Occassion they woud inspire the Militia with Confidence & enable us to repel the Enemy. The Want of Supplies of every kind in that Quarter will greatly embarrass every Measure & I fear that with our utmost Exertions we shall fail in collecting a sufficiency of Provission for the Troops that it may be necessary to keep in the Field in this Emergency.[30]

From Philadelphia on Oct. 16th, President Huntington forwarded copies of the Acts of Congress regarding the supply of provisions for the army in response to letters from the Senate and Assembly of New York State written on Sep. 21st requesting adjustments to the quotas required to support the war effort.

> ... signifying their Approbation that the State of New York may substitute Flour in Lieu of any quantity of Beef which may be deficient on the first Day of November next, of the Quota allotted to that State agreeable to the restrictions & Proviso expressed in the Act...
>
> ... Whereas the State of New York was required by an act of Congress of the 25th Feb'y last to furnish eleven thousand two hundred Ct.Wt. of beef [508 metric Tonnes]; and whereas it will be of public advantage to procure flour as near as possible to the military posts & quarters of the army...[31]

The letter then reiterated the agreement to substitute flour for beef, but advised -

> ... that the said State shall continue to provide & deliver the quantity of beef requested to be furnished by the Committee of Congress lately with the army in their letter of the second of June last and eleven hundred & twenty five head of beef cattle in addition thereto.[32]

Huntington also advised -

> ... that the Committee to whom was referred the application of the State of New York... for the relief of the Treasury... report their opinion... "That if the application should be granted the like benefit may be claimed for other States; that there is reason to fear that a compliance with such demands would involve the United States in the greatest difficulties, and that it cannot therefore by complied with."[33]

Nonetheless, the substitution of flour for beef was approved in favour of New York State. Of course, the State Congress was expecting that the bountiful harvest in the Mohawk region — the grain bowl of New York — would allow this to take place.

The rebel commissary general, Colonel Ephraim Blaine, wrote to President Samuel Huntington on Oct. 17th advising that the army's magazines were destitute of the necessaries of life.

> Permit me thro' your Excellency to remind Congress about the supplies of our army which gives me much

real concern and uneasiness; they are now fed from day to day, and scarcely a week has passed this three months, that they have not been one or two days wanting either bread or beef.

Your magazines are now destitute of Flour, Bread, Beef, Pork, Fish, Salt, Rum and none upon the continent, to my knowledge, can furnish one day's supply. The States of New Hampshire and Massachusetts-bay are our principal dependence for Beef; the French being stationed at Rhode Island has deprived the agent of that State from giving any assistance; indeed he is hard put to it, to find [supply, provide, furnish] the continental troops on that Station...

I have no relief from the State of New York for the main army; they have not been able to furnish their frontier posts with Beef...

[New] Jersey can furnish but little Beef and not a large quantity of flour...

Pensylvania as yet have delivered very little flour, no salt nor do I know of their buying any cattle.

All the garrisons & posts of the middle department are destitute of provisions, and no means in my power of relieving them. The season is now advanced and passing, in which quantities of Beef ought to be procured and laid in at these places, otherwise the troops must disband for want of subsistance.

I am distressed to think how the army is to be kept together thro' the winter; it will be impossible without large quantities of beef is laid in upon the North [Hudson] River contiguous to West Point, and at the magazines in Jersey...[34]

Governor Clinton's report to General Washington on his attempt to pursue and cut-off Sir John Johnson includes the following -

The morning after the action [Klock's Field], I arrived with the militia under my immediate Command; but they were so beat out with fatigue, having marched at least 50 miles in less than 24 Hours, as to be unable to proceed any further. I, therefore, left them & put myself at the head of the advanced Troops & continued the pursuit til within ab't 15 miles of Oneida, & if we cou'd possibly have procured Provission to have enabled us to have persisted one or two Days longer,

there is little Doubt but we might have succeeded at
least so far as to have scattered their main Body &
made many Prisoners, but there was no supplies, but
such as I was oblidged to take from the Inhabitants on
our Route & these was inadequate & the Collection of
them attended with Delay, nor could the Pack Horses
with the small Quantities procured in this disagreeable
manner, overtake us in so rapid a march through a
perfect wilderness. I was, therefore, oblidged tho'
reluctantly to return, most of the Troops having been
near two Days utterly destitute & unable to proceed.[35]

The situation throughout the States had not improved by December as
reports found in the papers of Sir Henry Clinton, British C-I-C North
America, dated the 18th, illustrate. A Lieutenant Vincent of the loyalist
regiment, the Guides & Pioneers, had escaped from the rebel Provost
at Fish Kill on the 11th and regained the British lines at New York City.
He brought intelligence that the Continental army and the citizenry
were "in the greatest distress for Cloathing & Provisions. The Congress
Regt. [Hazen's Congress's Own Canadian Regiment] have been a fort-
night without drawing any flour."[36]

This brief review of correspondence reveals that the supply system related to provisions, particularly that of beef and flour, was in
critical disarray across the northern states and, in particular, in New
York. It is also obvious that these desperate straits were brought on,
not by a lack of livestock or grain, but because of a breakdown in
finances and the general will of both the Continental Congress and
the people. That the British should set the destruction of grain and
livestock, the latter by killing or removal, as a strategic target should
be of no surprise. As well, the reduction of the supply of grain for
flour, and livestock for fresh and salted meat, further inflated the
value of what was left, making it more expensive to procure for the
army.

It remains to say that undeniably, the loyalist troops, white and
native, who were so often given the task of destruction, were frequently motivated by parallel considerations; however, that fact in no
way denies the military legitimacy of the strategy of ruining the
resources themselves, disrupting their husbandry and, in the case of
grains, their milling.

Governor Clinton summarized the disaster visited upon the New
York frontier as follows —

The news Papers will give you a pretty just account of
the late Progress of the Enemy on the Frontiers,

except as to the Devastations committed by them which it might not be so prudent to publish. They have destroyed at least 200 Dwellings & 150,000 bushels of wheat, with a proportion of other Grain & Forage... [37]

TO PAY THE PIPER - THE PRICE OF NEGLECT

The ruinous state of the Continental currency, the lack of will or inability of the various states to sufficiently support their Continental regiments and the evils resulting from short term enlistments, so obviously feared by General Washington, all came to a head in the new year. On January 1st, 1781, ten of the eleven regiments of the Pennsylvania Line mutinied. These regiments were in winter quarters at Mount Kemble (Morristown), New Jersey. The eleventh regiment was spared the disgrace by being in garrison on Pennsylvania's northern frontier. There had been minor mutinies before. In January of 1780, about one hundred Massachusetts' men, who declared their enlistment terms were finished, marched away from the garrison at West Point. They were overtaken and forcibly returned to The Point, where most were pardoned and a few punished.[38] In May of 1780, two regiments of the Connecticut Line encamped at Morristown in New Jersey had paraded under arms with the intent to leave the camp to search for provisions. This affair, a matter of "protest and expostulation",[39] was quickly dealt with by their officers and a show of force by the Pennsylvania brigade. As the citizenry of the various states were not always enamoured of each other, this interference by Pennsylvanians was deeply resented by the Connecticut men. In early June of the same year, in a protest over lack of pay and inadequate clothing, thirty one men of the 1st New York deserted with their arms from the isolated garrison at Fort Stanwix on the Mohawk River. Their stated intention was to join the British at Oswegatchie on the St. Lawrence River. The deserters were overtaken by a detachment from the garrison and a body of Oneida Indians and, in a bloody confrontation, their attempt was foiled.[40]

In comparison, the 1781 mutinies were far more extensive and portentous. Alarmingly, the Pennsylvania affair opened with a number of officers and men being killed and wounded and several fieldpieces being seized by the mutineers.[41] The Pennsylvania Brigade of 11 regiments represented the second largest commitment of men for Continental service of the thirteen states. Only Massachusetts, with a brigade of 15 regiments, made a greater contribution, while Virginia also furnished 11.[42] Should one of the largest state brigades in the

Continental service desert to the enemy, a possibility greatly feared at the time, or attack the Congress, the results would be utterly disastrous. However, there is very little evidence that any of the dissatisfied men had a serious intention to join the enemy. Their grievances were focused on the Continental and their home-state governments. Once it became clear that the Pennsylvanians had no thought of desertion, all thought and action was turned towards stopping these significant disturbances from spreading, for it seemed very unlikely that the somnolent British would not rouse themselves to take military action.

While rebel concerns of overt British military action were off the mark, the British did do their best to foment further unrest by employing secret agents to infiltrate amongst the mutineers and amongst the other Continental camps. It was, of course, impossible to prevent the news of the mutiny spreading and the New Englanders reacted in a quite different manner. Although they had been equally misused and were as angered as the Pennsylvanians, their approach for a redress of their grievances was quietly circumspect and unaccompanied by open rebellion against authority. Their petitions were courteously received and many of their complaints were quickly acted upon.

On the other hand, the three regiments of the New Jersey brigade, who were in winter quarters at Pompton, New Jersey, copied the Pennsylvanians' actions in late January and rose in arms. General Washington hesitated not a moment and ordered out New England troops from West Point to march to New Jersey and quell the mutiny. The commander-in-chief then wrote instructions to one of his New Jersey commissioners in which he encouraged the Colonel "to employ all your influence to inspire the militia [of New Jersey] with a disposition to cooperate with us [to reduce the mutiny], by representing the fatal consequences of the present temper of the soldiery, not only to military subordination but to civil liberty. In reality both are fundamentally struck at by their [the Continentals] undertaking in arms to dictate terms to their country."[43] The Jersey mutiny was quashed without resort to bloodshed, but the bitterness over the very real grievances suffered by the men of all the state brigades remained, even though several measures were taken by their home governments and Congress to address them.

No claim can be made that the raids that raged across the New York frontier in October 1780 were a direct cause of the mutinies in the Continental Line. The Continental soldiers' anger was nurtured by years of political mismanagement and wanton neglect. Lack of pay, clothing, shelter and spirits; gross unfairness in enlistment practices, especially the payment of bounties for short term men — all of these contributed to the uprising as much as the terribly inadequate supplies of food. Nonetheless, there can be little doubt that the destruction of supplies of grain, forage and livestock in New York State had a substantial impact.

NOTES

CHAPTER I — BACKGROUND

1   Gustave Lanctot, **Canada & the American Revolution** (London, Toronto, Wellington, Sydney: George G. Harrap & Co. Ltd., 1967) Chpts. 5-10.

2   Brig.Gen. Ernest A. Cruikshank and Gavin K. Watt, **The King's Royal Regiment of New York** (Toronto: Gavin K. Watt, 1984) p.32. Originally published, Ontario Historical Society, 1931. Hereafter, "Cruikshank & Watt, KRR NY."

3   WO17, 1573(1), p.187.

4   **The Sullivan-Clinton Campaign in 1779** (Albany: The University of the State of New York, 1929) pp.12-15.

5   ibid.

6   E. Cruikshank, **Butler's Rangers and the Settlement of Niagara** (Welland: Lundy's Lane Historical Society, 1893) p.63.

7   Research of Kim R. Stacy, (recreated 2Bn, 84th Regt) Detroit, Michigan. ex a transcript of a letter from Lt Archibald MacLaine, Light Infantry subaltern of the 1st Bn, 84th, to his brother Capt Murdock dated December 1780, but more likely 1779. Archibald advises that his commanding officer, Capt George McDougall, ("who behaved so gallantly at the Siege of Quebec") had died from the rigors of the campaign while aboard ship on Lake Ontario on a return voyage to lower Quebec. His letter is the only source of information yet found that confirms the participation of the 34th & 84th Light Coys in the 1779 campaign against the Sullivan expedition. Stacy advises that McDougall was a 35 year veteran of the army who was 60 when he died, an incredible age for a Light Infantry officer.

8   Sullivan-Clinton, **op.cit.,** p.10. Flick wrote the introduction to this publication.

9   Cruikshank, Butler's Rangers, **op.cit.,** pp.63&64. During the assembly stages of the Sullivan-Clinton expedition, Capt John McDonell, and his company of Butler's Rangers, alarmed the settlements on the Mohawk River and a little later, with the Seneca warchief John Montour, they struck Fort Freeland on the Susquehanna. Ranger Lieut Andrew Thompson's detachment, with a party led by Seneca warchief, Rowland Montour, scoured the Susquehanna region for cattle. Lieut John Johnston of the Indian Department led a party that brought in 18 prisoners from the frontier. A Ranger recruiting officer secured 20 new men off the streets of Albany and another enlisted 70 from the farms and towns on the east side of the Hudson River.

10 Cruikshank & Watt, KRR NY, **op.cit.,** pp.85-95. In 1782, Major Ross of the 2nd Battalion, King's Royal Yorkers brought a large force to Oswego and rebuilt the fort there; **ibid,** pp.97-99. The rebels attempted capture the fort at Oswego after the end of hostilities without success.

11 Archibald M. Howe, **Colonel John Brown of Pittsfield, Massachusetts, the Brave Accuser of Benedict Arnold, An Address Delivered before the Fort Rensselaer Chapter of the D.A.R. and others at the Village of Palatine Bridge, New York, September 29, 1908** (Boston: W.B. Clarke, 1908) p.15.

CHAPTER II — THE CAMPAIGN OPENS

1   Barbara Graymont, **The Iroquois in the American Revolution** (Syracuse: Syracuse University Press, 1972) p.224.

2   Howard Swiggett, **War Out of Niagara, Walter Butler and the Tory Rangers** (Port Washington, NY: Ira J. Friedman, Inc., 1963) p.212.

3 Graymont, **op.cit.**, pp.17-25, 232; One of the most detailed descriptions of native warfare is found in a Doctoral dissertation and is consequently not readily available. This is - Paul Lawrence Stevens, "His Majesty's 'Savage' Allies, British Policy and the Northern Indians During the Revolutionary War, 1774-1778", Department of History, State University of New York at Buffalo, 1984. pp.41-58

4 Franklin B. Hough, **The Northern Invasion of October 1780, A Series of Papers Relating to the Expeditions from Canada under Sir John Johnson and Others against the Frontiers of New York** ... (New York: 1866) p.22.

5 Butler reported leading 20-30 Indian Department rangers into the ravine. Capt Steven Watts' Light Infantry Company, KRR was there at the outset and, in mid afternoon, Capt.Lt John McDonell led a reinforcement of the Colonel's Coy, KRR and detachments from several other companies to the battle site.

6 Graymont, **op.cit.**, index. Old Smoke is an anglicized version or translation of Sayenqueraghta, as is Cornplanter of Gayentwahga.

7 Cruikshank, Butler's Rangers, **op.cit.**, p.41.

8 **ibid**, pp.41-43. This source suggests that only two companies were completed at that time. This being the case, the Major's Coy and Caldwell's are the most likely, as prior to Walter's arrival, Caldwell had been senior Capt, a position he regained after Walter's death in 1781.

9 Graymont, **op.cit.**, p.165. Graymont points out that Walter Butler was given his Captaincy in the Rangers at this time, but did not immediately accompany the regiment on campaign. Instead, he travelled to Quebec to transmit intelligence to Carleton, the Governor of Quebec.

10 Cruikshank, Butler's Rangers, **op.cit.**, p.43.

11 Isabel Thompson Kelsay, **Joseph Brant 1743- 1807, Man of Two Worlds** (Syracuse: Syracuse University Press, 1984) p.216; Cruikshank, Butler's Rangers, **op.cit.**, p.41.

12 **ibid**, pp.45-46.

13 Kelsay, **op.cit.**, pp.216-217; It is interesting to read Graymont's account of the Cherry Valley incident, **op.cit.**, p.166.

14 Cruikshank, Butler's Rangers, **op.cit.**, p.53.

15 Elizabeth Cometti, ed., **The American Journals of Lt. John Enys** (Syracuse: The Adirondack Museum - Syracuse University Press, 1976) pp.23-34. Excellent details of this excursion, although there is little information about the smaller loyalist detachments. Cited hereafter as "Enys"; another excellent account, Ida H. Washington & Paul A. Washington, **Carleton's Raid** (Canaan, NH: Pheonix Publishing, 1977) passim.

16 Christopher Carleton was a nephew of Guy, the Governor of Quebec from before the war until 1778 and again, as Lord Dorchester, from 1784 to 1795.

17 The Historical Section of the General Staff, eds, **A History of the Organization, Development and Services of the Military and Naval Forces of Canada, etc** ... (3 Vols, Ottawa: n.p., n.d.) II,p.73. Future citations - "General Staff." ex NAC, Haldimand Papers, B, Vol.132, pp.3&4. Haldimand's instructions to Maj Carleton, 17Oct78; A mantelet is a small fieldpiece, perhaps a one pounder, with a strong shield to protect the gunners from musketry. It was often used in direct support of infantry, however in this situation, as so few artillerists were assigned to the detachment, the mantelets may simply have been the shields and carriages to which the Cohorns were mounted. See Captain George Smith, **An Universal Military Dictionary or A Copious Explanation of the Technical Terms, etc** ... (London: n.p., 1779) p.158.

18 General Staff, **op.cit.**, p.82. From Haldimand's report to Lord George Germain, 21Nov78.

19 Cruikshank & Watt, KRR NY, **op.cit.**, p.24.

20 BM, HP, AddMss21765. Pay List, 24 Dec. 1777 - 24 Oct. 1778. This document lists five full, and one part, companies.

21 As the fighting strength of the Six Nations dwindled in the 18th Century, a number of small groups, which were the remnants of various eastern Algonkian-speaking nations, were invited to settle in Iroquoia by the League. They became loyal friends of their benefactors and could be counted upon to supply fighting men when needed. Some of these remnants were the Nanticokes, the Tuteloes and the Mahiconnucks. As some settled near to the rebel Oneidas, they became most closely allied to that nation and took side in its interest.

22 AO, HP, AddMss21770.

23 Swiggett, **op.cit.**, pp.216&217. ex The Papers of James Madison (New York, 1841) I, p.47. Madison writing to Thomas Jefferson.

24 General Staff, **op.cit.**, pp.8-17.

25 Cruikshank & Watt, KRR NY, **op.cit.**, p.264. Sutherland, an NCO in the 26th Regt captured at Sorel in 1775, escaped to Johnstown and then came away with Sir John in May 1776. He joined the KRR NY on its founding date, 19Jun76. As a Volunteer, he served as Adjutant of the battalion in 1776 & 77. Being without independent means, he could not buy his commission and he determined to earn it by merit, taking on the hazardous duties of a secret service scout. By 8May80 he had been promoted to Ensign having conducted successful missions to the Mohawk Valley in 1778, 79& 80. For his past & further services, he was promoted to second senior Lieutenant in the 2nd battalion on 13Nov81.

26 **ibid**, pp.36&37.

27 **ibid**, p.41.

28 T.W. Egly, Jr., **Goose Van Schaick of Albany, 1736-1789 - The Continental Army's Senior Colonel** (the author, 1992) p.81.

29 Hough, **op.cit.**, p.25. Due to the shortage of Continental Infantry, a measure was adopted by Congress to raise men for the defence of the frontiers by calling up drafts of men from the militia to serve for terms as long as 9 months. "In the summer of 1779, two regiments of 500 men each were raised in New York State. These were replaced by 800 men by an enactment of 4Apr80; p.38. "The governor of New York was authorized to issue press warrants for taking cattle, flour, grain, teams and labor, as the emergencies of the service required; p.41. "In matters relating to discipline, pay and rations, were placed on a par with the Continental troops; Egly, Van Schaick, **op.cit.**, p.81. "The Levies were made up of drafts from the militia regiments as well as men recruited directly from the civilian population. While similar to the militia in many respects, the Levies could be called upon to serve outside their home state during the entire term of enlistment. Levies had been sent to the Northern Department from other areas and were part of the troops being relied upon for the defense of the frontier." This explains the service of Massachusetts Levies in the Mohawk region; One suspects that the training of these men was not much better than the militia. However, they had two benefits. They were most frequently officered by ex Continentals and the length of time the various companies spent together gave them the opportunity to develop a team spirit that the very short term militiaman often lacked.

30 **TCM Newsletter, Vol.XV, No.9 (May 1995)** James F. Morrison research from the BM, HP, AddMss21842, Secret Intelligence.

31 **NAC, MG23, B23,** Call sign - Royal Regiment of New York. The Orderly Book was a gift to the Archives by Judge J.F. Pringle, a noted 19th Century Canadian historian and author, who noted that the book had belonged to Capt Samuel Anderson's Light Infantry Company, which several entries tend to confirm.

32 **ibid.**

33 **ibid.**

34 **WO17, 1574(2), p.75.**

35 Cruikshank & Watt, KRR NY, **op.cit.**, p.40.

36 **ibid**, p.41.

37 Hough, **op.cit.**, p.27.

38 Kelsay, **op.cit.**, p.291. ex Public Papers of George Clinton, Vol.V, p.740. Col Jacob Klock to BGen Abraham Ten Broeck. p.741, Klock to New York Governor Clinton. p.742, Maj Wemple to Col Goose Van Schaick ...

39 Hough, **op.cit.**, pp.29&30. This source gives some detail of the forces raised in pursuit of Johnson and the reasons for their lack of success.

40 Swiggett, **op.cit.**, p.127. ex Clinton Papers, V, p.769.

41 Cruikshank & Watt, KRR NY, **op.cit.**, p.43. Haldimand to Germain, 12Jul80.

42 James F. Morrison research.

43 Graymont, **op.cit.**, pp.234&235; This coercion of the Oneidas and their friends had quite questionable results. The following Chapters will give accounts of Oneida deserters who compromise the activities of Crown units; **Public Papers of George Clinton, First Governor of New York 1777-1795-1801-1804** (7 vols, Albany: The State of New York, 1902) VI,pp.480-482. This is a report from Col Weissenfels, the

commandant at Fort Stanwix, dated 9Dec80 which advises that a principle Oneida warrior named Jacob Reid had just brought his family and five Oneida warriors from Niagara. Their conversion to loyalism had obviously been a very thin veneer. He reported that he had been amongst 20 Oneidas who had been 'persuaded' by Brant, Peter and Skenandon to join the Crown Indians at Niagara. Further, he told that one of them had been killed on Sir John's October expedition and five had come off with himself. When asked how the Indians were being provided for at Niagara, he answered, "Well in every sense of the word." He also advised that the October raid had been aimed at Schenectady and, as an attack on that place had not occurred, the town would be the target of the next year's campaign.

44   Graymont, **op.cit.**, p.235; Kelsay, **op.cit.**, pp.292-295; Cruikshank, Butler's Rangers, **op.cit.**, pp.79&80.

45   Graymont, **op.cit.**, p.236.

46   Cruikshank, Butler's Rangers, **op.cit.**, pp.80-81.

47   Graymont, **op.cit.**, pp.242-244.

CHAPTER III — EXPEDITIONS ON LAKE CHAMPLAIN

1   While some historians, including Franklin Hough, have attempted to link Benedict Arnold's attempted betrayal of the fortress at West Point with the expeditions from Canada, the West Point affair occurred the month before. This is not to suggest that these events were totally unrelated, as Sir Henry Clinton, British C-I-C, may have intended to take action in the Hudson Highlands when West Point fell into British hands and asked Haldimand to give every assistance possible from Canada; however, no evidence of this request has been found.

2   Cruikshank, Butler's Rangers, **op.cit.**, p.82. This letter is quoted without stating to whom it was directed; General Staff, **op.cit.**, pp.21&22; Cruikshank & Watt, KRR NY, **op.cit.**, p.45. Letter from Haldimand to SJJ dated 24Aug80 with similar details.

3   **ibid**, p.55.

4   **ibid**, p.45.

5   Mary Beacock Fryer, **Buckskin Pimpernel, the Exploits of Justus Sherwood, Loyalist Spy** (Toronto & Charlottetown: Dundurn Press, 1981) p.106.

6   General Staff, **op.cit.**, p.22.

7   **ibid.**

8   Horatio Rogers, ed., Lieut. James M. Hadden, **A Journal Kept In Canada and Upon Burgoyne's Campaign in 1776 and 1777** (Albany: Joel Munsell's Sons, 1784) pp.20fn&21fn. "Christopher Carleton was a nephew of Sir Guy Carleton ... born at Newcastle upon Tyne, in 1749, and entered the British army as an ensign, Dec. 12, 1761. Feb. 12, 1762 [he entered] the 31st Foot. In that corps he was promoted to be lieutenant, July 29, 1763; captain-lieutenant, Dec. 25, 1770; captain, May 25, 1772; and major of the 29th Foot, Sept. 13, 1777. He accompanied the 31st to America in the spring of 1776, was appointed an aide-de-camp on the staff of Sir Guy Carleton, May 11th of that year, and served in Canada and on the northern frontier during the remainder of the Revolutionary war ... a lieutenant-colonel in the army Feb. 19, 1783; and ... died at Quebec, Thursday night, June 14, 1787"; Christopher Carleton is sometimes confused with his uncle, LtCol Thomas Carleton, also of the 29th Regt, who served simultaneously in Canada and was later the first Lieut.Gov. of the province of New Brunswick; Stevens, Savage Allies, **op.cit.**, X, p.648. Christopher Carleton was "the son of Guy Carleton's eldest brother" and had "recently married the elder sister of the governor's beloved wife."

9   **ibid.**

10   **ibid.**

11   **ibid**, X,p.649.

12.   William L. Stone, tr., **Letters of Brunswick and Hessian Officers During the American Revolution** (Albany: 1891) reprinted, Da Capo Press, 1970, p.65. A letter dated St. Anne, 9Mar-20Apr77.

13   Stevens, Savage Allies, **op.cit.**, X, p.649. ex Long, Voyages & Travels, p.36.

14   General Staff, **op.cit.**, III,p.19.

15   Ida H. & Paul A. Washington, **Carleton's Raid** (Canaan, NH: Pheonix Publishing, 1977) p.90. In the Washingtons' transcript of Carleton's report of the 1778 raid, the

Maj refers to an officer in the 29th Regt named Farquar. This is very likely the same man referred to in Enys' journal. The transcript of Enys' journal illustrates that he spelled phonetically as did so many of his contemporaries. As a more common spelling of the name would be Farquhar this is used throughout this text.

16 This detachment is likely from Von Kreutzbourg's Hesse Hanau Jaeger battalion, however there are other possibilities such as Von Barner's Brunswick Light Infantry battalion.

17 Maj Edward Jessup acted as the senior Provincial officer on this expedition. His activity and service on this occasion, as well as his previous performance, led Governor Haldimand to name him Major Commandant of the newly created Loyal Rangers in 1781. This corps was an amalgamation of the King's Loyal Americans, the Queen's Loyal Rangers and elements of the American Volunteers and the Loyal Volunteers. In this role, Jessup superceded his brother Ebenezer, who had commanded the KLA and was judged inadequate by Haldimand. John Peters, who had commanded the QLR, had offended the punctilious Governor and was reduced in rank to the Capt-commandant of the LR's Company of Pensioners, in which Ebenezer served as a supernumerary Capt. E. Rae Stuart, "Jessup's Rangers as a factor in Loyalist Settlement", **Three History Theses** (Ontario Department of Public Records and Archives, 1961) p.46.

18 Mary Beacock Fryer, **King's Men, the Soldier Founders of Ontario** (Toronto and Charlottetown: Dundurn Press Limited, 1980) pp.202,203,251. This source confirms that Majs Edward Jessup and James Rogers were in attendance.

19 Brig.Genl. E.A. Cruikshank, "The Adventures of Roger Stevens, A Forgotten Loyalist Pioneer in Upper Canada", **Ontario Historical Society Papers & Records, Vol.XXXIII (1939)** pp.11-37. Stevens was from the Grants and had refused to lead his militia company against the King and was jailed in Connecticut from where he escaped to join the Crown forces in 1777 under Burgoyne. He acted as a guide for Von Riedesel's German Brigade en route to Castleton and thereafter as wagonmaster and purchasing agent for General Burgoyne. He was captured attempting to escape to Canada after the capitulation of Burgoyne's army and was held at Bennington under very trying circumstances until he again escaped through the assistance of his brother Abel. He arrived at St. John's in Mar78 and was examined by Maj Carleton who found him truthful and well informed. He served as a guide for Maj Carleton's 1778 expedition against Otter Creek and again in 1780 against Forts Ann & George. He came to the attention of Maj Jas Rogers who promised him a commission if he could raise sufficient recruits. Stevens was able to raise 23 men who did service in the Rangers, but Rogers was not able to gain permission for a fourth company which meant that at the war's end, Stevens was returned only as a supernumerary Ens of the King's Rangers. In 1781 & 82, Stevens had many harrowing exploits in the Secret Service related to the negotiations with Vermont for which he received much well-deserved praise. After the death of his wife, he turned to womanizing while on scouts in enemy territory which caused his removal from Secret Service work, although he always continued to enjoy the highest opinion of the staid Governor who, remarkably, exhibited an understanding of, or a blind eye towards, his indiscretions.

20 Enys, **op.cit.,** pp.35-51. This source provides a table of the force as prepared by Enys. The names of many officers of various British regiments are taken from Enys' diary as is mention of Claus' Rangers being with Munro. Enys also recorded that the majority of the Canada Indians accompanying Carleton were from Akwesasne; General Staff, **op.cit.,** III,p.26. This source advises that some of the Indians were drawn from Caughnawaga (Kahnawake) and Lake of the Two Mountains (Kanehsatake). Akwesasne is not mentioned!

21 Cruikshank & Watt, KRR NY, **op.cit.,** pp.55-58. Report of Capt John Munro to Gov Haldimand; **WO17, 1574, p.175**. The exact number of Royal Yorkers on the expedition comes from this source as does the names of the subaltern officers. The Return lists the following on the expedition: 2 C, 3 L, 2 E, 1 Adj, 7 S, 2 Dr, 114 R&F.

22 There has been much recent debate over the identity of the Fraser commanding the party of Rangers who accompanied Munro. A Capt Alexander Fraser, 34th Regt, was seconded to the Quebec Indian Department in 1776 and also commanded a corps of select British marksmen during and after the Burgoyne campaign. In these capacities he led mixed bodies of warriors and marksmen in an advanced corps. Was this Alexander the Fraser with Munro? There was a Capt William Fraser of Jessup's King's Loyal Americans who, like Robert Leake, was given an

independent company command, in Fraser's case, of Rangers. This command was granted by Haldimand in 1778. In 1780, Fraser's company was composed of 3 officers, 3 Sjts, 3 Cpls and 52 R&F. See, **HP, Ms622, Reel 109, p.52 and HP, MG13, WO28, Vol.10, Pt2, p.254.** William Fraser was a farmer from outside of Ballstown. See, J. **Fraser, Skulking for the King, A Loyalist Plot** (Erin, Ont: The Boston Mills Press, 1985) pp.38,index. He had been very active with Capt Daniel McAlpin in the raising of the American Volunteers and later as a Capt in the King's Loyal Americans. As he was recognized by the Scott family at Ballstown during the raid, the finger points to William as the Fraser on the raid, not Alexander, who was not an inhabitant of New York.

23 **WO28/5, p.98.** Patrick Langan ranked as an Ens in the 1Bn KRR NY on 4Oct79 and as a Lt in the 2Bn on 12Nov81; **WO28/10, p.406.** List of Indian Dept Officers. Langan ranked as a Lt and Adjutant in the Six Nations' Indian Dept on 30Mar78; **Dictionary of Canadian Biography** pp.253-257 & Cruikshank & Watt, KRR NY, **op.cit.**, pp.6,30,75,87-89,92,120. John Deserontyon (Odeserundiye) was born in the Mohawk Valley in the 1740's. As a young boy he fought under Sir William Johnson and John Butler at the siege of Fort Niagara in 1759 and the next year in the campaign against Montreal. During the Pontiac Uprising, he helped to guard white settlers against the Seneca and in 1764 he went on Bradstreet's mission to Detroit to impose the peace on the Delawares and Shawnees. Before the rebellion, Deserontyon became a chief of the Mohawks' Fort Hunter settlement. He sided with the British at the outset and was amongst the loyalists who left the valley in 1775 with Guy Johnson. During the defence of Quebec, he barely escaped from Fort St. Johns when the British capitulated to rebel General Montgomery. In 1776, it was Deserontyon who obtained intelligence for Sir John Johnson which enabled him to assemble his friends and tenants and escape to Canada. In the spring of 1777, Captain John went to Quebec City and met with General Burgoyne. Deserontyon joined the St. Leger's expedition, during the approach stages of which, under the orders of LtCol. Daniel Claus, he led a party to Ft Stanwix and obtained detailed intelligence of the rebels' preparations which St. Leger chose to ignore. Deserontyon fought at Oriskany and, after St. Leger's retreat from Stanwix, he set out to travel across the valley to remove the Fort Hunter families to Quebec. En route, Deserontyon was so gravely wounded that he could not take to the field until 1779. Most of the Fort Hunter families withdrew to Quebec and settled at Lachine. Sufficiently recovered, Deserontyon went with Sir John on his abortive relief mission against Sullivan in 1779 and in May 1780 went to Johnstown with Johnson's large expedition. This book details the actions of the Fort Hunter band at Ballstown in Oct80. In 1782, Deserontyon led his men to the Mohawk Valley to destroy Ellice's mill, one the last grist mills operating on the New York frontier and later that year, he and his men, accompanied Brant and Capt Geo Singleton, LtCoy 2KRR NY, on the last foray of the war to the Mohawk region. After the peace, when the decision was made to settle the Mohawks in Quebec, Deserontyon favoured a location not far from Fort Frontenac on the Bay of Quinte. Brant disagreed, choosing instead a site on the Grand River near Fort Niagara where the Mohawks would be closer to their Seneca and Cayuga brothers, who chose to remain on their lands in Indian Territory, and nearer to the Western Indians. Deserontyon was not swayed and the Governor instructed Capt Wm Redford Crawford, 2KRR NY, to treat with the Mississaugas for the Cataraqui region tract. In 1783, Deserontyon led a secret mission to the Fort Hunter chapel where his party dug up the Anglican Communion plate given to his nation in 1712 by Queen Anne which the Mohawks had buried before removing to Quebec in 1777 and brought the service to Canada where it was divided between the Quinte and Grand River Mohawks. This plate continues to be used to this day on ceremonial occasions. Deserontyon was one of the many prominent and extremely effective Mohawk Captains whose career was overshadowed by the education and polish of Jos Brant. Capt John died at the Quinte settlement in 1811.

24 Enys, **op.cit.**, pp.35-52. The majority of the details of the Carleton-led wing of the expedition are taken from the Enys journal. Other details are endnoted separately and page references to the Enys Journal are not given unless confusion is likely with other sources.

25 Hough, **op.cit.**, p.43. This source gives the number of craft involved; **NAC, HP, B144, pp.140-9.** "General Return of Vessels on Lake Champlain, 1st January, 1779". This return lists 2 Ships, 3 Schooners, 1 Brig, 6 Sloops, 7 Hoys, 1 Galley, 16 Longboats, 16 Cutters and 2 Barges. Total guns - 152, total swivels - 102. Six of the larger vessels

had been taken from the rebels in the 1776 campaign, most of those after the battle of Valcour Island.

26   Fryer, King's Men, **op.cit.**, pp.251&252. The use of Indian trade muskets to supplement the arms needed by Provincials was a common measure. The first issue of firelocks to the newly formed 2Bn, KRR NY was of trade muskets. Of course, the trade musket could not mount a bayonet and, consequently, the use of that firelock prevented the proper training of Line infantry. On the other hand, the trade musket was a well made, lightweight firearm and, although not as robust as Land service arms, was quite suitable for rangers; Official Land, or Army, pattern muskets for Provincials were often in short supply. During the Burgoyne campaign, McAlpin's Corps of American Volunteers were partly equipped with "old french Muskets without Baynets." McAlpin to Haldimand, Sorel 26Jul79. **HP, AddMss21820, f.29**.

27   **HP, AddMss21821, f.5.** Eben & Edward Jessup, Samuel Adams, Robert Leake and Jeremiah French wrote to Haldimand on 2Dec78 requesting that the blue coats faced white not be issued to their various Corps as "many fatal accidents might happen from mistakes by Indians and our own Scouting Parties, as was actually the case several times Past Campaign." These corps even offered to "defray the Expense of Carriage" from Britain if "Red Clothing" could be supplied; **ibid, f.87.** McAlpin, in his role as overseer of all the small loyalist Corps noted in a letter to Haldimand dated at Montreal, 8Jun80, the last clothing issue for most of the men had been November 1778; **NAC, HP, MssAdd21818, p.9**. In 1777, Jessup's King's Loyal Americans had been supplied by Maj Gray of the KRR NY. Gray provided red coats, "the cheapest that could be got, at Montreal, very Common Red stuff turn'd up with Green as Red seemed to be their favourite colour, and being got rather cheper that any other I gratified their taste". Being of poor material, they did not wear well and led to many complaints. It is believed that Peter's Queen's Loyal Rangers were similarly equipped.

28   Cruikshank & Watt, KRR NY, **op.cit.**, p.56.

29   Enys, **op.cit.**, p.37. Enys gives Johnson's rank as Lt and his regt as the 47th; **AO, HP, AddMss21770**. A Return of Pay for Officers, Interpreters, etc.. for the Quebec Indian Dept dated 1Jul-24Dec78. This return gives Johnson's rank as Ens and his regt as the 29th. A Return dated 24Dec83, while not specifically naming him, suggests a promotion had taken place by that year. See, AO, HP, Ms622, Reel 113, **op.cit.**, f.51; The articles of capitulation for Fort George include "Wm. Johnston, Lt. 47 Regt." Clinton Papers, **op.cit.**, VI,p.291.

30   Oscar E. Bredenberg, **Military Activities in the Champlain Valley after 1777** (Champlain, NY: Moorsfield Press, 1962) p.29. Bredenberg advises that this man was Richard Houghton; Stevens, Savage Allies, **op.cit.**, p.2134, en24. Confirms Houghton's given name as Richard.

31   Enys, **op.cit.**, p.37.

32   **ibid.**

33   Cruikshank & Watt, KRR NY, **op.cit.**, p.56. Munro in his report refers to these men as "Mr.", a common designation for Volunteers. Thomas Smith (Smyth) was appointed Ens 15Nov81 and Lt 24Oct83. On disbandment he ranked as 11th senior in the 1st Bn. His father, Dr. George Smyth, was a very active servant of the Crown having remained behind rebel lines as a spy until 1781. Upon being discovered, he escaped incarceration and came to Canada. The father served as the Officer directing the Secret Service efforts in New York State as well as in the role of Surgeon to Jessup's Loyal Rangers. Church had served in the Queen's Loyal Rangers in 1777 and entered the KRR as a Vol on 25Jul78. He was promoted to Lieut on 21Nov81. He spent a period seconded to the Secret Service in which dangerous activities he earned his commission. On disbandment he ranked as 10th senior in the 2nd Bn.

34   Hadden's, **op.cit.**, p.82. A tip-in map of the 1777 attack on Ticonderoga showing, "H - a Boom & Bridge of Loggs chained together and Secured by Piles at equal distances."; a drawing of this bridge is found in, Ralph Nadding Hill, **Lake Champlain, Key to Liberty** (Taftsville, VT: The Countryman Press, 1977) p.108.

35   Many of Jessup's and Roger's men would have intimately known this waterway, as might some of Fraser's company of the 84th who were loyalists from New York.

36 This decision has every appearance of an afterthought on Carleton's part. Why would they not have been left behind at Ti or Crown Point with instructions to come ahead a few days later? Was Carleton afraid they might be discovered and give the game away? Why was it now safe for this small detachment to row the length of Lake George on their own? Very mysterious.

37 James F. Morrison research, **The New York Packet, October 19, 1780**. Newspaper accounts of the action at Fort Ann are so distorted as to create the immediate suspicion that the rebel populace was considered utterly unable to absorb bad news. The following is the account in the Packet. "FISH-KILL, October 19. Another party of about 800, commanded by Major Carleton, nephew to Gen. Carleton, came down the Lakes from St. John's, and advanced to Fort-Ann, which was garrisoned by 70 men, among whom were 14 continental soldiers; — they having cannon with them, and the fort being only stockaded, every shot made a breach: — It was, however, defended by Capt. Sherwood, with the greatest gallantry, until two thirds of his men were slain, when he surrendered. This party also destroyed several houses, killed some men, and took the women and children prisoners. They were pursued by Col. Livingston as far as Bloody Pond, but too late, they having retreated to their boats and made off. — So far the reports from that quarter, which we hope, are not so bad as related: — In our next, we expect to have a more exact narrative of this unhappy affair."
   If the populace only knew!

38 Enys, **op.cit.**, p.44; T.W. Egly Jr., **History of the First New York Regiment 1775-1783** (Hampton, NJ: Peter E. Randall, 1981) p.153. Capt Sherwood reported that his men had 10 rounds of ammunition each. No matter which officer was correct, an issue of 4 or 10 rounds was neither sufficient to produce confidence or to offer a stiff resistance; Dr. Asa Fitch, collector & Winston Adler, ed., **Their Own Voices: Oral Accounts of Early Settlers in Washington County, New York** (Interlaken, NY: Heart of Lakes Publishing, 1983) p.101. An account by Austin Wells, a local militiaman, describes Fort Ann as "simply a picket fort without ditch or earthy embankment around it. It was square and enclosed about half an acre's space. Within the fort was a single barrack, one story high, some sixteen feet wide and thirty or forty feet long — a framed and clapboarded building."

39 **ibid.**

40 Enys, **op.cit.**, p.44.

41 William H. Hill, **Old Fort Edward Before 1800, An Account of the historic ground now occupied by the Village of Fort Edward, New York** (Fort Edward: n.p., 1929) p.336. Hill provides details of Adiel Sherwood, his father Seth and the Carleton attack; Clinton Papers, **op.cit.**, VI,p.354.

42 Egly, 1 NY, **op.cit.** pp.152&153.

43 Hill, **op.cit.**, p.336.

44 Fryer, King's Men, **op.cit.**, p.202; W. Bruce Antliff, researcher and transcriber, **Loyalist Settlements, 1783-1789, New Evidence of Canadian Loyalist Claims** (Ontario: Ministry of Citizenship and Culture, 1985) p.122. The posthumous claim of David Jones entered by his brother Solomon, dated Montreal, 27Jun87.

45 Burt G. Loescher, **Roger's Rangers**, (2 vols: n.p., 1969) II,p.187.

46 Enys, **op.cit.**, p.45; Fitch & Adler, **op.cit.**, p.97. Jacob Bitely recollections.

47 Fryer, King's Men, **op.cit.**, p.202.

48 **Stone Arabia Battle Chapter, SAR Newsletter, (Dec 1993)** Thus, Jones' men destroyed the home of the brother of his murdered fiancee, Col. John McCrae (McRae), OC 13th (Saratoga District) Albany County Regiment. The 13th Albany were drawn from the Stillwater/Saratoga area.

49 Loescher, **op.cit.**, II,p.189.

50 Details of George Campbell's service can be found in **HP, AddMss21827, B167a, Pt.1**, 24Jan77 and, **ibid, 13Jul-8Aug77** and, **ibid, 25Jun77-24Oct77**; Re the Tuttles. George is found in **HP, MG13, WO28, V.10, Pt.1**, p.198, as being sworn at Point Clair, 30Jan77. His name is not found in McAlpin's or Jessup's after 24Oct77. Solomon and Ebenezer Tuttle served at various times in the KRR NY. Joseph and Nathaniel Tuttle in Wm Fraser's Coy, of Jessup's Loyal Rangers and Stephen, John and William Tuttle in Maj Edward Jessup's Coy of same. see Mary Beacock Fryer & William A. Smy, **Rolls of the Provincial (Loyalist) Corps, Canadian Command American Revolutionary Period** (Toronto and Charlottetown: Dundurn Press, 1981); Hazel M.

Mathews, **Frontier Spies - The British Secret Service, Northern Department, during the Revolutionary War** (Fort Myers: the author, 1971) p.53. Mathews gives this name, "The Great Burning." She mixes the Munro and Carleton raids together as well as the 1781 raid on Ballstown by Joseph Bettys, the famous loyalist spy; Fitch & Adler, **op.cit.**, p.97. Jacob Bitely, a local resident, uses "The Great Burning" in his reminiscences and names Campbell and the Tuttles as miscreants.

51 Frederic F. Van De Water, **Lake Champlain and Lake George** (Indianapolis & New York: The Bobbs-Merrill Company, 1946) p.223; Parkman, Montcalm & Wolfe, **op.cit.**, I, pp.308&309. The pond lay to the south-east of the fort close to the Fort Edward road. The corpses of Canadiens and Canada Indians who were killed in a sanguinary skirmish in the late afternoon of the famous 1755 Lake George battle were thrown into this body of water, thus giving it its name. The famous New York partizan leader, Teady McGinnis died in this afternoon battle.

52 **Washington Papers, MfReel 72.** A detailed report of affairs from Col Seth Warner to Washington dated Bennington 30Oct80.

53 **ibid;** William L. Stone, **Life of Joseph Brant-Thayendanegea, Including the Indian Wars of the American Revolution** (2 vols, New-York: Alexander V. Blake, 1838) II,p.134. Hereafter, "Stone, Brant." A letter from Col Gansevoort to Maj Carleton reveals that the garrison was from Col Seth Warner's regiment; Fryer, Pimpernel, **op.cit.**, p.113. Chipman was a Yorker, not a NH man; J.A. Roberts, **New York in the Revolution as Colony and State** (Albany: 1897) p.61. Roberts lists Warner's Regiment - the Green Mountain Boys - as an "additional corps" of the New York Line although by 1780, the unit had lost much of its original character.

54 B.F. DeCosta, **Notes on the History of Fort George During the Colonial and Revolutionary Periods, with Contemporaneous Documents** (New York: J. Sabin & Sons, 1871. pp.50&51. Chipman was extremely aware of public, political and military censure arising from his loss of Capt Sill's party and the subsequent surrender of Fort George. He wrote a lengthy letter of explanation which he forwarded to the Connecticut Gazette. It was published on 16Feb81. He notes with strong displeasure that he had received no warning of Carleton's force. "Monday the 8th of October, Capt. Sherwood, who commanded at Fort Ann was informed by his Scouts of the Approach of the Enemy, which Intelligence he Immediately communicated to Col. Henry Livingston [this name is common to many New York regiments. This man is the 2-I-C of Graham's Levies], who commanded at Fort Edward; but Col. Livingston not forwarding the Intelligence to me, I was totally in the Dark with respect to the Enemy's Incursion into the Country against Fort Ann and the Vicinity." Chipman had received word of two ships being seen at Crown Point and sent a scouting party by bateau north on Lake George to investigate. They got within 8 miles of the Landing when they discovered themselves to be cut off by Lt McFarlane's two bateaux with the mortars. The scouts ran their craft ashore and escaped overland.

55 Van De Water, **op.cit.**, p.223.

56 **Historical Magazine, New Series, Vol.II, No.VII (December 1867)** Henry B. Dawson, ed., Morrisania, NY. Orderly Book of the Officer Commanding. From the order's wording, one could conclude that it was written into the Orderly Book 'for the record' after the events were concluded.

57 Loescher, **op.cit.**, II,p.189.

58 Enys, **op.cit.**, p.45.

59 Loescher, **op.cit.**, II,p.189.

60 DeCosta, **op.cit.**, p.51. Chipman explained Sill's actions as follows. "Capt. Sill immediately marched, but unfortunately taking a Rout different from his Orders, he passed the Enemy on their Approach, and on his Return fell upon their Rear, which effectually prevented a Possibility of his Return to the Fort, and reduced him to the desperate Alternative of attacking a Body of at least thirty to one, or to march off through the Woods and expose himself to the infamous Reflections of Ignorance and Detraction; like brave Men they unanimously agreed on the Former and formed their Line, advancing (each Officer in command of his proper Section) near a Mile upon the Enemy, when they formed and were instantaneously attacked by this handful of brave Men who soon forced them to give way, and advanced on with charged Bayonets; but their Numbers being now known to the Enemy they soon surrounded and killed or took the whole, except Ensign Grant with 14 Men who made their

escape, and wisely kept clear of the Garrison, Capt. Sill and two Ensigns [Alexander McLowry and Martin Eno] fell in the Action ... " There is an element of fantasy in this report. For example, the odds quoted are ridiculous - Carleton did not deploy 1440 men against Sill which 30 to 1 odds would suggest. If Sill was a mile away from the detachment Carleton sent against him, how did Sill know to form his line with every officer "in his proper section"? Just who was having "infamous reflections"? One suspects that Sill's detachment were simply 'bounced and trounced' and all of Chipman's defensive bluster couldn't explain it.

61 Enys, **op.cit.**; Van De Water, **op.cit.**, p.223; DeCosta, **op.cit.**, Chipman claimed that 14 escaped.

62 Stone, Brant, **op.cit.**, II,p.135. A letter from Maj Carleton to Col Gansevoort dated "Mile Bay" 6Nov80 written in response to accusations made by the deserter Van Driesen claiming the Major had condoned the torture of a captive. From Gansevoort's description of the victim's wounds, he would seem to have been the deserter from the 29th who is mentioned in the text. As Enys mentions in his journal, this man was brought to the main party after suffering scalping and wounding.

63 Enys, **op.cit.**, p.45.

64 **ibid**, p.46. This man died a few days after being taken aboard a ship on Lake Champlain.

65 **ibid**, pp.45&46; James F. Morrison research. The New York Packet, **op.cit.**, October 26, 1780. Endnote #37 quoted a fanciful report of the fall of Fort Ann as reported in the Oct. 19 issue of this paper. The following is the Oct. 26 report of the fall of Fort George. It was introduced as follows — "The following extract of a letter from a correspondent at Albany, gives a more correct account of the enemy's procedures at Fort Ann and Fort George, than was inserted in our last." The body of the report follows — "Albany, October 21, 1780. Last week we were alarmed with an account that the enemy had taken Fort Ann, on which our militia marched to Half-Moon; when we were ordered to return as the enemy had re-crossed Lake George. —- They came down South-Bay, and summoned Fort Ann to surrender, which it did immediately: —- From thence they marched to Fort George, garrisoned by 80 of Warner's regiment, who were all, except 14, on a scout; who, we hear, were mostly cut to pieces; —- the officer refused to give up the Fort until he capitulated — obtaining his parole, with liberty to take off the women and children."

66 **ibid**, p.46; Hough, **op.cit.**, p.44; Warner to Washington, 30Oct80, **op.cit.**, In this report, Seth Warner advises Washington that his regiment has been "furloughed" until December due to its small numbers, its naked condition and its financial losses. He wrote that the Paymaster, one William Sherman, had 'eloped' and despite considerable measures to apprehend him, he remained at large. He further decries the loss of the unit's "Accounts and other papers at the Surrender of the Fort notwithstanding the Articles of Capitulation to the Contrary ... " As Enys recorded that Barrett left the garrison, apparently with all that had been requested, one has to wonder if some 'fiddling of the books' was underway and the occasion was found convenient to disguise some wrongdoing.

67 If Chipman entered his explicit order to Capt Sill after the fact, his concern about having the Regiment's Orderly and Account books sent south would have been to ensure that his superiors could see that he had taken suitable precautions in his orders. Chipman intimated in his open letter to the newspaper which has been recorded in an endnote above, that Sill had failed to follow his instructions and was cut off from a retreat to the fort. By implication, this was not Chipman's fault. Further, Sill's disobedience led to Chipman not having enough men to make a defence and ensured the fall of the fort. Of course, Sill was dead and could not refute any of these claims.

68 Clinton Papers, **op.cit.**, VI,p.354. Perhaps the Governor approved of Chipman's surrender as it was formalized by a list of written articles signed by Carleton, Kirkman and Johnston as the Crown's representatives, unlike Sherwood's capitulation at Fort Ann where no formal document had been prepared and accepted. However, it is tempting to think that Chipman was excused because he was a serving Continental whereas Sherwood had resigned his Continental commission and was only an officer of the Levies. It is difficult to see the fine points of the 'honour' gained by Chipman.

69 Enys, **op.cit.**, p.46; The complete articles of capitulation may be found in the Clinton Papers, **op.cit.**, VI,pp.290&291.

70 Enys advised that Fort George was sited not more than 200 yards from where the Seven Years War installation of Fort William Henry had stood. Many will recall the tragic events that attended the surrender of William Henry to the French in 1757. The garrison of soldiers and followers was allowed to march out for a withdrawal to the southwards when the Canada and Lakes Indians fell upon them. While some French officers attempted to halt the massacre, the killing was extensive. Some accounts indicate over fifty were killed out of hand, hundreds were wounded and 200 were carried off to captivity. Memories of that terrible event must have been very much in Carleton's mind. See, Francis Parkman, **Montcalm & Wolfe** (2 Vols, Boston: Little, Brown, and Company, 1884) I,pp.503-513,513fn&514fn.

71 Clinton Papers, **op.cit.**, VI,pp.289&307. Of some interest, LtCol Henry Livingston of Graham's NY Levies wrote to Albany from Fort Edward on Oct. 12th, to advise that he was surrounded by Indians & Tories, who were at least 400 in number, and that they had invested the place for the last twelve hours. He sent a sally of 20 men out of the fort, but they had returned after finding the enemy too numerous. Fort Edward was an installation near the community of the same name. Carleton had supposedly ignored it. Livingston reported that the raiders were burning about seven miles from his fort and his garrison only numbered 60 men fit for duty. Probably, Livingston was referring to the activities of the day before and, clearly, the raiders could have reduced this post as well. As it was, after this fright, the Levies in the garrison insisted that their terms were up. The stores were removed and the post abandoned six days later. Even without direct action, another frontier post had been temporarily lost to the rebel cause.

72 Enys, **op.cit.**, p.47.

73 Van De Water, **op.cit.**, p.223. The prisoners were taken to Canada and held in the prison at Coteau-du-Lac. Some of them managed to escape from there and were retaken by a party of Indians and Rangers. Cpl Cyrenius Parks of the King's Rangers was with the pursuit when the party fell upon the escapees in the night. Bill Harris of the Lake George settlement resisted with courage, grappling with an Indian and throwing him into the dregs of the fire. For his efforts, he received a blow across the head from Parks, who had previously been his neighbour from Lake George. Harris was left for dead with a broken arm, cut head and a bayonet wound in the chest. He revived after the pursuit had left, discovered two other prisoners who had evaded recapture and successfully travelled through the wilderness to return home. Harris was said to have born a deep antipathy towards Parks and Indians for the rest of his life.

74 Fitch & Adler, **op.cit.**, pp.98-103. The accounts of Fowler & Wells.

75 Clinton Papers, **op.cit.**, VI, p.408.

76 Enys, **op.cit.**, pp.47-49.

77 Cruikshank & Watt, KRR NY, **op.cit.**, p.55.

78 Fryer, Pimpernel, **op.cit.** p.139. ex HP, B179, Pt.1, p.72. Mathews to Sherwood 5Jun81. This letter named Sherwood as the officer commanding the Canadian Secret Service. His title was Supervisor of Spies and Prisoner Exchanges. As noted above, Dr. George Smyth served as his deputy.

79 **ibid,** pp.222-242. After the settlement of Upper Canada, Sherwood's opportunities for employment in the Government were poisoned by Munro and his associates; in addition to Fryer's biography of Justus Sherwood, one of the best sources of information regarding the struggle in the New Hampshire Grants and the personalities involved is the rare book, Mathews, Frontier Spies, **op.cit.**

80 Fryer, Pimpernel, **op.cit.**, pp.19,35,36,60. This source confirms that Justus Sherwood had an uncle Adiel in the rebel service. This Adiel is possibly the brother of Seth, the father of the commandant at Fort Ann; Roberts, **op.cit.**, p.74. This lists an Adiel Sherwood as a Capt in Malcom's Regiment of Levies who may have been the father of Adiel of Fort Ann and the uncle of Justus.

81 **ibid,** pp.112-120.

82 Mathews, Frontier Spies, **op.cit.**, p.112fn. ex Vermont Historical Society (1924-28), pp.96&97 and HP, B176, p.125. A letter from Sherwood to Mathews, 2Jun81; In view of Chipman's later dissembling apologia noted in the endnotes above, it is not difficult to question his sense of honour.

83 Clinton Papers, **op.cit.**, VI,pp.334-338.

84 Details of Jacob Schell being dispatched on a Secret Service mission are found in the following Chapter.

85 NAC, HP, MG21, AddMss21827, Pt.2, ff275-276. John Man was an Ens in the KLA.

86 Victor Hugo Paltsits, ed., **Minutes of the Commissioners for detecting and defeating Conspiracies in the State of New York, Albany County Sessions, 1778-1781** (3 vols, Albany: State of New York, 1909) I,p.416. Hereafter, "Minutes ... Conspiracies."

87 An Alexander McIntosh was a Pte in Capt Wm Fraser's Coy of Loyal Rangers in 1783.

88 **AO, HP, AddMss21827, pp.138&139.** A return of McAlpin's dated 1Aug77 does not list a Van Dusen or Van Driesen; **AO, Ms622, r.85, AddMss21827.** An account of monies paid by the late Maj McAlpin to the men in his corps up to 24Jun80 and **ibid**, p.290. A return of McAlpin's men who were at "brocken time unpaid" dated 25Jun80-24Dec81. Neither of these list a Van Dusen or Van Driesen.

89 If Van Driesen was actually at the Bloody Pond fight, he would have been serving in the King's Rangers, assuming Loescher's contention that the loyalists in the fight were only King's Rangers is correct. However, Van Dusen/Driesen is not listed on the King's Rangers roll dated 8Sep80. See, Loescher, **op.cit.**, II,pp.196&197. ex BM, HP, AddMss21820, p.66. As Carleton recorded that there was a deserter from Roger's Corps, by elimination, Van Dusen/Driesen must be that man, the conclusion has to be that he transferred from McAlpin's to Roger's after the KR's muster roll taken on 8Sep80.

90 HP, MG21, AddMss21827, Pt.2, ff275-276. William Moffat is carried on this 1May81 roll of "the Corps of Royalists Commanded by Ebenezer Jessup Esquire", the KLA, as a Volunteer; Fryer & Smy, Provincial Rolls, **op.cit.**, pp.82-96. In this Roll of the Loyal Rangers prepared at Rivière du Chêne on 1Jan83, William Moffet was still serving in the ranks as a Pte soldier (which was always the case for Volunteers awaiting a commission) in Capt Jno. Jones' Coy. For all of his dangerous work behind rebel lines as a recruiter and intelligence gatherer, he had been unable to earn his commission in a regiment which had been created by the amalgamation of several small corps, each with an abundance of active and deserving men who had been officers earlier in the war.

91 A Joshua Lowsey was returned as a Pte soldier in Capt Jno Jones' Coy of Loyal Rangers in 1783. Was this Joshua Jr.? If this was Losee, the past militia Capt, an election to that rank had not earned him a commissioned rank in the loyalist regiment, as was often the case. Distrust of any man, who had taken an oath to serve the State & Congress, would have been one reason, but also, a contempt for the rebels' method of selecting commissioned officers was another; Berthold Fernow, ed., **Documents Relating to the Colonial History of the State of New York** (Albany: Weed, Parsons and Company, 1887) State Archives, Vol. I,p.271. Fernow advises that a Joshua Losee was replaced as the Captain of the 4th Coy, 12th Albany by Thomas Hicks as he had been "appointed by mistake." Unfortunately, the date of this change is not quoted, so we do not know if his exposure by Van Driesen caused his removal.

92 A Jasper Moore was returned in the KLA in 1781.

93 In 1783, Archibald McNiel was returned as a Pte in Capt Wm Fraser's Coy of Loyal Rangers; Minutes ... Conspiracies, **op.cit.**, II,p.595. As a result of Van Driesen's testimony, an order was issued on 7Dec80 for the apprehension of both Archibald and "Alec" McNeal of Scotch Patent.

94 John Gilchrist, 33 was a Sjt in Capt Jno Jones' Coy on the 1783 roll of the Loyal Ranger's and Peter Gilchrist, 35 was a Pte soldier in Capt Peter Drummond's Coy. Neither of these men could be considered a 'young fellow.' John did not appear to settle in Canada. Two Peter 'Gillchrists' are returned at CT#2 in 1785. Unfortunately, their ages are not recorded. See, Norman K. Crowder, **Early Ontario Settlers, A Source Book** (Baltimore: Genealogical Publishing Co., Inc., 1993) p.108.

95 Fraser, **op.cit.**, p.128. A Robert and William Brisbin both came off with the Jessup brothers in 1776 as McAlpin was ill and could not travel. The two men first enlisted in the KLA in 1777, but chose to rejoin McAlpin when he came into Burgoyne's camp; John Brisbin was returned as a Pte soldier in Maj Edward Jessup's Coy of Loyal Rangers in 1783. See, Fryer & Smy, Provincial Rolls, **op.cit.**, p.83.

96 Clinton Papers, **op.cit.**, VI,p.336.

97 **ibid.**

98 Conspiracy Commission, **op.cit.**, II,p.554.

99 Clinton Papers, **op.cit.**, VI,p.337.

100 **ibid**, VI,pp.337&338.

101 **ibid,** VI,p.338.

102 When word was received in late November by Captain John Munro regarding Jacob Schell's execution at Albany, he also was advised that the "Prisoners [taken by the rebels] on the Late Expedition to Schohary are allowed only half Rations." Was this a punishment or simply a reflection of the rebels' acute shortage of provisions? **HP, AddMss21821, f.169.** Munro to Mathews, 30Nov80.

103 Conspiracy Commission, **op.cit.,** II,p.558.

104 Clinton Papers, **op.cit.,** VI,pp.358-363.

105 **ibid,** VI,p.359.

106 **ibid,** VI,pp.362&363.

107 This was Capt John Dafoe (De Veau,Devoe,Dafoot,Defoot) of the King's Rangers, a very accomplished scout and Secret Service agent. Dafoe was used repeatedly to carry dispatches from New York City to Quebec and return. He was worn out from his extensive utilization, and the attendant exposure and stress, and died in 1783. See, Mathews, Frontier Spies, **op.cit.,** pp.78,81,86. Mathews states that Dafoe was from Pownal, not Hosick (Hoosic.) One might be sure that the Commissioners were quite clear where Dafoe had resided; Mary Beacock Fryer, **Loyalist Spy, the Experiences of Captain John Walden Meyers during the American Revolution** (Brockville: Besancourt Publishers, 1974) p.240,passim; Fryer, Pimpernel, **op.cit.,** pp.148&149; Fryer, King's Men, **op.cit.,** pp.85,262; Fryer & Smy, Provincial Rolls, **op.cit.,** pp.97-103. The ranks of the KR's carried Wm Davo 24, Martin Davo 30, John Dafoe 23, Wm Dafoe Jr. 20, Jacob Dafoe 22, Wm Dafoe 23 and Cpl Abraham Dafoe - a prolific family. Three of these were John Sr.'s sons.

108 In 1784 Henry Ruiter was the 3rd Senior Capt in the King's Rangers and a John (likely the son of either Henry or John Sr) & Philip Ruiter were listed as Volunteers in his Coy. John Ruiter (Ritter) Sr was 10th Senior Lt in the Loyal Rangers; **HP, MG21, AddMss21827, Pt.1. f.102.** Henry & John Sr had been mustered in 1777 as Capts in Van Pfister's Loyal Volunteers; **HP, MG21, AddMss21827, Pt.2, ff.278-279** and HP, MG21, Vol.167, Pt.1, p.192. By combining these two documents, it may be seen that when Leake received a warrant to raise an Independent Coy to operate with the 1Bn, KRR NY, both Henry & John were not chosen for active service and were left at Sorel with 8 other officers, 6 NCOs, a drummer and 35 R&F. In 1781, when the Loyal Rangers were created by the amalgamation of several smaller units, John was unable to hold his more senior rank and fell back to a Lieutenant. Henry instead chose Roger's King's Rangers where he was favoured with a Captaincy.

109 Van Driesen stumbled over this name in his testimony; **MG21, B155,** pp. 34-37. On a list of men employed in the Engineering Department at St. Johns on 10Jan79, James McIlmoyle is found as a Carpenter. Was James a brother of John?; **ibid,** pp.59-62. A James Micha'l Moyle of McAlpin's Corps was returned on a list of men proposed to form two companies of Artificers in 1780. Obviously, 'Micha'l Moyle' is 'McIlmoyle', as is 'Muckle Miles.'

110 **HP, MG21, AddMss21827, Pt.2, ff.275-276.** O'Neal (O'Neil, O'Niel) was a Lieutenant in the KLA and had served in that regiment since the 1777 campaign.

111 Fryer & Smy, Provincial Rolls, **op.cit.,** p.89. Abraham Ostrander was a Cpl in Capt Wm Fraser's Coy of Loyal Rangers in 1783; little can be found about John Gregs (Gregg,Grig) except the note on a roll in Crowder, **op.cit.,** p.193, which indicates that ... Gregg had been "a Loyalist express in the war." ... Gregg settled in the Detroit region.

112 Most likely Lt Thomas Fraser of McAlpin's and later 9th senior Capt in the Loyal Rangers.

113 Loescher, **op.cit.,** II,p.196. In the King's Rangers return of 8Sep80, David Palmer is listed as a Private soldier "recruiting in ye Colonies." By 1784, he was returned as a Cpl in Capt James Breakenridge's Coy. Perhaps Van Driesen wasn't the only blowhard found in the loyalist regiments.

114 Lieut.-Col. H.M. Jackson, **Roger's Rangers, A History** (n.p., 1953) p.202. ex HP, AddMss21820. Was John Lantman [Lampman?] a relative of Abraham Lampman, Sr. & Jr., who were found in the ranks of the Ruiter's Coy, King's Rangers in 1784.

115 Found on Jessup's May 1781 roll are Ens Wm Snyder and three Private men, Wm Jr., Abram and Peter. On a 1784 roll of the King's Rangers, there is a Christian Snyder. Are these relatives of Hans?

116 Loescher, **op.cit.**, II,p.198. In this 1784 roll, John and George Hix are returned as Pte men in Maj Roger's Coy (Capt Jas Breakenridge's) of King's Rangers. Are these from the Newtown Hicks family?

117 Crowder, **op.cit.**, p.95. A John Gilles is noted as settling at Sorel, Que. in 1785.

118 There were Klines (Clines) in the KRR NY and Butler's Rangers.

119 Mathews, Frontier Spies, **op.cit.**, pp.58&160. Mathews marvels at how the Lansingh family, with the exception of Philip, managed to escape serious persecution during the war. The father, Abraham, and two of the sons, Jacob A. and Levinus were instrumental in Dr. George Smyth's escape to Canada in Feb. 1781; Fryer, Pimpernel, **op.cit.**, p.171. Fryer notes that Jacob Lansing, in the company of James Breakenridge Jr. of the King's Rangers, carried intelligence to Capt Justus Sherwood in Canada in Aug 1782 and Lansing was taken to visit Haldimand. Jacob was carrying a proposal from Vermont's Gov Chittenden and Ethan Allen regarding the negotiations. A very risky business indeed, considering the loyalist propensity to gossip.

120 Cruikshank & Watt, KRR NY, **op.cit.**, p.44. Philip P. Lansingh fled to Montreal, arriving on 22Jul80. Sir John reported his arrival, stating "the Sheriff of Charlotte County, having been obliged to fly from His Country and Property on account of his Loyalty, and the support and assistance he gave to friends of Government, and to the Scouts sent from this Province ... " He also advised that most of the letters and newspapers brought by the Secret Service into Canada had passed through Philip's hands and had been forwarded "at considerable personal expense and risk"; **ibid**, pp.68&69. Lansingh operated with the Secret Service and was involved in plans to establish a 'safe-drop', or depository, for intelligence to the west of Fort Edward. Sir John advised Haldimand on 3May81 that he planned to send off Lansingh on May 10 with "about Sixteen men with him, four of them Mohawks, with a view to destroy the Mills, Buildings, &c. at Saratoga, and to bring off Mr. Schuyler, if there, he thinks he can accomplish both errands at the same time." What came of these plans is unknown, however, General Schuyler was not attacked by a group led by Lansingh; **ibid**, pp.130&131. For his extensive and dangerous services to the Crown, a very deserving Philip Lansingh was given a Lieutenancy in the 2Bn, KRR NY and upon disbandment was the 8th senior in that rank.

121 Stone, Brant, **op.cit.**, II,pp.129-136. These pages quote all of the subject correspondence; The description of this prisoner fits closely with Enys' account of the British deserter who had been taken prisoner at Bloody Pond and brought to Fort George. Other than fear for his life, it is difficult to imagine why Van Driesen would accuse Maj Carleton of complicity in this man's maltreatment. Was he 'playing to his audience?' Carleton was not present when the man was wounded. Assuming that Enys' journal is correct, the man received no additional wounds after being brought to the fort, and was given substantial care, albeit to no avail.

122 Minutes ... Conspiracies, **op.cit.**, II,572&636.

123 Cruikshank & Watt, KRR NY, **op.cit.**, p.268. Rudolph (Rolph, Roloof) Van der Varkin, a brother or cousin of Albert's, had been appointed an officer in a brigade recruiting for Sir John Johnson in 1777 and brought recruits to the regiment after raiding German Flats with Joseph Brant in Sep78. His commission was not confirmed by Sir John. He is found on a return of deserving loyalists recommended to Haldimand for subsistence dated 1Jul79. His employment thereafter, if any, is unknown. Ruloff Vandicar was returned as a settler in 1786 at Cataraqui Township No.3. This is likely a different man, as Van De Kar is a known surname.

124 Loescher, **op.cit.**, II,p.196. Vol Albert Vanderwerker was returned on the King's Rangers roll of 8Sep80 as "recruiting in the Colonies."

125 Chris McHenry, compiler, **Rebel Prisoners at Quebec 1778-1783** (1981) pp.4,9 Peter Seets had been taken on the Mohawk River on 3Jun78 and Michael Cannon at Cherry Valley on 11Nov78. Neither man had been "in arms." While McHenry's compilations include some exchange lists and dates, none was found for Seitz and Cannon; Stone, Brant, **op.cit.**, II,p.130. ex letter from BGen Powell to Col Van Schaick dated 22Sep80. This letter mentions a Matthew Cannon being exchanged with several other civilian prisoners. Stone says he had been taken at Cherry Valley by the Indians.

126 Todd W. Braisted, "Captain Samuel Hayden: New Jersey Volunteer, King's American Ranger, Watchmaker & Tyrant", **The "Greens", The Newsletter of the 4th Battalion, New Jersey Volunteers, Vol.IV, No.1** (July 1992) Braisted, the indefatigable researcher, throws more light on Robert Rogers activities to raise his battalions.

One of his first actions was to recruit a few officers who had previously served with him in the Queen's Rangers, plus all of the unemployed officers of the New Jersey Volunteers, 14 in total, (ex 1780 North American Army List) who had found themselves 'seconded' when their regiment of 1200 men was reduced from six weak battalions to four. Rogers somehow finagled all of these men their commissions in violation of his beating orders. In Jun79, the other ranks of the entire regiment numbered 1 Sjt & 9 Ptes (NAC, RG8, "C" Series, V1862, f123). The 1st Bn transferred to Nova Scotia and in Dec81 mustered 4C, 2L, 2E, 1Adj, 1QM, 1Surg, 9Sjt, 3D & 120R&F (Huntington Library, American Loyalist Papers, HM15227 & HM15229) while James struggled on in Quebec. The 1Bn never grew beyond this strength; NAC, HP, B160 (AddMss21820) p.153-156. After disbandment, dated at St. John's 27Jan84. James' 2Bn mustered 3 companies with 1M, 3C, 3L, 3E, 1Surg, 6Vols, 10Sjt, 9Cpl, 1D, 176R&F. In trying circumstances, he had done considerably better than Robert, who in 1781 had left Nova Scotia for England in disgrace. The firm hand of Governor Haldimand is apparent in the composition of James' small battalion as there was no superfluity of officers or NCO's.

127 Jackson, **op.cit.**, pp.181-190; Fryer, King's Men, **op.cit.**, pp.237-262.

128 **HP, Ms622**, p.249 & **AddMss21874**, p.184. These are very detailed memorials of Messrs John Peters, Edward Jessup & Wm Fraser against Jas Rogers' recruiting methods.

129 **TCM Newsletter, Vol.XIX, No.8 (Apr 1990)** ex Misc Mss, Malcom, NY Hist Soc, NYC. Writing from Albany on 11Oct80 to Gov Clinton, Malcom refers to "a son of a B ....h of a Tory Lt." brought down by Lt. Lawrance." Is this referring to William Laird?; Morrison research — Laird was a 1Lt in Capt Andrew Wemple's Coy, 3rd Regt formed in 1776. Wemple deserted in May80 and was later a Capt in Butler's Rangers.

130 The King's Rangers roll of 8Sep80 records, [?] Leard as a Volunteer, "Recruiting in the Colonies."

131 Minutes ... Conspiracies, **op.cit.**, II,pp.591,628,643,682,707&708.

132 Jeptha R. Simms, **History of Schoharie County, and Border Wars of New York; containing also A Sketch of the Causes which led to the American Revolution; and Interesting Memoranda of the Mohawk Valley; together with much other Historical and Miscellaneous Matters, never before published** (Albany: n.p., 1845) reprinted Schoharie County Council of Senior Citizens, 1974, p.434. Hereafter, "Simms, Schoharie."

133 See Lt Patrick Langan's letter to Daniel Claus later in this book. It gives some additional detail regarding Van Der Werkin.

134 Information regarding Melchart Van Dusen and Peter Boon is found in Penrose, Mohawk Valley, **op.cit.**, see index; Melchart's relationship to James Van Dusen has not been determined.

135 Just where did Robert Snell go? He isn't found in the KRR NY, Butler's, the Loyal or the King's Rangers. He didn't settle in Canada after the war. He obviously isn't fictitious, as Van Der Werkin's story of him living with Maj Fonda would have been easily confirmed or denied. A mystery.

136 Simms, Schoharie, **op.cit.**, p.434; Peter Bowen's relationship to Hank & William who appear in this book has not been established.

137 Cruikshank & Watt, KRR NY, **op.cit.**, p.55.

138 See Chapter 4, Benjamin Burton testimony.

139 **ibid**, p.58. There are three explanations given by Munro of this adjustment to the provisions. The first says the men were completed to 30 days provisions. A second says that one day's provisions were left in the cache and the third clearly states he halved the per diem ration. Of course, there is no contradiction between the first and third statements. He could have issued 30 X 1/2 normal rations. The second reference is the puzzler. This text ignores the confusion of the second statement.

140 It is somewhat comical, depending on one's point of view, that no matter how the infanteer's combat load is pared and massaged, this order of magnitude in weight has been common from the 18th to the late 20th century. For example, while the weight of the soldier's firearm has been reduced dramatically, he is now expected to 'man-pack' electronic gear, or extra mortar or anti-tank ammunition.

141 The Sacandaga (Sacondaga) River flows into the Hudson about 20 miles as the crow flies northeast of Johnstown. Sir William Johnson built a summer house retreat on the

river, and further east, a Fish House where he enjoyed fishing. The summer house was nine miles above Johnson Hall. The river and its banks became a regular route for loyalist and Indian incursions during the war. In 1779 the rebels built a blockhouse, sometimes called Fort Fisher after the Mohawk Regiment's commander, about 2 1/2 miles south of the river which was regularly occupied by militia and/or Levies in an attempt to prevent the use of this route. When Marinus Willett came to command the Mohawk Valley region in 1781, he christened the Blockhouse 'Fort Folly' as a mark of his opinion regarding its lack of utility. It was soon-after abandoned. Munro must have located his rendezvous point well downriver from the Blockhouse which he would have known was occupied and from which he could expect regular patrols would be sent. TCM Newsletter, **Vol.IV, No.6 (Dec 1985)** James F. Morrison, "The Sacondaga Blockhouse"; TCM Newsletter, **Vol.XVII, No.7 (Mar 1996)**, A letter dated 17Mar80 from senior Col Jacob Klock to Col Visscher of the 3rd Tryon passing on orders from Gov Clinton. " ... I am directed to Keep guards at the severall Forts and Posts, particularly at Sacondago, and to continue the same till further orders. Request therefore you will order a Party to Sacondago to keep a guard there and scouting parties. I shall not prescribe to you the Number but leave it to your own Judgement ... " Morrison found this document in the BM, HP, Mss 21842, Secret Intelligence. Clearly, Munro would have known to be concerned about scouts from Sacandaga Blockhouse. This intelligence had been brought to Canada in Apr80 by "Mr Oneil", the James O'Neil of Jessup's KLA who is mentioned earlier in the text.

142 **Montgomery County Dept of History and Archives, Fonda NY, Claus Papers, Vol.III, pp.200-203.** A letter from Lt Patrick Langan to LtCol Daniel Claus dated Crown Point 31Oct80. Langan names Hank Bowen in this letter; **AO, Ms622, Reel 51**. A Return naming all of the Claus' Rangers dated 8Apr82 lists Henry Bowen. Hank is a common diminutive of Henry; Fryer & Smy, Provincial Rolls, **op.cit.**, p.61. Smy notes that Henry Bowen of Caughnawaga had deserted from Butler's Rangers on 24Oct78. Smy's later research suggests that Henry Bowen decided not to enlist in the Rangers and to serve instead with Claus. See, **NAC, MG19, F1, Claus Papers, Vol.3**. Claus wrote to Maj RB Lernoult on 14May81, "he [Henry Bowen] endeavoured to get away in the spring of 1777 ... and accordingly engaged two men to guide him to Niagara where, on his arrival, Colonel Butler allowed him half a dollar a day as a useful [he most likely spoke an Indian language] person in the Indian Department, but upon Colonel Butler's falling on the scheme of raising a Corps of Rangers, Bowen left him and joined me at Fort Stanwix ... " These two Rangers must have been part of Claus' Six Nations Dept in Canada; Jeptha R. Simms, **The Frontiersmen of New York showing Customs of the Indians, Vicissitudes of the Pioneer White Settlers, and Border Strife in Two Wars with a Great Variety of Romantic and Thrilling Stories never before published** (2 vols, Albany: Geo. C. Riggs, 1883) II,p.220. Simms names a Tory who travelled with the Fort Hunter Mohawks in a June 1778 excursion as being William Bowen. (**HP, AddMss21827, p.353.** A Return of the Officers of the Indian Dept (n.d.) lists William Bowen as the senior 1st Lieut) He mentions that William had a brother, but according to Claus, it is not Henry, who was an only son. One gathers from Simms' account that Wm Bowen was very familiar with the Mohawk people and that he perhaps spoke the language. The Bowen family were likely involved in the prewar department or the Indian trade; Luke Bowen was a Royal Yorker in the 1Bn, Col's Coy and he hailed from Philadelphia Bush near Johnstown where the Ross excursion spent much time in 1778; Simms, Frontiersmen, **op.cit.**, II,p.327. Henry & William Bowen, whom Simms reported to have been brothers, were believed to have led a wing of the May 1780 expedition to attack and destroy their home vicinity of Tribes Hill.

143 Langan, **op.cit.**, Langan names the second man as Maybee; **AO, Ms622, Reel 51**. There is no Maybee on this 1782 return of Claus' Rangers, however the name was common in the Valley; "Lewis Maybie" had served with John Butler as an Indian Dept Ranger in 1777 and had joined Butler's Rangers at its founding later that year. See **NAC, MG11, 'Q' Series, Vol.13, p.331.** "A List of Persons Employed as Rangers in the Indian Department June 15, 1777" and **BM, HP, AddMss21765.** "Pay Lists, 24 Dec. 1777 - 24 Oct. 1778, Capt Walter Butler's Company". Lewis Mabee is listed as a Sjt; Census of Niagara, **op.cit.** Lewis Maybee is again returned as a Sjt in John Butler's Coy; Further along in the text of this book, Staats Springsteen is mentioned in the attack at Ballstown. As he is also found in John Butler's Coy in the 1777-78 Pay Lists, along with Lewis Maybee, it is not stretching credulity to conclude that a secondment of John Butler's Rangers had been sent to Daniel Claus in lower Quebec as

a temporary transfer between the two subdivisions of the Six Nations' Indian Dept. This small detachment could have included Lewis Maybee and Staats Springsteen; WO28/4, p.10, **op.cit.** The Butler's Rangers Return dated 6Oct80 notes 2 Sjts and 20 Rangers on command at Carleton Island. The three men noted, and perhaps a few more, may well have come from the island to assist Claus.

144 Cruikshank & Watt, KRR NY, **op.cit.**, p.58.

145 **ibid**, p.56. Munro's report to Haldimand.

146 **ibid**, p.58. No matter how rigorous their march had been to this point, they could hardly have worn out all of their clothing. One suspects Munro of exaggeration to better excuse his alteration to his orders.

147 Josephine Mayer, "The Reminiscences of James Gordon with a Preface and Biographical Sketch", **New York History, Vol.XVII, No.3 (July 1936)** Hereafter cited as "Gordon Reminiscences." Gordon emigrated from Ulster in 1758 and arrived in America in the midst of the Seven Years War. He was soon occupied as a Sutler to Robert Roger's Corps of Rangers. This experience took him into the Indian trade where he served under Askin and Rogers, a well established firm from Schenectady. Gordon learned the trade and prospered. In 1770, after a brief visit to Ulster, he returned to New York to take up lands in Ballstown, bringing his mother, aunt, an unmarried niece and his brother-in-law, George Scott, his wife Jane (née Gordon) and their family. A year later Gordon married Mary Ball, the daughter of Rev Eliphalet Ball, the founder of Ballstown.

148 Roberts, **op.cit.**, p.120; **1780 - 1980 The Bicentennial Book of the Schoharie and Mohawk Valley Raids** (Montgomery County, NY: Klock's Churchyard Preservation Group, 1980) James F. Morrison, "The October 1780 Campaign of Sir John Johnson into the Schoharie and Mohawk Valleys". Hereafter "Morrison, Raids." A quote from a letter from Colonel W. Malcom (Malcolm, Malcomb) to Henry Glen Esq. the Quarter Master General at Schenectady dated at "6 miles above Fort Hunter" on 20Oct80. p.5.

149 Cruikshank & Watt, KRR NY, **op.cit.**, p.59. Munro advised in his 20Nov80 supplementary report that Capts Collins and Benedict had both been commanding officers at Fort Chambly in 1775 and had "used Colonel Campbell and Major Dunbar very roughly"; Claus, 2Nov80, **op.cit.**, "Among the Prisrs is one Capt Benedict & 2 his Sons[,] the Father commanded at Chamblee in 1775 when the Rebels were in Canada[;] he had then the Montreal Gentlemen such as Col Campbell, Mr St. Luc, Majr Dunbar[,] Majr Geor DeBre under his confinement." John Campbell was the Superintendent of the Quebec Indian Department. St. Luc was St. Luc de la Corne, the famous Canadien Indian officer and member of the Governing Council of Quebec and DeBre was LtCol. St. George Duprée of the Quebec Militia; Fernow, **op.cit.**, p.271. This source advises the Coy number.

150 Fraser, **op.cit.**, p.44.

151 **ibid**, p.59. Found in Munro's 20Nov80 supplementary report.

152 Fraser, **op.cit.**, pp.35-36; John Chester Booth, Violet B. Dunn & Beatrice Sweeney, eds, **Booth's History of Saratoga County, N.Y., 1858** (Saratoga County Bicentennial Commission, 1977) pp.83-85. Booth includes transcripts of Fraser's trial and that of some of his men.

153 Fryer, Loyalist Spy, **op.cit.**, pp.127-137. Gov Haldimand was persuaded by George Smyth, father of Vol Thomas Smyth of the Munro expedition, to approve the attempted capture of several significant rebel personalities in July 1781. Smyth reasoned that if these influential men could be removed from their role in the rebellion, rebel morale and leadership would suffer a great blow. Targeted were MGen Philip Schuyler of Albany, Dr. Samuel Stringer from below Ballstown and John Bleecker of Hoosic Falls. The latter two men sat as Commissioners for Detecting Conspiracies in Albany County. The attempt on Schuyler came close to success, the other two were fluffed; see also, Mathews, Frontier Spies, **op.cit.**, pp.63-77 and T.W. Egly Jr., **General Schuyler's Guard** (the author, 1986) pp.6&7.

154 Clinton Papers, **op.cit.**, VI,pp.334-338.

155 Morrison research, **HP, Reel 92, AddMss21840**. Van Schoonhoven to Mitchell dated Halfmoon, 11Oct80.

156 Katherine Q. Briaddy, **Shadows, the Life and Times of Eliphalet Ball, The Founder of Ballston** (the author, 1991) pp.102&103.

157 Cruikshank & Watt, KRR NY, **op.cit.**, p.56.

158 **ibid;** American accounts maintain that Shew was simply hunting with his friend Palmatier. Munro says otherwise. Claus reported on 2Nov80 "one of the 2 scalps was taken of a Rebel deserter they came across hunting in the Woods near Balls Town". It appears that the Indians accepted Shew's version, although his perfidy in taking flight from Canada was his death warrant.

159 Simms, Frontiersmen, **op.cit.,** II,pp.216-224,227&228; McHenry, **op.cit.,** p.3. This lists the men taken on this scout and held in prison in Quebec and notes that six others were "in possession of the savages."

160 There is little doubt that Capts Aaron and David Hill were with Munro as they were principle war chiefs of the Fort Hunter Mohawk. In any event, there were many others who would have recognized Shew.

161 Simms, Frontiersmen, **op.cit.,** II,pp.477-479. Needless to say, Simms recording of Shew's death varies considerably from the Crown accounts. For example, Simms mentions that Shew was not scouting for tracks of the enemy at the time of being taken. He was hunting deer in a chestnut grove and taken by Indians who had been advised of his intent to be there by John Palmer of the Royal Yorkers who in turn had been told of this by one Tuttle (who seemed to get blamed for a great deal), a local Tory. Simms further states that a Mina Vrooman, a Tory who returned to the town of Mohawk after the war, had been present when Shew was captured. Vrooman said that Shew only surrendered his firearm when promised by his captors that they were the total of the enemy force. Shew was taken to the encampment of the enemy who were in large numbers. He was slapped in the face by one Indian, who was reproved for so doing, as Shew was marked for death. Vrooman claims that when he was killed, Shew was picking wintergreen berries; there is no Mina (diminutive of Myndert) Vrooman mustered in Capt Wm Fraser's Independent Coy on 1Dec80 at Verchères. See, **HP, MG13, WO28, V.10, Pt.2, p.254.** Mina Vrooman does not appear in the Claus' Rangers muster of 1782 mentioned previously. The KRR NY had only one man named Vrooman. His given name was Thomas and he was captured near Fort Windecker on the Mohawk River on 20Oct80. A Mends Vrooman is found in the settlement at Niagara in a roll dated 20Jul80. He was likely the young son of Sjt Adam Vrooman of Butler's Rangers and not the man, Mina. See, Crowder, **op.cit.,** pp.90&91. So, just who was Mina Vrooman?; Simms maintains that John Shew had left the Johnstown area to visit his close friend Isaac Palmatier so they could enjoy the hunt together. One suspects that both of the men were asked by the local militia leaders to scout out the enemy and they complied with fateful results; Cruikshank & Watt, KRR NY, **op.cit.,** p.56.

162 Morrison, Raids, **op.cit.,** p.5; William L. Stone, **Reminiscences of Saratoga & Ballstown** (New York: 1875) p.415.

163 **ibid.**

164 **ibid,** p.414.

165 Simms, Frontiersmen, **op.cit.,** II,p.413.

166 Morrison, Raids, **op.cit.,** p.5; Roberts, **op.cit.** p.97.

167 Simms, Frontiersmen, **op.cit.,** pp.413&414; Simms, Schoharie, **op.cit.,** p.315.

168 Stone, Ballstown, **op.cit.,** p.414.

169 Cruikshank & Watt, KRR NY, **op.cit.,** p.58.

170 **ibid,** p.56.

171 Morrison, Raids, **op.cit.,** p.5.

172 Cruikshank & Watt, KRR NY, **op.cit.,** p.56; this tactical gambit bears some investigation. If Munro drew up his 130 Royal Yorkers at 6 ft. apart, they would extend for 780 ft. Supposing that Gordon's house was 90 ft. square and the men kept a distance of 72 ft. (26 yds) from the windows, likely a safe distance in the night when marksmanship is poor, a circle ascribed by those dimensions would have a circumference of 735 ft. Therefore, the 130 Royal Yorkers could easily have surrounded Gordon's house.

173 James Scott, "The Raid on Ballston, 1780, Memoranda of Reminiscences, 1846", **The Bulletin of the Fort Ticonderoga Museum, Vol.VII, No.4 (July 1946)** Hereafter, "Scott Memoranda." Melinda Walker (née Gordon) offered "Corrections and additions to the foregoing", (ie. Scott's recollections). Hereafter "Walker's Corrections." Walker recalled the officer who blocked the fall of the tomahawk as either Munro or Fraser, obviously from family discussion, as she was too young at the time to recollect personalities. As Fraser was at Collin's house, it must have been Munro.

174 Claus, 2Nov80, **op.cit.** Claus wrote " ... and brought off one Barlow, son of a loyalist, who was taken by the Oneidas at Oswego and was prisoner at Ballstown and intends going to his parents living at Carleton Island ... "; **NAC, HP, Mss B127**, p.338. A return of loyalists at Carleton Island dated 26Nov83 shows Grace Parlow aged 16 and Ann Parlow aged 8. Their entry is indented below that of "Montreal a Negro Man" aged 27 who had perhaps been entrusted to care for the girls while the parents went elsewhere to organize their affairs; Gordon Reminiscences, **op.cit.**, New York History, Vol.XVII, No.4 (1936) The relationship of Parlow to Gordon is an interesting one. During Gordon's activities as an Indian trader, he entered a partnership with a Laurence Parlow at Oswego in 1767. This suggests that Gordon agreed to offer succour to young Parlow when his loyalist father was taken prisoner by the Oneidas.

175 Stone, Ballstown, **op.cit.**, p.415.

176 **The Loyalists of Quebec 1774-1825, A Forgotten History** (Montreal: United Empire Loyalist Association, 1989) pp.212-215. "Return of Negroes and Negro Wenches brought into the Province by Parties under the Command and Direction of Lieut. Colo. Sir John Johnson, Bart." See the comments column. It appears that Ann, the wench, was retained by Sir John Johnson until Col Gordon redeemed her by exchanging a black child.

177 Scott Memoranda, **op.cit.**, p.16.

178 Claus, 2Nov80, **op.cit.**

179 Morrison, Raids, **op.cit.**, p.6; Walker Corrections, **op.cit.**

180 Scott Memoranda, **op.cit.**, pp.15&16. Scott gives Collin's son's name as Mannapole or Maner; Morrison, Raids, **op.cit.**, p.6.

181 Josiah Hollister, **A Journal of Josiah Hollister, A Soldier of the American Revolution and a Prisoner of War in Canada** (Romanzo Norton Bunn, 1928) pp.21&22.

182 **ibid**; Stone, Ballstown, **op.cit.**, pp.415&416; Morrison, Raids, **op.cit.**, p.6; Simms, Schoharie, **op.cit.**, p.316; Scott Memoranda, **op.cit.**; All of these accounts differ in the details of this affair, but in all cases the final result was the same.

183 **ibid.**

184 Scott, Walker's Corrections, **op.cit.**

185 Cruikshank & Watt, KRR NY, **op.cit.**, p.57.

186 As endnoted previously, Capt Benedict had been a commanding officer at Fort Chambly in 1775 and had the reputation of abusing two British Regular officers.

187 Briaddy, **op.cit.** pp.104&105.

188 Scott Memoranda, **op.cit.**

189 Like Bowen & Maybee, the presence of Springsteen on the Ballstown raid is a bit of a mystery. From such a positive identification by George & Mary Scott, coupled with such a unique combination of names, it is not at all probable that an error in identity was made. **BM, HP, AddMss218765**. "Butler's Rangers, Pay List, 24 Dec. 1777 - 24 Oct. 1778" Staats Springston is listed as a private in John Butler's Coy. As the extant returns for Butler's are few and far between, there is no other record yet found of his service. Springsteen is reported by Smy to have settled near Long Point, Ontario which must have been after 1790 as he is not found in Crowder's lists. See Fryer & Smy, Provincial Rolls, **op.cit.**, p.76. Nor is he on Claus' Ranger's roll of 8Apr82 or on any of the small lists of Brant's Volunteers. The latter are of interest as a 4Aug82 roll of Claus' small unit notes that 8 men had formerly been with Joseph Brant. Nor does Springsteen appear on Wm Fraser's roll dated 1Dec80. One can only postulate that Springsteen was on secondment from Butler's to Claus' Rangers, perhaps as he was one of Butler's men who spoke a native language. As noted previously in the endnotes for Bowen and Maybee, it is sensible to believe that John Butler's own company was one of the two in his battalion that were recruited from men able to speak a native tongue. Men from those two companies would be the most likely for a secondment to Claus.

190 Scott Memoranda, **op.cit.**, p.17. The dog survived his wounds for three days.

191 **ibid**, p.18. The observant young James also noted amongst the Mohawks an Oneida, whom he recognized by a calico patch on a garment. He recalled this Indian and others of his nation had encamped a few rods east of the Scott's house some weeks before and spent some time hunting. Was young Scott correct? As the Oneidas were most often pro-rebel, might this particular warrior have travelled to Canada to offer intelligence? And, considering the many written strictures by

Haldimand, Guy Johnson, Claus & Sir John against the perfidious Oneida nation, it seems unlikely that one of their men accompanied the expedition. However, the natives had rules of their own, and restrictions and warnings from the white leadership might well have been ignored if the chiefs believed the man was trustworthy.

192 **ibid.**

193 **ibid.**

194 **ibid**; Morrison, Raids, **op.cit.**, p.7; Stone, Ballstown, **op.cit.**, pp.416&417; Bredenberg, **op.cit.**, p.29; again, these four accounts differ somewhat in detail.

195 Briaddy, **op.cit.**, p.107. Two weeks later she delivered her first born.

196 Hollister, **op.cit.**, pp.22&23. Although he did not seem to encounter Munro during the retreat to Canada, he heard of him as a prisoner in Quebec and described him as "a poor old, drunken, sore eyed vagabond, who goes strowling rounde the streets." That there was very little reconciliation between rebels and loyalists after the peace is not at all surprising.

197 Scott Memoranda, **op.cit.**, p.16.

198 **ibid**, p.19; It's interesting to speculate on the identity of these two Royal Yorkers. There were at least three men in Munro's Coy who were Irish in birth — Florence McCarty aged 38, William McCormick 33 and Alexander Reed 49. The youthful recruit was possibly either Stephen Steneburgh aged 17 who had enlisted 4Apr80 or Peter Dopp 18 who joined on 22May80.

199 Cruikshank & Watt, KRR NY, **op.cit.**, p.58. Munro's report to Maj Richard Lernoult, Adjutant General, dated at Lachine 20Nov80 after Carleton's force had been withdrawn from the Champlain frontier. Munro exhibited concern that his management of the expedition might not have met with the approval of Haldimand as he had failed to join with Johnson, nor had he come to grips with the enemy. In this report he states that it was six days since the time appointed to join with Johnson, however it is unclear where his base comparison date lay.

200 **ibid.**

201 Stone, Ballstown, **op.cit.**, p.419.

202 Cruikshank & Watt, KRR NY, **op.cit.**, p.57; Simms, Schoharie, **op.cit.**, p.316; Hollister, **op.cit.**, p.23. Hollister recalls that all but one yoke of oxen were killed at the first stop. The prisoners were allowed to take some meat and roast it on sticks.

203 Cruikshank & Watt, KRR NY, **op.cit.**, p.58; Fraser, **op.cit.**, p.71. Quote of J. Fraser.

204 **ibid.**

205 Stone, Ballstown, **op.cit.**, p.421. Stone doesn't give the size of this party, but names a Patchin, a Gordon and a Holmes as participants.

206 **ibid**, pp.419&420.

207 Hollister, **op.cit.**, p.23.

208 Stone, Ballstown, **op.cit.**, p.419. Stone advises that Munro was dismissed the service for giving such an inhuman order; Bredenberg, **op.cit.**, p.30. Bredenberg advises that Munro was rebuked on his return to Canada for giving this order; Both of these accounts would seem to be entirely incorrect. There is no extant evidence that Munro was censured in any way. He continued to serve in the 1Bn, KRR NY for the rest of the war and upon disbandment was ranked as the 2nd senior Capt. He later served as the Sheriff of Lunenberg District in Upper Canada, and was a judge of the Court of Common Pleas and a member of the Land Board. Lastly, he was a member of the Upper Canada Legislative Council. Munro was one of the province's most respected citizens. (Cruikshank & Watt, KRR NY, op.cit., pp.128&131) One suspects his superiors, if they thought of it at all, viewed the order as a sensible precaution in view of the many prisoners who had been either able to disrupt retreat marches or effect escape; Hollister, **op.cit.**, p.23.

209 Scott, Walker Corrections, **op.cit.**; The identity of the old German soldier of Munro's may have been Jacob Shires aged 47, John Van (recognizing that Van is usually Dutch) Snell 48 or Henry Waggoner 41. This accepts that Gordon's use of 'old' was meant in experience as much as age. It was also common amongst some folk to think of Dutch and German interchangeably.

210 Scott Memoranda, **op.cit.**, p.18.

211 ibid; Stone, Ballstown, **op.cit.**, p.420.

212 Scott, Walker Corrections, **op.cit.**, p.24. An additional comment by James Scott advises that Caleb Benedict returned to Ballstown after the war and soon went back to visit his adoptive native family in Canada where he was greeted with great affection. After his second return to Ballstown, his native father sent him various presents until the older man suffered an untimely death.

213 Gordon Reminiscences, **op.cit.** Gordon provides the list of men taken by the Mohawks; Morrison, Raids, **op.cit.**, p.8. Morrison gives the names of every man captured, including those allowed to return; Simms, Frontiersmen, **op.cit.**, p.415.

214 Cruikshank & Watt, KRR NY, **op.cit.**, p.57.

215 Hough, **op.cit.**, p.46.

216 Stone, Ballstown, **op.cit.**, pp.421&422.

217 Cruikshank & Watt, KRR NY, **op.cit.**, p.57.

218 **ibid.**

219 There was no man named Joseph Bonner taken at Ballstown, however a Joseph Bonett or Bennett was taken at Ft. George by Carleton. While at first blush Hollister's comments seem to be referring to the distress of the prisoners when they arrived at Munro's cache of provisions and found them either consumed or infested, the event may well have occurred after Munro & Carleton's forces were recombined, at which time Joseph Bonnet and Hollister could have been together. Of course, another possibility is that Joseph Bonner was a loyalist soldier. According to extant records, no one of a similar name served under Fraser or Claus. The closest to that name would be Joseph Benedict who served in Munro's Coy as Cpl in 1781-82. There is no record found of whether he served under Munro in 1780, but it is likely. Bonner and Benedict are quite dissimilar in sound, but one must consider the possibility that Hollister altered the man's name to save him from recriminations after his journal was published, yet he would only have done so if the man was a fellow rebel. If he had been a loyalist guard, Hollister would have had no compunctions about giving his correct name; If Joseph Bonner was the fellow prisoner, Joseph Bonnet, it is very interesting to read Hollister's quotation of his utterly blasphemous refusal to share some rations and compare that to his earlier description of his Tory captors as the "offscouring of the earth" etc ... Beauty is indeed in the eye of the beholder.

220 Hollister, **op.cit.**, pp.23&24.

221 Briaddy, **op.cit.**, p.103.

222 Cruikshank & Watt, KRR NY, **op.cit.**, p.57.

223 Claus, 2Nov80, **op.cit.** It is apparent from Claus' report that at least some of the Fort Hunter men continued on to Canada as he reported them arriving on 1Nov80 with 9 prisoners and 2 scalps. Whether Carleton had hoped that Langan would return with all of them, part of them, or only himself is not recorded.

224 Langan, **op.cit.**

225 **ibid,** Langan reported the arrival of only one Bower and does not record his given name. Both Gasper and Peter Bower are recorded as enlisting on 16Oct80 and being recruited by Langan.

226 Peter Jost (Yost) was a Johnstown man who had gone to Canada with Sir John after the May '80 raid. Jost argued that he had been taken prisoner and had at no time joined with the enemy. As we have seen, this explanation was accepted and he was set free, although Langan's letter sheds much doubt on his allegation. He did not settle in Canada after the war.

227 Cruikshank & Watt, KRR NY, **op.cit.**, p.208. There were several Helmers in the KRR NY who may have been considered young; **CO42/490, pp.36-39**. This evidence suggest that 'young Helmer' is the 21 year-old John P. Helmer of the LtCoy who was frequently employed in the Secret Service. He had been taken in 1779 after suffering three bayonet wounds, one to the thigh, one to the abdomen and another to the left shoulder. He succeeded in escaping with the help of his guard who was his girlfriend's brother and brought off several recruits. As he had made the trip back to Canada with his men, he was presumably fit enough to conduct another scout the year following.

228 Cruikshank & Watt, KRR NY, **op.cit.**, p.254. In 1780, Peter Service (Servos,Serviss) would have been 30. He enlisted in the KRR NY on 22May80 and served in the 2Bn until disbandment. His family were in Montreal in 1784 and he had gone to the States with Sjt John Service (likely his brother) with the intention to "take up the King's lands

in the fall." No record has been found of these men returning to Canada. It is very unlikely that Peter abandoned his large family. Both men were possibly the fatal victims of rebel reprisals.

229 **ibid**, pp.129,131,181. William Claus was the 8th senior Lt in the 1Bn on disbandment. In postwar years, he became Sir John's closest confidant in the management of the Indian Dept. See, Thomas, **op.cit.**, passim; **Toronto Star**, Tues. Oct.10, 1995, p.A10. During the last year of Sir John's 88 year life, the management of the late Wm Claus was under investigation. He was found guilty of transferring Indian Department funds to his son. What a disappointment this must have been for his mentor.

230 Gordon Reminiscences, **op.cit.**, NYH, Vol.XVII, No.4.

231 **ibid.**

232 Cruikshank & Watt, KRR NY, **op.cit.**, p.58.

233 While a handful of blacks served in the northern loyalist corps, this golden opportunity to raise serious numbers for the King's service was never pursued. One suspects that the white administration had no desire to take the risk of training and arming such a large number of men of colour. Prejudice and fear transcended need.

234 Munro was in no way exaggerating. For a very one-sided account, see, Henry W. De Puy, **Ethan Allen and the Green-Mountain Heroes of '76 with a sketch of the Early History of Vermont** (Buffalo: Phinney & Co., 1853) pp.116-196.

235 Cruikshank & Watt, KRR NY, **op.cit.**, p.59. The quotation is Cruikshank's interpretation of Mathew's letter.

236 Zadock Steele, **The Indian Captive or a Narrative of the Captivity and Sufferings of Zadock Steele Related by Himself to which is prefixed an account of the Burning of Royalton** (Montpelier: the author, 1848) p.7; **HP**, AddMss21770. A Return of the Officers, Interpreters, etc.. employed in the Indian Dept under LtCol Campbell. No given name is recorded, however Joseph Marie LaMothe was a noted Canadien interpreter, Indian leader & scout who had been captured at the defence of Fort St. Johns in 1775 and later released.

237 Bredenberg, **op.cit.**, pp.28&29.

238 As with so many of the shadowy figures of the revolution, there is no record of a man named Hamilton serving in any of the Loyalist regiments which were with Burgoyne. The Rolls for Jessup's KLA's, Peter's QLR's, McAlpin's AV's, Van Pfister's LV's, Adams Rangers and John McKay's, Hugh Munro's & Peter Van Alstine's Companies of Bateauxmen show no man of this surname. There were many Hamiltons serving in Butler's Rangers, but the evidence of Steele's account indicates that Hamilton was intimately knowledgable regarding Charlotte and Gloucester Counties of New York. Butler's men were drawn predominantly from the Mohawk Valley region and Pennsylvania. The Hamilton of this account is not likely one who served later with Butler; Crowder, **op.cit.**, p. 99. Perhaps Collin Hamilton who who settled at RT#2 in 1785.

239 Steele, **op.cit.**, p.7.

240 De Puy, **op.cit.**, p.399.

241 Hadden's Journal, **op.cit.**, pp.4&5fns. Horatio Rogers, ed. gives many details of this event, quoting from Anbury's Travels and Wilkinson, one of Gen Gates' aides. Also, details from Whitcomb himself.

242 George F.G. Stanley, **Canada Invaded 1775-1776, Canadian War Museum, Historical Publications Number 8** (Toronto & Sarasota: Samuel Stevens Hakkert & Company, 1977) p.80.

243 De Puy, **op.cit.**, p.400. De Puy gives that name as Hannah Handy. Steele spells the surname as Hendee and provides no given name.

244 **ibid**, p.40; An instance of another "inhuman" order, yet no one claimed that Richard Houghton was dismissed the service, or censured by his superiors, or was an old, decrepit vagabond wandering the streets of Montreal.

245 **ibid**, p.59.

246 **ibid**, p.60.

247 **ibid**, p.63; Stevens, Savage Allies, **op.cit.**, I,p.89.

248 Steele, **op.cit.**, pp.66-130. Steele was incarcerated on Prison Island at Coteau-du-Lac, with several of his fellow prisoners from the Houghton raid. The post and island were garrisoned by the Royal Yorkers. There were a large number of men imprisoned there who had been taken from early in the war and during the many raids of the 1780 campaign. After some brutal experiences, in part brought on by their own uncompro-

mising behaviour as well as vengeful, loyalist bitterness, a number of them prepared an escape tunnel. Steele and Simeon Belknap, both of Randolph with John Sprague of Ballstown and William Clark, a Virginian, banded together and with about 30 other men managed to escape the island on 10Sep82, almost two years after the capture of the Randolph and Ballstown men. Their four-man party travelled an agonizing and desperate 22 days before reaching succour and safety — an ordeal immeasurably more difficult than their march into Canada, however their trial had at least been made of their own free will.

249 General Staff, **op.cit.**, III,p.179.

250 Van De Water, **op.cit.**, p.224; Bredenberg, **op.cit.**, p.29; Stone, Brant, **op.cit.**, II,p.129. Stone states that several of the pursuing militia were killed.

CHAPTER IV — "BANDITTIE" IN THE SCHOHARIE

1 Morrison Raids, **op.cit.**, pp.3-67.

2 Cruikshank & Watt, KRR NY, **op.cit.**, p.45.

3 **ibid.**

4 One suspects Sir John was being disingenuous in this comment. The Jaegers, who were all woodsmen by profession, were far more likely to have proven uncooperative rather than unable to withstand physical effort. Certainly, the Hesse Hanau Jaegers had been very difficult to manage at Fort Niagara, from which post they were sent down in some disgrace to Fort Haldimand on Carleton Island. The men assigned to Sir John were usually from Von Kreutzbourg's Hesse Hanau Jaeger battalion; On the Hesse Hanau attitude, see Mary Beacock Fryer, **Allan Maclean, Jacobite General, The Life of an Eighteenth Century Career Soldier** (Toronto & Oxford: Dundurn Press Limited, 1987) p.164. ex BM, AddMss21789, p.54 & AddMss21791, p.43.

5 Cruikshank & Watt, KRR NY, **op.cit.**, p.46; Sir John's opinion about the efficacy of moccasins on campaign was not commented upon by the Governor, however the Oswego pincer has been said to have been equipped with two pair of shoes per man as prisoners taken on the raid were found by the incredulous rebels to have an extra pair in their knapsacks. See also in the text details of a Royal Yorker whose knapsack was hit by a ball from a canister discharge at the Lower Fort. Sir John's observation about preferring shoes appears to have been accepted.

6 **ibid,** p.47.

7 Lanctot, **op.cit.**, pp.194&195. Azariah Pritchard, "a skilful counter-spy" was active in this discovery. He was the second senior Captain in the King's Rangers.

8 J. Watts De Peyster, **The Life & Misfortunes & the Military Career of Brig. General Sir John Johnson Bart.** (New York: Chas. H. Ludwig, 1882) pp.clviii&clix.

9 **ibid,** p.clix. De Peyster quotes from Von Eelking II,p.197. There is only one volume of the works of Von Eelking held in the Toronto Reference Library and p.197 does not include this topic. Perhaps the editions of his works, contemporary to De Peyster's writings, were in two volumes.

10 Cruikshank & Watt, KRR NY, **op.cit.**, p.48.

11 **ibid,** p.47.

12 **ibid.**

13 **ibid,** p.48.

14 **ibid;** Cruikshank, Butler's Rangers, **op.cit.**, pp.82&83.

15 Cruikshank & Watt, KRR NY, **op.cit.**, p.50.

16 **ibid,** pp.49&50.

17 Kelsay, **op.cit.**, pp.295&296.

19 Smy research, **NAC, HP, MfReel A-680.** Bolton to Haldimand, Niagara 30Sep80. Haldimand had ordered Bolton to reinforce Carleton Island. The Colonel responded, "I shall send every man of the 34th Regiment able to do duty to Carleton Island, and the sick as fast as they recover. But this will oblige me to call [in] every party cutting firewood, making hay, &c, &c, which will distress many in the winter. And even were it peaceful times, I should wish to have, and think it prudent to have, men in this fort when we have not less than 2,600 Indians [warriors] in our neighbourhood." Obviously, the Pontiac uprising of 1763 was in Bolton's mind.

20 James F. Morrison research, **Miscellaneous Manuscripts, Malcom, New York Historical Society,** NYC, NY. Letter of Sep 20 to Clinton.

21 Cruikshank & Watt, KRR NY, **op.cit.**, p.51. As noted above, these details and quotations are from Sir John's after-action report to Haldimand unless otherwise noted.

22. **ibid**, p.48. Haldimand had suggested a timetable for Bolton & Guy Johnson which was based on it taking 16 days for Sir John to reach Carleton Is. and another 6 to arrive at Oswego. The Governor had foreseen about 5 days of preparation on Carleton Is. before sailing to Oswego. He had personal experience with all of these waterways having commanded at Oswego in 1759.

23 Morrison research, **Washington Papers Microfilm, Reel 71**. Col Wm Malcom to Washington, 22Sep80.

24 Kelsay, **op.cit.**, p.295.

25 NAC, HP, Mf Reel A-680, 30Sep80, Bolton, **op.cit.** "The Garrison and Rangers are at this time extremely sickly with fluxes, fevers and agues. I never remember to have had anything like such a number of ill at the same time. Colonel Butler's family and several Officers of his Corps are also extremely ill ... Captain Butler is so ill that I have given him leave to go down to Montreal."

26 **ibid.**

27 **ibid.**

28 **ibid.**

29 This compilation is prepared from several sources, viz - **WO17, 1574(2)**, pp.170&175; Graymont, **op.cit.** pp237&238; Cruikshank, Butler's Rangers, **op.cit.**, pp.83-88; Cruikshank & Watt, KRR NY, **op.cit.**, pp.47-54. These pages include Sir John Johnson's personal correspondence during the planning for the expedition and his highly detailed report after completion of the raid.

30 The term 'Hat' Company was used to denote the eight standard infantry companies in a battalion as opposed to the two flank companies, ie. the Grenadiers and the Light Infantry. Two of the 'hat' companies were normally referred to by their commanders' ranks, viz the Colonel's and the Major's, the other six by their Captains' surnames.

31 **Shorter Oxford English Dictionary**, spelled as Coehorn or Cohorn after Baron Coehorn, a Dutch military engineer. A small mortar designed to throw grenades, ie. hollow shells, which are fused to explode above or in a target; The 'Royal' or Cohorn was the smallest mortar in service and fired a shell of 4.5 inch diameter. It was mounted on a solid wooden flatbed, however it could be removed from the flatbed and mounted on a light travelling carriage and used as a howitzer. In this deployment it was known as a 'Mortizer.'

32 Adrian B. Caruana, **Grasshoppers and Butterflies: The Light 3 Pounders of Pattison and Townshend** (Bloomfield, Ont: Museum Restoration Service, 1979) The Grasshopper was a light 3 pounder Fieldpiece mounted on a wheeled 'travelling' carriage and was readily disassembled and reassembled. The Grasshopper and its mate the 'Butterfly' were deployed with infantry which had difficult terrain to traverse. When disassembled, the gun was moved by pack animals or in the bed of a wagon; **HP, AddMss21819**. Haldimand and Johnson had been in correspondence regarding artillery during the planning stages for the 1779 expedition to relieve the Six Nations. Haldimand wrote to Sir John on 9Sep79 "Your idea of the Carronades is a very good one, but I have not one to furnish you with - those ordered for you are Grass Hoppers, they are easily transported, but too small for reducing any place - they will however go thro' any Stockades the Rebels can have erected, but will not beat them down, if well directed they may do great execution." A carronade was a short-barrelled, large-bore gun firing case or canister and most often used in fortifications and aboard vessels as anti-personnel weapons.

33 Cruikshank, Butler's Rangers, **op.cit.**, p.83. John Butler had been seriously ill since the 1778 expedition to the Wyoming Valley, an affliction which was made worse by the rigours of the 1779 Sullivan invasion. Since then, he had been not active in the field until this expedition of October 1780; **ibid**, p.50. Cruikshank quotes a description of John Butler. "A fat man, below the middle stature yet active; through the rough visage of the warrior showing a rather agreeable than forbidding aspect. Care sat upon his brow. Speaking quickly, he repeated his words when excited. Decision, firmness, courage were undoubted characteristics of the man"; **OA, Drawer 7, Reel 601**. General Orders. John Butler was promoted to LtCol Commandant of the Corps of

Rangers, 14Feb80.

34 Andrew Thompson had a noteworthy lineage. His father was Samuel Thompson, the husband of Elizabeth McGinness, the daughter of Sarah Kast McGinness. Samuel and Elizabeth, with the assistance of Sarah, conducted a very successful Indian trade business on the old Kast property in German Flats. When Guy Johnson withdrew from the Mohawk Valley in 1775, he travelled first to Samuel Thompson's with the intention to hold a Six Nation's council there. Like his grand-mother, and likely his father and mother, Andrew very probably spoke several Iroquoian dialects. Andrew was an Indian Department Lieutenant under John Butler during the 1777 campaign. Andrew was a 1Lt in Walter Butler's Coy in 1778 and was promoted to Capt on 25Dec79.

35 Number of Rangers: Smy Transcripts, Monthly Return of Butler's Rangers, dated Niagara.06Oct80, **NAC, W028/4**; Barent Frey: Frey was promoted to captain, 02Oct80. For evidence of his presence on the expedition, see **NYHA, Glen Papers.** Letter from Maj Christopher P. Yates to Henry Glen, 27Oct80.

36 Of the Indian Department officers, only McGinn (McGinnis, McGinness) has been found in the reports as a participant. Guy Johnson, the Indian Superintendent, had created seven 'companies' amongst the Six Nations & dependents at Niagara and assigned Captains to head each for administration. Brant was named for the Mohawks and Oneidas (and likely Tuscaroras) and received a formal commission as a Captain. The rest were white officers. Capt Wm Johnston was nominated to care for the Upper (Genesee) Senecas, John Powell for the Lower (Alleghany) Senecas and Robert Lottridge for the Cayugas. Those nations which participated in the expedition, were perhaps accompanied by their Capts although Brant is the only one currently confirmed.

37 Edward A. Hagan, **War in Schohary** (the author, 1980) p.35. Hagan does not quote a source.

38 Family legend says that Hendrick Nelles saved the Palatine Church near Caroga Creek from being burned and he is consequently listed with the expedition; For a strange, haunting and powerful novel about Hendrick Nelles, see Douglas Glover, **The Life and Times of Captain N.** (Toronto: McClelland & Stewart Inc., 1993) Glover repeats the legend.

39 All of Brant's Volunteers, whether white or native, are enumerated amongst the total of warriors.

40 In view of Powell's comments regarding the Niagara garrison's health and the report that Butler had to sweep the hospital to get close to the originally planned numbers, the number from Niagara was likely lower than planned and this total reflects that likelihood.

41 This odd spelling of Morrison with a single 'r' is found in Morison's signature. If Maj Gray was preoccupied with the battalion, Morison would have lead the company.

42 Capt Angus McDonell did not accompany the expedition and his company was com-manded by Lt James McDonell.

43 WO17, 1574(2), **op.cit.**, p.175. A KRR NY Regimental Return indicates that 1 LtCol, 1 Maj, 3 Capts, 4 Lts, 4 Ens, 1 Surgeon, 13 Sjts, 4 Drs & 196 R&F = 227 all ranks went on the expedition from Oswego. Therefore, this subtotal is in excess of the sum of the individual companies which denotes Rankers only.

44 Robert Leake, a half-pay officer of the 60th 'Royal Americans', had served as a Capt in Francis Van Pfister's Loyal Volunteers which had joined Brunswick Col Baum's expedition to Bennington during Burgoyne's campaign of 1777. In the famous battle of that name on 16Aug77, Van Pfister lost his life and it is likely that Leake brought the remnants of the badly mauled unit off the field. Command of the Loyal Volunteers was then given to Capt Samuel McKay, an officer of consider-able merit, who had also served in the 60th Regt in the previous war. Leake was likely his junior in grade. Upon the death of McKay, Leake assumed command and in 1779 he was instructed by Governor Haldimand, who would have known of him from the 60th, to raise from the remnants of the Loyal Volunteers a reinforced company, chosen from the best and most robust men, to be attached to Sir John's 1st Battalion, Royal Yorkers for active service. Leake was the husband of Lady Johnson's sister Margaret and, thereby, Sir John's brother-in-law. It was not said what role Leake's Company would play, but it seems doubtful that they were rangers, but more likely an additional flank company. In keeping with either of

those two roles, rangers or flank, the company officially mustered two Lieuts. Leake's Independent Company was stationed at Carleton Island from late 1779. Leake's was later absorbed into Sir John's 2nd Battalion with Leake becoming the senior Capt, which status must have been granted due to the merger. John Ross was returned to the 34th Regt in 1783 and on Oct. 24, Leake was made Major-commandant of the 2nd Battalion. It is likely this promotion was also promised to him prior to the merger in view of his long service. During the October 1780 expedition, it appears that Capt Alexander McDonell's Coy, 1Bn, KRR NY were sent with the bateaux brigade up the St. Lawrence to replace Leake's Coy in the garrison at Carleton Island; **NAC, HP, MG13, WO28, V5**, p.161. Leake's Independent Coy mustered 1 Capt, 4 Lts, 1 Ens, 5 Sjts, 2 Drs & 80 Rank & File on 4Jul79 at "St. Genevive", Quebec.

45 This total was soon eroded by the loss of 16 sick men. Then, 20 Cayugas deserted before the raiders reached the Schoharie. These losses were in part made up by the addition of 23 loyalist recruits who joined the column on Oct. 16 (see Appendix 4) A simple sum suggests that Sir John had 875 men when he entered the Schoharie Valley; Morrison, Raids, **op.cit.** pp.33&34. ex testimony of a Butler's Rangers deserter dated 17Oct80. The presence of the "Green Yagers" is noted as are 20 "Loyalists." Therefore, although Sir John had distinctly requested that no German "Chasseurs", ie. Jaegers, be included, a platoon was sent; **ibid**, p.40. A letter from Volkert Veeder mentions 80 Brant's Volunteers.

46 Cruikshank & Watt, KRR NY, **op.cit.**, p.51. ex Sir John's highly detailed report of Oct 31 to Governor Haldimand.

47 **ibid**, p.44. In early Aug., Thomas Smyth had been sent to Albany to collect intelligence from his father, Dr. George Smyth. Thomas found that his father and several other loyalists had been imprisoned for suspicious activities. Thomas also discovered that many of the Albany City militia had refused to turn out when ordered to do so by Governor Clinton.

48 See Chapter III for details of Schell's misadventure.

49 **NAC, HP, MG21, AddMss21827 (B167a, Pt.1) p.109.** In this undated return, William McKay is noted as the senior Lt of the Loyal Volunteers during the Burgoyne campaign, joining the corps on 1Aug77; **ibid**, MG13, WO28, Vol.10, Pt.1, p.123. This return is dated at Charleburgh (possibly the settlement just outside Quebec City) 28Jul78 and gives McKay's appointment as Lt by Gen Burgoyne on 17Aug77 and his date of joining as 22Aug77. He is also returned as the unit's Adjutant; **ibid**, MG21, Vol.167, Pt.1, p.192. This return is dated Sorel 3Jun79 and was taken just prior to the Independent Coy being created. Those men noted for that duty were said to be going on Secret Service. Wm McKay is noted as the senior Lt slated for that purpose; Cruikshank & Watt, KRR NY, **op.cit.**, p.128. It is noted that McKay had spent 7 years in the 21Regt as a Sjt and Volunteer. At the time of amalgamation of Leake's with the 2Bn KRR, McKay's commission in the latter corps was dated 14Nov81. He was 3rd senior Lt on disbandment.

50 James F. Morrison, **Colonel Jacob Klock's Regiment, Tryon County Militia** (Gloversville: the author, 1992) p.20. A report by A. Frasier (Alexander Fraser, 2-I-C Quebec Indian Dept) dated Carleton Island, 27Oct80.

51 **NAC, HP, MG21, AddMss21827 (B167a, Pt.1)** p.109. In this undated return, Henry Young is ranked as the senior Ensign of the Loyal Volunteers; **ibid**, MG13, WO28, Vol.10, Pt.1, p.123. This return is dated at Charleburgh 28Jul78 by which time Young had been promoted to Lt. The document states that his commission was granted by Col Pfister and dated 15Jul76, which would have made him senior to McKay, if correct. One suspects that this was the date of his Ens' commission. Like McKay, he joined the corps on 15Aug77; Cruikshank & Watt, KRR NY, **op.cit**, p.275. Young is noted as serving in the Seven Years' War at Ticonderoga, Fort Frontenac and Montreal which suggests he served in the New York Provincial Regiment in 1758 & 59. His commission as Lt of the 2Bn KRR was dated 16Nov81 and upon disbandment he was 5th senior in that rank. He had served in Capt Crawford's Coy in the 2Bn.

52 **ibid**; Cruikshank, Butler's Rangers, **op.cit.**, p.83.

53 Cruikshank & Watt, KRR NY, **op.cit.**, p.51; Was this Col Lewis Dubois' regiment of New York State Levies?

54 **Washington Papers Microfilm, Reel 71.**

55 Hough, **op.cit.**, pp.42&43. The Oneida deserter arrived at Fort Stanwix and was interviewed by Major Hughes, the commandant. His presentation of the empty mortar shell lent great weight to his story and all of the posts in the Mohawk Valley were placed on alert, however the Indian was not aware of the expedition's route and had advised that Stone Arabia and Fort Stanwix itself were primary targets. While the former was true, the latter was an incorrect supposition.

56 Kennanagara Creek is named as the entry point in Roberts, **op.cit.**, opposite p.xviii. A map entitled, "Map of the Schoharie and Mohawk Valley Showing the Route Traversed by Col. Sir John Johnson in his Raid of October, 1780", Wm. B. Wemple, Compiler. This superb map is only found in the early editions of this work.

57 Cruikshank & Watt, KRR NY, **op.cit.**, p.52.

58 **ibid.**

59 Smy research, **Schoharie County Historical Review, Spring Summer 1993,** ex "Recollection of Blacksnake, Seneca Chief", Lyman C. Draper Manuscripts. Further citations as 'Blacksnake.'

60 **ibid.**

61 **ibid.**

62 **ibid.**

63 Cruikshank & Watt, KRR NY, **op.cit.**, p.52.

64 See Appendix 4 for a list of these recruits.

65 Hazel C. Mathews, **Mark of Honour, Canadian Studies in History and Government No.6** (Toronto: University of Toronto Press, 1965) pp.42,45,47&73. Hereafter, "Mark." John McKay is an example of a local Scot who assisted the expedition. John had 'been out' with John McDonell (Scotus) in 1777, but had chosen to return to his large family rather than travel to Canada to join the KRR. He was recognized by the rebels as having participated in the 'uprising' and was strongly persecuted for it, being imprisoned on three separate occasions. In his claim to the government for losses incurred, dated at Montreal in 1787, he specifically mentions that "he was obliged to fly for furnishing Provisions to the Army under Sir John Johnson" and noted that he had not joined the British Army before 1780 because of his family. As his enlistment date is 12Dec80, he obviously was not one of the men who came off directly with the expedition. He likely chose to once again return home to Harpersfield Patent and then was driven off. A Hugh McKay of nearby Kortright's Patent must have suffered a similar ordeal, as his enlistment date is the same as John's. See, Alexander Fraser, Provincial Archivist, **United Empire Loyalists, Enquiry into the Losses and Services in Consequence of their Loyalty, Evidence in Canadian Claims, Second Report of the Bureau of Archives for the Province of Ontario** (2 vols, Toronto: L.K. Cameron, 1905) reprinted, Genealogical Publishing, Baltimore, 1994. I,p.357 and Cruikshank & Watt, KRR NY, **op.cit.**, pp.237&238.

66 Jeptha R. Simms, **History of Schoharie County and Border Wars of New York; containing also a Sketch of the Causes which led to the American Revolution and Interesting Memoranda of the Mohawk Valley; together with much other Historical and Miscellaneous Matter, never before published** (Albany: Munsell & Tanner, 1845) reprinted by the Schoharie County Council of Senior Citizens, 1974, pp.399&400; Blacksnake, **op.cit.** The Seneca's memory of the halt is quite different than that reported by Sir John. Blacksnake recalled, "After dark in the evening they approached the border [Upper?] fort, which they passed and avoided, 4 miles from the village, keeping quiet in the movement as possible, and went a mile beyond, and lay down in the woods, without a fire. The sentinels at the fort they had passed thought they heard some unusual noises, and suspecting the cause, two men were sent from the fort that night to Schoharie Village to notify them of the enemy's approach, as the Indians found out afterwards. Consequently, the village was abandoned, except the two stone houses occupied as forts. The women and children all left, many of them to the fort 6 miles beyond".

67 For Company assignments and enlistment dates, see Cruikshank & Watt, KRR NY, **op.cit.**, p.224. The Master Roll notes Henry Merkill (Merckley), born 1761, as joining on 15Aug77. This has proven to be incorrect and should read 17Nov80.

68 **New York State Archives, Albany, Rufus Grider papers.** A sketch with explanatory notes by R.A. Grider dated Feb.13, 1888; Hagan, **op.cit.**, p.7.

69 **ibid**, p.36; Morrison, Raids, **op.cit.**, p.28; All numbers for the various Companies of the 15th Albany County Regiment were obtained from Richard A. Sherman of the recreated 15th Albany, Burning of the Valleys Military Association.

70 Massachusetts Pension W21686 of Bethuel Bond submitted in 1832. This is the only source to mention Massachusetts men being in the garrison at the Upper Fort. Bond wrote, "We who were stationed at the Upper Fort followed the enemy up the [Mohawk] river to Fort Plain near the German Flatts ... " He refers to a Lt Harrison Richmond of Foord's who may have been in command of the Upper Fort detachment; Howe, op.cit., p.26. Howe's roster of Foord's Coy does not include a Harrison Richmond.

71 Clinton Papers, op.cit., II,p.238.

72 Hagan, op.cit., pp.7&8. Hagan notes that Simms recorded that two 9 pounders were in the fort. He points out that the weight of a 9 pr piece was in excess of what would readily be mounted in a frontier blockhouse. Hagan concludes that as Col. Butler of the Pennsylvania Continentals brought two 3 prs with him in 1778, these were the guns used in the blockhouses.

73 Clinton Papers, op.cit., VI,p.265. "Weekly Return of the detachments of Foot Levies of Colo. Graham's, Colo. Jacobs & Colo. Brown's Regements Commanded by Major Woolsey." Jim Morrison advises that the riflemen stationed at the Middle Fort who are returned as "Capt. Bogart['s] Riflemen" were from Harper's Regiment. Thus, elements from four different regiment's of Levies were present at the fort.

74 Hough, op.cit., p.48&fn. Woolsey had been appointed as a Major of a regiment of New York State Levies on 1Jul80. He signed the Return noted in the above endnote as "Mel. L'd Woolsey, Major."

75 Howe, op.cit., pp.26,27&31. In this detailed study of the Third Berkshire Regiment of Massachusetts Levies commanded by Colonel John Brown, Howe advises that Foord's Company comprised 63 private men and totalled 76, all ranks. The size of the Upper Fort detachment is unknown and assumed to be no more than a platoon of 16.

76 TCM Newsletter, Vol.VI, No.1 (Mar 1987) James F. Morrison research from Miscellaneous Manuscripts, Malcom, NY Hist Soc, NYC, NY; TCM Newsletter, Vol.III, No.4 (Dec 1984) "Muster Roll of Capt. Jacob Jno Lansings Compy ... October 1780"; Morrison, Raids, op.cit., pp.28&29; Hagan, op.cit., pp.36&37.

77 ibid, p.8.

78 Morrison, Raids, op.cit., pp.23&31. Morrison advises there were two Volkert Veeders ranked as LtCols. How they were related is unknown. On Oct 17, the one served in the 5th Albany at the Lower Fort and the other in the 3rd Tryon at Klock's Field on Oct. 19.

79 ibid, p.10.

80 Both of these field officers wrote reports of the raid while stationed at the Lower Fort. See later in this text.

81 ibid, pp.30&31.

82 Hagan, op.cit., p.40. Hagan does not give direct references for his conclusions.

83 Lester E. & Anne Whitbeck Hendrix, Sloughter's Instant History of Schoharie County 1700-1900 ... (Schoharie: Schoharie County Historical Society, 1988) p.45. This booklet is a compilation of a number of many resource books - Simms, Brown, Roscoe, Warner & Hagan. Cited hereafter as "Sloughter's."

84 Hough, op.cit., p.49. Hough suggests the attack was expected to fall on the Lower Fort first, which would have reversed the route of the expedition and made any action in the Mohawk Valley almost impossible.

85 Cruikshank & Watt, KRR NY, op.cit., pp.172&173.

86 ibid p.52.

87 Sloughter's, op.cit., p.45.

88 ibid; Morrison, Raids, op.cit., p.28. Morrison lists a Peter Feeck in Hager's Company which garrisoned the Upper Fort; Simms, Schoharie, op.cit., p.400.

89 Hagan, op.cit., p.98. Hagan's book prints a photograph of a plaque commemorating this sacrifice; Cruikshank & Watt, KRR NY, op.cit., p.223. John and Nicholas Mattice had joined in the Schoharie 'uprising' in 1777. In 1780, John was serving in Capt Samuel Anderson's Light Infantry and Nicholas in Capt John McDonell's (Scotus) Grenadiers. Their relationship to Frederick Mattice has not been established. Abraham, Adam, another John, another Nicholas and William Mattice served in Butler's Rangers during the war (see, Fryer & Smy, Provincial Rolls, op.cit. p.71.) This second Nicholas transferred to the 2nd Bn, KRR NY before the war's end and a Henry Mattice also served in the 2nd.

90   Simms, Schoharie, **op.cit.**, p.411.
91   Blacksnake's account is confusing. It is difficult to assess whether he is speaking of Middleburgh, the first village the column entered, or Schoharie, which they didn't enter until late afternoon.
92   Blacksnake, **op.cit.**
93   **ibid.** Blacksnake makes so many outrageous claims that his accounts must be treated with care. He follows this tale of entering "the fort" by saying that a "hasty council was held in the big road near the fort in which the British and Indians participated. It was decided to pursue "the fleeing Americans ... the Indians alone started off on the run, headed by [Old Smoke] and Brant, with nearly all the Indian force. About 4 miles off they overtook a party of Americans, killed about 100 of them, took some prisoners and a good many escaped from the battlefield". When Old Smoke and Brant returned to Schoharie town, they "found they had only lost one Indian killed and 2 wounded, had killed 180 Americans and took 40 prisoners, got a good many horses, cattle, flour from 2 grist mills (both which were burnt)". He then claims that "[they] started on their return and found the upper fort deserted, 4 miles from the village, which had been passed on the outward march. It was set afire and burnt." Surely, his memory was playing tricks!
94   Cruikshank & Watt, KRR NY, **op.cit.**, p.52.
95   Simms, Schoharie, **op.cit.**, pp.401&402.
96   Sloughter's, **op.cit.**, pp.39,40,46. While the nonsense in this source regarding Burgoyne's army is not to be credited, the details of Murphy are of interest; For much information regarding BGen Simon Fraser, see Horatio Rogers, ed., **Lieut. James M. Hadden, Roy. Art., A Journal Kept in Canada and Upon Burgoyne's Campaign ...** (Albany: Joel Munsell's Sons, 1784) p.li&passim.
97   Hough, **op.cit.**, p.50; Simms, Schoharie, **op.cit.**, pp.402&403.
98   **ibid.**
99   **ibid**, p.401.
100 **ibid**, p.403.
101 TCM Newsletter, **Vol.III, No.4 (Dec 1984)** James F. Morrison research. In a Return of Lansing's Company dated at Schenectady, 26Oct80, 16 men all ranks were 'on command' at Schoharie with one noted as having been killed in action on 17Oct80. All of the other ranks were noted as being under a 3 months term.
102 Lansing's Company's Muster Roll.
103 Simms, Schoharie, **op.cit.**, p.404.
104 Cruikshank & Watt, KRR NY, **op.cit.**, p.52; Original sources advise that the expedition started with two 'Royal' Cohorn mortars, yet in Sir John's report to Haldimand, the Baronet uses the singular rather than the plural. What might have happened to the first mortar is unknown.
105 The Beckers are a prime example of a family split by the rebellion. Seven Beckers from the Schoharie had joined with Capt John McDonell (Scotus) and Lieut Adam Crysler in the August 1777 'uprising', five of these were later mustered in McDonell's company of the KRR NY. A sixth Becker entered the KRR in June 1780. see, Cruikshank & Watt, KRR NY, **op.cit.**, p.170. A seventh served in Butler's Rangers. In the rebel garrisons of the Schoharie, Maj Becker served at the Lower Fort, Peter Becker at the Middle Fort and Jacob Becker at the Upper. Morrison, Raids, **op.cit.**, pp.29-31
106 Sloughter's, **op.cit.**, p.46.
107 Cruikshank & Watt, KRR NY, **op.cit.**, p.52; Judging from the accuracy of the gunnery which the Royal Artillerymen displayed at the Lower Fort, the "understanding" that they lacked was exactly where to apply their shot to achieve the collapse of the Middle Fort's walls, although Haldimand's earlier advice to Johnson suggests that a Grass Hopper could not be expected to "reduc[e] any place" and would "go thro' any Stockades ... but will not beat them down."
108 Simms, Schoharie, **op.cit.**, pp.404&405.
109 **ibid**; Morrison research, **Massachusetts Pension Application S13044.** The application was written 56 years after the event, thus the accuracy of these recollections is questionable. Foote advises that he served in Capt Marsh's Coy of Brown's Levies, but Howe, **op.cit.** makes no reference to a Capt Marsh and places Asahel Foot in Foord's Coy.

110 Simms, Schoharie, **op.cit.**, p.405. The march air "Yankee Doodle" was regularly played by both sides during the conflict. Often, the Crown Forces used the tune on occasions where a fine sense of derision was required. Perhaps this was the case at the Middle Fort, but nothing to suggest it has been recorded.

111 Malcom Ms, **op.cit.**, Malcom to Clinton Sep 16. "I find some militia about Schoharie pretending to be in service [gaining shelter in the fort and drawing rations] - they will not obey Woolseys orders & I have directed him to discharge them especially as provisions are scarce." Obviously, Woolsey had been in difficulty with members of the garrison before.

112 Morrison, Raids, **op.cit.**, p.10. ex New York Pension application of Nicholas Rightor, no. S14309.

113 Vrooman was Woolsey's junior by virtue of the latter holding a commission in the Levies; Sloughter's, **op.cit.**, pp.46&47; Simms, Schoharie, **op.cit.**, pp.405-407. Simms claims that Woolsey was motivated by personal fear. Hough ignored that opinion as have I, **op.cit.**, p.48fn. He notes that Woolsey continued in the confidence of State Governor George Clinton and subsequently held the rank of BGen of militia; Malcom Manuscripts, **op.cit.**, Col Malcom reported to Gov Clinton on Oct. 11 that he had requested BGen Ten Broeck, in whose brigade Schoharie's militia were mustered, "to order Vrooman to support Woolsey at Schoharie if needfull ... " This suggests a strained, or perhaps too independent, relationship between the Levies and the local militia. Malcom's report continued "I am only uneasy about that place."

114 Simms, Schoharie, **op.cit.**, p.408.

115 Sloughter's, **op.cit.** p.46. Some American historians record that Sir John ordered that the Churches not be burnt. No record of this order has been found and the many churches which were lost belies the comment, however some Anglican/Episcopalian churches were spared and this was likely at Sir John's specific order. The Hendrix's (and Simms) write that William Crysler of Butler's Rangers set fire to the Low Dutch Church about 1/2 mile from the Middle Fort as he held a grudge against some members of its congregation; William was a brother of Lieut Adam Crysler of the Indian Department who had been a mill owner on Breakabeen Creek north of the Upper Fort. William was mustered in Capt George Dame's Coy of Butler's Rangers in a Roll dated Niagara, 30Nov83. See United Empire Loyalist Assoc., Hamilton Branch, ed., **Census of Niagara 1783** (UEL Association, 1975). As noted, Capt Dame's Coy was on this 1780 raid.

116 Simms, Schoharie, **op.cit.**, p.408.

117 **ibid**, p.409.

118 **ibid**; This is a mysterious story. As there were no Canada Indians with Johnson, who was this captive? As a "French" Indian, he may have been from one of the Lakes' Nations. What language was he speaking that no one in the fort could understand other than Denny? If a dialect of Iroquois, surely someone in the garrison would have understood. Was it French, as Simms designation for him suggests? A man named DeCouagne, a name of French origin, was an Interpreter with John Butler and Joseph Brant in the Six Nations' Department in 1773 and a Damange, another French surname, was employed in the same role in 1777. See **OA, HP, Ms622, Reel 113 and NAC, CO, MG11, "Q" Series, Vol.13, p.331.** These men would usually be employed when Algonkian dialects or French, a common language amongst the Canada and Lakes Indians, was expected to be spoken. Was such the case in the Schoharie or Mohawk Valleys?

119 Simms, Schoharie, **op.cit.**, pp.409&410.

120 Sloughter's, **op.cit.**, p.47.

121 Cruikshank & Watt, KRR NY, **op.cit.**, p.52. There was much bravado and contempt in Sir John's claim as fifty yards was well within effective musket range, however, this is not to suggest that this order was not given precisely as phrased.

122 **ibid**.

123 Hagan, **op.cit.**, p.40.

124 Simms, Schoharie, **op.cit.**, pp.412&413.

125 Captain George Smith, **An Universal Military Dictionary** ... (London: J. Millan, 1779) p.141. Smith advises that Tin Case-shot, in artillery, is formed by putting a great quantity of small iron shot into a cylindrical tin-box, called a canister, which just fits the bore of the gun. Leaden bullets are sometimes used in the same manner ... Case-

Shot, formerly, consisted of all kinds of old iron, stones, musket-balls, nails, &c. and used as above.

126 Simms, Schoharie, **op.cit.**, p.415.

127 **ibid**, pp.415&416. Simms reports that a Capt Snyder assumed command in the belfry. Morrison advises that the only commissioned officer named Snyder was a 1Lt. See Morrison, Raids, **op.cit.**, p.30.

128 Simms, Schoharie, **op.cit.**, p.416.

129 **ibid**, pp.416&417; Hagan, **op.cit.**, p.41. According to Hagan, the first round struck the church's stone wall and shattered.

130 Simms, Schoharie, **op.cit.**, p.417.

131 **ibid**.

132 **ibid**, pp.418&419.

133 Roberts, **op.cit.**, Johnson invasion map.

134 Sloughter's, **op.cit.**, p.50. ex letter of James Madison, 14Nov80.

135 Graymont, **op.cit.**, p.238.

136 TCM Newsletter, **Vol.V, No.2 (Jun 1986)** Transcribed by James F. Morrison from the Henry Glen Papers, NY Hist. Assoc., Cooperstown, NY. All quotations which follow this endnote, which are part of this description of Burton's questioning, are taken from the transcript.

137 Cruikshank & Watt, KRR NY, **op.cit.**, p.65. The term 'New Levies' was used by Haldimand in his letter to Sir John in November, 1780 wherein he referred to loyalist corps. It is not frequently encountered in original British correspondence and it is puzzling that the rebels were also employing the term. One supposes that New Levies denoted loyal American regiments as opposed to the older, established British corps.

138 See Appendix 3.

139 Smy research, **NAC, HP, MfReel A-682.**

140 Simms, Schoharie, **op.cit.**, p.420; Cruikshank & Watt, KRR NY, **op.cit.**, p.206. A KRR return of prisoners corroborates Haines' capture in 1780. He was later exchanged and after disbandment was at Lachine, Quebec, in 1784.

141 After the ambush at Oriskany in 1777, the Tryon County Militia Brigade underwent a very difficult period with much acrimony and recrimination occurring between its various officers and the County Committee. In 1778, Governor Clinton intervened in and ordered the merging of the Tryon County militia regiments with the Albany County Brigade. In 1779, a second Albany County Brigade was created, in which the Tryon regiments served with Robert Van Rensselaer as their Brigadier. From the unpublished research of James F. Morrison, Gloversville, New York.

142 Morrison research, ex Throop Wilder, **The Glen Letters, That we may Remember.**

143 Hough, **op.cit.**, pp.198-207. Proceeding of a Court of Enquiry upon the Conduct of General Robert Van Rensselaer. Testimony of "Aid-Major" John Lansing Jr. dated 16Mar81. NOTE: for future references where an officer's name is mentioned for the first time, an endnote will advise where his testimony may be found. Thereafter, there will be no endnote unless some circumstance dictates that a degree of precision is required.

144 Morrison, Raids, **op.cit.**, p.36. "Robt Vn Rensselaer to Lt Colonel V. Veeder or Officer Commanding at Lower Fort Schohary" dated Schenectady 18Oct80. ex Volkert Veeder Papers, Mohawk-Caughnawaga Museum Ms, Fonda, NY.

145 Sloughter's, **op.cit.**, p.49.

146 Hough, **op.cit.**, pp.178-180. Testimony of A/QM Henry Glen, 12Mar81.

147 **ibid**, pp.186-193. Testimony of Major Lewis R. Morris, 12Mar81; TCM Newsletter, **Vol.VI, No.1, March 1987.** James F. Morrison research ex Miscellaneous Manuscripts, Malcom, NY Hist Soc, NYC. Col Malcom writing to Governor George Clinton states, "Lewis Morris is a fine young fellow - I[t] would be an acquisition to have him established in the line of your militia - his present Rank is a shadow ... "

148 Morrison, Raids, **op.cit.**, p.35. ex Clinton Papers, VI,p.303. Veeder to Glen, 17Oct80.

149 Clinton Papers, **op.cit.**, VI,p.352. Clinton's report to Washington dated "Pokeepsie, Oct'r 30th 1780."

CHAPTER V — "BLOOD-HOUNDS" IN THE MOHAWK VALLEY

1   Clinton Papers, **op.cit.**, VI,p.348. Quoted from a letter by Col Jno Lamb to Gov Clinton in a letter written 29Oct80, viz — "We are anxiously waiting to hear, what success you have had, in driving Johnson, and his Blood-Hounds, out of the State."

2   TCM Newsletter, Vol.VI, No.1 (Mar 1987), **op.cit.**, a Letter from Col Wm Malcom to Gov Clinton dated at Fort Rensselaer, 3Oct80. "The Roads are very bad. The Bridges broke down, so that in the fall it will be almost impracticable to pass — " While Malcom was writing about the roads in the upper Mohawk Valley, there is no reason to suspect that the condition in the lower valley was any better.

3   Again Sir John reports on the fate of only one mortar, not two; TCM Newsletter, Vol.V, No.2 (Jun 1986), **op.cit.**, Burton interrogation states, "one 4 inch Cohorn"; Clinton Papers, **op.cit.**, VI, p.355. Clinton to Washington. Clinton reports "two brass mortars for 4 3/4 shells which they concealed on their Route from Schoharie"; The shells were later found by the rebels and the powder inside of them salvaged for use.

4   TCM Newsletter, **Vol.XIX, No.8 (Apr 1990)** Senate House Mss, fr 2751,no.3648, Kingston, NY. Malcom's Levies dated at Fort "Ransler", 13Oct80. Five days before the raid, Capt Blaksley, 3 Lts & 28 ORs were on command at Fort Hunter. There were likely militiamen there as well; **NA, Washington, MF Reel 72, RevWar Rolls 1775-1783.** A Roll of Officers of 1st Regt NY Levies for Sep/Oct 1780 indicated that Capt Blakesly and his 3 Lts noted above were all discharged on 15Oct80. Were they gone by 18Oct when Thompson and Brant raided? Very likely.

5   Cruikshank & Watt, KRR NY, **op.cit.**, p.52.

6   Simms, Schoharie, **op.cit.**, pp.421&422. Simms reports that the destruction of Glen, perhaps a later place-name, was accomplished by Indians under Brant. As Brant and Thompson were detached to Fort Hunter on the east side of the Schoharie Kill, they were not likely responsible. The rebels tended to view all Indians as being under Brant's command and ignored the senior Seneca leaders whose men probably formed the party referred to.

7   **ibid**, pp.422&423. It has previously been noted that the expedition had been forced to eat the majority of its horses while on their approach march. Putman's description of the lighting of the fires begs the question whether any of the raiders actually carried pre-prepared torches of rags smeared in pine or spruce gum or made from pitch-pine knots. Or, was it simply relied upon that a fire could always be found in the hearth, or readily created outside, into which brands could be shoved to provide a torch?

8   Cruikshank & Watt, KRR NY, **op.cit.**, p.52.

9   Roberts, **op.cit.**, map.

10 Simms, Schoharie, **op.cit.**, p.423; Cruikshank & Watt, KRR NY, **op.cit.**, p.253. David Schrambling had enlisted in the Spring raid on 22May80 and was assigned to the 2Bn. Was the killed man a brother or father?

11 Stone, Brant, **op.cit.**, II,p.114.

12 Roberts, **op.cit.**, map. It must be remembered that measuring linearly on a map in no way accounts for the constant ups, downs and diversions that were inevitable.

13 James F. Morrison research.

14 **Claus Papers, V.III**, pp.199-200. A letter from Lt Patrick Langan to Col Claus dated Crown Point, 31Oct80. Referred to hereafter as "Langan."

15 Cruikshank & Watt, KRR NY, **op.cit.**, p.193. In 1776, when the Royal Highland Emigrants were being first raised, John Munro (later second senior Capt 1Bn, KRR NY) was LtCol Allan Maclean's first officer recruited and he led Maclean through the Hudson Highlands and across country to Sir John's estates on the Mohawk where, with the full blessing of the Baronet, Maclean raised amongst Johnson's tenants a number of recruits. En route, Munro had led Maclean to Richard Duncan's home in Schenectady and from there Duncan (later fourth senior Capt 1Bn, KRR NY) guided the pair through the Mohawk District of Tryon County to Johnson Hall.

16 Morrison, Raids, **op.cit.**, pp.98&99. Robert Gram notes that the church in Caughnawaga was used as a fort in 1778.

17 Hough, **op.cit.**, p.54fn.

18 Fort Johnson was Sir William Johnson's second Mohawk Valley home which he had built in 1748 about 17 miles west of Schenectady. William Johnson had occupied this house before erecting Johnson Hall in Johnstown. Fort Johnson had been Sir John's home before his father's death and he had lived there in a common-law relationship

with Clarissa Putman, a local Palatine woman, whose family members later proved to be ardent rebels. See, Earle Thomas, **Sir John Johnson, Loyalist Baronet** (Toronto & Reading: Dundurn Press, 1986)

19 Hough, **op.cit.**, pp.185&186. Testimony of Sampson Dyckman, 12Mar81. The condition of Chuctinunda Hill was the subject of many questions at the Hearing because of the several hours delay encountered in waiting for the moon to rise.

20 Roberts, **op.cit.**, pp.111&116. This source shows Maj Jno McKinstry in the 8th and LtCol David Pratt in the 9th; Morrison, Raids, **op.cit.**, p.25. This source indicates that both men were in the 9th; Pratt and McKinstry appear to have alternated in the conducting of this command, the one leading the advance for a period, then the other taking another body of men for the next period.

21 Roberts, **op.cit.**, p.112. Roberts lists Sampson Dyckman as a Private soldier which as a Vol would be the case. He also noted that his lists were incomplete below the rank of Lt, so it may be that Dyckman was an Ens.

22 Hough, **op.cit.**, pp171-177. Testimony of William Harper, 12Mar81.

23 **Montgomery County Historical Society Newsletter, Fort Johnson, Vol.1, No.1 (Jan 1982).** NY Pension Application of Daniel McGraw No.S9947.

24 **AO, HP, Mss622 Reel 51.** Two returns dated 1782 list 11-12 Rangers and 55 Mohawks under arms (208 all souls) "under the immediate Direction of Daniel Claus Esqr Agent for the Six Nations in Canada."

25 Simms, Schoharie, **op.cit.**, p.431. Simms advises that two 9 pounder pieces were taken from Schenectady. His is the only source to mention the weight of the ordnance; Cruikshank & Watt, KRR NY, **op.cit.**, p.53. Sir John reported that papers found on Brown's body stated that three Fieldpieces were with Van Rensselaer.

26 Roberts, **op.cit.**, p.116. The 8th is the only Albany regiment to muster a William Wood. His rank is not recorded.

27 Hough, **op.cit.**, p.187. Morris testimony.

28 Cruikshank & Watt, KRR NY, **op.cit.**, p.52. While this is a quotation from Sir John's report, in the early morning of the 19th he was unlikely to have known, first, where the men deserted to, and second, what they told John Brown. This information either came from prisoners taken after Brown's defeat or was found in Brown's pockets; Some American historians suggest a much smaller number of men ventured out with Brown. Numbers like 100-200, eg. see Simms, Schoharie, **op.cit.**, p.426. Simms gives 150-200. If so, Brown was extremely overconfident. One suspects that the numbers ascribed to Brown's force were deliberately reduced to make Sir John's troops appear overwhelming, and by doing so explain away the Baronet's easy victory.; **Newsletter of the Fort Klock Historic Restoration Project, Vol.III, No.3 (Sep 1990)** An account of the Stone Arabia battle by James F. Morrison gives Brown's strength at about 340 men; Lou D. MacWethy, **The Battle of Klock's Field, October 19, 1780 ...** (St. Johnsville, NY: Enterprise and News, 1930) p.12. Hereafter, "MacWethy, Klock's." As part of his study, MacWethy reprints an article by W.N.P. Dailey in which the number of Brown's men is given at 381.

29 Stanley, **op.cit.**, passim, see index; Lanctot, Canada & the American Revolution, **op.cit.**, passim, see index; **Newsletter of the Stone Arabia Battle Chapter, SAR, March 1975.** Robert L. French, "Colonel John Brown 1744-1780".

30 Hough, **op.cit.**, p.57fn; William L. Stone, **The Campaign of Lieut.Gen. John Burgoyne and the Expedition of Lieut.Col. Barry St. Leger,** (Albany: 1877) reprinted De Capo Press, 1970. pp.346-352. Appendix X; **Bulletin of the Ticonderoga Museum, Vol.II, No.1 (Jan 1930),** pp.31-40; Brown had early experience with Ticonderoga having served under Arnold during the fort's capture in 1775. He was given the pleasant task of riding to Congress with word of this success.

31 **ibid,** p.27.

32 Howe, **op.cit.**, pp.7-11,20-25. Complete details of Brown's problems with Arnold and his accusations of Arnold's misconduct.

33 Howe, **op.cit.**, pp.26-32. These pages present a detailed study of John Brown's (Third Berkshire) regiment of Levies. It contains no reference to a Capt Wright, although a Capt White and a Capt Warner are listed. Howe advises that White's Company of 64 men, all ranks, was engaged at Stone Arabia and lost 29 men killed, 1 wounded and 1 taken prisoner. Howe maintains that Warner's Company was not there and gives no casualties for it. However, the Pension Application of Isaac Blackmore, which is

referred to later in this chapter, claims that Warner's Company was sent across the Mohawk River to Brown from Fort Planck before the battle and Blackmore also claims he saw service in the battle at Stone Arabia. The question arises — is the Wright mentioned in Dubois' letter either White or Warner? Certainly Wright and White are phonetically similar. Or, did Dubois send two Massachusetts companies to Brown's aid — those of Wright/White and Warner? If Howe concluded that Warner's Company was not in the Stone Arabia battle because it returned no casualties, another interpretation could be that Warner's men were the rearguard of Brown's column and they were able to retreat towards the river and Fort Plain (as stated in Blackmore's pension application) without casualties. Howe lists an Isaac Blackmer as a Private in Warner's Company.

34 TCM Newsletter, **Vol.V, No.8 (Dec 1986).** Research of James F. Morrison. Haldimand Papers, Letters from Officers of the Royal Regiment of New York, Reel A-746; Ironically, General Van Rensselaer received the blame for luring Col Brown out of Fort Paris to attack Sir John's column, however, if Brown needed encouragement, Lewis Dubois' message was the more likely cause; Roberts, **op.cit.,** p.77. Jacob Bockee was a Lt in Dubois' Levies.

35 This strange place-name is biblical and Dutch in origin. Steen Rabi was one of many early spellings. The name was first given to a place on the east side of the Hudson R. not far from present day North Troy. It is thought the name transferred from there to the new settlement, which is the focus of this account. Fort Klock Newsletter, **Vol.III, No.9 (Sep 1991)** ex The Palatiner, August 1951.

36 Howe, **op.cit.,** pp.14&36. "Fort Paris, Dec. 19, 1776, Capt Christian Getman's Rangers, Tryon County militia, were stationed at Stone Arabia, and were ordered, when not ranging, to cut timber for building a fort, under direction of Isaac Paris, Esq. It was a palisaded enclosure of stone and [sic] block-houses for a garrison of from two to three hundred men."

37 **Symposium Forum on the Battle of Stone Arabia,** notes prepared by the local historian, Willis (Skip) Barshied Jr. The house was built in 1750 by Richard H. Wood for O. Hannes (Johannes) Keyzer according to an inscription found on two large stones taken from the building in 1858. In the latter year, the owner of the building, John A. Failing salvaged the stone to build his home. Failing gave the following as a description. "The main building of the fort was about 40 feet long and 35 wide ... There were about 10 port [loop] holes in it; the wedge shaped blocks taken from them, lay about the premises years after it was taken down ... two large rooms, no hall-way, a large stone fire place ... chimney of stone; the gables, from the collar-beam up were of wood; the roof was plain, the shingles about three-fourths of an inch thick. The lower rooms were about ten feet high in the clear, the upper room about 8 feet to the collar beam, and it was about 4 feet higher to the peak of the roof." Several original stone buildings remain in the Mohawk Valley as historic sites. All are quite similar to that described except that the gables are often of stone; Howe, **op.cit.,** p.17. Howe reports that Ft Keyser was held by "Captain Ziel[i]e with 8-9 men after Brown's defeat.

38 Hough, **op.cit.,** p.36. Hough reports that on 5Aug80, 500 Massachusetts Levies were ordered into the Mohawk Valley by Congress. Considerably less than 500 arrived, perhaps 300. In keeping with common practice of the period, the regiment was broken up into parcels which were distributed from the Schoharie, to Stone Arabia, to Fort Rensselaer, to Fort Planck. Hough gives the figure of 130 Mass Levies at Fort Paris; Howe, **op.cit.,** pp.26-32. Howe's study indicates that Capts Ely's (81 all ranks), Spoor's (72) & White's (64) companies were engaged in the battle and took casualties. It appears that Ely's & Spoor's were in garrison at Fort Paris and Wright's was sent from Fort Rensselaer and Warner's from Fort Planck (this latter from Isaac Blackmore's Pension Application) the night before the battle. In the absence of a garrison return, the sum of Ely's & Spoor's strengths has been taken for the garrison - ie. 153; Morrison, Raids, **op.cit.,** p.18. Capts Ely and Spoor are noted in this source. While Capt Wright is not listed, sufficient Subalterns and NCO's for three companies are noted; We have seen that Dubois sent Capt Wright from Fort Rensselaer to reinforce Brown; Morrison research, **Massachusetts Pension Application S5285 of Isaac Blackmore,** This source indicates that a second company of Brown's was dispatched by Dubois to Stone Arabia from below the Mohawk. It had been stationed at Fort Planck under the command of Capt Warner and mustered 88 men all ranks.

39 Morrison research, **New York State Pension No.S14760.** This record was submitted by Lt Henry J. Vanderberg of Capt Lee's Company who recorded that he was wounded

in the battle and two men from his company were killed; Roberts, **op.cit.**, p.77. This source confirms that Thos Lee was a Capt of Dubois' Levies.

40 Morrison, Raids, **op.cit.**, pp.20. Morrison's roster of men who participated in the Stone Arabia battle lists Captains Severinus Klock and Henry Miller. Miller had served as an Ens in the 3rd Coy and Klock of the 4th in 1777; Simms, Schoharie, **op.cit.**, p.426. Simms records that Zielie was in command at Fort Keyser. In 1777, he had served in the 5th Coy.

41 Howe, **op.cit.**, p. 426; Silas Underwood, **MAPA, S14744.**

42 Simms, Schoharie, **op.cit.**, p.426; Morrison, Raids, **op.cit.**, p.13; Simms recorded that Fort Keyser's small garrison was under the command of Captain John Zielie (Zeely) and Morrison agrees. Of course, Zielie could have stayed at the Fort with a skeleton crew while Getman took the majority on Brown's attack. Morrison does not list Zielie as a participant in the battle; Anne Moyer quote, in Barney Young, **NYPA, W22715.**

43 Langan, **op.cit.**, Langan reported that the detachment on the south side had crossed to join Sir John the night before. Perhaps he only meant that the senior Company officers did so in order to attend the celebration.

44 Hough, **op.cit.**, p.55; Roberts, **op.cit.**, map.

45 Morrison, Klock's, **op.cit.**, pp.20&21. The intelligence brought into Fort Haldimand by McKay was remarkably detailed. (Jim Morrison points out that these small garrisons were in constant flux and consequently he questions the value of the information) McKay brought with him two militia prisoners taken from Klock's 'Palatine' Regiment, Cpl Conrad Lawer and Pte Jno Lawer. These men gave precise details of the new 300-man garrison of nine months men at Fort Stanwix. They also advised that one Helmer and another "Low Dutchman" had been sent express from Stanwix on the 10th with details of Sir John's column obtained from the Oneida deserter who had run off with the mortar shell. They told that the people in the Valley had long known that Sir John was coming, but they knew not by what route. 600 "Regulars" had been sent into their District, ie. the Palatine precinct, and they were stationed as follows.

"Encamped at Stoneraby [Stone Arabia] 400

In Fort Plain opposite to Stonrabie	400
In Fort Fox	27
Fort Nellis	10
Fort Hess	22
Fort Clock	10
Clock's House	8
Nellis his Blockhouse	10
Fort Timberton	21
Fort Willeord [Walroth?]	7
Fort House	15
Fort Harkimar	24
Fort Vendecker [Windecker]	8
Fort Plank	6
	968"

Further, "In each of three of the above Forts there was one three pounder — all those Forts [lay] in the compass of nine Miles ... "

46 Roberts, **op.cit.**, map.

47 Morrison research, Massachusetts Pension Application S13044, **op.cit.**, The applicant, Asahel Foote, of Capt Marsh's Company was stationed at the Middle Fort in the Schoharie. He was with the relief column which marched to Stone Arabia the day after the battle there. His application was 56 years after the events, so his memory was likely playing him some tricks. He recalled that the Indians lured Brown out of Fort Paris and then led him into an "ambuscade in a notch where they arose upon them and slaughtered almost all of them - Colo Brown fell the first fire and was deposited in his grave the day before we arrived." On the march from Schoharie to Stone Arabia, Foote recalled "many cattle lay slaughtered[,] hardly an animal to be seen living[,] Houses smoking in ruins & when we arrived at Stone Robby, many Inhabitants laying in their gore yet unburied ... "

48 Simms, Schoharie, **op.cit.**, p.426. In almost every particular of topography, Simms reverses the positions of Brown's and Johnson's forces. He writes that it was

Johnson's men who enjoyed the cover of some woods and the fence. It is Brown's force which crossed through an open field. This was supposedly concluded from the recollections of veterans of the battle. The comparison of Johnson's & Simms' accounts is quite amazing. Sir John was a participant and wrote his report scant days later. In his recording of these quite specific details to his superior, Johnson had nothing to prove one way or the other regarding how the topography lay. He had won a clear victory. What did it matter who had the field and who the trees except on Simms' part to explain how the Crown Forces won such a quick & decisive victory? Or, did Simms misunderstand the American veterans? Did he somehow reverse who was where simply in error?; Howe, **op.cit.,** p.17. So many American historians search for an answer to Brown's defeat by turning to explanations of treachery on the part of 'patriots' and carefully laid ambushes on the part of the Indians. Howe claims that Brown was "deceived by the false advice of persons pretending to be patriots, [the deserters?], he was led to turn aside from the road upon which he marched out into a somewhat narrow clearing in the forest near a small work called Fort Keyser, and was killed nearly two miles from Fort Paris, being attacked on every side in what amounted to an ambuscade."; Rev. Garret L. Roof, "Colonel John Brown, his Services in the Revolutionary War, Battle of Stone Arabia", **Papers of the Oneida Historical Society (1884),** pp.15&16. Roof does not promote the theory of an ambuscade. He offers a colourful account of warnings given to Col Brown by his subordinate officers against venturing out from Fort Paris, including the telling of a dream of evil portent experienced by one of the soldiers. Unlike Howe, Roof maintains that the march to Fort Keyser was purposeful. (to pick up Getman's men?) He then notes that an Indian was discovered in the act of killing and scalping a woman who was fleeing from her home and that he was killed by one of Brown's "brave volunteers." This shooting opened a general engagement in which Brown's men 'were less effective than that of the enemy on account of their exposed condition.' " ... he was attacked by an overwhelming number, who were gaining upon his flank ... "; discussions with Stone Arabia historian Willis Barshied.

49   Roof, **op.cit.,** p.4. John Brown was born Oct. 19, 1744 at Haverhill, MA; Howe, **op.cit.,** p.3.

50   Langan, **op.cit.**

51   These are rather strange statistics as Howe reports that 15 men from Ely's company of 81 all ranks were killed in the battle. If Howe's report of the killed from Spoor's and White's companies are included, the total rises to 27 rankers. Adding Brown & Ely brings the total killed to 29. Of course, these figures assume that Howe's research is more correct than the veterans' memories, **op.cit.** pp.31&32.

52   Morrison, Raids, **op.cit.,** p.100. Reverend Robert Gram, "The Reformed Church and Johnson's Great Raid." This boulder now carries an inscription which reads, "On the Morning of Oct. 19, 1780 on the Stone Arabia Battlefield surrounding, fell thirty defenders of their Country with their Commander, Col. John Brown whose body was found 410 yards W.S.W. of this stone - 1886."

53   Jeptha R. Simms, **Frontiersmen of New York ...** (2 Vols, Albany: George C. Riggs, 1883) II,p.457.

54   Simms, Frontiersmen, **op.cit.,** II,p.445; Howe, **op.cit.,** p.28. Samuel Woolworth is on the roster of Capt Ely's Coy.

55   Cruikshank & Watt, KRR NY, **op.cit.,** p.53. To the raiders, some casualties may have appeared dead and others may have feigned death. However, as the Americans had the task of burying and accounting for the slain, one suspects their number to be accurate. Also, both sides always exaggerated the losses of their foe; Massachusetts Pension Application S5285, op.cit. Isaac Blackmore, a Private in Capt Warne's (Warner's) Company of Brown's Levies claimed that 150 men were lost. His is the only rebel account consulted which quotes such a large number of rebel dead. His application was filed 57 years after the battle; Hough, **op.cit.,** p.56. Hough reports the loss of 39 men killed plus Col Brown; MacWethy, Klock's, **op.cit.,** p.12. Dailey reports 30 Massachusetts Levies were killed and gives their names. The loss of the Tryon County men is not given; Morrison, Fort Klock Newsletter, **op.cit.** Morrison gives the killed at 35, wounded about 12; see also, TCM Newsletter, **Vol.III, No.10, June 1985.** James F. Morrison research. "Anecdotes of the Battle of Stone Arabia on October 19, 1780". Pension depositions of three men of Brown's regiment and one of a Palatine man describing his attempt to join with Brown.

56 Simms, Frontiersmen, **op.cit.**, II,p.443. This source claims that when on the march Col Brown had second thoughts about carrying Van Rensselaer's letter on his person lest it fall into the hands of his enemies and that he dispatched a messenger carrying the letter back to Ft Paris. Simms says that this messenger never arrived and theorizes that the messenger deserted to Sir John. But, the Baronet's report is clear. He found a letter in Brown's pocket with explicit information about the pursuit. Another mystery.

57 Morrison, Raids, **op.cit.**, p.14; Henry Genter, a German prisoner from Burgoyne's Army, and Peter Sutz/Sits manned the Ft Paris cannon. Adam A. Loucks, **NYPA, W16637** and Johann Henry Genter, **NYPA, S43591.**

58 Hough, **op.cit.**, p.50fn; as the KRR NY had been uniformed in red in 1779, this could have been one of its companies, or the British Regulars; The local historian, Willis Barshied, found a badly eroded KRR NY ranker's waistcoat button a few yards from the rebuilt Lutheran Church.

59 **ibid**, p.187. Morris testimony; Roberts, **op.cit.**, map.

60 **TCM Newsletter, Vol.XIII, No.4 (Apr 1993).** Research of James F. Morrison entitled, "Men from the Third Battalion who Served in the Levies"; Maryly B. Penrose, **Mohawk Valley in the Revolution** ... (Baltimore: Liberty Bell Associates, 1978) p.34; MacWethy, Klock's, **op.cit.**, p.16enB; **ibid**, Vol.IV, No.7 (Jan 1986). A letter from Wm Seeber, Chairman of the Tryon County Committee of Safety, and co-signed by 14 committee members of note including 3 Cols, 2 Majs, 3 Capts and 4 Lts, recommending Wallace for a commission. A very well thought of, young man indeed.

61 Hough, **op.cit.**, p.165fn; TCM Newsletter, Vol.XIX, No.8 (Apr 1990), **op.cit.**, Return of Malcom's Regiment dated 13Oct80. This shows Maj "Bunschoten" at Fort Paris and Capt. McKinstry, Lts Delong and Utley with 85 all ranks at Fort Herkimer. As Benschoten & McKinstry serve with Col Dubois on Oct 19, it is clear that the Levies assembled at Fort Rensselaer were from both Dubois' and Malcom's regiments.

62 Hough, **op.cit.**, pp.165&166. Part of the John Harper's testimony, 12Mar81.

63 It is interesting to compare what Sir John said he learned from the letter in Brown's pocket to the information given in Lansing's letter to Col Dubois. Some American historians maintain that both Brown and Dubois had letters written to them from Van Rensselaer and sent from Fort Johnson the day before. But, why would Brown's letter, which was more likely to be intercepted by flank-guards of Sir John's forces, contain so much more specific data than that sent to Dubois? As Sir John was destined never to see three fieldpieces, let alone two, it cannot be that he wrote his report from the benefit of hindsight - rather it would appear that he was quoting with some accuracy from a letter found on Brown's body which he had retained. Quite mysterious.

64 **ibid**, pp.187&188. Morris testimony and p.173. William Harper testimony, 12Mar81; Richard Young **NYPA, S11923.**

65 Johnson's, Butler's and Leake's men were on a much different footing than the rebel militia and indeed, the State Levies. Although many of the individual militia officers and men had seen Continental service, as units they were marginally trained when compared to the British Provincial troops. The militia were called out for short term emergencies, the Levies for longer terms such as nine months, but the British Provincial corps, soldiers and rangers, signed on for the duration of the war, however long that may be. Even the Continental Regiments had men enlisted for mixed terms, some the duration and others only months - an organizational nightmare. A loyalist only left his regiment by being discharged as too old, sick or crippled to do duty, or as a deserter or to transfer to another service such as the engineers, the Provincial Marine, the bateaux companies, etc ... Of course, British Regulars were also 'in for the duration' and only left their regiments for similar reasons. Military discipline was consistently harsh and demanding. The soldier became hardened to his duty. For the loyalist with strong political convictions, his motivation on campaign was very high. In short, the British Army in North America enjoyed a continuity of service that almost guaranteed proficiency in operations; **ibid**, p.25. Hough notes that in the Spring of 1780, "the commander-in-chief [Washington] was at this time embarrassed by the expiration of the period of enlistment of many troops in the Continental Army ... "; See Chpt 6 for Washington's comments on this topic.

66 **ibid**, p.202. Lansing testimony.

67 Clinton Papers, **op.cit.**, VI,p.305.

68 **ibid**, p.188. Morris testimony and p.173. Wm Harper testimony; There is no reason to believe that all of the prisoners examined by Van Rennselaer were in uniform. Any

suspicious person at large in the country may have been taken up as a suspected loyalist sympathizer.

69 Graymont, **op.cit.**, pp.149,155,197. This source gives some details of Col Louis' services; Stevens, Savage Allies, **op.cit.**, II,pp.569,637&640. Details of Atayataghronghta's activities in 1775&76.

70 Hough, **op.cit.**, p.202. Lansing testimony and p.173. Wm Harper testimony.

71 Driskell is not recorded in Roberts as having served in the New York Artillery. In testimony given at the Van Rensselaer hearings, his rank is noted as both Lt and Capt. However, Driskill records his rank as Lt and includes his given name in his report of ordnance taken at Klock's Field which is endnoted later.

72 **ibid**, p.174. Wm Harper gives himself and Maj McKinstry credit for discovering the enemy and on p.188, Morris testimony, Morris claims he and Pratt saw the enemy first.

73 **ibid**, p.193. Edward S. Willet testimony.

74 **ibid**, p.188. Morris testimony.

75 **ibid** and also p.174. Wm Harper testimony.

76 Clinton Papers, **op.cit.**, VI,p.319.

77 **ibid**.

78 The identity and regiment of this Maj Schuyler is confusing. Roberts, **op.cit.**, passim. This source does not list a Maj named Schuyler in any of the seventeen Albany militia regiments. On p.101, Roberts notes a Philip P. Schuyler as the Col of the 3rd Albany; Morrison, Raids, **op.cit.** on p.24 confirms the presence of the 3rd Albany Regiment at Klock's Field and names six participants. From these sources, one concludes that this Schuyler named by Dyckman is the Col of the 3rd Albany and he has identified the rank incorrectly.

79 The transcript of the testimony shows "Yale's", not Yates. However, the surname Yale is not found in the Valley whereas Maj Christopher P. Yates was a noted citizen, having been a Tryon County Committeeman in 1775, a Maj in the 1st New York ContLine in 1775 and in the Commissary Department thereafter. See, Penrose, Mohawk Valley, **op.cit.**, p.356 and Egly, 1st New York, **op.cit.**, pp.51,74,81.

80 Hough, **op.cit.**, p.203. Lansing testimony; **ibid**, pp.174&175. Wm Harper testimony and p.189. Morris testimony and p.194. Samuel Clyde testimony.

81 Mathews, Mark, **op.cit.**, pp.12,38-41,43,47,48. The irascible, passionate John Harper had been educated at Dr. Eleazor Wheelock's Indian School in Lebanon, CT. He had attended with Joseph Brant and a number of other Tryon County natives. He was a most active politician/soldier in favour of the rebellion. At one point he served as a Committee of Safety member and later as chairman, simultaneously as a Capt of Rangers with his brother Alexander. At another time he was active in the Schoharie having a primary role against the McDonell-Crysler 'uprising' of 1777. Like his brother William, he was a Tryon County commissioner of sequestration; TCM Newsletter, Vol.VI, No.1 (Mar 1987) **op.cit.**, and Vol.XV, No.9 (May 1995), **op.cit.**, James F. Morrison research. John Harper was the past commander of the 5th Regiment of Tryon County's militia, however by May 1780 he was in command of a regiment of New York State Levies which relieved the 1st NY Continental Line as the garrison of Fort Stanwix (Schuyler) on 3Oct80. Col Malcom, the senior Levies' officer in the Mohawk region in 1780, wrote to Governor Geo Clinton from Albany 14Sep80 and says, "Genl Renslear will tell you that Harper is a blockhead ... " See next endnote for indications that Harper was not well thought of by his peers. However, none could have doubted his devotion to the rebellion.

82 James F. Morrison research, **Library of Congress, Washington Papers, Series 4, reel 71, item 153-336.** "Weekly Return of a Regiment of New York State Levies Comanded by Lieut Coll John Harpur, now in Garrison at Fort Schuyler" dated 1Oct80. Under "Absent Officers", LtCol Harpur is returned as sick at Schenectady, having already been away for 15 days; Malcom Manuscripts, **op.cit.**, a derogatory letter written by Malcom dated at Fort Rensselaer on 25Sep80 to Gov Clinton states that he had given Harper a furlough and intimated that Harper was welcome to claim illness so long as he wasn't with his regiment.

83 Morrison, Raids, **op.cit.**, p.14.

84 Hough, **op.cit.**, pp.166&167. Jno Harper testimony; Amos Weller, **NYPA, W25952.**

85 **ibid**. Harper, ever a firebrand, was vitriolic in his testimony and an obvious spokesmen for those who felt Van Rensselaer had performed poorly. His brother William, who was of similar temperament, was not quite so blatantly accusatory.

86 **ibid**.

87 **ibid**, p.180. Dubois testimony.

88 **ibid**, p.168. Jno Harper testimony and pp.194&195. Col Clyde Testimony , 16Mar81.

89 **ibid**, p.189. Morris testimony.

90 As events transpired, it was indeed fortunate for the raiders that the artillery was left on the south bank. If the pieces had been brought into action and well served, the rebels could have sat back and pounded the Crown's infantry with devastating effect and brought about a quite different result than that which unfolded.

91 Clinton Papers, **op.cit.**, VI,pp.304&305; **ibid**, VI,p.258. As late as Oct. 31st Schuyler was being alarmed by Carleton's force. He wrote a secret letter to Gov Clinton on that date advising that "Allen has disbanded his militia, and the Enemy in number upwards of 1600, are rapidly advancing towards us ... Intreat Gen. Washington for more Continental troops ... "

92 TCM Newsletter, **Vol.XV, No.8 (Apr 1995)**. James F. Morrison, editor. "Pension Application of William Van Slyke". See fn#10 in second section.

93 Morrison, Raids, **op.cit.**, p.78. Milo Nellis, "Unpublished Tory Report of the Battle of Klock's Field." The Nellis account first appeared in the Enterprise and News, July 27, 1944.

94 Cruikshank & Watt, KRR NY, **op.cit.**, p.53.

95 Daniel Hess, **NYPA S22826**. Hess stated, "gun shots were exchanged...One of Sir John's men being killed in the exchange."

96 Simms, Frontiersmen, **op.cit.**, II,p.383; John Leonard Crouse, **NYPA, W16935.**

97 Hough, **op.cit.**, p.190. Morris testimony.

98 **ibid**, p.168. Jno Harper testimony.

99 **ibid**, p.195. Clyde testimony.

100 **ibid**, p.190. Morris testimony.

101 Clinton Papers, **op.cit.**, VI,p.352. He referred to the party of Oneidas as being small. At this stage in the war, that would not have been the Oneidas' perception.

102 Morrison, Raids, **op.cit.**, pp.22-24. Morrison lists participants from the 1st, 2nd & 3rd Tryon and Casselman's & Gray's companies.

103 The exact structure of the three columns has not been discovered. None of the American accounts have recorded the number of men deployed and only fragmentary evidence has surfaced which places certain regiments in each column. There is no doubt that Cuyler's and Van Alstyne's were in the left column as both are mentioned in that context during the Van Rensselaer hearing. The same can be said for Whiting's and Van Rensselaer's in the Centre Column and Dubois', Graham's and Clyde's in the Right Column. Obviously Schuyler's 3rd Albany was somewhere on the field as his presence is noted in the testimony. Morrison's research places the 2nd & 3rd Tryon in the fight as well as Wemple's 2nd Albany & Van Ness' 9th Albany. A 150 man detachment of Wemple's was stationed at Ballstown on Oct. 13th and it is unlikely that they were recalled to march into the Mohawk. Casselman's Ranger company from the Stone Arabia garrisons may well have been the van of Dubois' Right Column as they would have known the country particularly well, although the Col fails to mention them; Amos Weller, **NYPA, W25952**. Weller claims there were five columns with "Col. McEnster" i.e. Maj McKinstry, at the head of one.

104 Morrison, Raids, **op.cit.**, p.24.

105 **ibid**.

106 James Morrison's research indicates that LtCol Veeder's 3rd (Mohawk) Tryon regiment contributed to the forces deployed at Klock's Field. It is most likely that these men would have marched with Clyde's.

107 Hough, **op.cit.**, p.204. Lansing testimony.

108 Clinton Papers, **op.cit.**, VI, p.220.

109 The conclusion that the height of land was Klock's orchard is taken from various testimony that follows. Sir John does not say so in his report.

110 Cruikshank & Watt, KRR NY, **op.cit.**, p.53.

111 MacWethy, Klock's, **op.cit.**, map entitled, "Battle of Klock's Field October 19th, 1780." Footnote #6 (there are two) to this map advises that the properties belonging

to Klock and Failing joined one another, with Failing's being to the west of Klock's. Therefore, Sir John sending a detachment to the high ground on Klock's properties and moving down from the hills through Failing's orchard is quite believable; TCM Newsletter, Vol.III, No.10, **op.cit.**, deposition of Lodowick Moyer of Col. Lewis Dubois Regt. of N.Y.S. Levies. This source confirms the battle was fought "in a field called Failings Orchard."

112 Dubois must have been referring to all troops in redcoats as regulars. As the KRR NY was then in red coats with blue facings, similar to those worn by the 8th Regiment, one can suspect that the rebels were either unable to differentiate, or indifferent to doing so, between British and loyalist line troops. The 34th were clothed in sleeved waistcoats trimmed in yellow. (research of Christian Cameron, OC recreated 34th Regt Light Infantry, British Brigade) All companies of the Royal Yorkers wore coatees, or jackets, as opposed to full length regimental coats, as the latter had proven to be less serviceable, their tails continually catching on brush in the woods. The KRR's disbanded men of flank and line companies were recorded wearing slouched hats in 1784 which indicates that the whole regiment did so from 1779 onwards. See, Cruikshank & Watt, KRR NY, **op.cit.**, p.152. The James Peachey watercolour at New Johnsto[w]n on the St. Lawrence (NAC, negative no.C-2001) illustrating the settlement of the companies of Capts Samuel Anderson and Patrick Daly offers excellent detail of the uniforms worn by the 1Bn KRR NY; Leaving the hat brim down, rather than cocked, provided protection for the face and neck from the sun. The practice of wearing coatees, or sleeved waistcoats, and slouched or flopped hats even by midwar was well established. Further details on uniforming may be found in, Hew Strachan, **British Military Uniforms, 1768-96, The Dress of the British Army from Official Sources** (London: Arms and Armour Press, 1975) and John Mollo & Malcolm McGregor, **Uniforms of the American Revolution in color** (New York: MacMillan Publishing Co., Inc., 1975)

113 Stone, Brant, **op.cit.**, II,p.121. Stone believes these riflemen were German Jaegers, the only regular riflemen in the British service in the north. From the deserter, Benjamin Burton, we have discovered that "Green Yagers" were with Sir John's raiders. No record of the colour or style of Leake's Independent Company's clothing in 1780 has yet been found, but if they continued to wear the green coats, which loyalist line troops such as the Royal Yorkers had ceased to wear in 1779, and if they wore slouched or cocked hats rather than caps like Butler's, they may have been taken for German Jaegers to the rebel observers. While confusion may have resulted on the part of rebel observers in identifying which troops were sent with Brant, this text assumes them to have been German Jaegers.

114 Hough, **op.cit.**, pp.181&182. Dubois testimony and p.175. Wm Harper testimony.

115 **The Manual Exercise as Ordered by His Majesty in 1764** ... (New-York: 1775) pp.19-22. The system of platoon firing delineated in the text is that used by small detachments. A regiment of 8-10 companies would regulate the firing according to the 1764 Manual. See also, Stuart Reid, Paul Chappell, **King George's Army 1740-93: (1) Infantry, Osprey Military Men-at-Arms Series No.285** (London: Osprey, 1995) p.22. Weapons and Tactics. A simplified explanation of the Platoon Firings.

116 Roberts, **op.cit.**, p.97.

117 Hough, **op.cit.**, p.194. Lt Garrett Van Schaick testimony, 16Mar81; **Library of the University of the State of New York, Albany, Mss 13329**. Excerpts of a diary of John Beebe Jr. prepared during the Revolutionary War years as transcribed by Richard C. Perry, 1983&89. Beebe was from New Concord, south-east of Albany. On Oct. 26th, 1780 he wrote, "thursday[,] militia Returnd from pursuing the Enemy up the mohawk River where they had a Sever Engagement for the Space of half an hour when the Enemy fled being Coverd by the night[.] [W]hat is to be Remarkd[,] not one of the militia killd but 2 or 3 wounded ... " So, while the musketry was certainly hot and heavy, neither side appeared to suffer to any great degree.

118 Roberts, **op.cit.**, p.97.

119 **ibid**. p.104.

120 MacWethy, Klock's, **op.cit.**, map of Klock's Field battle.

121 Cruikshank & Watt, KRR NY, **op.cit.**, p.53; These horses were part of the plunder.

122 Hough, **op.cit.**, p.169. Jno Harper testimony.

123 The evidence in the testimony names no more than two regiments, although circumstantially there were one or two more.

124 Cruikshank & Watt, KRR NY, **op.cit.** p.53; Brant's Vols abandoned much plunder including Col Brown's scalp which was interred with his body. Amos Weller, **NYPA, W25952** and John Vanderburgh, **NYPA, S16279**.

125 TCM Newsletter, Vol.XIX, No.8 (Apr 80), **op.cit.**, ex Senate House Manuscripts, folder 2751, no.3648, Kingston, NY. "Weekly Return of the first Regiment of the State of New York Commanded by Colo. William Malcom - Fort Ransler Oct 13th, 1780."; Maj Elias Van Benschoten had served as a Captain of the 1st Coy, 3NY at Fort Stanwix during the 1777 siege by St. Leger. Benschoten had played an important role in Willett's sortie from the fort on the afternoon of August 6 at which time the Royal Yorker and Indian camps were thoroughly plundered.

126 **ibid**.

127 **ibid**.

128 Hough, **op.cit.**, p.206. Lansing testimony.

129 Cruikshank & Watt, KRR NY, **op.cit.**, p.53. Sir John's own words.

130 Simms, Schoharie, **op.cit.**, p.433. Many years after the war, Richard Duncan, a substantial landowner and member of the Legislative Council and Land Board of Upper Canada, decided to risk a permanent return to the United States. Perhaps business or old family interests compelled him. In a private meeting with some of his pre-war friends, against whom he had been in arms during the revolution, Duncan delivered his story. Possibly, in deference to his audience, his version did not mention why the loyalist officers had declined to surrender.

131 Robert's, **op.cit.**, map; Morrison, Raids, **op.cit.**, p.80. Milo Nellis argues that the Crown Forces forded the river at the site of the battle and offers much evidence to support his contention. He also claims that the regular ford further upriver at Christie's was guarded by two forts, one on either side of the Mohawk, which he implies would have prevented a crossing there. Nellis also claims that the retreat "was every man for himself"; however, an enemy that is broken and flees with 'every man for himself' does not reunite in utter darkness and then continue with a well disciplined withdrawal the very next morning, completely eluding the pursuit. Nellis was 'dreaming in technicolor.'

132 Cruikshank & Watt, KRR NY, **op.cit.**, p.54.

133 Hough, **op.cit.**, pp.196&197. Clyde testimony.

134 Cruikshank & Watt, KRR NY, **op.cit.**, p.54; Cruikshank, Butler's, **op.cit.**, p.86; **OHS Paper & Records, Vol.22 (1925)** pp.36&37. Ernest Cruikshank, "A Memoir of Lieutenant-Colonel John MacDonell." An odd sequel to this spirited attack by Capt McDonell was the Court Martial of 1Lt Peter Ball. Ball had command of the rear of McDonell's force that attacked the rebel militia at Fort Herkimer. He was accused of refusing to support the Capt, saying "it was too dangerous", and to have prevented the men from doing so. McDonell, who had recuperated in lower Quebec during the winter, returned to Niagara only to find himself thrust into Ball's Court Martial. John Butler reported that McDonell had been unaware of "Why the Rear did not support him as he would wish" until he rejoined the corps. Col Butler wrote to Haldimand (2Jul81) that "should Lieut. Ball be acquitted for what he has been Tryed, the Corps will not do Duty with him till he clear up this." Peter Ball was able to successfully defend his position and returned to full duty with the Rangers. In 1783, he was the 1Lt in Capt Jno McKinnon's Coy mustered at Niagara (Census of Niagara, op.cit.) and at 4Nov81 he was noted as the 7th senior 1Lt with a commission date of 15Aug80 (**OA, HP, Ms622, Reel 36**). By disbandment he had advanced in this very active corps to 4th senior 1Lt (**HP, AddMss21827, p.348**). On 1Jun82, John Butler wrote to Haldimand's military secretary asking that McDonell's commission date be put ahead of Capt Ten Broeck's as the former was "always thought to be the eldest [senior]" and was "the most capable officer in the Corps to command in my absence". Further, that he "is also the best liked by the Indians who soon after the death of my Son [Capt Walter] desired in a very pressing manner that he should step in my son's place ..." Very high praise indeed!

135 Morrison, Raids, **op.cit.**, p.26. Morrison reports M'Kean serving in Harper's Levies in 1780.

136 TCM Newsletter, **Vol.XV, No.7 (Mar 1995)**. James F. Morrison research. "Deposition of Henry H. Pickard, George Van Slyke's Pension Application", S10016, NA, Washington. In fn#6, this article contains excerpts from the Pension Application of Jacob A. Young with details of Sir John's waiter, or servant; **"The Burning Issues", Newsletter of the Burning of the Valleys Military Association, March 8, 1995,**

James F. Morrison, "Deposition of Henry H. Pickard ... " Offers some additional information; Cruikshank & Watt, KRR NY, **op.cit.**, p.269.

137 Stone, Brant, **op.cit.**, II, pp.122&123; Simms, Schoharie, **op.cit.**, p.433. Simms quotes Cass as stating there were seven captors, but the pension deposition of Pickard, a non-participant, gives only five.

138 Clinton, **op.cit.**, VI,pp.322&333.

139 Hough, **op.cit.**, p.197. Clyde testimony. Responses to questions set by Genl Van Rensselaer and p.207. Lansing testimony.

140 MacWethy, Klock's, **op.cit.**, p.17fnF. One presumes Clinton received the following report when at Fort Rensselaer. It read:
"A Return of Ordinance and Stores taken from the British army Commanded by Sir John Johnson.
Fort Rensselaer, Oct. 19, 1780
1 piece Brass Ordinance 3 pd. with Emplm'ts Comp.
23 rounds, Round Shot fix'd

10 -do-, Canister	1 Quadrant
1 Scale Beam	1 mallet and set
20 fuses	1 seane marlin
2 port fires	1 cole chisel
1 augur	1 Seane Quick Match
100 wt corn powder	1 drudging box
Jo. Driskill, Lt. Artillery"	

141 TCM Newsletter, Vol.V, No.8 (Dec 1986), **op.cit.** James F. Morrison research ex Glen Papers, New York State Association, Cooperstown, NY.

142 **ibid**, James F. Morrison research. Miscellaneous Manuscripts, Clinton, NY Hist. Soc., NYC.

143 Hough, **op.cit.**, p.207. Lansing testimony; NOTE: Events that occurred after Gov Clinton assumed command are not dealt with in the hearings into Gen Van Rensselaer's conduct. Only sparse details regarding the subsequent pursuit are found in the works of 19th century historians such as Stone & Simms.

144 Stone, Brant, **op.cit.**, II,pp.123&124. The events are taken from this account without any of the vitriol which is heaped upon Van Rensselaer, whom we have seen was not even in command at this time.

145 TCM Newsletter, **Vol.VI, No.10 (Dec 1987),** ex Pennsylvania Gazette of 8Nov80.

146 Morrison, Raids, **op.cit.**, p.17.

147 TCM Newsletter, Vol.VI, No.1 (Mar 1987), **op.cit.** James F. Morrison research from Miscellaneous Manuscripts, Malcom, NY Hist Soc, NYC. Col William Malcom relieved the 1st New York Continental Line at Fort Stanwix (Schuyler) in early October 1780 with Harper's Regiment of NY Levies leaving Major James Hughes as Commandant.

148 In the north, the leaves of the Sumach tree are a bright scarlet in the Fall and would be a source of 'Red Boughs'. These would be stuck into the men's hats as a cockade to provide a common identity as the clothing being worn was varied. The choice of red as a colour of identification was an odd choice as it was commonly associated with loyalty to the Crown. The reader will recall that the men in the Helleburgh chose red cockades to denote loyalty to the established government.

149 **ibid**, James F. Morrison research ex Haldimand Papers, Reel A-746. Letters from Officers of the Royal Regiment of New York.

150 From an unpublished study prepared by James F. Morrison, Gloversville, NY.

151 Morrison, Klock's, **op.cit.**, p.20. Intelligence gathered from Cpl Conrad Lawer and Pte Jno Lawer of Klock's Regiment; Morrison research, **Malcom Ms, New York Historical Society, NYC, NY** A letter from Col Wm Malcom to Gov Clinton dated Albany Sep. 16.

152 Malcom Manuscripts, **op.cit.**

153 **ibid**, p.54; Some American historians are convinced that Staring (Starring) was a loyalist who sought a method of deserting Vrooman as an opportunity to bring intelligence to Sir John. This is very doubtful. How would he have known where to meet the raiders? No George Staring is found in the rolls of the KRR NY, Butler's or Leake's. Neither is the name found amongst the prisoners held in Quebec Province. See, McHenry, **op.cit.**, passim. As he was supposedly sick, did the raiders leave him at Old Oneida?

154 Peter W. Johnson research collection, from **OA, UCLP, E Bundle, 18, #35**. The Petition dated 1834 of Andrew Embury in his 75th year. Embury had joined at Crown Point in 1776, likely with a group led by Justus Sherwood. He was attached to the Royal Yorkers over the winter and joined John Peter's Queen's Loyal Rangers in June 1777, serving in Capt Justus Sherwood's Coy. Embury went on the Burgoyne Campaign that year and saw action at Hubbardton (Jul.7) and Bennington (Aug.16). In the former action, Sherwood's Coy served as the advance corps which located the rebels who were then brought to action. At Bennington, Sherwood's Coy was again the advance corps and was heavily engaged. Embury transferred to the Loyal Volunteers under Capt Samuel MacKay on Aug.24 to be with close friends. As the competition for men was fierce amongst the loyalist corps, Embury was mustered in both the QLR and the LV over the period Aug.1 to Oct.24. He was one of the men chosen by Capt Leake for his Independent Coy on 28Jul78. Leake's Coy was absorbed into the 2nd Bn, Royal Yorkers in 1781 and Embury participated in Maj John Ross' Expedition of October that year. After the battle at Johnstown, Oct.25, there was a rigorous retreat march during which the men "travelled for a no. of days through the Snow; and had to lay down on it at night in the open wilderness when the weather was very Severe." It appears that he served as a Sjt in Capt Geo Singleton's Light Coy and, if so, would have been on the last raid against the Mohawk Valley in July 1782 under Capt Joseph Brant. Therefore, after such a long, action-packed military career, the remembering of the taking of Vrooman's party would indicate its great significance and suggests a direct involvement in the capture. Andrew Embury is returned as a Serjeant in the 2nd Bn, KRR NY on 28Feb84 at age 25, height 5' 7 1/4".

155 Pomroy Jones, **Annals and Recollections of Oneida County** (Rome, NY: Pomroy Jones, 1851) p.365. In his account of this affair, Jones makes many ridiculous assertions to enhance the conduct of Vrooman's party. One useful piece of information he provides is that the party was taken "while taking their dinner"; Clinton, **op.cit.**, VI,pp.332&333. A letter from Capt Jno Lawrence, Jr., to Col. Saml Drake, likely the father of Capt Joshua Drake of Vrooman's detachment. The letter was dated at Fort Schuyler (Stanwix) 24Oct80, sheds some further light on these affairs. " ... was sent out in order to harass the Enemy's front & flank & if possible to destroy the Boats in Onondaga Lake, which could it have been effected, would have been the means of the whole of their force falling into the Hands of Genl. Rensselaer who was following them in their Rear. On their arrival at Canasheaga, the[y] found the Enemy had just moved off, & that 7 men of the [Vrooman's] Party had deserted, & finding the Enemy to be numerous by their Tract & the militia not pursuing their Rear so close as they had Reason to expect, the Officers agreed to retreat back to the Fort; they had returned three miles destroying the Indian Settlements when unfortunately, my unhappy friend with the Party were surrounded by about 500 who they discovered not until the Enemy gave the Indian Shout. Two of the Party, after the Enemy begun to disarm them, pushed thro' them, who fired several Shots, but fortunately they escaped; one of them was my man, who Joshua [Drake], had taken as a waiter; he arrived about an Hour since."

156 Cruikshank, Butler's, **op.cit.**, p.87; Hough, **op.cit.**, p.62. This source gives a different number, ie. taken prisoner, 2 Capts - 1 Lt - 8 NCOs & 55 privates. Killed, 1 Lt - 3 Ptes; the list of prisoners held in Quebec Province that were taken on this raid includes 43 names from Vrooman's party. See McHenry, **op.cit.**

157 Cruikshank, Butler's, **op.cit.**, p.87.

158 Clinton Papers, **op.cit.**, VI,p.347.

159 Simms, Schoharie, **op.cit.**, p.431fn.

160 H.C. Burleigh, **Deforests of Avesnes and Kast, McGiness** (n.d., the author) p.11. From a memorial by George McGinness dated June 1782.

161 **ibid**, pp.4,5,11&12. He was discharged from the Indian Dept in 1782. McGinness' memorial states, "received a shot through the knee, which deprived him of the use of his leg." He was in Montreal until the settlements of 1784 at which time he and his wife and two children took up land in CT#3. Unable to cope with clearing and farming, he retired to Amherst Island on a grant provided for his family by Sir John and lived to "a ripe old age"; Cruikshank, Butler's, **op.cit.**, p.88. Cruikshank provides the name of McGinness' companion - Mannerly. No record of this name is found in the Butler's Rangers rolls or those of the Indian Department. Crowder does not list the name in his study. No one of that name made a loyalist petition.

162 Cruikshank, Butler's, **op.cit.**, p.87.

163 Cruikshank & Watt, KRR NY, **op.cit.**, p.54.

164 **ibid**, p.62.

165 **NAC, HP, MfReel A-688.**

166 Cruikshank & Watt, **op.cit.**, p.54.

167 Minutes ... Conspiracies, **op.cit.**, II,pp.554-558,560.

168 Of the list of prisoners with the rebels recorded in the KRR NY records, two men fit the description of 'being taken prisoner by the enemy' in the May '80 raid. One of these was John Martial (Marshall) who enlisted on 22May80, however he is carried on the regiment's rolls through to 1783. He may have been a contingency man (a fictitious name allowed to be carried on the company roll as an extra to draw certain allowances.) John Cogden enlisted on 25May80, perhaps a clerical error in the recording of the date, and he is not returned on later rolls. While the slim evidence points to Cogden being the mystery man, his case is complicated as he was returned on the KRR prisoner list as being in Munro's Coy. Of course, Munro's Coy was at Ballstown and no prisoners were taken by the rebels from that secondary expedition. ex Cruikshank & Watt, KRR NY, **op.cit.**, Master Muster Roll.

169 Clinton Papers, **op.cit.**, VI,pp.369&370.

170 James F. Morrison research.

171 Enys, **op.cit.**, p.94.

172 **AO, Microfilm, Drawer 7, Reel 566.** Haldimand, General Orders, Headquarters Quebec 28May81. Proceedings of a General Court Martial at Montreal, 6Jun81.

173 The plot described in the text is from evidence given at the Court Martial; Fitch & Adler, **op.cit.**, pp.94&95. A rebel account gives quite a different view of this affair. "Several of our prisoners had enlisted into the British service. Two of these, Hugh Pennel of Salem and John Garter — where Garter was from I don't remember — and possibly others were among the guard of Montreal [NB. not Coteau-du-Lac] jail. With this influence in the guard to join them to an attempt to escape from Canada. John Simpson, also of Salem, was one of the foremost of the prisoners in concerting this scheme. Arms and provisions were procured for supplying the whole of them well, the prisoners giving the guard their last farthing to buy provisions, et cetera, for their journey. The night was approaching, when John Simpson seeing a stranger among the guard, beckoned to him and communicated the whole plot. The guards were flogged most severely, I saw their backs just after and it was the worst sight I ever saw — their backs were torn as though a pack of hungry dogs had gnawed and mangled them. The whole were then banished to Cote de Lac Island. John Simpson never returned home after this." How remarkable! Who was Pennel? He was not a Royal Yorker. Was the Court Martial evidence of the betrayal by a Canada Indian offered to somehow protect Simpson? Certainly, banishment was not to prison island at Coteau-du-Lac, as their Court Martial directs them to foreign parts. No John Simpson settled in Canada.

174 Nathaniel Benton, **History of Herkimer County**, pp.90&91.

175 James F. Morrison research. A Sefferenus Tygert entered a US Pension claim in 1832, but this is not likely the same man; McHenry, **op.cit.**, p.67. A Sefferenis Tyger is listed as a prisoner "forwarded from Ticonderoga to their respective States, July 18, 1783." He was taken at German Flats in Oct81 and was aged 14 years in '83. This is likely the man who made the pension claim in 1832.

CHAPTER VI — REFLECTIONS AND CONSIDERATIONS

1 Thomas, **op.cit.**, p.107.

2 Clinton Papers, **op.cit.**, VI,p.351.

3 **ibid**, VI,p.319.

4 **ibid**, VI,pp.322&333.

5 J.A. Houlding, **Fit For Service, The Training of the British Army, 1715-1795** (Oxford: Clarendon Press, 1981) pp.117&118. " ... normal enlistments before 1795 were for life ... "

6 **ibid**, Chapter II, "The Condition of the Corps: Men and Arms". Houlding's exhaustive study of the army includes very specific details of longevity of service amongst the Officers and the men. The Army's system of drafting trained men from various home regiments to bring up the strength of overseas units is explained.

7   Montgomery, who, as the General (MajGen??) officer commanding the invading American army died at its head in the attack on Quebec City on New Year's Eve in 1775/76, had retired from the British Army as a Captain of the 17th Foot. To move from leading a peace-time company of 60-70 men to leading an army of thousands was a tremendous leap in responsibility. A.L. Todd, **Richard Montgomery, Rebel of 1775** (New York: David McKay Company, Inc., 1966)

8   Clinton, **op.cit.**, VI, pp.309-317.

9   What has not been quoted from Washington's letter is his excellent enumeration of the many occasions where the British high command's "supineness and folly" and lack of "a little enterprise and industry" instead of "torpid inactivity" might have ended the war. He cites as examples the 75/76 "loss of Canada to the Union" when Montgomery risked everything in an attack on Quebec City on the night of New Year's eve because much of his army's enlistment terms fell due on Jan. 1st — the 1776 campaign in the Jerseys where he had only 2000 men to oppose the Crown's massive army — the 1777 events at Valley Forge where a handful of men wintering in pitiful conditions were all that stood between the British and victory. Washington's arguments are compelling, because they are so aptly illustrated.

10 Peter Betz, "York State, 1776 ... The embattled frontier farmer", **American Agriculturist,** (September 1975). Betz addresses this question in some depth. To quote —

> The grain, ground at the local mills, and shipped to the continental storehouses was vital for feeding our army ... and it was just as vital to the British to destroy this crop, on the realistic theory that an army that can't find food, can't fight.
>
> Thus, from the start of the war, our government turned to the farmers of the Mohawk, Schoharie, Cherry and Hudson valleys for grain and each year bought every last sack that could be obtained. New England produced the horses and cattle that were required, but no large amount of grain came from there.
>
> It would seem that our struggle for independence would bring prosperity to the farmer, and for a time it did. But the British quickly realized the military importance of eliminating the production of wheat, and the raids began.
>
> There were large and small raids. For many years, our history books have lumped them all together and called them grudge attacks, but recent research has produced evidence suggesting the raids were a carefully-organized, systematic effort to eliminate our grain-producing ability.
>
> There were three ways to do this. Burning the crops in the field or barn was the most common, and accounts for why most of the large raids occurred in October. The mills ranked equally as targets, for a mill in ruins cannot grind wheat. Many of the smaller raiding parties that were made up of disaffected Loyalists and Indians cut more directly to the heart of the matter by eliminating the farmer and his family.
>
> ... By 1781, only one grist mill west of Schenectady remained unburned, out of around 100 operating in 1776.

11 Egly, Van Schaick, **op.cit.**, p.81.

12 James F. Morrison research, **Washington Papers Microfilm, Reel 70.**

13 Morrison research, Malcom Manuscripts, **op.cit.**

14 **ibid.**

15 Clinton Papers, **op.cit.**, VI,pp.226&227.

16 **CO42, V.40, MG11, Reel B-35, f173.** Haldimand to Germain dated Quebec 12Jul80.

17 Malcom Mss, **op.cit.**

18 **ibid.**

19 **ibid.**

20 Washington Papers, **op.cit.**, Reel 71.

21 Stanwix was abandoned in 1781 after a mysterious fire which destroyed a portion of the barracks.

22 Malcom Mss, **op.cit.**

23 Clinton Papers, **op.cit.**, VI,p.286.

24 Washington Papers, **op.cit.**, Reel 71.

25 Clinton Papers, **op.cit.**, VI,p.289.

26 Washington Papers, **op.cit.**, Reel 71.

27 Clinton Papers, **op.cit.**, VI,p.292.

28 **ibid**, VI,p.291.

29 **ibid**, VI,p.293.

30 **ibid**, VI,p.294.

31 **ibid**, VI,pp.296&297.

32 **ibid**.

33 **ibid**.

34 **ibid**, VI,pp.298-301.

35 **ibid**, VI,p.353.

36 Todd A. Braisted research, **Sir Henry Clinton Papers, Vol.134, item 18.** University of Michigan, William L. Clements Library.

37 Clinton Papers, **op.cit.**, VI,pp.349&350. Clinton to MajGen Heath dated at Poughkeepsie on 30Oct80. The emphasis is the author's and speaks volumes as to Clinton's opinion of the fragility of the morale of the people in his own State, if not the country at large.

38 Carl Van Doren, **Mutiny in January, The Story of a Crisis in the Continental Army now for the first time fully told from many hitherto unknown or neglected sources both American and British** (New York: The Viking Press, 1943) p.20.

39 **ibid**, pp.22&23.

40 **ibid**, p.20; Egly, 1st New York, **op.cit.**, pp.154-156.

41 Van Doren, **op.cit.**, pp.32-203.

42 Harold L. Peterson, **The Book of the Continental Soldier, being a compleat account of the uniforms, weapons and equipment with which he lived and fought** (Harrisburg, PA: The Stackpole Company, 1968) pp.258&259. In 1776, Massachusetts and Virginia furnished 15 one-battalion regiments for the Continental Line and Pennsylvania 12. In May 1778, Congress reformed the army leaving Massachusetts with the burden of 15 and reducing Virginia and Pennsylvania to 11 each. Another reorganization was agreed to in October 1780, as a number of the regiments were far below full strength. It was decided that the new programme would be implemented in January 1781, the same month as the mutinies. Massachusetts would field 10 regiments, Virginia 8 and Pennsylvania 6. This compression was to incorporate all of the NCOs and rankers, at that time under arms, and the supernumerary commissioned officers would be somehow provided for. Regimental strength would be 699 men, all ranks. As so much of this study deals with New York State, it is of interest to note that New York was only expected to field 4 regiments in 1775, 5 in 1778 and 2 in the final reorganization of 1780/1. By the war's end, there was the equivalent of 4 full-sized battalions of New Yorkers under arms for the King in the Canadian Department alone. In the Central Department out of New York City, there was at least the equivalent of 6, not including the city's militia units. There is no need to wonder why New York State was unable to furnish more than two battalions in the late war.

43 Van Doren, **op.cit.**, p.215.

APPENDIX 1
MYSTERIOUS TALES OF NEW DORLACH[1]
OCTOBER 17-19, 1780

Two seemingly unrelated events occurred in the settlement of New Dorlach at the same time as Sir John's expedition entered the Mohawk Valley. We have already noted that Jacob Merckley, a man with relatives in New Dorlach, was sent from Johnson's camp with instructions to raise a band from amongst the loyalists of that settlement and march them to join with the expedition. Jacob set off from Kennanagara Creek at some time on the 16th or 17th to follow the Indian trails north to the settlement. The second New Dorlach tale began a day or so later and involved another inhabitant of that small place. His story is told first.

PHILIP CRYSLER'S MISSION[2]

It will be recalled that when Sir John's force finished its work of destruction in the Schoharie Valley late the evening of Oct. 17, they marched north to encamp at Harman Sidney's mills. That night, Philip Crysler, a Butler's Ranger, and the Schoharie Mohawk, Seth's Henry, prepared a small party for a mission to New Dorlach. This settlement lay about 16 miles from the camp near Sidney's mills at Fly Creek. The party would start early the next morning and follow Indian trails through the woods, arriving at Dorlach about noon. Whether this venture was officially sanctioned by Butler or Johnson is unknown. No mention of it is found in Sir John's report.

★★★

The strangely interwoven background to both of the Crysler and Merckley ventures started four years earlier in Tryon County when on June 19th, 1776 — the very day Sir John Johnson was receiving his official beating order at Chambly, Quebec for his 1st Battalion, King's Royal Yorkers — the Committee of Safety noted that a number of men were "judged inimical to the Liberties of America and dangerous to remain [in] the County and are ordered... to be sent down to Albany to be disposed of as General Schuyler shall direct."[3] While Jacob Merckell [Merkle, Merckley, etc...] and Henry Merckell Jr. were found on the list of eleven "inimical" men, their subsequent activities suggest that they were either able to elude capture or had been taken and then escaped confinement.

About a month later, several men from New Dorlach were arraigned before the committee to be examined for disaffection. To save their skins, they were remarkably forthcoming with denunciations of their friends and neighbours, so much so that their frankness suggests a concerted method of defence. Henry Haynes (Haines) advised that -

> "Conradt Brown told him that there was Some Secret Matters or News come from Sir John Johnson that was not to be made Publick on the Penalty of Death... that such persons as were Willing to Remain Good Subjects to this Britannic Majesty & Enjoy the Libertys they formerly Enjoyed must give their Names & Sign an Association to Join Sir J. Johnson — that when he came to the House of P.[eter] Sommer — he asked for a sight of the Association but Mr. Sommer told them he knew nothing of any such doing — George Walker & Jacob Merckle were the persons appointed to carry the Association to the Squaw Molly [Brant] to be by her sent [to] Sir John Johnson... "[4]

William Young was sworn and he gave testimony that "Captain Jacob Miller & Lieut. Pet. Sommer & some other persons would Sign an Association to Join Sir John Johnson." When Conradt Brown was sworn he testified that "Captn Jacob Miller asked him on last Thursday Morning if he was willing to Acknowledge his Brittannic Majesty... and if he was Willing to... sign an Association to be sent to Sir John Johnson Who had a post that brought him Constant Intelligence every Twenty four Hours... It was Death for the Person who made it Publick... that same Evening George Walker and Oatman would Carry the Association to the Squaw... "

George Walker was interviewed next and advised "this County was in great Danger, & the people knew not what way to help themselves, unless by signing an Association & sending to Some of the officers in the British army, then perhaps they might be saved alive otherwise not... "[5] Many of the men, who gave this evidence, would appear as true or quasi-loyalists in the years to come.

An event of great significance to the fabric of these stories occurred in August 1777 when Captain Jacob Miller, the commander of the 8th (New Dorlach area) Company, 1st Regiment of Tryon County Militia, received orders from his brigade commander, General Nicholas Herkimer. Miller was to assemble and bring his men to German Flats to join with the rest of the Tryon brigade. The brigade would march from there to relieve the garrison at Fort Stanwix which at the time was surrounded by a Crown force led by Brigadier General Barry St. Leger.

Either by design or by accident, Miller's Company did not make the assembly at German Flats. Consequently, they missed the disastrous and bloody battle in the ravine at Oriskany. It is easy to conclude that Miller and his officers conspired to ignore Herkimer's summons, as several days later, they led their company to join St. Leger's forces in the siege lines at Fort Stanwix.

In Jacob Miller's New Dorlach area company were the two Crysler brothers - Philip and John. Philip was one of Miller's Sergeants; John one of the privates.[6] A third Crysler brother named Adam lived and prospered in the Schoharie Valley. At the same time as Miller marched his men to Stanwix, Adam was planning for the loyalist "uprising" in the Schoharie. Inexplicably, rather than joining Adam, his brothers, Philip & John, left New Dorlach with Miller.

Of the 85 New Dorlach-area men who made that trip; 40 joined the Royal Yorkers, 9 the Indian Department and 36, a few days after their arrival, mysteriously and secretly left the siege lines and returned home. The men who chose to enlist were readily absorbed into the KRR NY and the Indian Department. Those with rank in the militia did not receive much recognition. Sergeant Philip Crysler was only mustered as a private in Major James Gray's Company alongside his brother John.[7] As the years rolled by, John remained with the Yorkers until disbandment, but Philip soon transferred to Butler's, perhaps to seek a better opportunity.

A fourth Crysler brother, William, did not participate either with Adam in the Schoharie, or go with Philip and John to Stanwix; however, he joined Butler's Rangers sometime after 1778 and served with Philip in George Dame's Company.[8]

In the Schoharie Valley, a skirmish known as the "The Flockey" abruptly ended the 1777 "uprising." Adam Crysler had been lightly wounded in the affray and he decided to winter with the Indians while he recovered. Adam came to Niagara in the spring of 1778 and was mustered in the newly-formed Butler's Rangers.[9] Later that same year, he transferred to the Indian Department and was commissioned a lieutenant, in which capacity he served with great activity until discharged on June 24, 1783.[10]

Previously in the text, it has been noted that the Major's Company of the Royal Yorkers, Dame's Company of Butler's and several officers of the Indian Department were on the October 17th expedition. Thus, it is possible that all four Crysler brothers were with Sir John; however, it would seem that only Philip went on the mission to New Dorlach.

★★★

What purpose was there to Crysler's venture? It is said that Philip had decided the time had come to remove his family from rebel territory and take them to refuge at Fort Niagara. He obtained the assistance of another member of Dame's Company named Berkley[11] and another Ranger who has remained unnamed. The Schoharie Mohawk, Seth's Henry, led a group of 17 warriors. During the 1777 "uprising", Henry and his men had assisted Philip's brother Adam[12] and, in turn, Adam had fed and lodged the Schoharie Mohawk band prior to the outbreak.[13] As a repayment of this debt, Henry may have felt an obligation to assist any Crysler when asked. A more sanguinary view might be that Philip was able to promise some easy plunder, prisoners and scalps which would be sufficient cause to tempt this active partizan and his following.

The party set off for New Dorlach on the morning of Oct. 18th. Their march took them due west, far from the route of the main body of the expedition. Philip travelled directly to his house to ready his family for the long trip to Niagara while the rest of the party made their appearance just after noon at Michael Merckley's[14] farm.

Michael was a known loyalist sympathizer. His eldest son, Jacob, and his brother, Henry, had joined the Major's Company of the Royal Yorkers at Fort Stanwix at the same time as Philip and John Crysler.[15] His son, Michael Jr., had joined the KRR the month before the events of this story. Perhaps to keep the local Committee of Safety at bay, Michael's fourth son (either John Merckly or Philip Merkle[16]) was a member of the garrison at the Schoharie Lower Fort. His youngest son, a 13 year old, was at home with a younger lad named Fox, who was living with the Merckleys. In addition, Michael Merckley had three daughters, two of whom continued to live at home. A nephew, Martin Merckley,[17] had arrived at the farm just that morning to borrow a leather-dressing knife. The two daughters, the youngest son, the lodger and the nephew were immediately taken prisoner by Seth's Henry's men.

When the Indians and Rangers arrived, Michael was en route home from visiting his married daughter in New Rhinebeck, a community north-east of New Dorlach. He had made the trip with his niece Catherine, a daughter of his brother Frederick, and another local girl named Betsey Frantz.[18] Michael returned to the farm ahead of his niece and rode into the yard. He saw Indians milling about the doorway of his house, but was in no way alarmed, as he felt he would be recognized as a friend. In this belief, he had good reason, for in addition to his older sons being in the loyalist forces, his farm had been used as a rallying point the previous July for an Indian party which captured a local rebel. Entirely unconcerned about his unexpected guests, he dismounted and was inexplicably shot dead and scalped.

Catherine was a distance behind. When she rode into view the deed had already been done. The two loyalists and some of the Indians hailed her to rein in. Either she saw her mangled uncle lying in the dirt, or she sensed something was amiss. She spun her horse and, as she rode off, Seth's Henry levelled his rifle and fired at her. She remained upright in the saddle. Believing he had missed, Henry tore a rifle out of the hands of one of his men and sent a second ball after her. She tumbled off the horse and the war chief ran to her and ripped off her scalp. Catherine was a noted beauty and her killer supposedly commented later that if he had known she was so handsome with such "long black hair", he would not have killed her.

A neighbour, Bastian Frantz,[19] hearing the repeated gunfire in the direction of Merckley's, laid his shoemaking tools aside and took down his firelock. He made his way through the woods to see what was happening at his neighbour's. He discovered that two Indians were already advancing down the road towards his farm and, recognizing that he could never outdistance them, he chose to go the Lower Fort for assistance. As the trip would take half a day, he may have been more interested in saving his skin than gaining help; however, this view could be entirely uncharitable, as the Indians rarely harmed submissive women and young children. Thus, trusting that his family were safe, Bastian may have concluded that local property was at the greatest risk.

As the two Indians drew near the Frantz's farm, they were attacked by the family's large watch-dog. One of them promptly shot and killed the animal. Two of Frantz's older boys, John & Henry, had watched this proceeding and may have urged the dog to do its duty. The second warrior quickly advanced to the boys and made them captive, then led them to the wood pile at the side of the house. Perhaps the Indians had been angered by the dog's attack, because when the first Indian came up, John Frantz was thrust at him. He aimed a toma-hawk blow at the youngster's head; young John blocked its descent with his arm, but a second blow felled him. Recognizing that both Indians were intent on killing, Henry broke loose and escaped, follow-ing his younger siblings who were running into the woods. His captor was immediately in hot pursuit.

The Indian who had struck John with his tomahawk did not stop to strip his scalp. Leaving the wounded lad, he crossed a nearby creek to visit the Hoffman's farm, whose owners had fled into the woods upon hearing the gunshots. The other Indian soon ran down Henry and the younger children and led them back to the front door of the Frantz house where the group was joined by six more of Seth's Henry's party. While one of them guarded the youngsters, the others rummaged through the house and found a number of pies in the cel-lar. Being extremely hungry, they brought these upstairs and began to eat them. Just as they started, a courageous Mrs. Frantz returned home from some errand, only to find her house occupied and her chil-dren threatened with capture.

Young Henry went to the assistance of his wounded brother John and tried to persuade him to hide under an outdoor oven. John was too weak to even crawl and Henry found he couldn't push him under the structure. Their mother was terribly distraught when she saw John at death's door and, in her great distress, she extracted promises from the Indians not to harm any of her other children.

While the Indians were distracted by eating, young Henry took advantage to again escape. A determined search failed to find him, so when the warrior who had attacked John returned from Hoffman's place, he was so angered to discover that Henry had escaped, he fini-shed John and tore off his scalp. One might imagine the mother's hor-ror and her fear for her other children.

Philip Crysler's farm lay beyond Hoffman's. He had been assisting his wife Elizabeth to pack up for the escape when she heard the gun-fire at Frantz's. She urged him to put on his Indian clothing (which he likely had been wearing when he arrived home) and rush to the Frantz farm to save the family. She told him that the Frantzes had given her and the children substantial support ever since he had left to join the Provincial army. Crysler did her bidding, donned his native dress and ran to assist his family's benefactors. He arrived at the same time as the warrior returned from Hoffman's, but was unable to prevent John's death and scalping. Crysler's disguise was so effective that he remained unrecognized by his former neighbours. Mrs. Frantz recalled a blue-eyed Indian as the man who persuaded the Indians to leave the rest of her family unharmed and her chattels virtually unplundered.

This was done with great reluctance on the part of the warriors, especially the man who had lost Henry as his prisoner. He was so disgruntled that he thrust a flaming brand into the hay in the Frantz's barn. Another Indian immediately pulled it out; however, the harm had been done, as some fallen embers soon became a raging fire which consumed the barn and two large barracks.

With Crysler's family now in tow, the party continued to a farm and mill owned by a Henry Haines (not the same man who came to the Lower Fort with burned feet) and captured a number of his slaves. Simms reported that they left the buildings unscathed, as Haines was a loyalist. When his neighbours later discovered that had received this favour, he was forced to run off. On the other hand, the Indians burned the home and barn of Michael Merckley, doubtlessly reasoning that if it was left standing, it would only fall into the hands of rebels.

The party then moved to the farm of William Spurnhuyer which was found empty; it was plundered and destroyed. A young heifer was found tied near the buildings and shot for food. The boy, Henry Frantz, after making his second escape, had run to Spurnhuyer's for safety and was incredibly fortunate to hear the shot which killed the heifer just before he left the cover of the woods. Otherwise, he might have blundered into the Indians. This warning allowed him to avoid capture for a third time.

From Spurnhuyer's, Crysler's party continued on. They had gone only a mile or two when the two boys, the youngest Merckley and his friend Fox, began to cry uncontrollably. They were inconsolable, either by the Merckley sisters or the threats of the Indians. One of the warriors grasped the two boys and fell out of the march. He soon rejoined with two bloody scalps hanging at his belt. The Ranger Berkley explained to the horrified Merckley girls that the Indians would not have killed the boys if they had stopped blubbering. As Simms phrased it - "Indians never fancy crying children."

The party apparently made no attempt to rejoin with Sir John's expedition and set off overland directly to Fort Niagara, suffering en route from the severe weather and lack of good rations. The decaying carcass of a horse, which was luckily found in their path, kept the party from starving. When they at last reached the Indians' camp, Martin Merckley was forced to run the gauntlet and was badly knocked about. In no way was he spared from the ordeal although his dead uncle had been a loyalist sympathizer and his first cousins were soldiers in the Royal Yorkers. It may be hoped that the orphaned Merckley daughters fared better as they subsequently accepted proposals of marriage and remained in Canada after the war.

It is a mystery that a party of Schoharie Indians and two Ranger confederates chose to attack and kill the loyalist Michael Merckley and take his family prisoners. Jeptha Simms, the 19th century Schoharie historian, believed he had discovered the answer. Simms maintained that a son of Michael Merckley had impregnated one of Philip Crysler's daughters when she was in service with the Barnharts, a local family. When confronted, the son refused to recognize his patrimony and Crysler took him to court to compel a marriage. Perhaps the girl was feeble-minded or possessed a loose reputation as the magistrate strenuously counselled her about the dangers of bearing false witness. After her evidence, the court's decision was to name Barnhart as the father. It is entirely possible that she was either a willing or forced recipient of Barnhart's advances and, in her fear, did not recognize the consequences of naming him. As he was already married, the pregnant girl faced double the shame and her child was born a bastard. Simms maintained that this outcome so rankled Philip Crysler that he sought vengeance upon the Merckley family. Therefore, when he made his plans to remove his family, he saw the opportunity and took it.

If Simms' hypothesis was true, why is it that Michael's sons never discovered the tragic circumstances of the deaths of their father, brother and cousin? Surely, the two sisters who remained in Canada would have passed on the story. It would be difficult to believe that any of them could have remained still if they had learned of the reasons for the deaths and believed them to be true, particularly as the two sisters, Christianne and Eve, were ransomed from the Indians at Niagara by Sir John Johnson and lived with him in Montreal as house servants until the end of the war.[20] If either of them suspected Crysler's role in their father's death, surely they would have sought, and received, justice through Sir John. On the other hand, if the action was suspected to be taken by the Indians entirely on their own, it would likely have been viewed as one of the misfortunes of frontier warfare.

Another story uncovered by Simms involved Crysler having left part of his valuables in the hands of the Hoffmans before he left New Dorlach in 1777. The Hoffman's young servant girl found Crysler's hidden treasure and purloined some of it. Simms theorizes that Crysler heard of this loss and concluded that the Hoffmans had somehow encouraged it. As seen above, the Indian who tomahawked young John Frantz went on to the Hoffman's farm for some purpose. Simms believed that this action was an attempt upon the Hoffmans' lives· encouraged by Crysler. As it transpired, the Hoffmans were killed by Indians during the 1781 campaign.

Was Philip Crysler the vengeful monster hypothesized by Simms? If he had given free rein to such a rage of revenge, could he really have kept his misdeeds quiet? If he had been discovered, could he have explained away his actions to his wife Elizabeth, who certainly had demonstrated her sense of conscience and obligation?

JACOB MERCKLEY'S 'COMPANY'[21]

As noted in the background to these stories, many of the men of Jacob Miller's New Dorlach-area militia company, who had travelled with him to the siege lines at Stanwix in '77, returned home a few days later. The reason for this withdrawal is unknown, but it certainly could not have been either encouraged or approved by the Crown authorities. These men were saved from a charge of desertion as none of them had yet taken the King's shilling.

One reason may have been the general level of discouragement which they found amongst the loyalist troops when they arrived on Aug. 14th. For the Provincials of the Royal Yorkers and the Indian Department, the euphoria of defeating the Tryon County militia at Oriskany eight days before had melted away as the attack against the fort turned into a regularized and monotonous siege. Progress was extremely slow. To make things worse, the expedition's lightweight artillery was seen to have little effect on either the works or the garrison.

The Royal Yorker's encampment had been stripped of its amenities by a sortie from the fort on the afternoon of Aug. 6th, so there was sparse comfort to be found and the temper of the troops would have mirrored the fact. Rumours flew that the expedition's commander, Brigadier General St. Leger, had refused to allow Johnson, Butler, Claus and the chief warriors of the Iroquois the opportunity to strike into the Mohawk Valley to finish the job which had begun so promisingly in the Oriskany ravine. Instead, St. Leger agreed to send Ensign Walter Butler of the 8th Regt., the son of Major John, with a small body of troops and Indians under a Flag of Truce to Fort Dayton in the German Flats to recruit the inhabitants — a fool's errand indeed. The whole party had been taken prisoner, flag of truce or not, and this news was the talk of the camp. In short, nothing was going well at Stanwix.

Another distinct possibility was that Miller's Company had received a lukewarm reception. While Miller and his two subalterns, Lieutenant John Peter Sommer and Ensign John Caldwell, had been elected as officers of the militia company on three different occasions,[22] this cut little ice with either Sir John or Major Gray. That they had signed an association to serve under Sir John would have carried weight, but not guaranteed the awarding of rank. The Company Commanders of the Royal Yorkers had been carefully selected prior to Johnson's flight to Canada and most of the positions for junior company officers had already been promised. Nonetheless, positions had been found for promising, English-speaking Canadians, British Regular officers and a few late-arriving American loyalists and this fact leads to the suspicion that the New Dorlach militia officers did not carry sufficient social standing to impress Johnson or Gray.

An appeal to Major John Butler would have yielded little as he was commanding a large body of Indian Department rangers, not the later corps which took his name. Therefore, he was not yet in need of captains or subalterns and the criteria for receiving senior posts in the Indian Department probably precluded naming Miller, Sommer and Caldwell to any position above the lowest paid ranger. On the other hand, it is entirely possible that the men in Miller's company saw themselves as soldiers, not men running in the woods with the natives, so an approach to Butler may have not been a consideration.

If low morale and a poor reception caused so many of the men to return to their homes, unfolding events certainly justified their decision. A few days later, the siege of Stanwix collapsed ignominiously and those of Miller's men, who had remained with the Crown's Provincials were broken up and drafted into six different companies of the Royal Yorkers. Miller became a sergeant in Duncan's, Sommer a sergeant in Daly's and Caldwell a private in Alexander McDonell's.

Obviously, the rebel authorities were outraged by the desertion of Miller with so many of his men. The 8th Company was quickly reorganized with 2nd Lieutenant John Mathias Brown being named as the new captain. He was an ardent rebel from New Rhinebeck and had not participated in Miller's defection to the enemy. Jacob Haines (Hahns), one of Miller's former private soldiers who had sheepishly returned from Stanwix, was named, or elected, to be the company's 1st lieutenant and Conrad Brown (a brother of John Mathias),[23] another former private back from Stanwix, became the 2nd lieutenant. All of the company's new sergeants and corporals were appointments from amongst the privates who had skulked back from Stanwix.[24] A small community did not have unlimited choices.

As it transpired, many of the men who had returned home continued to hold loyalist sympathies or were ambivalent toward the rebel cause. Some remarkable revelations of their activities came to light when one of them, William Sommer, the son of Dominie Sommer who held services in the Schoharie Valley,[25] was imprisoned in 1781 on suspicion of disaffected behaviour. To secure a lighter sentence for himself, he revealed a complex story regarding the activities of the New Dorlach loyalists and quasi-loyalists.[26] William Petrie, the Justice of the Peace who heard Sommer's testimony, was understandably scandalized to find that so many of the County's citizens were double-dealing while serving in the militia, right under the noses of the Committee of Safety.

Germane to the account of Sir John's October raid into the Schoharie and Mohawk Valleys was Sommer's revelations about a Jacob Merckley,[27] a former Dorlach resident. Previously, we have noted that a Jacob Merckley had joined Sir John's expedition on Oct. 16th and been ordered to return to New Dorlach and bring off the loyalists from there to join the column in the Schoharie. Sir John notes in one of his reports to Haldimand that "I left a few trusty men in different parts of the Country to Pilot off such men as they could collect, one of which men[,] I was informed while I was at Schoharie, had gone off with twenty or thirty men from the Back of Canajoharie but what Route they had taken I could not learn but imagine that to Carleton Island."[28] It would appear that this man was Jacob Merckley.

Sommer advised that Jacob Merckley had appeared in New Dorlach just before the Oct. 17 invasion into the Schoharie, bringing word that Sir John's force was "coming down... [and] they were very strong and intended to murder every man[,] Woman and child before them." Sommer testified that 25 Dorlach men formed themselves into a company under this Jacob Merckley with the intention of joining Johnson.

Of these men, 12 had previously gone to Stanwix with Miller in 1777. Conrad Brown, the 2nd lieutenant in the Dorlach militia company, was one of them, as were seven of the company's nine non-commissioned officers.

★★★

While the assembly of Merckley's volunteers was taking place at New Dorlach, the settlement's militia captain, John Mathias Brown, had travelled to the Schoharie Valley to visit with his wife, who had been sheltering in the Lower Fort for some two years. As he later admitted that his Tory sister had advised him of Sir John's coming two days before the event,[29] it is difficult not to conclude that Brown's visit with his wife had a special purpose. Brown assisted the garrison in its preparations against the arrival of Sir John's raiders in the early morning of the 17th, perhaps to allay any suspicions. Then, he and his wife mounted their wagon and rode off to Livingston's Manor on the Hudson, a notoriously Tory Community, to visit her relatives. He did not return to the area until after the war.

In the process of departing, Brown evinced a great reluctance to leave the garrison, while his wife, a strong-willed woman, sat atop the wagon outside the pickets and "declared her intention to remain there and be shot rather than again enter the fort... " He quarrelled with her, but to no avail.[30] Was all of this an elaborate show staged to excuse Brown's removal at a time of grave emergency, or was the scene quite genuine? No matter which was true, how was his wife's obvious lack of zeal for the rebellion and his desertion in the face of the enemy accepted so calmly by the community? Why was it not branded as Toryism or blatant cowardice?

John Mathias Brown was appointed a County Judge of the First Bench of the Common Pleas in 1795 and he became the first print-historian of the Schoharie Valley in 1816[31] — in short a very well-respected citizen. Was it not a remarkable coincidence that Brown arrived at the fort and removed his wife to safety at Livingston's Manor while Jacob Merckley assembled loyalist recruits from Brown's company, including Brown's brother Conrad, to run off to Sir John?

★★★

On Oct. 19th, Merckley's "company" set off for the Schoharie and were met on the road near the Upper Fort by four of the Valley's inhabitants, "Jost Brown, Isaac Vrooman, Brassler Crysler and Old Jocham,"[32] whom they took prisoner. These men told the "company" that Sir John had already been and gone. Undaunted, Jacob Merckley decided to carry on to find the expedition. Somehow, word of Merckley's attempt reached Sir John while the expedition was still in the northern end of the Schoharie Valley,[33] although this proved to be of no assistance to Jacob.

There is no record of how long or far the "company" travelled before the majority gave up; however, one suspects they were discouraged in the attempt to cross the Mohawk Valley, which would have been alive with the comings and goings of Van Rensselaer's and Clinton's troops. Of Merckley's 25 men, only George Riddich,[34] Henry Merckley and David Frauts continued with him, while the rest turned about and again went home. After a harrowing trip through the wilderness of the upper regions, George Reddick [Riddich] and Henry Merckley [Merkil] enlisted in the 1st Battalion, KRR NY on Nov. 17th. David Frauts [Frats] is recorded as joining two days later, which may have been a clerical error. The three men served in Captain Richard Duncan's Company.[35]

In a letter written to Acting Quartermaster Henry Glen on Oct. 20th, LtCol. Volkert Veeder advised that "Old Joacum Van Valkenburg and two others was taken prisoners about the upper Fort But where [were] since Let at Liberty, they Where taken by a Party of about thirty men, Indians and Tories." Veeder continued, "this moment I was Informed that the Settlement [of] Thourlough [Dorlach] was Laid into Ashes[.] We he[a]r that this was Done By the party that took Joacum prisoner... "[36]

William Sommer doesn't mention any Indians being with Jacob Merckley's "company." Of course, the natives reported by Joacum Van Valkenburg may have been white loyalists dressed as Indians. We have seen in the Crysler story that Philip managed to disguise his identity from a close neighbour by dressing as a native. Also, William Sommer's testimony in 1781 continued with the description of a later foray by the New Dorlach men against the nearby settlement of Currytown during which all of them were dressed as Indians.

★★★

One of the many mysteries of the Philip Crysler and Jacob Merckley stories is their relative timing. Crysler's and Seth's Henry's arrival at about noon on Oct. 18th must have occurred at the same time as Jacob Merckley made efforts to assemble his "company." It would seem that Merckley's men didn't leave until sometime on Oct. 19th, as the trip to the Upper Fort would not have taken much more than a half day. While Crysler was organizing his family to leave New Dorlach and Seth's Henry's band were killing Merckleys and Frantzs, Jacob would have been gathering together the men who were willing to join with Sir John.

Was the community of New Dorlach so spread out that two quite large groups of men could gather there and not be seen or heard by each other? Could Seth's Henry's men repeatedly discharge their firelocks without arousing the suspicions, or the curiousity, of Merckley's group? Could the houses and barns be set afire and Jacob Merkley's men not see the smoke arising?

As opined above, if the Simms' accounts and hypotheses were accurate, surely the Merckley family would have sought some form of redress for the killings of their family members. *Or, were these two ventures in some way related, and Simms' interpretations entirely incorrect?*

ROSTER OF JACOB MERCKLEY'S
NEW DORLACH 'COMPANY'

The following table compares lists of the names of men from New Dorlach who participated in various roles mentioned in the text. The first column lists the men taken by Capt Jacob Miller to Fort Stanwix in Aug. 1777 and who chose to return home rather than enlisting in the Crown Forces. The second column contains the men who were assembled into a "company" by Jacob Merckley in Oct. 1780 and who travelled to the Upper Fort on the 19th of the month. The third column notes the men who left New Dorlach in 1781 to assist Captain Joseph Brant and Captain Barent Frey in the reduction of nearby Currytown. The last column is the roll of No.8 Coy, 1st Regt Tryon County Militia. Many of these names weave a common thread.

During the examination of William Sommer on July 15, 1781, Justice of the Peace, William Petrie, wrote -- "He appears Intelligent, but is no doubt a great villian." It is easy to sympathize with Petrie's observation when one considers that Sommer, and so many of his associates, could live ostensibly in peace amongst their rebel neighbours and then rise against them and commit depredations only to later return home and re-assume a cloak of innocence. Their duplicity is quite outrageous.

JACOB MILLER'S PETITION — Those who left w/o enlisting	WM SOMMER'S TESTIMONY — Jacob Merckley's 'Company'	WM SOMMER'S TESTIMONY — The Currytown Party of 1781	No.8 Company, 1st Tryon Regt (James F. Morrison research)
Robert	Robert Aurson		Cpl John Angell
Hermanus Asten			George Angell
Philib Barnhart			Robert Arsen
Barnhart			Hermanus Barnhart
Hendrik Borst	Michael Bost		
		Godleap Bowman	
		Martis Bowman	
Conrad Brown	Lt Conradt Brown	Conradt Brown	2Lt Conrad Brown
			Capt John M. Brown
		John Conradt	John Conrad
	Jacob Coughman	Jacob Coughman	
			George Crouse
			Peter Crouse
Cristian Ettinger			Isaac Falk
Andras Ficker	Jacob Fester	Andreas Fichter	Cpl Andrew Fighter
	Abdries Fichter	Michael Fichter	
Santer Flind	Christopher Fraunce	Jacob Fraunce	Sjt Chris'r France
Cristoffer Frantz	Jacob Fraunce		Jacob France
Jacob Frantz	David Frauts		
Pastian Frantz			
Hendrik Fratz	Ernest Frats	Henry Frauts	Sjt Ernest Fretz
Ernst Fretz	Michael Frederick	Earnest Frets	Cpl Michael Frederick
Mikal Fridarik	George Frymin*	Michael Fredericks	
	Michael Frymin		
Jacob Hahns	Jacob Hanes	Henry Hanes	1Lt Jacob Haines
Jacob Hahns jr.	Jacob Hanes jr.	Henry Hanes jr.	Sjt Jacob Heyntz
William Hains		Jacob	William Heyntz
		Christian Hanover	

J JACOB MILLER'S PETITION Those who left w/o enlisting		WM SOMMER'S TESTIMONY Jacob Merckley's 'Company'		WM SOMMER'S TESTIMONY The Currytown Party of 1781		No.8 Company, 1st Tryon Regt (James F. Morrison research)	
John	Hass	Jacobus	Happer	Jacobus	Hopper	John	Hess
Cobus	Hobber			Conrat	Hopper	Jacob	Hopper
						Philip	Hoffman
						Adam	Jordan
						Mathias	Junk
						Peter	Junk
						Zachariah	Junk
David	Kaufman						
Karl	Kerwagon			Charles	Hearwagon	Charles	Herwag
Ludwig	Kling					Sjt Lodowick	Kling
						Christian	Lain
						Christian	Lane
						Cornelius	Lawke
Cornelius	Louks			Henry	Loucks	Cornelius	Loux
Peter	Louks						
Friderik	Markle	Henry	Mirch	Frederick	Mirch	Frederick	Merkle
Hendrik	Markle	Mathias	Mirch	Henry	Mirch		
Mathu	Markle	Michael	Mirch	Matthias	Mirch	Cpl Mathais	Merkle
Mickel	Markle			Michael	Mirch	Cpl Michael	Merkle
						Michael F.	Merkle
Sandy	McHave						
Christian	Otman	Christian	Otman	Christian	Olman	Christian	Meinard
Cristoffer	Rettig	Christopher	Riddich	Christopher	Riddich	Christian	Otman
Georg	Rettig	George	Riddich			Christopher	Rettig
William	Sommer	William	Sommer	William	Sommer		
				John	Sommers		
Friderik	Strobak					Frederick	Strobeck
Adam	Strobak						
						Jacob	Van Dewerke
Georg	Walker	George	Walker	George	Walker	George	Walker
						Ens Jeremiah	Young

◆ A George Freemire (Freemyer) served in the 4th Company, 15th Albany County Regiment in 1778 and fought against Joseph Brant and Lieutenant John Dochstader at Cobuskill.

Notes

1 Like so many German placenames, the spellings for this settlement are legion, all variations starting with "D" and "T", eg. Thorlough, Torlach, Torlock, Dorlach.

2 The events of this next story are found in Simms, Schoharie, **op.cit.**, pp.434-444. Simms concluded that Crysler took his family to Canada - in fact, one might conclude that any loyalist who left the Valleys always went to Canada. All evidence points to Crysler taking his family to Fort Niagara where Butler's Rangers were headquartered.

3 Penrose, Mohawk Valley, **op.cit.**, p.84.

4 **ibid**, p.85.

5 **ibid**.

6 **AO, HP, Ms622, r.109, AddMss21874, pp.112-113**. The petition of Jacob Miller ... to Gov Haldimand. Hereafter referred to as "Miller's Petition"; of interest, John Crysler settled in Royal Township No.4, or Williamsburgh; George F.G. Stanley, **The War of 1812, Land Operations, Canadian War Museum Historical Publication No.18** (National Museum of Man, National Museum of Canada and Macmillan of Canada, 1983) pp.259-265. The farm that John settled and cleared became the site of the famous Battle of Crysler's Farm of the War of 1812 on 11Nov1813 at which place the British Regulars, Canadian Militia and Indians (800) soundly defeated a substantially stronger force of American Infantry (1800).

7 Cruikshank & Watt, KRR NY, **op.cit.**, p.181.

8 Census of Niagara 1783, **op.cit.**

9 Butler's Rangers' Pay Lists, **op.cit.**, Adam Krysler (Crysler, Chrysler, Creislor, Chryslair) is mustered in Capt Wm Caldwell's Coy.

10 **AO, HP, AddMss21827, f.353**. Again, the surname is spelled as Krysler. His length of service was noted as 6 years in this document, which backdated his joining to 1777, thus allowing his activities in the Schoharie to show as service. However, he is clearly noted as leaving the colonies in 1778.

11 This surname is found in Simms' account. In 1783 there were four men named Berkley (Barkley) in Capt George Dame's Coy of Butler's Rangers. They were Andrew, Evort, Job and Peter. Census of Niagara 1783, **op.cit.**

12 Simms, Schoharie, **op.cit.**, p.241.

13 James J. Talman, ed., **Loyalist Narratives from Upper Canada** (Toronto: The Champlain Society, 1946) p.56. The Journal of Adam Crysler.

14 The surname Merckley is one of those names of German origin which, perhaps due to its pronunciation, has taken a remarkable number of spellings over its history in America. According to an article in the Loyalist Gazette the following variant spellings for the surname Merckley have been encountered: Maracle, Marckel, Markal, Markell, Marking, Markle, Markley, Marquel, Marrikle, Merckle, Mercle, Merkill, Merkle, Merkley, Van Marckell. From the author's research in Original, Transcripts and Secondary documents, the following variants have been recorded. March (O), Marcle (O), Markill (T), Markley (O), Markly (O), Marrico (O), Marrile (O), Maskell (T), Maskley (T), Mercle (S), Mercly (T), Merkel (O), Merkil (O), Merkill (O), Merckley (T), Merkly (O), Mirch (T), Mircle (O), Mockley (T), Morcal (T), Mortley (T). In Simms' books, Merkley, Mercle & Mericle. Tracking the Merckley stories is a challenge.

15 Miller's Petition, **op.cit.**; Cruikshank & Watt, KRR NY, **op.cit.**, p.224; Alexander Fraser, ed., **United Empire Loyalists, Enquiry into the Losses and Services in Consequence of their Loyalty, Evidence in Canadian Claims, Second Report of the Bureau of Archives for the Province of Ontario** (Baltimore: Genealogical

Publishing Co., Inc., 1994) first published, Toronto, 1905. pp.395,396,1100. These petitions establish the relationship between Michael and his sons.

16   Morrison, Raids, **op.cit.**, p.31; not surprisingly, there is no mention of a fourth son of Michael in the loyalist petitions. Of course, if the fourth son had remained behind in New York, his existence would have no impact upon the petitions. In addition, he may have been virtually disowned as a rebel by his brothers.

17   Simms advises that Martin was the son of Frederick Merckley, the brother of Michael. As it has not been possible to discover how many families of Merckleys lived in New Dorlach, it is difficult to know if the Frederick Merckley who joined the Royal Yorkers in 1777 from Jacob Miller's Company was Martin's father, brother or cousin. This same problem also applies to the identity of the other Frederick Merckley of Miller's Company who chose to come home from Stanwix rather than enlisting.

18   Simms, Schoharie, **op.cit.**, p.434. Simms gives this name as "France"; Miller's Company, **op.cit.** France is obviously a phonetic spelling of Frantz. Cristoffer Frantz, Jacob Frantz and Pastian Frantz had been amongst those of Miller's Company who returned home from Stanwix in Aug. 1777. How, and if, these men were related has not been determined; Hagan, **op.cit.**, p.54. The transcript of Wm Sommer's July 1781 testimony spells this name as "Fraunce."

19   Perhaps the Pastian Frantz who had gone to Fort Stanwix with Miller and Crysler. See Miller's Petition, op.cit.; James F. Morrison research, **Enterprise and News, St. Johnsville, NY (Dec. 4, 1935)**, Wm. A. Brinkman, "New Dorlach Massacre 1780." This newspaper article claims that Bastian France was a member of the Committee of Safety for New Dorlach and a private in the 3rd Albany Regt. during the unit's service between 2Oct79-4Nov81.

20   Audrey Martin McCaw, "Beating the Drums for Sir John", **The Loyalists of the Eastern Townships of Quebec** (Stanbridge East, Que: Sir John Johnson Centennial Branch, UEL Association, 1984) p.111. McCaw's version of the murder of Michael Merckley and his young son is very similar to Simms. She advises that after the war, Christianne "married happily and settled in Eastern Ontario [and] lived to be 98." Her husband was Jacob Ross, 1 Bn, KRR NY.

21   Hagan, **op.cit.**, pp.53-56. ex Clinton Papers. Testimony of William Sommer dated at Canajoharie, 15Jul81. In the record of this testimony, New Dorlach is spelled Torloch and the Merckley surname is spelled Mirch. In the interest of clarity, the spelling of both of these names have been changed in this text.

22   Miller's Petition, **op.cit.**

23   TCM Newsletter, **op.cit.**, Vol.I, No.9 (Sep 1983). A brief biography of John Mathias Brown by Jim Morrison; personal letter from James F. Morrison, 12Feb96.

24   James F. Morrison research.

25   Morrison, Raids, **op.cit.**, pp.93&94. Robert Gram's account of the Raid gives details of Dominie Sommer of St. Paul's Evangelical Lutheran Church at Schoharie. Gram explores the antipathy between the members of this sept and those of the Reformed faith which may have led to the burning of the Low Dutch Reformed Church in Middleburgh by William Crysler.

26   Hagan, **op.cit.**, pp.54-56. ex Clinton Papers. The testimony of William Sommer dated Canajoharie, 15Jul81. Sommer's count of the number of men who travelled with Miller to Stanwix in '77 is only 26. Sommer advised that Miller had written to Joseph Brant before making the trip. As Adam Crysler was also in correspondence with Brant at this same time, one can conclude that Joseph was party to much of "the King's business" in the region. Sommer testified that he and Harmonus Barnhout (Barnhart) had returned home together five days after arriving in the siege lines.

27   This could be the Jacob Merckley, son of Michael, who enlisted in the Royal Yorkers in Aug77. It may also be the Jacob Merckley who enlisted in the KRR on 16Oct80, the night before the expedition entered the Schoharie Valley. The text and index assumes the latter.

28   Cruikshank & Watt, KRR NY, **op.cit.**, p.60.

29   Simms, Schoharie, **op.cit.**, p.400.

30   **ibid**, p.415fn.

31   TCM Newsletter, Vol.I, No.9 (Sep 1983), **op.cit.**

32   Morrison, Raids, **op.cit.**, pp.39&40. Letter from Veeder to Henry Glen from the Lower Fort dated 20Oct80.

33   Cruikshank & Watt, KRR NY, **op.cit.**, p.60. Johnson to Haldimand.

34   The Hagan transcript of William Sommer's testimony gives this name as George Mirch, but no such name is on the list of Merckley's "company." The only George found on the list is Riddich (Reddick), who enlisted in the KRR on the same day as Henry Merckley.

35   Cruikshank & Watt, KRR NY, **op.cit.**, p.198.

36   **ibid**, the burning of a few buildings hardly constituted laying the whole settlement into ashes.

APPENDIX 2
REBEL MILITIA REGIMENTS ENGAGED AT KLOCK'S FIELD

THE ALBANY COUNTY MILITIA

LEFT COLUMN

1ST (ALBANY CITY)	COL ABRAHAM CUYLER	300
2ND (SCHENECTADY)	COL ABRAHAM WEMPLE	250♠
3RD (1ST RENSSELAERWYCK)	COL PHILIP P SCHUYLER	325
7TH (KINDERHOOK DISTRICT)	COL ABRAHAM J VAN ALSTYNE	240
	TOTAL	**1115**

CENTRE COLUMN

8TH (1ST CLAVERACK)	COL HENRY I. VAN RENSSELAER	325
9TH (2ND CLAVERACK)	COL PETER VAN NESS	445
17TH (KINGS DISTRICT)	COL WILLIAM B WHITING	530
	TOTAL	**1300**

THE TRYON COUNTY MILITIA♥

RIGHT COLUMN

1ST (CANAJOHARIE)	LTCOL SAMUEL CLYDE♣	192
2ND (PALATINE)	COLONEL JACOB KLOCK	206
3RD (MOHAWK)	LTCOL VOLKERT VEEDER♣	224
	TOTAL	**622**

♠ It must be remembered that 150 men of this regiment were on duty at Ballstown under 1Mjr Abraham Switts circa Oct. 13th. As Carleton's force remained "on the lakes" as a threat to the Champlain and upper Hudson Valleys, it is unlikely that this detachment had been recalled from there to march against Sir John.

♥ This Return of 9Jul80 did not include the 4th (Kingsland & German Flats) Regiment under Col Bellinger who had not been able to forward his documents in time.

♣ Col Samuel Campbell was the commander of the Canajoharie Regiment, but was not in the area during the Johnson Raid and therefore did not lead his unit at Klock's Field. Col Frederick Visscher commanded the Mohawk Regiment, but he was recovering from wounds received during the May 1780 raid.

NOTES:

1. The total men in each Albany County regiment is an arithmetic average of two returns noted in the sources. As little action occurred involving this Militia Brigade between Mar79 and Oct80, it is felt that these numbers are indicative of the regiments' potential turnout. It must be recognized that complaints were constant about the inability of the regimental commanders to achieve a full turnout of their companies. It is an open question whether 30%, 50%, or 70% actually answered the summons to assemble, although comparing the above totals with the number ascribed by historians to BGen Van Rensselaer's army at Fort Klock would suggest less than 50% was the turnout achieved.

2. The two Returns consulted are prior to the 1779 amalgamation of the Tryon County Militia regiments with those of Albany County and the subsequent splitting off into two brigades which was ordered on 29Jun80. The Tryon Militia was incorporated into the second brigade under Robert Van Rensselaer.

    There is no mention of the 4th Regiment of Tryon being in action against Johnson's column at Klock's Field. Perhaps the 4th was not expected to move eastwards from German Flats as the raiders were headed in their direction.

SOURCES:

ALBANY COUNTY MILITIA

Clinton Papers, **op.cit.**, IV, p.654. "A Return of the Militia in the City and County of Albany commanded by Abraham Ten Broeck Brigadier General. Albany 20th March 1779."

ibid, IV, p.680. "Return of Brigadier General Ten Broeck's Brigade of Militia in the City & County of Albany." 19Feb78.

Berthold Fernow, ed., **Documents relating to the Colonial History of the State of New York** (Albany: 1887) State Archives, Vol.I, Vol.XV, pp.262-273.

James F. Morrison, "The Tryon County Militia - 1778", **"The Burning Issues", Newsletter of the Burning of the Valley Military Association (September 1993)**

TRYON COUNTY MILITIA

Clinton Papers, **op.cit.**, V,p.804. "A Return of the Militia of Tryon annexed to General Rensselaer's Brigade... Stone Arabia, Fort Paris 9th July 1780"

APPENDIX 3
CASUALTY ANALYSES OF THE JOHNSON EXPEDITION

Part 1

RETURN OF KILLED, WOUNDED AND MISSING OF THE DETACHMENT ON THE EXPEDITION TO THE MOHAWK RIVER, UNDER THE COMMAND OF LIEUTENANT COLONEL SIR JOHN JOHNSON IN OCTOBER 1780

REGIMENT	KILLED	WOUNDED	DESERTED	MISSING W/COMMENTS
ROYAL ARTILLERY				1
8TH REGT	1			4 (1 DRUMMER & 3 PTES)
34TH REGT				13
CHAUSSEURS				4 (2 KNOWN WOUNDED)
KRR NY	3	1	3	13
RANGERS				18 (1 CAPT, 1 SJT, 16 PTES - 3 KNOWN WOUNDED)
INDIANS	5	1 (CAPT JOS BRANT)		
TOTAL	9	2	3	53

The above details correspond with Sir John's detailed report of the expedition prepared for submission to Governor Haldimand on 31Oct80 in Montreal. The only variance is in the number of missing, Johnson reporting 52 while this table records 53. See text, Chapter 5.

NOTES:
1   This Return was prepared prior to Capt George Dame arriving at Oswego in early November with 9 soldiers, including himself, and reporting that 5-6 more were coming in by a different route, two of which were wounded. Capt W Butler's report of 24Dec80 returned 10 men, 2 killed and 8 still missing. A much later report dated 7Jun81 (LtCol Butler to BGen HW Powell, NAC, HP, MfReel A-681) advised that 5 Rangers "taken by the rebels last fall on the expedition with Sir John Johnson" had returned to Niagara. As Capt Butler does not report any NCOs as missing, the Sjt noted above must have come in with Dame.
2   There were no fatalities recorded in the KRR NY Regimental Return of Casuals prepared at Point Clair on 17May81 for the period of 17-24Oct80 when the regiment was in action against the enemy. The above table may very well have enumerated Royal Yorkers who were believed dead, but who returned with Dame later.

Only one fatality is recorded on the 17May81 return which falls into the overall time frame of the expedition. This is Pte Thomas Adams, who died on 24Sep80. On that date, the expedition lay at Oswego awaiting the arrival of the shipping from Fort Niagara. Adams had been previously recorded as serving in the Colonel's Company which did not participate on the expedition; however, it is not impossible that he had been with the force and died of an illness or accident at Oswego. Nonetheless, dying of an illness or accident is not being "killed" in action and given the fact that comments have been entered to expand on some of the entries, we could expect to have Adam's non-combat death explained, if he had been with the expedition.

Whatever was the case, given this evidence, the notation of three men killed in the KRR NY should perhaps have been entered under "Rangers", as two of Butler's men were believed killed, although both of the men named as dead are found in Canada at the war's end. See also Appendix 3.

SOURCES:

James F. Morrison research, **Bulletin of the Fort Ticonderoga Museum, Vol.VII, No.4 (July 1946)** p.26. Original source unstated.

William A. Smy research, **NAC, HP, MfReel A-688.** Capt Alex'r Fraser to Haldimand dated Carleton Island, 8Nov80.

••

Part 2
CASUALS OF BUTLER'S RANGERS DURING OCTOBER 1780 RAIDS

NAME	WHEREABOUTS AT END OF WAR	COMMENTS
Pte Benjamin Burton (Butts,Button,Benton)	unknown	taken, 16[17]Oct80, Schoharie, claimed to be a deserter
Pte Peter Ferrou (Feero,Feirro)	at Fort Erie	taken 19Oct80
Pte Thomas Griffon (Griffiths)	unknown	taken 16Oct80, claimed to be a deserter
Pte John Harris (Harrison)	at Niagara?	taken and killed♣, 19Oct80
Pte Chris Higbie (Highbie)	at Niagara	taken, 19Oct80
Pte John Holden	unknown	taken 19Oct80
Pte Daniel Holdenforff	unknown	taken 19Oct80
Pte James Hoghdaline (Hoghtelling)	at Niagara	killed♥ at Schoharie, 17Oct80
Pte Robert Livingston	unknown	taken 19Oct80
Pte Robert Reynolds♣	unknown	claimed to be a deserter
Pte Jacob Salisbury	unknown	taken 19Oct80
11 Men		

NOTES:

The above list totals 11 men, yet only 10 were returned by Capt Butler. Sir John's Return of losses indicates that 18 Rangers were missing. When Dame returned in early November, he brought "nine soldiers" plus himself and "above 20 Indians". Perhaps 8 had been Rangers, as Capt Butler returned that 10 were still missing on 24Dec. Of those 10 outstanding, 5 more were reported returned from the expedition by LtCol Butler in Jun81. The wording of the Colonel's report suggests that these 5 had been captured and then escaped to hide in the country where they were found by a recruiting party which brought them to Niagara.

♣ See the chart "Prisoners held in Pennsylvania... " in Appendix 4. A Butler's Ranger named Harraison was captured at Fort Windecker on 19/20Oct80. This is very likely John Harris and the return showing him as dead was incorrect. A John Harris was returned in Capt Andrew Bradt's Coy at Niagara 30Nov83 and is at Murrays District, Niagara 14Dec86.

♥ James Hoghtalin, aged 56, is returned at the Niagara settlement in Capt Jno McDonell's Coy of Butler's at Niagara 30Nov83, perhaps indicating that "rumours of his death may have been greatly exaggerated."
♣ Not found on Capt W Butler's return of 24Dec80.

SOURCES:
William Smy research, **NAC, HP, MfReel A-682.** Capt Walter Butler to Capt Robt Mathews dated Niagara 24Dec80.

Mary Beacock Fryer & LtCol William A. Smy, **Rolls of the Provincial (Loyalist) Corps, Canadian Command American Revolutionary Period** (Toronto & Charlottetown: Dundurn Press, 1981) pp.53-79. Smy's master roll of Butler's Rangers.

Minutes of the Commissioners for detecting and defeating Conspiracies in the State of New York, Albany County Sessions, 1778-1781 (2 vols, Albany: State of New York, 1909) pp.554-709.

Norman K. Crowder, **Early Settlers of Ontario, A Source Book** (Baltimore: Genealogical Publishing Co., Inc., 1993)

••

Part 3
"LIST OF THE PRISONERS WITH THE REBELS OF THE KING'S ROYL REGT OF NEW YORK"

COMPANY	NAME	ENLIST'T DATE	WHEREABOUT AT END OF WAR	COMMENTS
Major's	Simon Swart	15Aug77	CT #1	captured at Ft Windecker, 20Oct80
	John Weaver	?	RT #4	do do do
	Alex Cameron	19Jun76	RT #2	
	Isaac Awson (Austin, Aerse)♣	15Aug77	unknown	captured at Schoharie, 17Oct80; claimed to be a deserter
	Henry Harris (Haines)	15Aug77	Lancaster	wounded, turned himself in 17Oct80 at Schoharie
	John Lassly (Leslie)♥	?	unknown	captured in Oct80; claimed to be a deserter
Capt Angus McDonell's	Hugh McMillan (McMullen)	18Aug77	unknown	
	Duncan McDonell	19Jun76	RT #2	
	Thomas Vrooman	18Aug77	unknown	captured at Ft Windecker, 19/20 Oct80
	James Lockwood	15Aug77	unknown	
	Peter Lockwood	01Jun79	unknown	
	John Lewis	15Aug77	unknown	
Capt John Munro's	John Cogden	25May80	unknown	noted as a deserter, 26Oct80
	Robert Thurnbull (Thrumbel)	18Aug77	unknown	
	John Maddock	11Aug77	unknown	captured at Ft Stanwix, 8Sep77
	John Freeland♣	11Aug77	unknown	do do do
Capt Pat'k Daly's	Charles Johnson	15Jun77	likely in Canada	
	Frederick Rice	15Jun77	"	
	William Empey	15Aug77	RT #7	

COMPANY	NAME	ENLIST'T DATE	WHEREABOUT AT END OF WAR	COMMENTS
Capt Richard Duncan's	Corp. Philip Cook	15Jun77	RT #2	captured at Ft Windecker, 20Oct80
	Cpl Jacob Shell (Schell)♦	15Jun77		surrendered while on Secret Service; hanged as a spy, 26Oct80
	Adam Shades❖	03Jul77	likely in Canada see note below	
	Dennis Sullivan	08May80	"	
	John Martell (Marshall)	22May80	"	captured at Ft Windecker, 20Oct80
	Adam Hobber (Huber,Hoofer)♠	25Oct77	"	captured at Schoharie, 17Oct80; claimed to be a deserter
Capt Alex McDonell's	Peter McDougall	06May77	CT #2	
	Nathaniel Crossley✛	13Jan80	RT #3	captured at Ft Windecker, 20Oct80
	Richard Freeman	14Aug79	likely in Canada	
Capt Jos Anderson's	John Dingwell	26Oct79	Lancaster	
	George Smith	22Aug77	CT #3	deserted 3NY ContLine, 22Aug77
	Peter Coss (Cass)✛	15Jun77	likely in Canada	captured at Ft Windecker, 20Oct80
	Hazelton Spencer Volunteer	15Aug78	CT #3	"now in Skenesborough"

♠ Isaac Aerse (Austin) and Adam Hoofer (Hobber,Huber) were arraigned before the Conspiracy Commission in Albany on 30Oct80 to test their claims to be deserters. Their fate is unknown.

♥ John Leslie (Lassly,Lessly) was arraigned before the conspiracy commission on 31Oct80 and claimed to be a deserter. He requested an audience with Gov George Clinton which was granted. More information has not been found.

♣ Freeland enlisted in the 3NY Continental Line on 23Apr77 and deserted into the Royal Yorker lines on 11Aug77. Like Maddock he was taken prisoner at Fort Stanwix 8Sep77 during the retreat. He was accepted back into the 3NY and deserted again on 18Jun80. A true malcontent.

♦ Jacob Schell is not found on the MG21, B158, fo415 list of prisoners although he was taken prisoner in October 1780. His capture and execution were not likely known in Canada at the time of the list's preparation.

❖ Shades was in a 3NY ContLine work detail at Fort Stanwix on 3Jul77 and captured by Indians. He enlisted in the Royal Yorkers 5Aug77; however, his name is not recorded in any KRR Company in 1778. He was taken prisoner by the rebels on 19Oct80. Capt Leonard Bleeker asked Gov Clinton on 2Nov80 to allow Shades to return to his company in the 3rd NY (Clinton Papers, VI,pp.369&370.) The results of this request are unknown; however, in 1781 he was mustered as a private Willett's New York State Levies and he deserted from that regiment that same year.

✛ Nathaniel Crossley and Peter Cass were known to have been taken on 20Oct80 at Ft Windecker, yet their listed companies were not present there. At the time of their capture, Alex McDonell's Company was at Ft Haldimand, Carleton Island and Joseph Anderson's on Lake Champlain with Carleton.

BASIC SOURCE AND EXPLANATIONS:

1 **NAC, HP, MG21, B158, fo415.** This source is an undated list of names with their Company designations. Its date of preparation had to be after 25May80, as that is the enlistment date of John Cogden. The list's preparation appears to be before the formation of the 2nd Battalion, as none of the men listed served therein. Also, it is prior to 1783, as Capt Jos Anderson resigned his commission on 24Dec82. The "comments" column is an addition, as are the enlistment dates, which have been taken from KRR NY, **op.cit.**, Master Muster Roll.

2   Their captures are not exclusive to the October 1780 raids as it is known that John Maddock of Munro's was captured in 1777. Of course, it is possible that he returned to Canada in 1779 or 1780, for which years no Returns have yet been found, and been taken prisoner a second time.
3   Also, two of the above listed Companies were not on the October 1780 expeditions, eg. Daly's and Alex McDonell's. Those men may have been taken at any time prior to 1780, perhaps at Stanwix in 1777 or while on a scout into enemy territory.
4   It is very, very strange that no names appear from the Colonel's, Grenadiers or Light Infantry Companies, as they were amongst the companies most exposed to enemy action.

LEGEND:

RT   This abbreviation is for Royal Township. There were eight of these founded on the north shore of the St. Lawrence River. The township immediately west of the Ottawa River was Lancaster.

CT   This stands for Cataraqui Township. In 1784 there were five of these townships.

unknown   These mens' names are not on the 1783 Return and they are suspected of remaining in the United States.

••

Part 4
LISTED DESERTERS OF THE KRR NY FROM THE OCTOBER 1780 EXPEDITION

COMPANY	NAME	DESERT'N DATE	COMMENTS
Capt Jno McDonell's	John Banger (Bangell)	26Oct80	capt'd on 23Jul79 while on a 1NY work detail.
Capt Jno Munro's	John Cogden	26Oct80	
unknown	Jacob Yacker (Youker)	26Oct80	previously in 2nd "Palatine" Regt, Tryon County

NOTE:

The question of who actually deserted and who was captured was always a difficult one. John Bangell later returned to duty in the regiment. Therefore, he may well have been captured rather than deserted. In contrast, as noted above, a number of the men officially listed as being prisoners made the claim with the rebels that they had deserted. Of course, they may have chosen to do so in order to avoid the penalty of death associated with spying. On the other hand, they did not return to Canada after the war, which suggests they had deserted as claimed.

SOURCE:
NAC, HP, MG21, B158, p.212, ff.247-248.

Part 5

RETURN OF BRITISH PRISONERS OF WAR IN PENNSYLVANIA TAKEN DURING THE OCTOBER 1780 EXPEDITION

NAMES	OTHER SPELLINGS	REGIMENT /COY	WHEN TAKEN	WHERE TAKEN
PATRICK BUTLER		8TH	20OCT80	FORT WINDECKER
JOHN FRAKER	FRISKER, PARKER	DO	DO	DO
JOHN HORNBY	HORNBE	DO	?	?
CPL BENITHORP		34TH♦	?	?
ROBERT BIGGS		DO	20OCT80	FORT WINDECKER
JAMES CLAFFRAY		DO	DO	DO
JOHN CONNOR		DO	?	?
MICHAEL GRIFFEN		DO	20OCT80	FORT WINDECKER
WILLIAM HOWARD		DO	?	?
JOHN JAMES		DO	20OCT80	FORT WINDECKER
ARTHUR LONG		DO	?	?
JOHN MEDLERN		DO	?	?
JOHN MCGAWLEY	MCGALEY	DO	20OCT80	FORT WINDECKER
GEORGE TAYLOR		DO	DO	DO
GEORGE TEED		DO	?	?
ANTHONY PECK	ANTHNA, HENRY	JAEGER	20OCT80	FORT WINDECKER
CPL PHILLIP COOK		KRR NY	DO	DO
CPL? JOHN MARSHAL♥	MARSHALL, MARTIAL	DO/DUNCAN'S	DO	DO
HUGH CARR♣		DO	DO	DO
PETER CASS	COSS	DO	DO	DO
NATHANIEL CROSLEY	CROSBY	DO	DO	DO
HENRY PLACE♦	BLOSS	DO/MAJOR LUKS	DO	DO
SIMON SWART✤	SEVART, SCHWART STEWARD,	DO/MAJOR LUKS	DO	DO
JOHN WEAVER		DO	?	?
..... HARRAISON+		BUTLER'S	20OCT80	FORT WINDECKER
AN INDIAN		......	26OCT80	TRYON COUNTY, YORK STATE

NOTES:

♦   The only prisoner return that lists the place at which the men were captured is that of 5Jan81. Unfortunately, two of the 34th's men's names are illegible due to a tear in the original document. That return lists a total of eight men of the 34th; however, combining the other lists in the above table indicates twelve men of the 34th. How could this be? It is possible that other men were taken in Oct. 80 and not returned until later. They may have been in hospital or in transit to the prison camps at "Reeding"/Lancaster. Only those men of the 34th whose names were legible on the 5Jan81 list are noted as being taken on 20Oct80. It is acknowledged that no men of the 34th were captured during the Carleton Expedition and the 34th did not see action again until the Ross expedition of Nov81; therefore, unless these four additional men had been captured prior to 1780, the twelve names listed were prisoners from the Schoharie/Mohawk Valley expedition.

♥   Martial (Marshall) is returned as a Cpl at Lancaster in 1782, but is not shown as such in any of the KRR NY regimental returns.

♣   Hugh Carr never reached Pennsylvania. He escaped from Fish Kill Gaol sometime in the week of 4Dec80 and appears to have infiltrated into the British lines at New York

City. There is no record of Carr rejoining his regiment or settling in Upper Canada. Two interesting documents are found in the Clinton Papers, Vol.VI, p.356. The first is a letter from Clinton to the Commanding Officer at Fishkill dated Oct. 30, 1780. It advises that 31 prisoners taken in Tryon County by the "militia & Levies of this State" were being forwarded to him. The second document is a receipt from a captain lieutenant of the Fishkill Provost advising that 30 prisoners had been received dated the same day. The escapee was Hugh Carr.

♦   Hendrick Plass (Place,Plaus) mustered in the Loyal Volunteers in 1777 and from the Company he was said to have belonged to, ie. Major Luks, it would seem he was with Leake's in 1780. He was carried on 2Bn, KRR NY rolls in 1782, although he is noted as being held in Lancaster, PA on 24Jun82.

❖   Swart is returned on the KRR NY list of prisoners with the enemy as being in the Major's Coy. His designation of being in Leake's Coy must be an error, as there is no record of him serving in that unit. He served in the Maj's Coy, KRR from 1777-83, and this may be the source of the confusion.

✛   John Harrison (Harris) is listed in Smy's master roll of Butler's as having been killed at Stone Arabia on 19Oct80; however, he is found on the 5Jan81 rebel prisoner list at "Reeding," PA as having been taken at Fort Windecker on 20Oct80. The latter must be correct. Harrison appears only on the first of the prisoner returns which suggests that he may have escaped. A John Harris mustered in Capt Andrew Bradt's Coy of Butler's Rangers at Niagara on 30Nov83 and was returned as a settler at Murrays District, Niagara on 14Dec86.

SOURCES:

The above table is a compilation by the author from transcripts prepared by Todd A. Braisted, Brigade of the American Revolution. The information was found in the following sources:

Library of Congress, Peter Force Papers, Series IX, Reel 106, pp.440&441. "Return of British Prisoners of War Sent from Reeding to Lancaster" dated at "Reeding," 5Jan81.

ibid, IX, p.739. "A List of the British Prisoners of War in Lancaster Barracks" dated 18Jul81.

ibid, IX, Reel 107, pp.4-8. "A List of the Prisoners in the Barracks" [Lancaster] dated 30Aug81.

Historical Society of Pennsylvania, Thomas Bradford Papers, Land and Naval Prisoners, p.103. "A Return of the British Soldiers Prisoners of War in the New Goal" dated at Philadelphia 5Feb82.

NAC, Ward Chipman Papers, MG23, D1, Vol.27, p.351. "Muster Roll of Different Regts. and Company's Prisoners of War Taken at the Cowpens &c." dated at Lancaster, 24Jun82.

Sir Henry Clinton Papers, Vol.134, item 18, University of Michigan, William L. Clements Library.

In addition:

Norman K. Crowder, **Early Settlers of Ontario, A Source Book** (Baltimore: Genealogical Publishing Co., Inc., 1993)

Mary Beacock Fryer & LtCol William A. Smy, **Rolls of the Provincial (Loyalist) Corps, Canadian Command American Revolutionary Period** (Toronto & Charlottetown: Dundurn Press, 1981) pp.53-79. Smy's master roll of Butler's Rangers.

Part 6

RECONCILIATION OF REPORTS OF THOSE MISSING & THOSE KNOWN TO BE PRISONERS

UNIT	FROM SIR JOHN'S EARLY REPORT	RETURNED AS DESER- TERS	REVIEWED BY CONSPIRACY COMISSION	HELD PRI- SONERS IN PENNSYLVANIA	ESCAPED	TOTAL W/REBELS
RL ARTILLERY	1	0	0	0		0
8TH	4	0	0	3		3
34TH	13	0	0	12		12
JAEGERS	4	0	0	1		1
KRR NY	13	3	4♠	7	1	13
BUTLER'S	18	0	3	1		4
INDIANS	0	0	0	1		1
TOTALS	53	3	8	26	1	37
BROUGHT IN BY CAPTAIN DAME	10♥					
STILL IN THE WOODS ON NOV.8	5-6					
YET MISSING	38-39					37

♠ As we have seen in the text, five Royal Yorkers were questioned by the rebel Commission; however, one of them was unnamed. The assumption has been made in these calculations that this man was one of the three deserters returned by the KRR NY in 1781.

♥ Sir John reported to Haldimand on 8Nov80 that Dame had arrived at Oswego with "fifteen of the missing soldiers and thirty Indians" (Cruikshank & Watt, KRR NY, p.62); however, Capt Alex Fraser of the Quebec Indian Department reported from Carleton Island to Haldimand three days earlier the arrival of "Captain Dame of the Rangers, with nine soldiers and above twenty Indians.... "(NAC, HP, MfReel A-688) As Fraser was closer to the scene, his numbers have been used although it should be recognized that Johnson may have been in possession of an official report.

SUMMATION:

According to Johnson's Returns & reports, some 39-40 men still remained missing from the expedition on Nov. 8th. In comparison, various rebel records indicated 37 men had been captured and were being held as prisoners, or had already escaped their custody, or had been welcomed as deserters. Sir John's return of the missing would not have included any men which he had sent "into the country" on recruiting or secret service work, whereas the rebel reports of prisoners would make no such distinction. Also, as noted previously, it is somewhat questionable whether or not that four of the prisoners of the 34th Regt. had been taken in Oct. 1780. Considering these explanations, the reconciliation may be seen to be reasonably close.

APPENDIX 4

RECRUITING IN THE KING'S ROYAL REGIMENT OF NEW YORK RESULTING FROM THE OCTOBER 1780 RAIDS

Part 1
THE EXPEDITION FROM OSWEGO

SUMMARY

Date of enlistment	Number enlisted	Expedition's Location at the Time
16 Oct	23	Encamped at south end of Schoharie Valley
24 Oct	2	On the return march beyond Old Oneida village
25 Oct	44	Primarily men of Vrooman's party of Levies & militia
26 Oct	1	Arrived at Oswego and sailed to Carleton Island
1 Nov	1	In bateaux on the St. Lawrence River
2 Nov	2	- do -
4 Nov	1	- do -
Subtotal	74	

SURNAME	OTHER SPELLING	GIVEN NAME	ENLIST' DATE	RANK	BATTN	COMMENTS	SETTLEMENT
Davis	Davies	Peter	16Oct80	Pte	2		RT #3
Frish	Frihart	Christian	16Oct80	Pte	2	taken prisoner✦	no record
Horn		Henry	16Oct80	Pte	2		no record
Merkill	Mircle	Jacob	16Oct80	Pte	2		no record
Parsons		John	16Oct80	Pte	2		no record
Phillips		John	16Oct80	Pte	2	in Crawford's Coy	CT #3
Rambough	Rambouch	William	16Oct80	Pte	2		CT #3
Rapole	Rawpole	George	16Oct80	Pte	2		no record
Robins	Robbins	Thomas	16Oct80	Pte	2		RT #2

SURNAME	OTHER SPELLING	GIVEN NAME	ENLIST' DATE	RANK	BATTN	COMMENTS	SETTLEMENT
Roof	Rufe	John	16Oct80	Pte	2	recruited by SJJ	no record
Young		Peter	16Oct80	Dr	2		CT #3
Moore		John	24Oct80	Pte	1	in Daly's Coy 81-83	no record
Showls	Shools	John G.	24Oct80	Pte	1	in Col's Coy 81-82	no record
Allen		Henry	25Oct80	Pte	2		no record
Archer		Edward	25Oct80	Pte	1	in Duncan's Coy 81-82	no record
Balks	Bork	John	25Oct80	Pte	2	4 yrs serv in Loyalists??	no record
Beetle	Beedle	Benjamin	25Oct80	Pte	2		no record
Berry	Barry, Besay	William	25Oct80	Pte	2	from Harper's Levies	CT #3
Boudish		John	25Oct80	Cpl	2		Lachine
Bussard		Henry	25Oct80	Pte	2		no record
Cooley		John	25Oct80	Pte	2		no record
Delong		John	25Oct80	Pte	2	from Harper's Levies	no record
Dogg		John	25Oct80	Pte	2		no record
Earhart		John	25Oct80	Pte	2	in Loyal Rangers 83	RT #8
Earhart		Nicholas	25Oct80	Pte	2		no record
Eastwood		John	25Oct80	Pte	2	from Harper's Levies deserted at Oswego, 1Sep83	no record
Eckler	Eglar	Leonard	25Oct80	Pte	2	from Harper's Levies	no record
Eckler		William	25Oct80	Pte	2	from Harper's Levies	Niagara, 1786
Edwards♥		William	25Oct80	Pte	2		no record
Flamsborough		William	25Oct80	Pte	2	from Harper's Levies in Loyal Rangers 84	RT #7
Hart		Joel	25Oct80	Pte	2		no record
Henry		Hugh	25Oct80	Pte	2	from Harper's Levies	no record
Howse♥		Peter	25Oct80	Pte	2	from Harper's Levies	no record
Jacque♥	Jacquay	Seth	25Oct80	Pte	2		no record
Klock	Clock	Adam	25Oct80	Pte	2	in Crawford's Coy	CT #3
Loft		David	25Oct80	Pte	2		CT #3
Martin		Robert	25Oct80	Pte	2		no record
Moss		Simon	25Oct80	Pte	2	from Harper's Levies	no record
McPherson	McPharson	Daniel	25Oct80	Cpl	2	in Crawford's Coy	CT #3
Naramore		Esau	25Oct80	Pte	2		no record
Oxburgher	Oxbury	John	25Oct80	Pte	2	in Crawford's Coy	no record
Piper		Jacob	25Oct80	Pte	2		no record
Sharpe♥		Peter	25Oct80	Pte	2	from Harper's Levies	no record
Smith♥		Nicholas	25Oct80	Pte	2	one of this name a Dr in Capt Dame's Coy BR's 83	no record
Start		Nathaniel	25Oct80	Pte	2		no record
Stata	Stoty	Phillip	25Oct80	Pte	1	in Duncan's 81; Gdr 82-83	RT #3
Tages	Tager	Stephen	25Oct80	Pte	2		no record
Tigert♥	Tygert, Dygert	Sefferenus	25Oct80	Pte	2	from Harper's Levies	no record
Truax		Isaac	25Oct80	Pte	2	from Harper's Levies	no record
Truax		John	25Oct80	Pte	2		no record
Truax		Nicholas	25Oct80	Pte	2		no record
Valentine		Alexander	25Oct80	Pte	2		no record
Van Wagner♥	Van Waggoner	Andrew	25Oct80	Pte	2		no record
Mills		John	26Oct80	Pte	2		no record
Howell		Warren	1Nov80	Pte	2	in Leake's & 2Bn 82	CT #3

SURNAME	OTHER SPELLING	GIVEN NAME	ENLIST' DATE	RANK	BATTN	COMMENTS	SETTLEMENT
Arginsinger	Arpensinger	Phillip	2Nov80	Pte1&2		rctd by SJJ; in Cols' 82	no record
Kane	Cain	John Sr.	2Nov80	Pte	2	recruited by SJJ	RT #1
McTaggart	McTagget	James	4Nov80	Cpl	2	in Crawford's Coy	CT #3

♠ Christian Frihart (likely Christian Frish) was taken prisoner by the rebels in the Schoharie Valley one or two days after his enlistment and was brought before the Conspiracy Commission in Albany on Oct. 27, 1780. As he would have been without uniform, he may well have been found guilty of spying, in which case he would have been hanged.

♥ These were the men who were involved in the conspiracy to commit mutiny at Coteau du Lac while in training for the 2Bn, KRR.

NOTES:

1 In addition to the willing recruits who joined the expedition during the march, there were numbers of rebel prisoners taken, some of which joined the Royal Yorkers rather than endure imprisonment. As noted immediately above, a few of these planned a mutiny during their training. On the other hand, many others continued to serve and settled in Canada after the war.

2 Some of the loyalists who joined the expedition may not have immediately chosen the life of a soldier in the hopes that other employment would be available in Quebec Province. While they may have entered the ranks at a later date, there is no way of relating them back to the expedition.

3 The enlistments into the KRR NY includes all recruits originally taken into Leake's Independent Coy which in 1781 was absorbed into the 2Bn KRR NY

4 One can presume that a similar influx occurred in Butler's Rangers. As enlistment dates for individual Rangers have not yet been found, an analysis has not been possible.

MUNRO'S BALLSTOWN EXPEDITION

SURNAME	OTHER SPELLING	GIVEN NAME	ENLIST' DATE	RANK	BATTN	COMMENTS	SETTLEMENT
Bower	Bowen	Adam	16Oct80	Cpl	2	rec'd by Lt Langan♠	CT #3
Bower	Bauwer	Gasper	16Oct80	Pte	2	rec'd by Lt Langan♠	CT #3
Cadman		John Sr.	16Oct80	Pte	1	in J Anderson's Coy 81-83	RT #3
Cadman		John Jr.	16Oct80	Pte	1	in J Anderson's Coy 81-83	RT #3
Chisholm		Allan	16Oct80	Pte	2	rec'd by Lt Langan♠	RT #1
Cromwell		Nicholas	16Oct80	Pte	2	rec'd by Lt Langan♠ in Crawford's Coy	no record
Davis		Henry	16Oct80	Dr	2	rec'd by Lt Langan♠	no record
Dublin♠		John	16Oct80	Pte	1	in Munro's Coy 81	no record
Earhart		Simon	16Oct80	Pte	2	rec'd by Lt Langan♠	St. John
Evans		Bolton	16Oct80	Pte	2	rec'd by Lt Langan♠ 14 yrs in 9th Regt	CT #3
Hoople		Hendrick	16Oct80	Pte	1	in J Anderson's Coy 81-83	RT #3
McCarthy	McCarty	Caleb	16Oct80	Cpl 2&1		in J Anderson's Coy 82	no record
Bartley		Isaiah	25Oct80	Pte	2	recruited by Capt Munro	CT #3
Bartley		Michael	25Oct80	Pte	2	recruited by Lt Langan	CT #3
Evans		Iry	25Oct80	Pte	2	recruited by Vol Church♥	no record
Hulbert		Jubil	25Oct80	Pte	2	rec'd by Mr Halbert♠	no record

♠ Lt Patrick Langan was the officer assigned to the work with the Fort Hunter Mohawks on the Crown Point raid. These men were recruited during this expedition.

♥   Vol Oliver Church was operating with Capt Munro. This recruit was taken during the Ballstown raid.

♣   Philo Halbert (Hulbert) had been a Lt in Peter's QLR in 1777 and served as a recruiting officer for the KRR NY in 1780. Jubil Hulbert was captured at Fort George.

❖   It is an odd coincidence that a black named Dublin (Bendict) was taken in Ballstown and reported by the rebels to have escaped.

NOTES:

1   In attempting to analyse which men were recruited in the Lake Champlain area as opposed to the Schoharie Valley, the researcher is assisted by knowing who recruited the men and in which companies they later served, eg. Lt Patrick Langan. Also, the companies of Capts John Munro and Joseph Anderson were the core of the Ballstown element of the expedition.

2   One suspects that the men recruited on 16Oct80 met the expedition at Crown Point and assisted as guides during the raid, then coming off to Canada and enlisting.

3   Capt Jos Anderson resigned his commission on 24Dec82 and command of his company passed to Capt Archibald McDonell. Thus, anyone serving in the Company in 1783 was actually reporting to Archibald McDonell, not Joseph Anderson.

SOURCES:

Cruikshank & Watt, KRR NY, **op.cit.**, Appendix III, "Master Muster Roll of the Officers, NCO's, Drummers & Private Men of the Two Battalions of His Majesty's Royal Regiment of New York. 19 June 1776 to 24 June 1784"

Norman K. Crowder, **Early Settlers of Ontario, A Source Book** (Baltimore: Genealogical Publishing Co., Inc., 1993)

MG21, B158, p.342, ff.404-405. "Roll of Recruits enlisted by Lieutenant P. Langan, at his Private Expense, For the Two Battalions of His Majestys Royal Regt of New York... "

••

Part 2
RECRUITING IN JESSUP'S & ROGERS' CORPS FROM THE REBEL PRISONERS TAKEN AT FORTS ANN & GEORGE OCTOBER 1780

The following list of names was submitted as potential recruits to Gov Haldimand's Military Secretary, Robert Mathews, in late 1780 by LtCol. Eben Jessup OC, King's Loyal Americans. Jessup advised that his brother, Major Edward, had assembled this list while still on service at Crown Point. The surnames and given names are as found in Eben Jessup's letter. These names have been compared to the prisoner lists from Forts Ann and George and where they were taken is noted. A search of various Muster Rolls for the King's Loyal Americans (and their subsequent unit, the Loyal Rangers) and the King's Rangers led to the comments noted below.

SURNAME	GIVEN NAME	WHERE TAKEN	COMMENTS ABOUT SUBSEQUENT SERVICE
AIRS	DANIEL	UNKNOWN	NO RECORD OF THIS NAME FOUND
CODDER	GEORGE	UNKNOWN	IF GEORGE CODNER/CADNER, IN KING'S RANGERS (ALBANY CTY, AGE 17)
CODDER	ISHMAEL	UNKNOWN	♣

GRAHAM	OLIVER	UNKNOWN	♥
GRANGER	JOSIAH	FORT GEORGE	IF ZACHARIAH GRANGER, IN KING'S RANGERS, SEE NEXT CHART
HUNT	WILLIAM	UNKNOWN	IF WM HYE/HIGH, IN KING'S RANGERS, SEE NEXT CHART
LAROVE	RICHARD	FORT GEORGE	LARABIE - DID NOT INLIST - RETURNED AS A PRISONER IN QUEBEC, 22JUL82 & OCT82.
MCPHERSON	ALEXANDER	UNKNOWN	NO RECORD OF THIS NAME FOUND
MORISSON	ALEXANDER	UNKNOWN	" " "
PRISS	SETH	FORT ANN	SETH RICE IN KING'S RANGERS, SEE NEXT CHART
SMITH	HENRY	FORT ANN	♣
STEWART	SOLOMON	FORT ANN	IN KING'S RANGERS, SEE NEXT CHART
WEBSTER	MILOW	FORT ANN	" " "
YOUNG	BENJAMIN	UNKNOWN	NO RECORD OF THIS NAME FOUND

♣ Inexplicably, an Ishmael Codner is returned in the King's Loyal Americans on 1May80. Had he deserted and returned home? He is then mustered in the King's Rangers on 10Jan82, on 21Jan83 as being from Connecticut and 14 in 1780 & finally on 27Jan84 in the Maj's Coy.

♥ Oliver Graham in returned in the King's Rangers 21Jan83, from See Brook, age 20 in 1780 & then on 27Jan84 in Ruiter's Coy. He is returned as a settler at Royal Township No.8 on 12Oct84.

♣ A Henry Smith is found on a Quebec prisoner list on 22Jul82. A man of the same name is in the King's Rangers on 10Jan82, therefore the conclusion must be that these are not the same man.

NOTES

1   Daniel Airs, George Codder, Ishmael Codder and Benjamin Young are not found on McHenry's List of Prisoners. The two Codders/Codners would seem to have enlisted for the King immediately; however, Airs and Young did not, nor were they held prisoners in Canada. Did they immediately enlist and then desert at the first opportunity? There was no Alexander Morrison returned amongst the prisoners held in Quebec, but a Jonathon Morrison was. Similarly, there was no Alexander McPherson listed, but there was a Donald. Are these actually the same men and their given names are entered incorrectly on Jessup's list due to sloppy clerical work, or are they different men altogether?

2   As those who did enlist were found in the King's Rangers, it appears that Major Roger's recruiting claims were favoured over Major Jessup's during the mandatory examination of recruits before their assignment to a battalion.

3   H.M. Jackson (p.187) advises that 16 of the men taken at Fort Ann joined the King's Rangers and brought the unit's strength to 133 all ranks. By 26Dec80, a total of 34 rebel deserters were in the ranks and Major Nairne inspected the corps on Haldimand's orders as rumours suggested that many of the men were too young to bear arms. See the following chart for ages of recruits in 1780. Major Nairne examined the 95 men recruited since 24Oct80 and passed all but three. Nairne offered the opinion that Roger's had followed instructions and added that he "has in his way much of [the] air [of the] old Soldier" and seemed to pay great attention to his men.

SOURCES

HP, AddMss21821, f.162. Eben Jessup to Robert Mathews.

—, **AddMss21827,** Pt.2, ff275-276. Roll of KLA's, 1May81.

—, **AddMss21820,** f.203. Roll of KR's, 27Jan84.

—, **AddMss21827,** p.285. Roll of KR's, 10Jan82.

Chris McHenry, compiler, **Rebel Prisoners at Quebec,** 1778-1783 (n.d., n.p.)

Norman K. Crowder, **Early Settlers of Ontario, A Source Book** (Baltimore: Genealogical Publishing Co., Inc., 1993)

Lieut.-Col. H.M. Jackson, **Roger's Rangers, A History** (n.p., 1953)

Part 3

NAMES OF MEN TAKEN AT FORTS ANN & GEORGE FOUND ON LOYALIST REGIMENTAL ROLLS DATED 10TH JANUARY 1782, 1ST JANUARY 1783 & 27 JANUARY 1784

NAME AS FOUND PRISONER LISTS	NAME AS FOUND IN MUSTER ROLLS	SERVED IN, CORPS & COMPANY	PLACE OF NATIVITY	AGE 1780	TAKEN AT
ANTHONY, RICHARD	ANTONEY	KING'S RANGERS PRITCHARD'S	RHODE IS.	18	FT ANN
BENNINGER, ISAAC		LOYAL RANGERS, SHERWOOD'S	AMERICA	21	"
BROWN, DAVID		KING'S RANGERS	DUCHESS CTY	16	FT GEORGE
BROWN, SAMUEL	BROWNSON, BRUNSON CPL	" ", MAJ'S	" "	20	FT ANN
..OR..	BROWNSON, SAMUEL	LOYAL RANGERS, PETER'S	AMERICA	64	
CAMPBELL, JOHN		LOYAL RANGERS, WM FRASER'S	IRELAND	21	FT GEORGE
DIBBLE, ESA	DRIBBLE, ASA	KING'S RANGERS, PRITCHARD'S	NEW MILFORD	22	"
DUNNAM, SAMUEL	DUNHAM	LOYAL RANGERS, JON'N JONES'	AMERICA	24	FT ANN
GRANGER, EZACH'R	ZACHARIAH	KING'S RANGERS, MAJ'S COY	♠		FT GEORGE
HARRIS, WILLIAM	FARRIS	KING'S RANGERS			FT ANN
HINES, CALVIN	HINDS	" "			FT GEORGE
HUNTER, MOSES		LOYAL RANGERS, JON'N JONES'	AMERICA	21	FT ANN
HYE, WILLIAM	HIGH	KING'S RANGERS, RUITER'S	JERSEY	17	"
KELLOCK, WILLIAM	KELLER	" "			FT GEORGE
LINTE, ALIAS	LINT, ELIAS	" "		22	FT ANN
MCDONALD, ALEX'R	MCDONOLD	LOYAL RANGERS, THOS FRASER'S	AMERICA	14	FT GEORGE
MILLETT, JONATHON	MILLER	KING'S RANGERS, MAJ'S	DUCHESS CTY	21	FT ANN
MITCHELL, JOHN	MICHEL	LOYAL RANGERS, JOHN JONES'	AMERICA	25	FT GEORGE
MORRISON, JONATHON	JONN	KING'S RANGERS	DUCHESS CTY	15	FT ANN
RICE, SETH		" "	HALIFAX	18	"
SIMPSON, ROBERT	SIMSON, ROBT SJT	LOYAL RANGERS, MEYER'S	AMERICA	28	"
OR SIMPSON, ROBERT		" ", JON'N JONES'	"	22	
STEWART, SOLOMON		" ", MAJ'S	HAMPSHIRE	15	"
SUTTERLY, JOSEPH	SATTERLY	KING'S RANGERS, RUITER'S			"
SWEET, NICHOLAS		" ", PRITCHARD'S	RHODE IS.	13	FT GEORGE
THOMAS, APHRIM	THOMSON, EPHRAIM	KING'S RANGERS			FT ANN
VENVAST, JELLES	VAN VORST, CALLIS TELLIS	LOYAL RANGERS, WM FRASER'S	AMERICA	36	FT GEORGE
WEBSTER, MYLOR	MYLO	" ", JOHN JONES'	"	16	FT ANN
WHITMAN, GEORGE		KING'S RANGERS, RUITER'S	RHODE IS.	16	FT GEORGE

♠   In Jackson's transcript of the 1784 roll, there is a Lachs Granger. Likely the "L" should have been read as a "Z". In his transcript, there is no other man named Zachariah. In Fryer's transcript of the 1783 roll, there is a Zacarh Crauzer. Could this be Granger? As there is no other Zachariah on the roll and there is no Crauzer on the 1784 roll, this also appears to be a transciption error. To anyone familiar with these old rolls, such interpretation problems are understandable. If these are all the same man, he was from Duchess Cty and 20 in 1780.

NOTES

1   Obviously, a number of these names are common enough in the time period that they may not be the same men taken on the Carleton expedition; however, in many cases there can be little doubt.

2   Those names from Eben Jessup's list which were not found in the McHenry prisoner lists do not appear in the above chart.

3   Certainly a number of these men were quite young in 1780 for active service; however, not abnormally so for this period.

SOURCES

MG13, WO28, V.10, Pt4, pp.459-465. A Size Roll &c. of Loyal Rangers, "River du Chene" 1Jan83.

HP, Ms622, AddMss21827, R.85, p.295. Return of King's Rangers, St. John's 10Jan82.

McHenry, Prisoners, **op.cit.**

Fryer & Smy, Rolls, **op.cit.**, pp.97-104. ex MG13, WO28, V.10, pp.490-491. A Size Roll of King's Rangers, St. John's 21Jan83. (gives birthplace & ages)

H.M. Jackson, **op.cit.**, pp.197-202. ex NAC, HP, B160, pp.153-6. Return King's Rangers, St. John's 27Jan84. (gives company assignments)

APPENDIX 5
REBEL PRISONERS TAKEN DURING THE FALL 1780 RAIDS

SURNAME	GIVEN NAME	RANK	DATE OF CAPTURE	RECORDED PLACE OF CAPTURE	COMMENTS
Sherwood	Adiel	Capt	10Oct80	Fort Ann	Graham's Regt, NY Levies
Sherwood	Seth	Capt	10Oct80	Fort Ann	Webster's Regt, Charlotte Cty Mil
Baldwin	Cornelius	Lt	10Oct80	Fort Ann	
Roberts	Ezekiel	Lt	10Oct80	Fort Ann	Graham's Regt, NY Levies
Gates	Samuel	Sjt	10Oct80	Fort Ann	
Sherwood	Newcomb	Sjt	10Oct80	Fort Ann	Webster's Regt, Charlotte Cty Mil
Fitz	Eliz	Cpl	10Oct80	Fort Ann	
Guy	Jno	Cpl	10Oct80	Fort Ann	Graham's Regt, NY Levies
Allan/Allen	David	Pte	10Oct80	Fort Ann	
Allan	James	Pte	10Oct80	Fort Ann	
Anthony	Richard	Pte	10Oct80	Fort Ann	
Archer	James	Pte	10Oct80	Fort Ann	
Benninger/ Bennington	Isaac	Pte	10Oct80	Fort Ann	Graham's Regt, NY Levies
Benson	John	Pte	10Oct80	Fort Ann	
Blowers	Samuel	Pte	10Oct80	Fort Ann	Graham's Regt, NY Levies
Brown	Samuel	Pte	10Oct80	Fort Ann	
Caldwell	John	Pte	10Oct80	Fort Ann	Graham's Regt, NY Levies
Carr	James	Pte	10Oct80	Fort Ann	
Caswell	Abner	Pte	10Oct80	Fort Ann	Graham's Regt, NY Levies
Caswell	David	Pte	10Oct80	Fort Ann	
Chichester	Nathanial	Pte	10Oct80	Fort Ann	
Cordenay	George	Pte	10Oct80	Fort Ann	
Cowan	William	Pte	10Oct80	Fort Ann	
C[a]vell	Isaac	Pte	10Oct80	Fort Ann	
Dealey	Samuel	Pte	10Oct80	Fort Ann	
Dunnam	Samuel	Pte	10Oct80	Fort Ann	
Edgar	Rachel		10Oct80	Fort Ann	
Foster	Jonathon/Jno	Pte	10Oct80	Fort Ann	
Fuller	Benjamin	Pte	10Oct80	Fort Ann	Graham's Regt, NY Levies
Gifford	John	Pte	10Oct80	Fort Ann	Graham's Regt, NY Levies
Gills/Gilt	William	Pte	10Oct80	Fort Ann	

SURNAME	GIVEN NAME	RANK	DATE OF CAPTURE	RECORDED PLACE OF CAPTURE	COMMENTS
Goodner	James	Pte	10Oct80	Fort Ann	
Guy	Timothy	Pte	10Oct80	Fort Ann	
Harris	Moses	Pte	10Oct80	Fort Ann	Webster's Regt, Charlotte Cty Mil
Harris	William	Pte	10Oct80	Fort Ann	
Hathaway	John	Pte	10Oct80	Fort Ann	
Haven	Elias	Pte	10Oct80	Fort Ann	
Hearth/Heath	Winslow		10Oct80	Fort Ann	Graham's Regt, NY Levies
Henderson	Alexander	Pte	10Oct80	Fort Ann	
Hopkins	Robert	Pte	10Oct80	Fort Ann	
Hunter	Moses	Pte	10Oct80	Fort Ann	
Hye	William	Pte	10Oct80	Fort Ann	
Linte	Alias	Pte	10Oct80	Fort Ann	
McNutt	Alexander	Pte	10Oct80	Fort Ann	Graham's Regt, NY Levies
McPherson	Donald	Pte	10Oct80	Fort Ann	
Millett	Jonathon	Pte	10Oct80	Fort Ann	
Moor	Paul	Pte	10Oct80	Fort Ann	
Morrison	Jonathon	Pte	10Oct80	Fort Ann	
Moss	Isaac	Pte	10Oct80	Fort Ann	
Knapp	Benjamin	Pte	10Oct80	Fort Ann	
Powell	Cyrus		10Oct80		
Ray	Rosell	Pte	10Oct80	Fort Ann	
Rice	Seth	Pte	10Oct80	Fort Ann	
Ronalds/ Renolds	John	Pte	10Oct80	Fort Ann	
Schoolcraft	Christopher	Pte	10Oct80	Fort Ann	
Scott	John	Pte	10Oct80	Fort Ann	
Sherwood	Seth	Pte	10Oct80	Fort Ann	
Simpson	Robert	Pte	10Oct80	Fort Ann	
Smith	Solomon	Pte	10Oct80	Fort Ann	
Smith	Henry	Pte	10Oct80	Fort Ann	
Smith	Richard	Pte	10Oct80	Fort Ann	
Stewart	Solomon	Pte	10Oct80	Fort Ann	
Sutterly	Joseph	Pte	10Oct80	Fort Ann	
Thomas	Aphrim	Pte	10Oct80	Fort Ann	
Umphrey	Emry	Pte	10Oct80	Fort Ann	
Uress	Benjamin	Pte	10Oct80	Fort Ann	
Van Corke	Roger		10Oct80		
VanTassel/ Vantash	Cornelius		10Oct80	Fort Ann	
Webster	Mylor	Pte	10Oct80	Fort Ann	
Williams	Job	Pte	10Oct80	Fort Ann	
Wyng	Daniel	Pte	10Oct80	Fort Ann	
Wyng/Wing	Benjamin	Pte	10Oct80	Fort Ann	Graham's Regt, NY Levies

All men listed as taken at Fort George were from Warner's Continental Regiment

Chipman	John	Capt	11Oct80	Fort George	Paroled & Exchanged, 19Oct80
Payne	Francis	Lt	11Oct80	Fort George	
Barrett	Oliver	Ens	11Oct80	Fort George	Paroled as part of the surrender
Garrett	Andrew	Ens	11Oct80		
Lighthall	William	Ens	11Oct80	Fort George	
Stephens	Ebenezer	Ens	11Oct80	Fort George	
Luddington	John	SjtMjr	11Oct80	Fort George	

SURNAME	GIVEN NAME	RANK	DATE OF CAPTURE	RECORDED PLACE OF CAPTURE	COMMENTS
Bonett/ Bennett	Joseph	Sjt/DMj	11Oct80	Fort George	
Rennel	Isaac	Sjt	11Oct80	Fort George	
Trowbridge	Stephen	Sjt	11Oct80	Fort George	
Venvast	Jelles	Sjt	11Oct80	Fort George	
Ammon	Markin	Pte	11Oct80	Fort George	
Barr (Burr)	Alexander	Pte	11Oct80	Fort George	
Brown	David	Pte	11Oct80	Fort George	
Burt	Cyrus		11Oct80	Fort George	chose to remain in Canada
Campbell	John	Pte	11Oct80	Fort George	
Castler	Mark		11Oct80		
Coon	John	Pte	11Oct80	Fort George	
Dibble	Esa	Pte	11Oct80	Fort George	
Force	Timothy		11Oct80	Fort George	
Gillis	William	Pte	11Oct80	Fort George	
Graham	William	Pte	11Oct80	Fort George	
Granger	Ezach'r	Pte	11Oct80	Fort George	
Granvison	Charles		11Oct80		
Henderson	Samuel	Pte	11Oct80	Fort George	
Hines	Calvin	Pte	11Oct80	Fort George	
Huston	George	Pte	11Oct80	Fort George	
Keeler	Isaac		11Oct80		
Kellock	William	Pte	11Oct80	Fort George	
Larabie	Richard	Pte	11Oct80	Fort George	
Lawrence	Elijah	Pte	11Oct80	Fort George	
Loff	David	Pte	11Oct80	Fort George	
McDonald	Alexander	Pte	11Oct80	Fort George	
Mitchell	John	Pte	11Oct80	Fort George	
Rowland	Lewis	Pte	11Oct80	Fort George	
Smith	Jeremiah		11Oct80	Fort George	
Southwick	David/Daniel	Pte	11Oct80	Fort George	
Staring	Henry		11Oct80		
Sweet	Nicholas	Pte	11Oct80	Fort George	
Tanner	Gidian	Pte	11Oct80	Fort George	
Thomas	John	Pte	11Oct80	Fort George	
Weakley/ Wrakley	Henry	Pte	11Oct80	Fort George	
Whitman	George	Pte	11Oct80	Fort George	
Wood	Iser'l	Pte	11Oct80	Fort George	
Bellener	Joseph		12?Oct80		

all men taken at Ballstown and listed with ranks were from the 12th Albany County Regiment

Gordon	James	Col	12Oct80	Ballstown	
Collins	Tyrannis	Capt	12Oct80	Ballstown	
Benedict	Caleb	Ens	12Oct80	Ballstown	
Brannan/ Barnham	Thomas	Sjt	12Oct80	Ballstown	
Davis	John	Sjt	12Oct80	Ballstown	A John Davis in Munro's Coy, KRR NY 1781-83.
Kennedy	George	Sjt	12Oct80	Ballstown	allowed to return due to lameness
Benedict	Elisha		12Oct80	Ballstown	previously Capt, 2 NY ContLine

SURNAME	GIVEN NAME	RANK	DATE OF CAPTURE	RECORDED PLACE OF CAPTURE	COMMENTS
Benedict	Caleb	Pte	12Oct80	Ballstown	
(Benedict)	Dublin		12Oct80	Ballstown	escaped
Benedict	Elias	Pte	12Oct80	Ballstown	
Benedict	Philip/Felix	Pte	12Oct80	Ballstown	
Fillmore	?		12Oct80	Ballstown	escaped
Galbraith	Jack		12Oct80	Ballstown	
Gordon	James Jr.	Pte	12Oct80	Ballstown	
(Gordon)	Ann		12Oct80	Ballstown	a black slave of Col Gordon's, the only female taken to Canada
(Gordon)	Jacob		12Oct80	Ballstown	a black slave of Col Gordon's
(Gordon)	Nero		12Oct80	Ballstown	a black slave of Col Gordon's
Higby	John	Pte	12Oct80	Ballstown	
Higby	Lewis	Pte	12Oct80	Ballstown	
Hollister	Josiah	Pte	12Oct80	Ballstown	
Kennedy	Thomas	Pte	12Oct80	Ballstown	
Palmatier	Isaac	Pte	12Oct80	Ballstown	
Parlow	John		12Oct80	Ballstown	
Patchen	Samuel		12Oct80	Ballstown	
Patchin	Jabez	Pte	12Oct80	Ballstown	
Pierson	Paul		12Oct80	Ballstown	allowed to return due to age
Pierson	John		12Oct80	Ballstown	allowed to return due to youth
Sprague	Ebenezer		12Oct80	Ballstown	allowed to return due to age
Sprague	Elisha/Elijah	Pte	12Oct80	Ballstown	
Sprague	John		12Oct80	Ballstown	
Waltrous (Waters)	Edward A.	Pte	12Oct80	Ballstown	
Wood	Enoch	Pte	12Oct80	Ballstown	

Many of men below were undoubtedly in the Gloucester County militia but identification has not been found.

Belnap/ Belknap	Samuel/ Simeon		16Oct80	Randolph	
Boileau	Abna		16Oct80	White River	
Brown	Charles		16Oct80	White River	a Charles Brown in King's Rangers, Pritchard's Coy in 1784.
Brown	Jonathon		16Oct80	Royalton	
Brown	Joseph		16Oct80	White River	a Joseph Brown in King's Rangers, Pritchard's Coy in 1784.
Curtis	Elias		16Oct80	White River	
Davis	Experience		16Oct80	White River	
Downes	Donald Sr.		16Oct80	White River	
Downes	Donald Jr.		16Oct80	White River	
Durkee	Adan		16Oct80	Royalton	died in Canada
Evans	Cotten		16Oct80	White River	
Evans	Joseph		16Oct80	White River	
Avery/Everay	George		16Oct80	White River	
Gibbs	Giles		16Oct80	Royalton	killed first day of captivity
Gifford	John		16Oct80	White River	
Gilbert	Nathaniel		16Oct80	Royalton	a Nathaniel Gilbert in the 2Bn, KRR enlisted 10Feb81, aged 14 in 1780.
Griffin	Joseph		16Oct80	White River	

SURNAME	GIVEN NAME	RANK	DATE OF CAPTURE	RECORDED PLACE OF CAPTURE	COMMENTS
Haskell	Prince		16Oct80	Royalton	
Hutchinson	Abijah		16Oct80	Royaltown/Tunbridge	
Hutchinson	Eliah		16Oct80	White River	
Hutchinson	John		16Oct80	White River/Tunbridge	
Kent	John		16Oct80	White River	
Kneeland	aged father		16Oct80	Royalton	released to warn the militia not to pursue
Kneeland	Joseph		16Oct80	Royalton	killed first day of captivity
Luce	Jonathon		16Oct80	Onion River	
Mason	Peter		16Oct80	White River	
Miles	Timothy		16Oct80	White River	
Parks	John		16Oct80	White River/Royaltown	
Parsons	Moses		16Oct80	White River	
Pember	Samuel		16Oct80	White River	
Rix/Rexx	Gardner		16Oct80	White River	
Waller	Daniel		16Oct80	Royalton	
Warren	Moses		16Oct80	Onion River	
Welden	Abraham		16Oct80	White River	
Steele	Zadoch		17Oct80	Randolph	

Schoharie & Mohawk Valley Prisoners

SURNAME	GIVEN NAME	RANK	DATE OF CAPTURE	RECORDED PLACE OF CAPTURE	COMMENTS
Lawer	Conrad	Cpl	17Oct80	Schoharie	2Bn, Tryon County Militia
Klock	John	Pte	17Oct80	Schoharie	2Bn, Tryon County Militia
Lawer	John	Pte	17Oct80	Schoharie	2Bn, Tryon County Militia
Fourburn	Fred		18Oct80		
Lewis	John		18Oct80	Caughnawaga	
Primiere	Jno		18Oct80		
Shoemaker	Jno		18Oct80		
Hatter	Nich		19Oct80	German Flats	
Root,Rool	Stephen		19Oct80	Stone Arabia	Massachusetts Levies
Rema	John		19Oct80	Klock's Field	1Bn, Tryon County Militia
Rema			19Oct80	"	1Bn, Tryon County Militia
Crowley	Jer'h		20Oct80		
Lachan	James		20Oct80		
Staring♦	George	Pte	21Oct80	Kanawolohale	Capt Putman's Coy, Harper's Levies
Drake	Joshua	Capt	23Oct80	Ganaghsaraga	Company Commander, Harper's Levies
Vrooman	Walter (Wm)	Capt	23Oct80	"	Company Commander, Harper's Levies
Atkinson/ Ackerson	Cornelius	Lt	23Oct80	"	Capt Lawrence's Coy, Harper's Levies
Hatch	William	Sjt	23Oct80	"	Capt Vrooman's Coy, Harper's Levies
Lattimore	Francis	Sjt	23Oct80	"	Capt Bogart's Coy, Harper's Levies
Post	Cornelius	Sjt	23Oct80	"	Capt Vrooman's Coy, Harper's Levies
Renex/Rynex	Andrew	Sjt	23Oct80	"	Capt Vrooman's Coy, Harper's Levies
Henry	Hugh	Cpl	23Oct80	"	Capt Harrison's Coy, Harper's Levies
Bell	Matthew	Pte	23Oct80	"	Capt Drake's Coy, Harper's Levies
Berry	William	Pte	23Oct80	"	Capt Putman's Coy, Harper's Levies

SURNAME	GIVEN NAME	RANK	DATE OF CAPTURE	RECORDED PLACE OF CAPTURE	COMMENTS
Blameless/ Blamely	William		23Oct80	Fort Stanwix	
Borst	Jacob J.	Pte	23Oct80	Ganaghsaraga	Capt Bogart's Coy, Harper's Levies
Brannan/ Brannon	Abraham	Pte	23Oct80	Fort Stanwix	Capt Drake's Coy, Harper's Levies
Brown/Bowen	Timothy	Pte	22Oct80	Ganaghsaraga	Capt Vrooman's Coy, Harper's Levies
Carpenter	Thomas	Pte	23Oct80	Fort Stanwix	Capt Drake's Coy, Harper's Levies
Cosley	Jacob		23Oct80	Mohawk River	
Cosley	Marks		23Oct80	German Flats	
Curknew	Jacob		23Oct80	Fort Stanwix	
Clements	Jacob		23Oct80	Ganaghsaraga	Capt Putnam's Coy, Harper's Levies
Delong	John	Pte	23Oct80	"	Capt Harrison's Coy, Harper's Levies
DeGraff	John		23Oct80	"	Capt Vrooman's Coy, Harper's Levies
Eastwood	John	Pte	23Oct80	"	Capt Harrison's Coy, Harper's Levies
Eckler/Eglar	Leonard	Pte	23Oct80	"	Capt Putnam's Coy, Harper's Levies
Flansburgh	William F.	Pte	23Oct80	"	Capt Vrooman's Coy, Harper's Levies
Hawkins	Stephen	Pte	23Oct80	"	Capt Bogart's Coy, Harper's Levies
Hill	Amasa	Pte	23Oct80	"	Capt Vrooman's Coy, Harper's Levies
Hogeboom	Peter	Pte	23Oct80	"	Capt Vrooman's Coy, Harper's Levies
House	Peter A.	Pte	23Oct80	"	Capt Putman's Coy, Harper's Levies
Keeler	Isaiah	Pte	23Oct80	"	Capt Drake's Coy, Harper's Levies
Kelsey	Ebenezer	Pte	23Oct80	"	Capt Harrison's Coy, Harper's Levies
Monross/ Munro	Jesse	Pte	23Oct80	"	Capt Drake's Coy, Harper's Levies
Moss	Simeon/ Simon	Pte	23Oct80	"	Capt Drake's Coy, Harper's Levies
Murray	Peter	Pte	23Oct80	"	Capt Vrooman's Coy, Harper's Levies
Newkirk	Jacob	Pte	23Oct80	"	Capt Putman's Coy, Harper's Levies
Potter	Rolland	Pte	23Oct80	"	Capt Drake's Coy, Harper's Levies
Rickard	Jacob	Pte	23Oct80	"	Capt Putman's Coy, Harper's Levies
Ross/Rose	James/	Pte	23Oct80	"	Capt Lawrence's Coy, Harper's Levies
Sharp	Peter	Pte	23Oct80	"	Capt Harrison's Coy, Harper's Levies
Stark	Nathan	Pte	23Oct80	Old Oneida	
Thomas/ Thom	Ludwick	Pte	23Oct80	"	Capt Harrison's Coy, Harper's Levies
Truax	Isaac I.	Pte	23Oct80	"	Capt Vrooman's Coy, Harper's Levies
Virgin/Virgil	Abijah	Pte	23Oct80	"	Capt Vrooman's Coy, Harper's Levies
Williams	Gilbert	Pte	23Oct80	"	Capt Lawrence's Coy, Harper's Levies
Winne	Kilian	Pte	23Oct80	"	Capt Bogart's Coy, Harper's Levies
Rivershoe	John Peter	Pte	23Oct80	Fall Hill	Capt Dygert's Coy, 1st Tryon
Schuyler	Jacob	Pte	23Oct80	"	Capt Dygert's Coy, 1st Tryon
Schuyler	Nicholas	Pte	23Oct80	"	Capt Dygert's Coy, 1st Tryon
Shafer	Adam	Pte	23Oct80	"	Capt House's Coy, 1TCM
Dennis	Jacob		24Oct80	German Flats	
Docksteader	George		24Oct80	German Flatts	
Lute	Stephen		24Oct80	Mohawk River	

NOTES

♠   The sick man taken at Kanawolohale who, being lame, was left in New York.

1   It is likely that all of the prisoners taken at Fort Ann were either from Graham's 3rd Regiment of New York Levies or Webster's Charlotte County Militia Regiment; however, definite identification has been found only for those noted. Morrison research.

2   The garrison at Fort George were from Warner's Continental Regiment which had been recruited in 1775 from the Green Mountain Boys of the New Hampshire Grants. Warner's saw action in Canada during that year's campaign and took heavy casualties from disease, the weather and enemy action. They were reformed under Warner in 1776 and saw heavy action during the Burgoyne campaign, of note at Hubbardton and Bennington. On 18Sep80, a Return by Nicholas Fish, Major 2NY & Inspector of the Line, listed six additional corps credited to the State of New York "as part of its proportion of the Continental Army." Warner's regiment was one of those additional corps. The unit continued as an entity until disbandment on 1Jan81. See, Fernow, Documents Colonial History of New York, **op.cit.**, I,p.247 and Walter S. Fenton, "Seth Warner", **Proceedings of the Vermont Historical Society, New Series, Vol.III, No.4 (December 1940).**

     Warner's Regimental Return to Washington's Headquarters dated 27Oct80 showed the unit to be remarkably understrength with a total of only 101 men reported as sick, furloughed, dead or captured. None were "on duty." The return indicates that the vast majority of men in the regiment were from Connecticut with a smattering from New York & Massachusetts. That New York State should be credited for a unit containing such a large proportion of out-of-State men is simply one of those mysteries. Upon disbandment, the Yorkers were transferred to the 2NY. Morrison research, **Washington Papers Mf Reels 72,** p.85 & 73,p.20.

3   As noted in the text, Vrooman was said to have commanded a detachment of 61 men all ranks, yet only 39 names have been identified. One source claimed that 52 men were captured and another source, 66, i.e. more men than comprised the detachment. Another mystery.

SOURCES:

Ken D. Johnson, Fort Plank Historian, **The Bloodied Mohawk, The American Revolution in the Words of Fort Plank's Defenders and Other Mohawk Valley Partisans** (Rockport, ME: Picton Press, 2000)

Chris McHenry, compiler, **Rebel Prisoners at Quebec, 1778-1783** (n.d., n.p.)

James F. Morrison, **1780-1980 The Bicentennial Book of the Schoharie and Mohawk Valley Raids** (Klock's Churchyard Preservation Group, 1980) pp.20,27,28,66,67

................., unpublished list of names & ranks Capt Walter Vrooman's detachment of Harper's Levies and Tryon Militia sent out from Fort Stanwix.

................., unpublished list of names and ranks of men of the 12th Albany Regt, taken at Ballston by Munro.

New York in the Revolution as Colony and State (2 Vols, Albany: NYS, 1904)

Zadock Steele, **The Indian Captive or a Narrative of the Captivity and Sufferings of Zadock Steele Related by Himself... The Burning of Royalton** (Montpelier, VT: the author, 1848)

BIBLIOGRAPHY OF CITATIONS

Listed in their frequency of citation;
sources cited less than five times are not listed

Unpublished Manuscript Sources (originals & transcripts)

Haldimand Papers

Colonial Office Records

War Office Records

Claus Papers

Malcom Manuscripts

Washington Papers

Published Manuscript Sources

Public Papers of George Clinton, First Governor of New York 1777-1795-1801-1804 (6 vols, Albany: The State of New York, 1902)

Census of Niagara 1783, United Empire Loyalist Association, Hamilton Branch, ed. (UEL Association, 1975) muster roll of Butler's Rangers & Brant's Volunteers, 1783.

Early Ontario Settlers, A Source Book, Norman K. Crowder (Baltimore: Genealogical Publishing Co., Inc., 1993) transcriptions of Loyalist Settlement Returns.

United Empire Loyalists, Enquiry into the Losses and Services in Consequence of their Loyalty, Evidence in Canadian Claims, Second Report of the Bureau of Archives for the Province of Ontario, Alexander Fraser, Provincial Archivist (2 vols, Toronto: L.K. Cameron, 1905) reprinted, Genealogical Publishing, Baltimore, 1994.

Loyalist Settlements 1783-1789, New Evidence of Canadian Loyalist Claims, W. Bruce Antliff, researcher & transcriber (Ontario: Ministry of Citizenship and Culture, 1985)

New York in the Revolution as Colony and State, J.A. Roberts (Albany: 1897) Maps found in 19th Century editions only. Reprinted without maps or illustrations (Rhinebeck: Kinship, 1993)

Rolls of the Provincial (Loyalist) Corps, Canadian Command American Revolutionary Period, Mary Beacock Fryer and Lieutenant-Colonel William A. Smy (Toronto and Charlottetown, Dundurn Press, 1981)

Documents relating to the Colonial History of the State of New York, Berthold Fernow, ed., Vol.XV, State Archives, Vol.I (Albany: New York State, 1887)

A History of the Organization, Development and Services of the Military and Naval Forces of Canada, etc..., with *Illustrative Documents,* The Historical Section of the General Staff, eds (3 Vols, Ottawa: n.p., n.d.) Vols.II&III

Secondary Sources

The King's Royal Regiment of New York, Brig.Gen. Ernest A. Cruikshank and Gavin K. Watt (Toronto: Gavin K. Watt, 1984) Text originally published, Ontario Historical Society, 1931.

The Northern Invasion of October 1780, A Series of Papers Relating to the Expeditions from Canada under Sir John Johnson and Others against the Frontiers of New York..., Franklin B. Hough (New York: 1866)

History of Schoharie County and Border Wars of New York; containing also a Sketch of the Causes which led to the American Revolution and Interesting Memoranda of the Mohawk Valley; together with much other Historical and Miscellaneous Matter, never before published, Jeptha R. Simms (Albany: Munsell & Tanner, 1845) reprinted by the Schoharie County Council of Senior Citizens, 1974

1780-1980 The Bicentennial Book of the Schoharie and Mohawk Valley Raids (Montgomery County, NY: Klock's Churchyard Preservation Group, 1980)

The Story of Butler's Rangers and the Settlement of Niagara, E. Cruikshank (Welland: Lundy's Lane Historical Society, 1893)

The American Journals of Lt. John Enys, Elizabeth Cometti, ed. (Syracuse: The Adirondack Museum -Syracuse University Press, 1976)

"The Raid on Ballston, 1780, Memoranda of Reminiscences, 1846", James Scott, *The Bulletin of the Fort Ticonderoga Museum, Vol.VII, No.4 (July 1946)*

The Iroquois in the American Revolution, Barbara Graymont (Syracuse: Syracuse University Press, 1972)

Reminiscences of Saratoga & Ballstown, William L. Stone (New York: 1875)

War in Schohary, Edward A. Hagan (the author, 1980)

Sloughter's Instant History of Schoharie County, Lester E. & Anne Whitbeck Hendrix (Schoharie: Schoharie County Historical Society, 1988)

A Journal of Josiah Hollister, A Soldier of the American Revolution and a Prisoner of War in Canada, Josiah Hollister (Romanzo Norton Bunn, 1928)

Life of Brant - Thayendanegea, Including the Indian Wars of the American Revolution, William L. Stone (2 vols, New-York: Alexander V. Blake, 1838)

Roger's Rangers, Burt G. Loescher (2 vols: n.p., 1969)

Frontier Spies - The British Secret Service, Northern Department, during the Revolutionary War, Hazel M. Mathews (Fort Myers, FA: the author, 1971)

Buckskin Pimpernel, the Exploits of Justus Sherwood, Loyalist Spy, Mary Beacock Fryer (Toronto and Charlottetown: Dundurn Press, 1981)

Joseph Brant 1743-1807, Man of Two Worlds, Isabel Thompson Kelsay (Syracuse: Syracuse University Press, 1984)

The Battle of Klock's Field, October 19, 1780..., Lou D. MacWethy (St. Johnsville, NY: Enterprise and News, 1930)

Lake Champlain and Lake George, Frederic F. Van De Water (Indianapolis & New York: The Bobbs-Merrill Company, 1946)

The Frontiersmen of New York Showing Customs, Indians, Vicissitudes of the Pioneer White Settlers, etc..., Jeptha R. Simms (Albany: Geo. C. Riggs, 1883)

The Indian Captive or a Narrative of the Captivity and Sufferings of Zadock Steele Related by Himself to which is prefixed an account of the Burning of Royalton, Zadock Steele (Montpelier: the author, 1848)

King's Men, Soldier Founders of Ontario, Mary Beacock Fryer (Toronto and Charlottetown: Dundurn Press Limited, 1980)

Skulking for the King, A Loyalist Plot, J. Fraser (Erin, Ont: The Boston Mills Press, 1985)

Mohawk Valley in the Revolution, Committee of Safety Papers & Genealogical Compendium, Maryly B. Penrose (Franklin Park, NJ: Liberty Bell Associates, 1978)

Military Activities in the Champlain Valley after 1777, Oscar E. Bredenberg (Champlain, NY: Moorsfield Press, 1962)

Colonel John Brown of Pittsfield, Massachusetts, the Brave Accuser of Benedict Arnold..., Archibald M. Howe (Boston: W.B. Clarke, 1908)

Index

KEY TO INDEX

GENERAL

1. Place names, features and persons which appear on maps or in illustrations are so noted by having the page number in bold.
2. The endnotes and appendices are indexed only for principle persons, occurrences, military units, items and places.
3. All military units are listed under the general topic "Army," eg. Army, British, Regular, 8th Regt. Similarly, all references to naval matters on the sea, rivers or lakes are indexed under "Navy."
4. All rivers, lakes and forts are listed under those classifications, eg. River, Mohawk; Lake, Champlain and Fort, Niagara.
5. Native-language, personal names are either enclosed by single quotation marks or square brackets.

LEGEND

1. When a name is followed only by the abbreviation of a State, eg. "NY," two possible conditions apply. Either the individual lived prior to the rebellion or, the specific revolutionary-war military service of that individual is unknown, but his/her political beliefs were believed to be in favour of the rebellion. Although information may not have been located, it should be recognized that virtually all males between 16 and 50 served in the militia.
2. If followed by a State abbreviation, eg. "MA," and an indication of service, eg. "Levies," the individual served in the Massachusetts Levies.
3. If the person's name is followed by a State abbreviation, a slash and the abbreviation "Loy.," or the reverse of this, eg. "Loy./CT," this indicates a split allegiance during the time period of the book.
4. If followed by "Loy.", the individual was either a loyalist by persuasion or circumstance. If followed by "Loy.?" this indicates the individual was suspected or accused of being a loyalist.
5. The double abbreviation "NY/VT," indicates a place which was in New York at the time of the Revolution, but was ceded to Vermont when the latter's Statehood was achieved.
6. For natives who fought with the British during the Revolution, their names are followed by the term "Crown." For those who sided with the rebellion, their names are followed by "Congress." As with some whites, both terms are applied to the same name when allegiances were known to have been split during the conflict. For men who espoused neutrality during the rebellion, their names are followed by "Neutralist," even though a number of these men were compelled to take up arms.

ABBREVIATIONS

MISCELLANEOUS

Cont. - Continental, ie. a U.S. Regular
Gov - Governor
Loy. - loyalist
OC - Officer Commanding

SJJ - LtCol Sir John Johnson
LC - Lower Canada
UC - Upper Canada

CPSIA information can be obtained
at www.ICGtesting.com
Printed in the USA
LVOW05s1916200517
535123LV00001B/8/P